PROPHECY AND WAR IN ANCIENT ISRAEL

by

Duane L. Christensen

* * *

BIBAL MONOGRAPH SERIES 3

p

PROPHECY AND WAR IN ANCIENT ISRAEL

Studies in the Oracles Against the Nations in Old Testament Prophecy

* * *

by

Duane L. Christensen

BIBAL Press
Berkeley, California

Prophecy and War in Ancient Israel

Library of Congress Cataloging-in-Publication Data

Christensen, Duane L., 1938-
Prophecy and war in ancient Israel.

(BIBAL monograph series; 3)
Previously published in Harvard dissertations in religion; no. 3.
Originally presented as the author's thesis, Harvard, 1971.
Bibliography: p.
1. Nationalism--Biblical teaching. 2. War--Biblical teaching.
3. Bible. O.T. Prophets--Criticism, interpretation, etc.
4. Bible. O.T. Prophets--History of contemporary events, etc.
I. Title. II. Series.
BS1199.N3C4 1989 224'.06'6 88-071437
ISBN 0-941037-06-1

Published by BIBAL Press, Berkeley, CA 94701
Printed at GRT Book Printing, Oakland, CA 94601

TABLE OF CONTENTS

FOREWORD

Though this book has been out of print for some time, the demand for it has continued, leading to the decision to include it in the BIBAL Monograph Series. No changes have been introduced here other than the addition of a selected bibliography of the author's publications since 1975, which have some bearing on the discussion. It should be noted that the method of "prosodic-textual analysis" utilized in this study has been superseded in recent years by a more sophisticated and sensitive method of analysis, which is spelled out in detail in some of these journal articles by the author. Nonetheless, the following comments by Charles D. Isbell, which appeared in a review published in the *Bulletin of the American Schools of Oriental Research* (No. 225 [February 1977], p. 77), remain apropos.

In this Harvard dissertation, the author traces the historical development of the oracle against a foreign nation (OAN) from its origin in the early military traditions of Israel down to its refinement as a form of prophetic speech. Using "prosodic-textual analysis," Christensen begins with early material related to "oracular divination" (pp. 19-22) and moves chronologically through Israelite history down to the early 6th century B.C. He observes two major transformations of the war oracle.

> In the 10th-8th centuries the war oracle as a tactical element in military strategy was transformed into the literary mode of a prophetic judgment speech against both military foes and the nation of Israel, together with her political allies. In the opening decades of the 6th century the war oracle was again transformed from the world of international politics to the trans-historical realm of early apocalyptic (p. 283).

In general it may be said that Christensen has sustained his theses with objective and balanced exegesis. In particular during the course of his rigorous historical presentation, Christensen has clarified several issues with respect to OAN materials which often bear on Old Testament studies in a more general way.

He provides an excellent summary of the contribution of Amos ("he has taken the earlier speech form of a war oracle, in the form of a judgment speech against a specific nation or people [cf. I Kgs 20:28], and transformed it into a judgment speech against Israel" [p. 71]) and Isaiah (he incorporated "Assyria and Egypt/Ethiopia into the traditional [i.e., ancient political structures addressed by Amos which stem from Israel's covenant league] roll call of the nations" [p. 132]) to the development of the OAN tradition. In addition, Christensen has addressed a difficult 8th century question–the date of Pi'ankhi's incursion into Egypt, setting the year at 723/22, seven years earlier than the widely accepted date proposed by Albright, on the grounds that it was "after Hoshea's appeal for aid in 724" and "before the defeat of Pi'ankhi's forces at Raphia by Assyria in 720" (p. 82). Further, Christensen's view of Isa 10:27c-34 as a picture of Yahweh leading the enemy force in battle against Zion itself (pp. 147-53) is convincing to this reviewer, as is his dating of Nahum to the period before rather than after 612 (Humbert, Lods, Sellin) on the basis of its position within the developing OAN tradition (pp. 166-67).

In dealing with Jeremiah, Christensen is particularly instructive. He has shown that "the ideology of holy war was formative in the prophet's self-understanding" and that Jeremiah's entire life as prophet, pacifist, intercessor, and theologian may best be grasped by viewing Jeremiah the way he understood himself, "as the herald of the Divine Warrior, proclaiming holy war against Judah and Jerusalem, and by extension, to foreign nations as well" (p. 193). The point is well taken. The reviewer further agrees with Christensen's conclusion that "cup of wrath" was not a formative motif for Jeremianic OAN material (p. 200) and accepts his defense of verse 11 in Jer 49:7-22 (against Edom!) as pre-Jeremianic or at least pre-exilic (see especially p. 232). And Christensen once again has rung the bell in pointing out that Jeremiah's advice concerning Babylon in 27:17 and his letter advising exiles to prepare for a lengthy stay in Babylon "are not in opposition to the sentiment against Babylon as portrayed in Jeremiah 50-51" (p. 262) if one understands "the major transformation for the entire prophetic tradition" immediately following 597 which moved from hope placed on the exiled human king to "the concept of the Davidic king as Yahweh's anointed, the Messiah" (p. 262).

PREFACE

The present study was presented to Harvard University in October 1971 as a doctoral dissertation in substantially its present form. Revisions have been made in line with subsequent published works by the author, and the bibliography has been updated. This dissertation was directed by Professor Frank Moore Cross, Jr., to whom I am profoundly grateful for the long hours of consultation given so generously in spite of a most demanding schedule. His ready accessibility and prompt thoroughness in response to my many queries stand as a challenging example I would hope to emulate.

I am especially indebted to the late Professor G. Ernest Wright for course work and consultation throughout my doctoral work which culminated in this study. I would also acknowledge my debt to Professor Mitchell Dahood, S.J., for his counsel on several textual matters during his sabbatical year in Cambridge in 1969-70; to Professor Shemaryahu Talmon, who discussed with me his class on "The Oracles Against the Nations" at Brandeis University; and to the late Professor Roland de Vaux, O.P., whose course on "The History of Ancient Israel" at Harvard in 1964-65 was a profound experience at a most critical juncture in my academic training. I also benefited from consultation with Professor Paul D. Hanson, whose work on the origins of apocalyptic was germinal in the formulation of my research objectives.

I would also take this opportunity to thank my colleagues at Bridgewater State College for partial subvention of this publication through the Scholarly Support Committee. My appreciation also goes to Professor Jordan D. Fiore, my divisional director, and to Professor John F. Myers, my departmental chairman, for their understanding these past several months in allowing me a teaching schedule which left adequate time to see this study through to publication. A further note of thanks is here expressed to Rabbi Baruch Goldstein of Temple Emmanuel in Wakefield, Massachusetts, without whose assistance I would not have gotten through the modern Hebrew literature cited here.

Finally, I would express my thanks to my wife Carol and our three girls -- Beth, Sharon and Julie -- who have been understanding of the many long hours of my "absence" and the many projects which got postponed so often. This book is dedicated to them.

Duane L. Christensen

Wakefield, Massachusetts
August 1975

ABBREVIATIONS

AAA	*Annals of Archaeology and Anthropology* (Liverpool)
AASOR	*Annual of the American Schools of Oriental Research*
AB	Anchor Bible
ABR	*Australian Biblical Review*
AfO	*Archiv für Orientforschung*
AJSL	*American Journal of Semitic Languages and Literatures*
ANET[2]	*Ancient Near Eastern Texts Relating to the Old Testament*, 2nd edition, ed. by J. B. Pritchard (Princeton, 1955)
ARAB	*Ancient Records of Assyria and Babylonia*, ed. by D. D. Luckenbill (Chicago, 1926-27)
ARM	*Archives Royales de Mari. Transcriptions et Traductions*, ed. by A. Parrot and G. Dossin (Paris, 1940-)
ARW	*Archiv für Religionswissenschaft*
ATD	Das Alte Testament Deutsch
AThANT	Abhandlungen zur Theologie des Alten und Neuen Testaments
BA	*The Biblical Archaeologist*
BANE	*The Bible and the Ancient Near East*, ed. by G. Ernest Wright (Essays in Honor of William Foxwell Albright, 1961)
BAR	*The Biblical Archaeologist Reader I, II and III*, ed. by G. E. Wright, D. N. Freedman and E. F. Cambell, 1961-70)
BASOR	*Bulletin of the American Schools of Oriental Research*
BDB	*A Hebrew and English Lexicon*, F. Brown, S. R. Driver and C. A. Briggs (Oxford, c1907)
BH[3]	*Biblia Hebraica*, ed. by R. Kittel
BHS	*Biblia Hebraica Stuttgartensia*, ed. by K. Elliger and W. Rudolph
Bib	*Biblica*
BIES	*Bulletin of the Israel Exploration Society*
BJRL	*Bulletin of the John Rylands Library*
BK	Biblischer Kommentar Altes Testament
BWA(N)T	Beiträge zur Wissenschaft vom Alten (und Neuen) Testament(s)
BZAW	Beihefte zur Zeitschrift für die Alttestamentliche Wissenschaft
Camb.-B	Cambridge Bible for Schools and Colleges
CBQ	*Catholic Biblical Quarterly*
CCK	*Chronicles of Chaldean Kings (626-556 B.C.)*, D. J. Wiseman (London, 1956)
DJD	*Discoveries in the Judean Desert, I-IV*, D. Barthélemy and others (Oxford, 1955-65)
EH	Exegetisches Handbuch zum Alten Testament (Münster)

EI	*Eretz-Israel* (Jerusalem)
ET	*The Expository Times*
ETL	*Ephemerides Theologicae Lovanienses*
FRLANT	Forschungen zur Religion und Literatur des Alten und Neuen Testaments (Göttingen)
FuF	*Forschungen und Fortschritte*
HSM	Harvard Semitic Monographs
HTR	*Harvard Theological Review*
H(z)AT	Handbuch zum Alten Testament (Tübingen)
HUCA	*Hebrew Union College Annual*
ICC	The International Critical Commentary
IDB	*The Interpreter's Dictionary of the Bible*, ed. by G. A. Buttrick (New York and Nashville, 1962)
IEJ	*Israel Exploration Journal*
JAOS	*Journal of the American Oriental Society*
JBL	*Journal of Biblical Literature*
JCS	*Journal of Cuneiform Studies*
JJS	*Journal of Jewish Studies*
JNES	*Journal of Near Eastern Studies*
JPOS	*Journal of the Palestine Oriental Society*
JThC	*Journal of Theology and the Church*
KAT	Kommentar zum Alten Testament
KB	*Hebräisches und Aramäisches Lexikon zum Alten Testament*, L. Koehler and W. Baumgartner
KHC	Kurzer Hand-Commentar zum Alten Testament
LBC	The Layman's Bible Commentary
LS	*Ha-Lashon ve-ha-Sefer* (Essays by Harry Torczyner, I-III, Jerusalem, 1948-1959)
LXX	The Septuagint
MT	Masoretic text
OAN	Oracles against the nations
Or	*Orientalia*
OS	*Oudtestamentische Studiën*
OT	Old Testament
OTL	The Old Testament Library
OuTWP	*Die Ou Testamentiese Werkgemeenskap in Suid-Afrika*
PEQ	*Palestine Exploration Quarterly*
POS	Pretoria Oriental Series
RB	*Revue Biblique*
RGG	*Die Religion in Geschichte und Gegenwart* (Tübingen)
RSV	Revised Standard Version (of *The Holy Bible*)

SBL	Society of Biblical Literature (and Exegesis)
SBT	Studies in Biblical Theology (London and Naperville, Ill.)
SP	The Samaritan Pentateuch
StANT	Studien zum Alten und Neuen Testament (München)
SVT	Supplements to *Vetus Testamentum*
ThZ	*Theologische Zeitschrift* (Basel)
UT	*Ugaritic Textbook*, C. H. Gordon (Rome, 1965)
VT	*Vetus Testamentum* (Leiden)
WMANT	Wissenschaftliche Monographien zum Alten und Neuen Testament (Neukirchen)
ZAW	*Zeitschrift für die Alttestamentliche Wissenschaft*
ZDPV	*Zeitschrift des Deutschen Pälastina-Vereins*
ZKTh	*Zeitschrift für Kotholische Theologie* (Innsbruck)

LIST OF MAPS

CHAPTER ONE

INTRODUCTION: THE PROBLEM IN PERSPECTIVE

The oracles against the nations (OAN) in Old Testament prophecy have received relatively little attention in biblical research of the past century. Since the major contribution of the prophetic movement was conceived to be the impulse of universal monotheism and moral values into the stream of the developing Judaeo-Christian tradition, the narrow nationalism of the foreign-nation oracles appeared to have little relevance for anyone. The OAN tradition constituted the dregs of the prophetic movement. As R. H. Pfeiffer of Harvard University put it in 1941:[1]

> Although such anathemas against the heathen were inaugurated by Amos . . . they reflect on the whole not the moral indignation of the great pre-exilic prophets, but rather the nationalism of the "false prophets" and of the later Jews chafing for centuries under alien rule.

This negative evaluation of the OAN tradition resulted in scholarly neglect, as illustrated by the important work of Claus Westermann on the forms of prophetic speech which gives less than two pages of text to what he himself describes as the "large and complicated body of oracles against foreign nations."[2]

By oracles against the nations (OAN) we mean that body of prophetic revelations in the form of oracular poems which stands apart as distinct from the bulk of the prophetic literature in that it is concerned with peoples other than Israel. The bulk of this material is concentrated in sizeable collections within the books of Isaiah (chs. 13-23), Jeremiah (chs. 46-51), and Ezekiel (chs. 25-32). However, with the possible exception of Hosea, no prophetic book in the Old Testament is without such material. Nor can a discussion of this material within the major prophets ignore material outside the formal OAN collections. What we are concerned with is a central form of prophetic speech which is so common that we must assume it to be a basic and integral part of the prophetic message and outlook.

---

[1] Robert H. Pfeiffer, *Introduction to the Old Testament* (New York: Harper & Brothers, 1941), p. 443.

[2] Claus Westermann, *Basic Forms of Prophetic Speech*,,trans. by Hugh White (Philadelphia: Westminster, 1967), p. 204; a translation of *Grundformen prophetischer Rede* (Muenchen: Chr. Kaiser Verlag, 1960).

Major Impulses to the Study of the OAN Tradition

The history of investigation of the OAN tradition is marked by a series of three major impulses and subsequent refinement in methodology, namely: 19th century German literary criticism, German form criticism, and the proliferation of extra-biblical materials which have made possible religio-historical study of prophecy in ancient Israel. A history of the OAN tradition, when it is in fact written, will benefit from the contributions of each of these major impulses and the refinement in methods of textual and historical study which have been emerging during the past three decades.

The major study of the OAN tradition produced by the school of German literary criticism is that of Friedrich Schwally,[3] who concluded that *all* of the OAN material in Jeremiah is post-Exilic and spurious. It is important to note that this particular study was Schwally's inaugural-dissertation, written at the University of Giessen under Bernhard Stade when Schwally was 25 years of age. As Paul Volz later commented, the question of authenticity of this material had been raised continually since the time of Vatke, a teacher of Wellhausen, and continued in the person of Stade.[4] Schwally clearly stands on the shoulders of his mentors and is in fact presenting the consensus of feeling within a school of thought in rejecting Jeremiah as the author of this material. Preoccupation with the problem of authenticity continued to dominate investigation of the OAN material into the 20th century. Paul Volz (1920-30),[5] though still convinced that the OAN material in Jeremiah was inauthentic and late, was so impressed with the homogeneous nature of these chapters that he posited a Deutero-Jeremiah, a follower of the prophet who composed these oracles shortly after the death of Nebuchadnezzar (around 560 B.C.), making use of Amos, Isaiah, and particularly Jeremiah. Bardtke, in a lengthy study published in two installments (1935 and 1936),[6] went still further and rejected Schwally's thesis altogether. Basing his arguments largely on Jeremiah's call as a prophet to the nations (Jer. 1:2-10), Bardtke argued that the OAN material was authentic but must be ascribed to Jeremiah's "youth," i.e. 617-615 B.C. Unable to assign these oracles to the mature years of the prophet alongside his other prophecies, Bardtke worked out a compromise which gained few followers. The pressure of a new impulse from

---

[3]Friedrich Schwally, *Die Reden des Buches Jeremia gegen die Heiden: XXV.XLVI-LI untersucht* (Giessen: Druck von Wilhelm Keller, 1888). Also published in *ZAW* 8 (1888), pp. 177-216.

[4]Paul Volz, *Der Prophet Jeremia* (Leipzig: Deichert, 1922), pp. 374-5.

[5]Paul Volz, *Studien zum Text des Jeremia* (BWAT 25, Leipzig: J. C. Hinrichs, 1920) and *Der Prophet Jeremiah*, 3rd ed. (1930).

[6]H. Bardtke, "Jeremia der Fremdvölkerprophet," *ZAW* 53 (1935), pp. 209-39; 54 (1936), pp. 240-62.

form critical study of the prophetic literature was at work, pushing the date of the OAN material back, thus undermining the dominant presuppositions of German literary criticism as expressed by Schwally.

The second major impulse to the study of the OAN tradition arose out of Hermann Gunkel's study of the Psalms (1904 ff.).[7] In 1905 Hugo Gressman, a disciple of Gunkel, applied the new method of form criticism to the prophetic literature and concluded that OAN material was early, and in fact a pre-classical prophetic *Gattung* which formed part of pre-8th century Israelite eschatology (as expressed in the concept of the "Day of Yahweh").[8] He considered the material to be composed by *Heilspropheten* connected with the royal court in ancient Israel. Gunkel expressed his views in 1915, 1917 and again in 1930 without any essential changes.[9] As Westermann has pointed out, the fact that Gunkel did not find it necessary to change his understanding of prophetic speech as a whole or in part over so long a span of time indicates the originality and far-reaching significance of his understanding; "but it is also a sign of the lack of essentially new impulses in this area over a long period of time."[10] The Gunkel-Gressman hypothesis as developed between 1905 and 1930 began to exert an increasingly strong influence in wider circles of scholarly endeavor. Though death prevented Gressman from completing his study of the OAN material, it is possible to reconstruct in outline his understanding of this body of literature from *Der Messias* (1929), published posthumously.

The form critical methodology initiated by Gunkel and Gressman steadily gained adherents in Germany prior to the outbreak of World War II. Schmökel's discussion of the OAN material (1934)[11] as *Heilsprophezeiung* from a Near Eastern court setting is strongly influenced by Gressman, but also reflects a refinement in methodology based on extra-biblical materials which promised to shed increasing light in subsequent research. Christian Schmerl, in a partially published dissertation at Heidelberg under Gustav Hölscher (1939),

---

[7]Hermann Gunkel, *Ausgewählte Psalmen* (Göttingen: Vandenhoeck & Ruprecht, 1904; 4th rev. ed., 1917); *Die Psalmen übersetzt und erklärt* (HzAT 11/2, Göttingen: Vandenhoeck & Ruprecht, 4th ed., 1926); *Einleitung in die Psalmen: Die Gattungen der religösen Lyrik Israels* (Göttingen: Vandenhoeck & Ruprecht, 1933).

[8]Hugo Gressman, *Der Ursprung der israelitisch-jüdischen Eschatologie* (Göttingen: Vandenhoeck & Ruprecht, 1905).

[9]Hermann Gunkel, in the introduction to the volume on the Major Prophets (revised by Hans Schmidt) in the old *Göttingen Bibelwerk* (1915); "Propheten II seit Amos," *RGG*[1] (1917) and *RGG*[2] (1930).

[10]C. Westermann, *op. cit.*, pp. 30-31.

[11]Hartmut Schmökel, *Jahwe und die Fremdvölker* (Breslau: Maruschke, 1934).

investigated the "abrupt style" of speech in the use of verbal imperatives in the OAN material and concluded that the manner of speaking points to the experience of ecstatic prophets.[12] He also raised the question of the history of the literary *Gattungen* in the OAN material, pointing out that there is no single literary *Gattung* as such in the OAN material but that other literary forms are taken over by the prophets and adapted to new uses. In particular he noted the military background for certain of the oracles against the nations.

After World War II it is difficult to trace the development of form critical methodology as it merges with older literary criticism, especially in Mowinckel's *Prophecy and Tradition* (1946), and with the new impulse from religio-historical investigation based on extra-biblical materials taking place in widely separated circles. A. Bentzen, in his article on Amos 1-2 (1950),[13] argued for cultic execration in ancient Israel in parallel with the Egyptian execration texts of the early second millennium B.C. Seeking a specific *Sitz im Leben* for such a cultic rite, Bentzen posited the enthronement ritual in the New Year Festival. In reaction to the stress on cultic execration other scholars turned toward the legal background of this material as the basis for understanding the OAN tradition. With the publication of Mendenhall's work on international treaty forms and their relation to the Old Testament (1954),[14] interest soon centered on royal treaties in the ancient Near East and specifically covenant treaty documents and curse motifs. Reventlow (1962)[15] spoke of Amos 1 as a *Völkerritual* at an assumed Covenant-renewal Festival. Fensham (1962 and 1963)[16] suggested the implications of treaty-curses for understanding the prophetic literature of the Old Testament. Hillers (1963 and 1964)[17] turned his attention more directly to OAN material

---

[12]Christian Schmerl, *Die Völkerorakel in den Prophetenbüchern des Alten Testaments* (Würzburg: Richard Mayr, 1939), a partial publication of his Inaugural-Dissertation at the University of Heidelberg.

[13]Aage Bentzen, "The Ritual Background of Amos 1:2-2:16," *OTS* 8 (1950), pp. 85-99.

[14]George E. Mendenhall, "Law and Covenant in Israel and the Ancient Near East," *BA* 17 (1954), pp. 26-46 and 49-76.

[15]H. G. Reventlow, *Das Amt des Propheten bei Amos* (FRLANT 80, Göttingen, 1962), pp. 111 ff.

[16]C. F. Fensham, "Malediction and Benediction in ancient Near Eastern vassal-treaties and the Old Testament," *ZAW* 74 (1962), pp. 1-9; "Common Trends in Curses of the Near Eastern Treaties and *Kudurru*-Inscriptions Compared with Maledictions of Amos and Isaiah," *ZAW* 75 (1963), pp. 155-76.

[17]Delbert R. Hillers, *Treaty-Curses and the Old Testament Prophets* (Rome: Pontifical Biblical Institute, 1964), which is the publication of his

as a whole and in the closing paragraphs of *Treaty-Curses and the Old Testament Prophets* posed a programmatic question:[18]

> Questions as to the nature and purpose of the oracles on foreign nations are raised by the fact that a high proportion of expressions with parallels in treaty-curses occurs in them. Does this mean that these expressions have become stock phrases which a prophet might use against anyone? Or is the implication present in some cases that these nations have broken treaties with Israel?

In the midst of this proliferation of studies, based primarily on extra-biblical materials, which was producing hybrid branches of form criticism of OAN material, important work in the older Gunkel-Gressman tradition continued to appear, particularly within a circle of Israeli scholars. Diman-Haran (1946/47),[19] in a comparative literary analysis of Isaiah 15-16 and Jeremiah 48, argued that both compositions represent elaborations of an "archaic fragment" found in Numbers 21, the so-called "Song of the Mošlîm," which, he maintained, was originally an Amorite victory song. Kaufmann (1947/48)[20] examined in detail the OAN material in Amos and Jeremiah and concluded that Amos 1-2 lacks the major characteristics of classical prophecy and in its original form reflects an historical situation prior to the time of the prophet Amos. He also found part of the Jeremiah collection (chs. 48:1-49:27) to be "archaic" or pre-Jeremianic in origin. Seeligman (1954),[21] in a study of the extent of mantic-prophetic influence on the classical prophets, concluded that the major literary influence is *via* the OAN tradition which he sees as basically "war-prophecy." The work of these Israeli scholars was published in modern Hebrew and, for several years, exerted little influence abroad. In 1960-61 Norman Gottwald, while on a Fulbright grant at the Hebrew University in Jerusalem, did the basic research for his subsequent book, *All the Kingdoms of the Earth* (1964). In this book, which made use of this modern Hebrew literature, particularly that of Kaufmann, Gottwald concluded that the OAN tradition "was one of the earliest, if not the earliest, form of Hebrew prophecy and that the style and motifs were taken over from

---

doctoral dissertation submitted to Johns Hopkins University in 1963.

[18] *Ibid.*, pp. 88-89.

[19] M. Diman-Haran, "An Archaic Remnant in Prophetic Literature" (Hebrew), *BIES Reader B* (Vols. I-XV, 1933-1950) (Jerusalem, 1965), pp. 250-58; published originally in *BIES* 13 (1946/47), pp. 7-15.

[20] Y. Kaufmann, *Tôldôt Ha-Emûnah Ha-Yisre'ēlît* (Heb.) (4 vols.; Tel Aviv: Bialik Institute-Dvir, 1937-56, III, pp. 38ff. and 415ff.

[21] I. A. Seeligman, "Concerning the Problems of Prophecy in Israel, its History and Character" (Heb.), *EI* 3 (1954), pp. 125-32.

non-Israelite prototypes, in some cases the actual foreign compositions were used."[22] Though he has not published his work on the subject, Talmon, another Israeli scholar, has played an important role in shaping the current discussion of the OAN material. His course on the oracles against the nations offered at Brandeis University subsequently led to a doctoral dissertation by Barry Margulis (1967),[23] written under the guidance of Talmon and Sarna. Margulis analyzed the literary style and motifs of the OAN tradition by means of a method he calls "stereotype analysis." His study also was intended to suggest, at least in broad outline, the literary history of the OAN tradition.

Toward a History of the OAN Tradition

Though the desire to reconstruct the history of the OAN tradition has been present from the beginning of modern critical study of the prophetic literature, that history as such remains to be written. The early literary critics imposed a preconceived history of the phenomenon of prophecy on this material and consequently relegated the OAN tradition to the Exilic or post-Exilic periods. The impulse from form criticism undermined the historical presuppositions of the literary critics and raised a series of important questions about the history of both prophecy and the OAN tradition. In Hegelian fashion the impulse from German form criticism reversed the picture, positing the OAN tradition as among the earliest forms of prophetic speech, a pre-classical *Gattung*. The resultant dialectic is yet to be fully resolved.

As early as 1924 Kraeling challenged the Hellenistic or Maccabean date commonly assigned to Zech. 9:1-10 and argued for a pre-Exilic setting among the circles to which the 8th century prophet Isaiah belonged.[24] More recently Ginsberg (1950)[25] and Malamat (1950-53),[26] among other noted historians and textual critics, took up the gauntlet seeking to pin down specific OAN material to pre-Exilic dates so as to make use of this material in historical research. More often than not such efforts met with but limited success.

---

[22]Norman K. Gottwald, *All the Kingdoms of the Earth* (New York: Harper & Row, 1964), p. 49.

[23]Barry B. Margulis, "Studies in the Oracles Against the Nations" (unpub. Ph.D. dissertation, Brandeis University, December, 1966).

[24]E. G. H. Kraeling, "The Historical Situation in Zech. 9:1-10," *AJSL* 41 (Oct., 1924), pp. 24-33).

[25]H. L. Ginsberg, "Judah and the Transjordan States from 734 to 582 B.C.E.," in *Alexander Marx Jubilee Volume*, English Section (New York: Jewish Theological Seminary of America, 1950), pp. 347-68.

[26]Abraham Malamat, "The Historical Setting of Two Biblical Prophecies on the Nations," *IEJ* 1 (1950-51), pp. 149-59; and "Amos 1:5 in the Light of the Til Barsip Inscriptions," *BASOR* 129 (1953), pp. 25-26.

As Margulis has observed, the use of this material is severely limited as long as the literary character and history of the material itself has not been established.[27]

The flood of extra-biblical material, particularly in the decade following the end of World War II, has exerted a powerful influence on the historical assessment of the OAN tradition. One of the most striking illustrations of this fact is the tablets of the Babylonian Chronicle published by Wiseman in 1956.[28] This invaluable historical document was known to the scholarly community since the appearance of L. W. King's *Chronicles Concerning Early Babylonian Kings* in 1907, but there were serious gaps in this text, which had originally covered the years 626-556 B.C. Wiseman's publication cast a brilliant new light on the years 626-23 and 605-594 and the response within certain circles of biblical scholarship is most instructive. The very year that Wiseman's work was published also saw the publication of Hyatt's commentary on Jeremiah in *The Interpreter's Bible*, where -- in the tradition of Vatke, Stade and Schwally -- virtually all of Jeremiah's OAN tradition was rejected as inauthentic and late. Later that same year Hyatt reversed himself in a journal article,[29] expressing reservations only about the oracles against Elam and Babylon. In 1960 Lawrence Hay, one of Hyatt's students at Vanderbilt University, completed his doctoral dissertation on "The Oracles Against the Foreign Nations in Jeremiah 46-51" in which he went even further, asserting "that only the oracle on Babylon can be conclusively denied to Jeremiah."[30] Unfortunately Hay's study was little more than a collation of six major commentaries on the text of Jeremiah 46-51 along with a reconstruction of the relevant political history of the period from *ca.* 669-582 B.C.

The obvious need for a new assessment of the entire OAN tradition was soon taken up by John Hayes at Princeton Seminary (1964).[31] Hayes' approach to the OAN tradition is essentially phenomenological and stands as an excellent introduction to the study of the OAN material, the best over-all treatment of the subject to date. Hayes displays remarkable control of the secondary literature and has presented a detailed synthesis of current scholarly

---

[27]Margulis, *op. cit.*, p. 10.

[28]D. J. Wiseman, *Chronicles of Chaldean Kings (626-556 B.C.) in the British Musuem* (London: The Trustees of the British Museum, 1956).

[29]J. Philip Hyatt, "New Light on Nebuchadrezzar and Judean History," *JBL* 75 (1956), pp. 277-84.

[30]Lawrence C. Hay, "The Oracles Against the Foreign Nations in Jeremiah 46-51" (unpub. Ph.D. thesis, Vanderbilt University, 1960), p. 201.

[31]John H. Hayes, "The Oracles Against the Nations in the Old Testament: Their Usage and Theological Importance" (unpub. Th.D. dissertation, Princeton Theological Seminary, 1964).

opinion.[32] He correctly notes the dominant military imagery in the OAN tradition and the holy war ideology in particular, making this the starting point of his analysis.[33] While observing that both classical prophecy and the OAN tradition have their roots in Israel's earliest wars,[34] he was also keenly aware of the fact "that usage of oracles against other peoples was not limited . . . to the sphere of warfare."[35] Thus considerable attention is given to the place of the OAN tradition within the royal and political life of the nation of Israel, in particular to the so-called royal ideology, national services of lamentation, and international treaties.[36] As a descriptive study of the phenomenon of oracles against foreign nations in ancient Israel, Hayes has made an important contribution.

Hayes has called attention to the fact "that the delivery of oracles against the nations was a prophetical function with a long history."[37] Like Margulis after him, Hayes has suggested the broad outline of that history, noting "that the earliest Israelite usage of oracles against other nations occurred within the realm of warfare"[38] and that the "usage of oracles against the nations in the monarchial period shows a development in the direction of judgment oracles."[39] In his discussion of Ezekiel's oracles against Egypt he also observed that "only the faint outline of historical existence" remains in this eschatologically oriented material.[40] The historical development from war oracle to judgment speech to early apocalyptic usage is thus implied. And yet the dictum which Hayes applied to the OAN material in Zechariah and Joel applies equally well to a good many of the OAN passages he has discussed: "Due to problems of dating, it is difficult to assign the material to any definite historical period."[41]

---

[32]It is unfortunate that Margulis (*op. cit.*) was unaware of this earlier work in his subsequent study at Brandeis. It would have provided a much needed corrective to some of the excesses in his rather cavalier treatment of non-Israeli scholarship on the subject. Note, in particular, such comments as: "the O.A.N. tradition belongs to that rare species of biblical literature which has failed to receive scholarly treatment from the very beginning of critical Biblical scholarship" (p. 1); "Scholarly interest in the O.A.N. virtually ceases with Gunkel's aforementioned essay [until Bentzen's article in 1950]" (p. 9); and "the most significant approach to the material yet to emerge . . . (emenates) from the circle of Israeli scholars and . . . cannot but have escaped the notice of all but a few of their European and American counterparts" (p. 15).

[33]Hayes, *op. cit.*, pp. 39-67. [34]*Ibid.*, p. 69.

[35]*Ibid.*, p. 93. [36]*Ibid.*, pp. 93-172. [37]*Ibid.*, p. 174.

[38]*Ibid.*, p. 93. [39]*Ibid.*, p. 80. [40]*Ibid.*, p. 269.

[41]*Ibid.*, p. 288.

Martin Kessler, in a paper read in 1969 at the SBL meeting at Toronto, raised the question of method as the central issue in regards the historical assessment of the OAN tradition.[42] Deeply influenced by James Muilenburg, Kessler selected the concept of "rhetorical criticism"[43] as a possible way out of what he called the "methodological quandry" with respect to Jeremiah 50-51. He does not reject form criticism as a legitimate method of inquiry into the study of the biblical text. Rather, he seeks to move beyond the limits inherent in the form critical approach and its atomistic tendencies, by giving primary attention to the larger rhetorical usage, where a number of various literary forms may be adapted to new purposes by a given author. Kessler suggests that we may be on the edge of a methodological breakthrough in the study of the OAN tradition.

Methodology, Objectives and Limits of the Present Study

A more promising way out of the so-called "methodological quandry"[44] has become evident in recent years, particularly in a series of studies over the past decade or so at Harvard University. The synthesis which promises eventually to resolve the methodological dialectic produced by the impulses from classical literary criticism and subsequent form criticism, and to reduce the OAN material to manageable proportions for historical research is a confluence of several important lines of inquiry. The dominant figure in the emergence of this methodological synthesis is Frank Cross.

The most primary need has been for a more objective control of the Hebrew text of the OAN tradition which includes "some of the finest poetry in the entire prophetic canon."[45] To the steady advancement in the fields of lexicography and historical grammar, Cross has added an important breakthrough in the study of Hebrew prosody. Building on the earlier work of Albright,[46] and the epoch making studies of Parry and Lord in the nature of

---

[42]Martin Kessler, "Oracles Against the Nations: Jeremiah 50 and 51" (paper read at the annual meeting of the Society of Biblical Literature in Toronto, November 19, 1969).

[43]James Muilenburg, "Form Criticism and Beyond," *JBL* 88 (1969), pp. 1-18.

[44]Borrowing Kessler's terminology, see note 42 above.

[45]John Bright, *Jeremiah* (AB 21, Garden City, New York: Doubleday & Company, 1965), p. 307.

[46]William F. Albright, "The Earliest Forms of Hebrew Verse," *JPOS* 2 (1922), pp. 69-86; "Some Additional Notes on the Song of Deborah," *JPOS* 2 (1922), pp. 284-85; "The Oracles of Balaam," *JBL* 63 (1944), pp. 207-33; "The Old Testament and the Canaanite Language and Literature," *CBQ* 7 (1945), pp. 5-31; "The Psalm of Habakkuk," in *Studies in Old Testament Prophecy*, ed. by

oral narrative poetry,[47] Professor Cross and some of his students have added much to our growing knowledge of the canons of ancient Hebrew poetry which in turn are rooted in Canaanite poetry.[48] As is so often the case in scientific endeavor, the man who builds a better theoretical model or who improves the symbolic representation of a given phenomenon through a more efficient system of notation, makes a profound contribution to the advancement of human knowledge. Thus the abandonment of the Ley-Sievers system of poetic scansion in favor of Cross's system of long (l) and short (b) cola based primarily on syllable count is a more important methodological step than the casual reader may realize.

A second line of inquiry which has also contributed much to the formulation of a more objective control of the Hebrew text is a more accurate understanding of the history of the biblical text itself which has grown out of studies in the Qumran literature during the past decade. Again Cross has been a central figure.[49] Though much work remains to be done in this area, the

---

H. H. Rowley (T. H. Robinson Festschrift, Edinburgh: T. & T. Clark, 1950), pp. 1-18; "A Catalogue of Early Hebrew Lyric Poems (Psalm LXVIII)," *HUCA* 23 (1950-51), pp. 1-40; "Some remarks on the Song of Moses in Deuteronomy XXXII," *VT* 9 (1959), pp. 339-46; "Archaic Survivals in the Text of Canticles," in *Hebrew and Semitic Studies*, ed. by D. Winton Thomas and W. D. McHardy (G. R. Driver Festschrift, Oxford, 1962), pp. 1-7; *Yahweh and the Gods of Canaan* (Garden City, New York: Doubleday & Company, 1968), pp. 1-52.

[47]Albert B. Lord, *The Singer of Tales* (New York: Atheneum, 1968); published originally as *Harvard Studies in Comparative Literature*, 24 (Cambridge: Harvard University, 1960). This book is the popular introduction to the study of Yugoslavian oral poetry on the part of Milman Parry and his disciple Albert Lord.

[48]Frank M. Cross, Jr., *Studies in Ancient Yahwistic Poetry* (Baltimore: Johns Hopkins University, 1950); "The Blessing of Moses," with David N. Freedman, *JBL* 67 (1948), pp. 191-210; "A Royal Psalm of Thanksgiving: II Samuel 22 = Psalm 18," with David N. Freedman, *JBL* 72 (1953), pp. 15-34; "The Song of Miriam," with David N. Freedman, *JNES* 14 (1955), pp. 237-50; "The Song of the Sea and Canaanite Myth," *JThC* 5 (1968), pp. 1-25; and *Canaanite Myth and Hebrew Epic* (Cambridge: Harvard University, 1973), *passim*. See also Paul D. Hanson, "The Song of Heshbon and David's Nîr," *HTR* 61 (1968), pp. 297-320.

[49]Frank M. Cross, Jr., "The History of the Biblical Text in the Light of the Discoveries in the Judaean Desert," *HTR* 57 (1964), pp. 281-99; "The Contribution of the Discoveries at Qumran to the Study of the Biblical Text," *IEJ* 16 (1966), pp. 81-95. Mention should also be made of the earlier work of W. F. Albright, "New Light on Early Recensions of the Hebrew Bible, *BASOR* 140 (1955), pp. 27-33.

broad outline of the early recensional activity in the transmission of the Hebrew text is apparent, and a new appreciation for the nature and worth of the various recensions of LXX has emerged. The study of John G. Janzen on the text of Jeremiah (1965)[50] is of particular importance in providing a more adequate basis for text critical work in Jeremiah.

These first two lines of inquiry are foundational in nature and shape our basic approach to the Hebrew text in matters of reconstruction and interpretation. A third line of inquiry has perhaps even more direct bearing on the problem of the historical development of the OAN tradition. New understanding of the history of military, political and religious institutions in ancient Israel has emerged in recent years which is of fundamental importance in any historical assessment of the OAN tradition. The most important of these institutions, as far as this study is concerned, is that of holy war.[51] From 1958 to 1965 a series of eight papers appeared in the Old Testament Seminar at Harvard University on warfare and holy war in ancient Israel.[52] The most important of these studies, for our purposes here, are those of Kaufman, "The Significance of Oracles Concerning Foreign Nations in Jeremiah," and Shenkel, "Jeremiah and Holy War," both of which were written in the Fall of

---

[50] John G. Janzen, *Studies in the Text of Jeremiah* (Cambridge: Harvard University, 1973); published form of Ph.D. thesis submitted in 1965.

[51] The starting point in any modern discussion of "holy war" is the important monograph by G. von Rad, *Der Heilige Krieg im Alten Israel* (Abhandlungen zur Theologie des Alten und Neuen Testaments, No. 20; Zürich: Zwingli-Verlag, 1951); available also in 4th ed. (Göttingen: Vandenhoeck & Ruprecht, 1965). See also von Rad's *Studies in Deuteronomy*, trans. by David Stalker (Studies in Biblical Theology, No. 9; London: SCM, and Naperville, Ill., 1953). Cf. also J. A. Soggin, "Der prophetische Gedanke über den heiligen Krieg als Gericht gegen Israel," *VT* 10 (1960), pp. 79-83; and the recent discussion of G. Ernest Wright, "God the Warrior," in *The Old Testament and Theology* (New York, Evanston, and London: Harper & Row, 1969), pp. 121-50.

[52] James D. Purvis, "The Holy War in Early Israel" (Fall, 1958); G. L. Vogan, "Yahweh Sebaoth and the Ark of the Covenant" (Fall, 1958); Patrick D. Miller, Jr., "Warfare in the Davidic Era" (Fall, 1959); Michael Stone, "The Language of Holy War in the Prophets of the 8th Century (Fall, 1961); Ivan T. Kaufman, "Holy War and Foreign Policy in Eighth Century Prophecy" (Fall, 1961); James D. Shenkel, "Jeremiah and Holy War" (Fall, 1962); Ivan T. Kaufman, "The Significance of Oracles Concerning Foreign Nations in Jeremiah" (Fall, 1962); and Marvin L. Chaney, "Mythology and Holy War in Isaiah 34:1-17 and 51:9-11" (Fall, 1965). Though unpublished, papers submitted to the Old Testament Seminar at Harvard University are bound and available in the Andover-Harvard Library, Harvard Divinity School.

1962. The year 1962 also saw the publication of an important study in Germany by Robert Bach.[53] In this particular study, Bach traced the literary history of two important forms of prophetic speech, the summons to battle and the summons to flight, and found their original *Sitz im Leben* within the ancient institution of holy war in Israel. In December of 1962 Professor Cross delivered a lecture at Brandeis University which was subsequently published as "The Divine Warrior in Israel's Early Cult."[54] Making use of this paper and other work done in the Old Testament Department at Harvard, Patrick Miller produced his important dissertation on "Holy War and Cosmic War in Early Israel" (1963).[55]

Meanwhile another line of inquiry, stemming in part from Kaufman's observations on the historical-legal background of Amos 1-2, as expanded by Professor Cross, [56] led to a programmatic summation by Professor Wright, "The

---

[53]Robert Bach, *Die Aufforderungen zur Flucht und zum Kampf im alttestamentlichen Prophetenspruch* (WMANT 9; Neukirchen: Neukirchen Verlag, 1962); which is the published form of his earlier dissertation, "Formgeschichtliche Untersuchungen zu den Fremdvölkerspruchen des Jeremiabuchs" (unpub. doctoral thesis, Rheinischen Friedrich-Wilhelms-Universität in Bonn, 1956).

[54]Frank M. Cross, Jr., "The Divine Warrior in Israel's Early Cult," in *Studies and Text III: Biblical Motifs*, ed. A. Altmann (Cambridge: Harvard University, 1966). See also *Canaanite Myth and Hebrew Epic* (1973), pp. 91-111.

[55]This study is now available in published form, *The Divine Warrior in Early Israel* (Cambridge: Harvard University, 1973).

[56]Ivan T. Kaufman, "The Significance of Oracles . . .," pp. 3-5. Cf. also the discussion of G. Ernest Wright in *Encounter* 26 (1965), p. 236. In a seminar situation it is often difficult to determine where one person's contribution or insight leaves off and that of another begins. From an examination of class notes taken during the seminar in question and conversation with two participants, it would appear that an original insight on the part of Kaufman was significantly expanded in the subsequent discussion, particularly by Professor Cross. Kaufman called attention to the system of vassal treaty relationships created in the Davidic Empire as the legal background for understanding the indictments against the nations concerned in Amos 1-2 (cf. in particular Kaufman's discussion on p. 4 of his paper). Professor Cross went on to suggest, in outline form, a typology of the OAN tradition as a whole. He suggested that two types of oracles against the nations can be observed, both of which are rooted in Israel's ancient Tribal League: 1) prophetic oracles in regard to national enemies, announcing defeat or victory in battle, and 2) summons to go to war on a member of the league itself. He went on to note that with Amos the OAN tradition has become a

Nations in Hebrew Prophecy" (1965),[57] which sets the stage for the present study. Building on the work of two of his students and the independent study of Mendenhall on the concept of *nāqām* ("vindication") and the *imperium* of Yahweh,[58] Professor Wright argued that prophecy in ancient Israel is essentially a political office:[59]

> The chief content of Israel's literature is the concern for the politics of God, that is for the *imperium* and the manner in which its power and purposes are made effective. During the period of Israel's monarchy the prophetic office, charismatic in function as it was, nevertheless played a primary role in the effective government of the *imperium*. Ecstasy was taken up into this office . . . . Yet the meaning given to the ecstatic in Israel, and the manner in which its more primitive features are overcome in the greater of the prophetic figures, can

---

type of literary mode, a vehicle of divine judgment. A new type of oracle then emerged in Israel, addressed to a foreign nation who was an ally and whose representative was in Jerusalem. Yahweh was to fight on the side of Israel in league with the nation(s) concerned. In the prophecies of Isaiah, Jeremiah and Ezekiel the horizon was greatly extended to include foreign enemies who were not former members of the empire of David. Both the Assyrian and Babylonian empires were envisioned as ordained of Yahweh, the suzerain of the nations.

[57]G. Ernest Wright, "The Nations in Hebrew Prophecy," *Encounter* 26 (1965), pp. 225-37.

[58]George E. Mendenhall, "God of Vengeance, Shine Forth!" *Wittenberg Bulletin* (Wittenberg College, Springfield, Ohio) 45 (Dec., 1948), pp. 37-42; "The Vengeance of God: A Bridge Between Faith and Reality," manuscript of address given at Harvard Divinity School (Fall, 1965); and "The 'Vengeance' of Yahweh," *The Tenth Generation* (Baltimore: Johns Hopkins University, 1973), pp. 69-104. For a brief summary of Mendenhall's views see Wright, *op. cit.*, pp. 231, 235-36. The term *imperium* is taken from ancient Roman law and refers to government by fiat. An *imperium* is a power to command which includes the power to exercise force; it is the "effective exercise of personal power, as distinct from our modern bureaucratic, elective, and representative type of officialdom in government" (Wright, *op. cit.*, p. 231). The *imperium* of Yahweh in ancient Israel was administered through bureaucrats and messengers: priests and prophets. The exercise of *imperium* takes place primarily through two means: war, declared through the prophet (Yahweh's messenger), against those who do not recognize the *imperium*; and law, with respect to those who are bound by it.

[59]G. Ernest Wright, "The Nations in Hebrew Prophecy," *Encounter* 26 (1965), p. 231.

> never be grasped apart from this basic and political conception of prophecy as an agency of an *imperium* conceived to control all things in the universe, as universal in its exercise of power as was the divine council of every polytheistic structure of the ancient Near East.

The recent assessment of the legal basis for indictments against foreign nations by Howard Macy (1970)[60] builds directly on the work of Wright and Mendenhall. Macy argues that, at least in some cases, the prophets utilized the covenant treaty metaphor to indict foreign nations for violation of specific international treaties. He notes, however, that "the larger and more inclusive category is the metaphor of indictment for violation of Yahweh's universal suzerainty."[61]

In Cross's publications of 1966 and 1968 he has outlined the history of the ritual conquest traditions which were apparently celebrated at Gilgal in the premonarchical period and in the subsequent Royal Fall Festival in Jerusalem.[62] This festival was a major carrier of holy war traditions throughout the period of the monarchy in Israel, as noted by William Millar who has reconstructed the Royal Fall Festival in greater detail in his study of the "Isaiah Apocalypse."[63]

Another line of inquiry has started from the other end of the time spectrum with respect to the OAN tradition, moving from the post-Exilic phenomenon of full-blown apocalyptic back to the early apocalyptic communities of the 6th century. The study of the origins of Jewish apocalyptic by Paul Hanson is the major contribution in this regard, and his work on Zech. 9:1-17 and Isa. 63:1-6 is of primary importance in any assessment of the OAN tradition as a whole.[64]

---

[60] Howard R. Macy, "The Legal Metaphor in Oracles Against Foreign Nations in the Pre-Exilic Prophets" (unpub. M.A. thesis, Earlham School of Religion, 1970).

[61] *Ibid.*, p. 57.

[62] Frank M. Cross, Jr., "The Divine Warrior . . .," pp. 14-16, 25-27, esp. notes 11, 12 and 59; "The Song of the Sea . . .," pp. 21-15; and *Canaanite Myth and Hebrew Epic*, pp. 99-111.

[63] William R. Millar, "Isaiah 24-27 and the Origin of Apocalyptic" (unpub. Ph.D. thesis, Harvard University, 1970), pp. 156-75. This dissertation is in the process of revision and is scheduled for publication by Harvard University Press. Isaiah 24-27 is a 6th century composition, closely related to the developing OAN tradition.

[64] Paul D. Hanson, "Studies in the Origins of Jewish Apocalyptic" (unpub. Ph.D. thesis, Harvard University, 1969), esp. pp. 200-209 and 269-98. This study has been published recently in revised form, *The Dawn of Apocalyptic* (Philadelphia: Fortress, 1975). See also Frank M. Cross, Jr., "New

The present study is not an attempt to write a history of the OAN tradition as such. At best it is intended as a prolegomenon to such a task. The focus of this study is the various forms of prophetic speech which constitute the war oracle in ancient Israel. Summons to battle, summons to flight, summons to mourn (because of impending destruction), battle curses, announcements of victory or defeat, victory songs and taunt songs against the enemy are among the more dominant speech forms found in the war oracle. It is the purpose of this study to trace the historical development of the war oracle in ancient Israel from earliest times to *ca.* 580 B.C. The OAN tradition of Amos 1-2 and Jer. 46-51 forms the two poles around which the present analysis takes shape. Two major transformations of the war oracle are observed. In Amos 1-2 the earlier war oracle has been transformed into a judgment speech against the nations of the idealized Davidic Empire, with particular focus on Israel. In the hands of Jeremiah, following the defeat of Judah and the exile of King Jehoiachin in 597, the war oracle experienced another transformation as the focus of attention shifted from judgment on the national foes of Yahweh, the suzerain of the nations, to the preservation of the Divine Warrior's people in exile and their ultimate restoration to Zion.

No attempt is made to move beyond Jeremiah to the important OAN traditions of Ezekiel, Second Isaiah and the other Exilic and post-Exilic writers of OAN material.[65] Within the limits set, the present study is an attempt to build on the work already done in the Old Testament Department at Harvard University, as outlined above. The relevant OAN material is subjected to detailed prosodic-textual analysis, form critical study and historical interpretation. Hopefully the end result is a firmer footing in the pursuit of a history of the large and important literary tradition known as the oracles against the nations in Old Testament prophecy.

Directions in the Study of Apocalyptic," *JThC* 6 (1969), pp. 157-65.

[65]Hayes, *op. cit.*, pp. 250-91, presents a good general survey of this material.

CHAPTER TWO

AMOS AND THE TRANSFORMATION OF THE WAR ORACLE

In his discussion of "War and Peace," G. F. Thomas almost instinctively turned to the oracles against the nations in Amos 1-2 to paint a terrible picture of the folly and cruelty of war.[1] Battle atrocities, broken treaty agreements, gross inhumanity and wanton destruction -- the evils of war as presented by Amos -- strike home with force; for the evils of war are all too evident to modern man. Nonetheless, as Roger Caillois has argued, war is not to be relegated to the profane as over against the sacred.[2] No matter how uncomfortable the idea may be to man today, war and the sacred are integrally related, especially in the religion of ancient Israel. The centrality of warfare in the development of the religion of Israel led Wellhausen, long ago, to posit the war camp as Israel's oldest sanctuary.[3] More recently R. Smend has argued, rather persuasively, that the *Jahwekrieg* was in fact the formative basis of the nation of Israel.[4] The concept of God as a "Divine Warrior" leading his hosts in battle against foes in both human and cosmic spheres is dominant in Israel's most ancient traditions and lives on as a central motif within the developing OAN tradition.

The earliest collection of OAN material in the prophetic literature is that preserved in Amos 1-2. In several respects this particular collection is unique in that six different foreign nations are treated together in a highly stylized manner, while the work as a whole focuses on Israel who faces divine judgment. War imagery dominates the oracles and the judgment on Israel presents the startling picture of Yahweh's holy war waged against his own people.

It is the intent of this chapter to examine the war oracle in ancient Israel, particularly within the context of the institution of holy war, so as

---

[1]George F. Thomas, *Christian Ethics and Moral Philosophy* (New York: Charles Scribner's Sons, 1955), p. 347.

[2]Roger Caillois, "War and the Sacred," Appendix III in *Man and the Sacred*, tr. by Meyer Barash (Glencoe, Illinois: Free Press, 1959), pp. 163-80.

[3]Julius Wellhausen, *Israelitische und jüdische Geschichte*, 7th Ausgabe (Berlin: Druck und Verlag von Georg Reimer, 1914), p. 28.

[4]Rudolph Smend, *Jahwekrieg und Stämmebund* (FRLANT 84, Göttingen: Vandenhoeck & Ruprecht, 1963). This important work was recently translated by Max G. Rogers, *Yahweh War & Tribal Confederation: Reflections upon Israel's Earliest History* (Nashville and New York: Abingdon, 1970).

to determine the role played by Amos in the development of the OAN tradition. Y. Kaufmann[5] and N. Gottwald[6] have argued, on literary and historical grounds, that the oracles in Amos 1-2 have a previous history. Further support for this conclusion will be presented in this chapter. Nonetheless, it will be argued that Amos 1:3 - 2:16 forms a literary unit composed in the 8th century by the prophet Amos. In so doing he transformed an earlier prophetic speech form, a war oracle in the form of a judgment speech against a covenant "brother," into an oracle of divine judgment against Israel.

War Oracles in Israel's Covenant League

As far back as prophecy and divination can be traced in the ancient Near East they stand in relation to political activity and war in particular. A *bārû*-priest was attached to each army contingent at 18th century Mari.[7] Before any decisive action was undertaken such as a declaration of war or the conclusion of a peace treaty, a *bārû*-priest was summoned to sacrifice a sheep and inspect its liver to determine whether the gods were favorably or unfavorably disposed toward the matter in question.[8] Prophecy and divination were closely linked, the former probably emerging from the latter as the personal endowments of individual interpreters allowed for innovative development.[9] War was a recognized instrument of foreign policy in the ancient Near East; and kings, realizing the need for contact with religious forces, drew prophetism into the court, thus helping to shape the political interest of the developing prophetic movement.

Within the context of the Israelite Covenant League four types of war oracles are found: divination-type responses to specific military questions, prophetic oracles of defeat or victory in battle, summons to battle in defense of the league or on a member of the league, and summons to flee from impending destruction. These oracle types are examined in relation to the developing OAN tradition.

---

[5]Y. Kaufmann, *op. cit.*, Vol. III/1, pp. 60ff.

[6]N. Gottwald, *op. cit.*, pp. 103-106.

[7]Cf. *ARM* II, no. 22 and *ARM* III, no. 80. For a discussion of omens and warfare in Mesopotamia see A. Leo Oppenheim, "Zur keilschriftlichen Omenliteratur," *Or* 5 (1936), pp. 208-211. See also the chapter on "Diviners and Omens" in the recent study of Albert E. Glock, "Warfare in Mari and Early Israel" (unpub. Ph.D. dissertation, University of Michigan, 1968), pp. 128-38 and 196-97.

[8]I. Mendelsohn, "Divination," in *The Interpreter's Dictionary of the Bible* (New York and Nashville: Abingdon, 1962), I, p. 857.

[9]Alfred Guillaume, *Prophecy and Divination Among the Hebrews and Other Semites* (London: Hodder and Stoughton, 1938), pp. 37-53 and 107-133.

1. Oracular Divination

Oracular divination is a wide-spread phenomenon in antiquity and persists in the religion of Israel, even after the emergence of true prophecy. With the Urim and Thummim and the ephod, techniques of divination were officially incorporated into Israel's priestly religious structures. When Joshua was commissioned to succeed Moses in the narrative of Num. 27:12-23, he was taken before the priest Eleazar who inquired "the judgment of the Urim before Yahweh" and invested Joshua with the authority of Moses as a political-military leader: ". . . at his word they shall go out, and at his word they shall come in, both he and all the people of Israel with him, the whole congregation." The picture is a military one. Joshua was commissioned as commander-in-chief to lead Israel in the wars of conquest (cf. also Deut. 3:18-22). The divine will in the matter was communicated through the Urim, the oracular media controlled by the priesthood.

Oracular inquiries in a military setting occur on occasion in the book of Judges. In Judges 1:1-2 the people of Israel consulted Yahweh to find out which tribe was to take the lead in the wars of conquest. The oracle designated Judah, though no explicit reference is made as to the means by which the oracle was received. Gideon's action with the fleece of wool was an attempt to receive divine assurance in his military commission against the Midianites (Judg. 6:36-40). The interpretation of a dream on the part of a Midianite soldier to mean that God had given Midian into Gideon's hand illustrates another popular means of oracular divination as a means of obtaining a war oracle (Judg. 7:9-14). The Danite spies sought an oracle as to the success or failure of their attempt to find a new home (Judg. 18:5). The Levite priest in the house of Micah had "an ephod, teraphim, a graven image, and a molten image" (Judg. 18:14), which were so valued by the warriors from Dan that they were stolen along with the Levite priest. In the war against Benjamin, which is discussed in greater detail later, the tribal council assembled at Mizpah to render judgment on the matter in question. When war was declared, the people of Israel went up to Bethel to find out who was to lead the battle. The oracle designated Judah (Judg. 20:23-27). The ark of the covenant is mentioned as the source of the divine oracle in this particular instance (Judg. 20:27-28).

The sacred lots as oracular media appear again in a military setting under Saul and David. When Saul discovered that Jonathan and his armor-bearer had gone up to battle alone against the Philistines, he called for the ephod[10] (I Sam. 14:18). While Saul consulted the priest, the tumult of Yahweh's battle in the Philistine camp increased. After the subsequent rout

---

[10]Reading "ephod" with LXX; cf. S. R. Driver, *Notes on the Hebrew Text of the Books of Samuel* (Oxford: Clarendon Press, 1890), pp. 83-84.

of the Philistines, Saul again turned to the sacred lots to determine whether the Israelites should pursue after the enemy (I Sam. 14:36-37). He received no answer because of sin in the camp. The Urim and Thummim were used to discover Jonathan's transgression (I Sam. 14:41-42).

David made use of oracular divination on several occasions. As a fugitive from Saul he "consulted Yahweh" twice to bolster the courage of his men in battle with the Philistines (I Sam. 23:1-4). He summoned the ephod again after the battle to determine whether or not to leave the town of Keilah (I Sam. 23:6-12). When Ziklag was destroyed, David summoned the ephod to inquire on the pursuit of the Amalekites (I Sam. 30:7-8). After he had been anointed king of Israel and had captured Jerusalem, David again "inquired of Yahweh" (II Sam. 5:19) on whether or not he should attack the Philistines.

Solomon banished the priest Abiathar, who "bore the ark of Yahweh before David" (I Kings 2:26), because of his complicity in the accession intrigue of Adonijah. After this particular incident, the sacred lots are not mentioned again (except for the ambiguous post-Exilic passage in Ezra 2:63 = Neh. 7:65) and apparently ceased to be used.

A further glimpse into the phenomenon of oracular divination in military matters is preserved in the fascinating story of Saul and the medium of Endor. When Saul "inquired of Yahweh," he received no answer "either by dreams, or by Urim, or by prophets" (I Sam. 28:6). Dismayed by the strength of the Philistines and failing to receive an answer by more customary means, Saul turned to witchcraft and summoned the ghost of Samuel. Apparently an oracle of success in battle was still of critical importance to maintain the morale of military troops in premonarchical Israel. The oracle was often of a mechanical nature administered by the priests, similar to the war oracle sought by other peoples in antiquity.

Allusions in the prophetic literature indicate that the use of divination continued throughout the monarchy, though not on an official basis. Hosea 4:12 is perhaps the most explicit such reference: "My people inquire of a thing of wood, and their staff (מקל) gives them oracles." The continued use of the ephod and teraphim for purposes of divination seems to be alluded to in Hosea 3:4 -- "For the children of Israel shall dwell many days without king or prince, without sacrifice or pillar, without ephod or teraphim." Even after the destruction of Jerusalem, the function of the "teraphim" and "diviners" (קוסמים) was apparently well known in Israel (cf. Zech. 10:2). In all such allusions, however, there is no clear indication that oracular divination as such was used routinely by the political-military leaders of Israel in time of war. It should be noted that in the attempted revolt against Babylon in *ca.* 594, Jeremiah made reference to prophets, diviners, soothsayers and sourcerers as the source of a war oracle among Judah's neighbors (Jer. 27:9-10); but when he turned his attention to King Zedekiah and the priests in Jerusalem, he mentioned only the word of the prophets as the source of the summons to revolt (Jer. 27:14).

As war became more secularized under David and Solomon with standing armies, professional soldiers, horse-drawn chariots, and mercenary troops; the king turned to professional advisers for council in military matters. The story of Hushai and Ahithophel as rival counselors for Absalom in his rebellion against David, illustrates the new situation (II Sam. 16:15ff). Both men were summoned before Absalom to give their advice in the battle against David. Absalom and the "men of Israel" weighed the advice given and chose a course of action. On the death of Solomon, Rehoboam sought advice from two opposing groups of advisers and his decision to heed the advice of the younger counselors precipitated the successful revolt of the northern tribes (I Kings 12).

A most instructive illustration of the change in the use of oracular divination which took place during the 10th-9th centuries in Israel is the account of Elisha's death-bed war oracle (II Kings 13:14-19). When Joash, king of Israel, learned of Elisha's terminal illness, he went to the prophet and wept, saying: "My father, my father! The chariots of Israel and its horsemen!" This exclamation is identical to that uttered by Elisha when Elijah was taken up by the whirlwind into heaven (II Kings 2:12). The statement probably refers to the prophet's role in the institution of holy war in North Israel in the 9th century, as suggested by P. Miller and S. Asami.[11] Though the statement itself is cryptic, it is clear that, from a military point of view, both Elijah and Elisha were more important and more powerful than mere chariots and horsemen. After this introductory exclamation on the part of Joash, Elisha ordered the king to take a bow and arrows. The king was told to open the window eastward and shoot. Elisha then uttered an oracle of victory in battle: "Yahweh's arrow of victory, the arrow of victory over Syria! For you shall fight the Syrians in Aphek until you have made an end of them" (II Kings 13:17). The king was then ordered to take the arrows and strike the ground with them. When he struck the ground only three times, Elisha was angry and exclaimed: "You should have struck five or six times; then you would have struck down Syria until you had made an end of it, but now you will strike down Syria only three times" (vs. 19). This incident is sometimes explained as belomancy and compared to the reference in Ezekiel 21:21 (in an OAN context), where: ". . . the king of Babylon stands at the parting of the way, at the head of the two ways, to use divination; he shakes the arrows, he consults

---

[11]Patrick D. Miller, Jr., *The Divine Warrior in Early Israel* (Cambridge: Harvard University, 1973), pp. 134-35; and Sadao Asami, "The Central Sanctuary in Israel in the Ninth Century B.C." (unpub. Th.D. thesis, Harvard University, 1964), p. 359.

the teraphim, he looks at the liver." It is more important to note the contrast with earlier oracular divination. The mechanical means of divination are unimportant. Elisha makes use of divinatory techniques, but it is with the authority of Yahweh himself that he speaks. It is the spoken word that is central. The precise means by which the prophet discerns this word are of no greater significance than the specific rod of almond or the boiling pot that led Jeremiah to conclude that judgment was coming on Israel out of the north (cf. Jer. 1:11-19).

War oracles in ancient Israel, at least in the period of the tribal league and early monarchy, were often obtained by means of oracular divination. Mechanical means of divination were used to ascertain the divine will, much as was the case among other peoples of the ancient Near East. The Urim and Thummim, the ephod, the teraphim, and the ark of the covenant were the central religious objects in such sacred rites. In the course of time, however, the techniques of oracular divination were displaced by the authoritative word of the prophet as Yahweh's divinely appointed spokesman, the official herald of Yahweh's *imperium*.

2. Prophetic Oracles of Victory or Defeat in Battle

Balaam is sometimes cited as Israel's earliest contact with prophecy.[12] In Numbers 22-24 he is described as a North Syrian diviner from the Euphrates valley hired by the king of Moab to curse Israel prior to its entrance into Canaan. The historical situation is difficult, if not impossible, to reconstruct in any manner of detail. Albright has stated the matter rather succinctly:[13]

> It is improbable that the material has been transmitted just as it was delivered or composed, since there are too many broken connections, obvious gaps and repetitions. We may suppose rather that the surviving remains of the Balaam Oracles, which had been transmitted orally, were carefully collected in traditional or conjectural order and were then reduced to writing.

On the basis of studies in early Hebrew orthography and Northwest-Semitic grammar, Albright has dated the first writing down of the poetic oracles attributed to Balaam to "in or about the tenth century B.C."[14] His analysis of the prosodic structure of the oracles suggests an original date of oral composition of *ca.* 1200 B.C.[15] It should also be noted that the historical

---

[12]Gottwald, *op. cit.*, p. 47.

[13]W. F. Albright, "The Oracles of Balaam," *JBL* 63 (1944), p. 226.

[14]*Ibid.*, p. 210.

[15]W. F. Albright, *Yahweh and the Gods of Canaan*, p. 15.

reference to the Kenites in Num. 24:21-22 makes sense only in the period before the time of David, as the Kenites were subsequently absorbed into Israel. But beyond these few remarks little can be determined with any degree of certainty as to the place of Balaam in early Hebrew history or the history of the Balaam tradition as preserved in the Old Testament.[16]

Albright has suggested that Balaam became a convert to Yahwism and that he later abandoned Israel, joining the Midianites in fighting against the Yahwists.[17] Such a conclusion is certainly a rational deduction but moves beyond the evidence at hand. Van Zyl presents a different conclusion on the matter:[18]

> The original words of Balaam which predicted disaster for the Moabites would not have been recorded in the land of Moab, nor would the Moabites have made known the contents of Balaam's predictions to the Israelites, because Israel could have applied them as a weapon against the Moabites themselves. Rumours about the favorable words which Balaam uttered for Israel would have penetrated to Israel and this could have given rise to the creation of the so-called oracle (*sic.*) of Balaam at a stage when it could have been successfully applied by Israel in their struggle against the Moabites.

In his suggestion of the war of liberation under Ehud as the occasion of the promulgation of these oracles,[19] van Zyl also has left the realm of fact for that of conjecture. R. F. Johnson is more cautious in his simple statement that the figure of Balaam "may have had a history not always associated with the oracles now attached to his name."[20] For our purposes it is only necessary to see the so-called Oracles of Balaam as part of the premonarchical war literature of Israel.

In the biblical record as it stands, Balaam utilized techniques of divination and appears as a Mesopotamian *bārû*-priest, at least in the earlier portions of the biblical narrative and the first two oracles. He presented a morning sacrifice. With his employer, Balak, remaining beside the sacrifice,

---

[16]For a competent discussion of these matters and a survey of the pertinent literature see the recent study of William Dumbrell, "The Midianites and Their Transjordanian Successors" (unpub. Th.D. thesis, Harvard University, 1970), pp. 155-57 and 176, n. 91. Dumbrell revives the older theory that Balaam was a Midianite sage. For an exhaustive bibliography on Balaam, arranged chronologically, see J. Coppens, "Les Oracles de Biléam," *Mélanges Eugène Tisserant* I (Studi e Testi 231, Vatican City, 1964), pp. 67-69.

[17]Albright, "Oracles of Balaam," p. 233.

[18]A. H. van Zyl, *The Moabites* (POS 3, Leiden: E. J. Brill, 1960), p. 12.

[19]*Ibid.*, pp. 12, 129-30.

[20]R. F. Johnson, "Balaam," in *IDB*, I, p. 342.

Balaam consulted the omens and undertook certain magical acts while walking. He saw his omena with unhindered vision and apparently fell down during the ceremony, perhaps in an ecstatic trance (cf. Num. 24:4, 16). However, in Numbers 24 the biblical account seems to present a different picture of Balaam. In delivering the last two oracles, Balaam abandoned divination as such and, at least within the received tradition, took his place in the prophetic stream as a true spokesman for Yahweh. The final oracle (Num. 24:15-24) is an unsolicited oracle of doom directed at Moab and her confederates. This particular oracle is of importance in the developing OAN tradition and is alluded to on occasion in the OAN tradition of Isaiah and Jeremiah. The following analysis and translation of the text of this oracle is dependent on the work of W. F. Albright.

<u>Numbers 24:15-24</u>

15	[And he delivered an oracle about him, saying:]		
	Utterance of Balaam, who is Beor's son,	נאם בלעם בנו[a] בער	8
	Utterance of the man whose eye is true;	ונאם [ ] גבר[b] ש-תָּמָּת[c] עין	8
16	Utterance of one who knows the words of El,	נאם שמע אמרי אל	7
	And knows the knowledge of Elyon;	וידע דֵעֹת[d] עליון	7
	He beholds visions of Shaddai,	מחזה שדי יחזה	6
	In a trance, with eyes unveiled:	נפל[e] וגלוי עינים	7
17	I see, but not this moment;	אראנו[f] ולא עתה	7
	I gaze, but it is not soon --	אשורנו[f] ולא קרוב	8
	When the star of Jacob shall prevail;	דרך כוכבם[g] יעקב	7
	And the scepter shall arise in Israel,	וקם שבט מישראל	7
	He shall smite the extremities of Moab,	ומחץ פאתי מואב	7
	And destroy all Bene-Shut.	וקרקר[h] כל בני שת	7
18	Edom shall be dispossessed;	והיה אדום יָרֵש[ ][i]	7
	Dispossessed shall be Seir,	והיה יָרֵש[ ] שעיר	7
19	Jacob shall rule over his foes,	⟨ו⟩[ ]ירדם[j] יעקב⟩[k] איביו	7
	And Israel shall have success;	ועשה ישראל[l] חיל	7
	Yea, he shall slay the remnant of Ar.	והאביד שריד מע[ ]ר[m]	7

---

[21]S. Daiches, "Balaam -- a Babylonian *bārû*," *Hermann Hilprecht Anniversary Volume* (Leipzig, 1909), pp. 60-70. Daiches understood ואלכה in Num. 23:3 as a ritual act and וילך שפי as "he went by pace or step by step," after Assyrian *šēpu*.

20 [And he saw Amalek and delivered an oracle about him, saying:]

Amalek was the first of the clans,	ראשית גוים עמלק	7
But his end is to perish forever.	ואחריתו עד יאבד[n]	7

21 [And he saw the Kenite and delivered an oracle about him, saying:]

	Perennial is your abode, O smith --	איתן מושבך ⟨קין⟩[o]	7
	Your nest is set in the cliffs;	ושים בסלע קנך	7
22	Nonetheless, it shall become fuel,	כי אם יהיה לבעד	7
	. . . . . ?	עד-מה אשור תשבך[p]	?

23 [And he saw Agag (?) and delivered an oracle about him, saying:]

	. . . . . ?	אוי מי יחיה משמו אל	?
24	. . . . . ?	וצים מיד כתים	?
	. . . . . ?	וענו אשור וענו עבר	?
	So he also shall perish forever.	וגם-הוא עדי אבד	7

Numbers 24:15-24 in Outline

A. Introduction to an Ecstatic Revelation (vss. 15-16; cf. Num. 24:3-4)

[1:1] An utterance of Balaam, the "seer,"
[1:1] Who heard a message from God,
[1:1] Who saw the vision clearly:

B. War Oracle: Blessing of Victory for Israel (vss. 17-19)

[1:1] "I see what will be."
[1:1::1:1] Israel will destroy Moab
[1:1::1:1:1] Edom will be dispossessed by Israel.

C. Battle Curses (vss. 20-24)

[1:1] Against Amalek: Amalek will perish forever.
[1:1::1:1] Against the Kenites:
Though apparently secure,
They, too, will be destroyed.
[1:1::1:1] ? Against some other southern people who will also perish forever.

Notes to the Text

[a]Interpreting the *waw* as the preservation of the nominative case-ending, with Albright; cf. also *JBL* 61 (1942), p. 117.

[b]Studies in the historical development of Hebrew poetry have shown that several prosaic particles which appear frequently in the received tradition were not at home in classical Hebrew poetry, especially the את direct object

marker, the relative particle אשר, the definite article (except when it has demonstrative force), and, in many cases, the *waw* conjunction. These particles are deleted here without further discussion in the notes.

[c]Following Wellhausen's explanation of MT שתם העין (*Die Composition des Hexateuchs*, p. 351). Albright confirms this reading with a parallel in a Phoenician incantation from Arslan Tash (see *BASOR* 76 (1939), p. 9, esp. notes 23-26; *BASOR* 84 (1941), p. 11; and Gaster, *Or* 11 (1942), p. 44, 61-63.

[d]Following Albright who proposed the plural form in parallel with the plural in *'imrê 'ēl*; cf. Job 36:4 and I Sam. 2:3 (*kî 'ēl dē'ôt Yahweh*, "for Yahweh is a God of knowledge").

[e]Reading an intransitive participle or derived adjective, and rendering "unconscious," or the like, with Albright; cf. Akk. *nabultu* (for *napultu*), "corpse," and Heb. **napîl*, "dead hero or shade" (Nephilim), **nipl* (*nefel*), "foetus." The diviner was subject to ecstatic trances in which he seemed like a corpse but possessed the gift of interior vision.

[f]Taking the *nun* in אראנו and אשורנו as energic, without the addition of the pronominal suffix, with Albright.

[g]Taking the *mem* as enclitic. According to the Amarna evidence this enclitic particle was vocalized *mi*, *me*, but the vowel had presumably been dropped by the time this oracle was composed.

[h]Albright and most commentators emend the text here with SP and the parallel line in Jer. 48:45 to read קדקד, "skull," in parallel with פאתי, "temples, sides of the head." It should be noted, however, that a verb is expected here and the root *qrr* II, "to tear down," appears in the reduplicated form in Isa. 22:5 (in an OAN context) -- מקרקר קר, "a battering down of walls" (RSV). Moreover, it should be noted that the text in Jer. 48:45 is dubious. It is missing in the Old Greek and the Lucianic recension reads ἐξηρευνησεν which may render a Pilpēl verbal form of קור, which would mean that the Jer. passage should be emended in line with Num. 24:17.

[i]Vocalizing *yarûš*, passive participle of *yrš* in the sense of "dispossess," with Albright. The root *yrš* appears in the Qal form in Jer. 49:2 with the same meaning.

[j]Reading enclitic *mem* on the root *rdh*, "have dominion, rule," with Albright who cites Ginsberg, *JBL* 62 (1943), p. 115 for a parallel in Ps. 29:6.

[k]The word איביו is out of place in MT. Restore the missing words which apparently dropped out by haplography and were restored after verse 18 in the received tradition.

[l]Following Albright who vocalized the verb as a perfect and transposed the verb and noun.

[m]Reading *'Âr*, a city of Moab, with Albright (so also Meek in the "Chicago" Bible). Ar of Moab is mentioned in the Balaam story itself (Num. 22:36) and in the Amorite "Song of Heshbon" (Num. 21:28).

[n]Following SP, with Albright; *ʿad* is adverbial accusative (cf. also *JAOS* 60 (1940), p. 288.

[o]Restoring קין from verse 22, with Albright. The play on words between *Qayn, Qên* and *qēn*, "nest," requires this transposition. Note also Obad. 4 and Jer. 49:16 where the words refer to Edom.

[p]The Hebrew text in this colon and in verses 23-24 is corrupt and perhaps beyond reconstruction. It seems preferable, as Professor Cross has suggested, to omit this material rather than adopt the rather forced translation offered by Albright [*JBL* 63 (1944), p. 226]. In *Yahweh and the Gods of Canaan*, p. 16, n. 40 Albright has offered the following translation of verses 23 and 24: "And he saw Gog and delivered an oracle about him, saying:

The isles shall be gathered from the north
  And ships from the farthest sea,
And they shall harass Aššûr and harass ʿEber,
  But he (Gog) will perish forever."

The fourth oracle of Balaam (Num. 24:15-24) differs from the other three in several respects. The term "songs of Balaam" which van Zyl applied to these oracles,[22] is a fitting description of the first three. There the tone is one of praise as Israel and her God are exalted. The imagery reflects ancient holy war tradition in that Yahweh caused his people to "storm like a wild bull " (Num. 23:22; 24:8) as he brought Israel from Egypt. No power was able to stop Yahweh and his people in their march of conquest. The exclamation "What hath El done!" (Num. 23:22) is filled with awe, for he has raised up a strong nation, a people "that doth attack like a lion" (Num. 23:24). Yahweh has brought his people from the south and has established them in a new land (Num. 24:5-7). The focus of the first three oracles is on Israel and her God. Reference to other peoples is couched in generalities. It is not at all difficult to envision the use of such material within the historical cultus of the Israelite Covenant League, particularly in the so-called ritual conquest tradition.

The fourth oracle of Balaam, however, presents several difficulties if one seeks to relate it to the same pattern of cultic celebration in ancient Israel. Here there is a note of invective, as specific peoples are singled out and cursed in an oracle of doom. The tone is that of judgment, not cultic celebration. The historical references to the peoples in question are specific, not timeless. The setting is more that of the military camp prepared to wage war against the peoples named. The literary background is that of the blessings and curses proclaimed within a military context. The fourth oracle is precisely what Balaam, in the narrative tradition, was called to

---

[22]van Zyl, *op. cit.*, p. 11.

proclaim -- only directed at Israel's foes.

Most attempts to date the oracles of Balaam are based on the historical allusions in the fourth oracle, particularly the reference to the Kenites (Num. 24:21-11) and the "Sea Peoples" (Num. 24:23). The "one perfect example of a repetitive pattern familiar from Ugarit (abc:acb')," cited by Albright,[23] is also found in this oracle. It is interesting to note that each of the examples cited by Albright where "etymological assonance has clearly begun to displace the older repetitive type" (Num. 23:8,10,20 and 24:4,7,10)[24] are found in the first three oracles. It could be argued that the fourth oracle is in fact all that remains of the original "utterance of Balaam," and that the other three oracles are later poetic constructions, based on the Balaam tradition. As it stands in the biblical text, the fourth oracle is akin to the literary genre of tribal blessings and curses spoken by the patriarchs.[25]

The fourth oracle of Balaam stands very much alone in the biblical record. More than three centuries separate it from the next group of recorded oracles of victory or defeat in battle which appear in connection with Ahab and Jehoshaphat in the ninth cietury B.C. There are numerous battles fought during this interim period and a number of war oracles are mentioned, particularly in connection with the battles of Saul and David; but, for the most part, such oracles are to be classified as oracular divination. Other war oracles during this period fall into the categories of summons to battle or summons to flight. Besides the fourth oracle of Balaam there are but four recorded occurrences of prophetic war oracles announcing victory or defeat in battle, prior to those delivered by unnamed prophets who appear before Ahab king of Israel in his wars with Ben-hadad of Aram. All four are problematic.

Two of these occurrences are oracles given to Moses by Yahweh, prior to the Oracles of Balaam in the Pentateuchal narrative. The first is found in Exod. 17:14 and comes at the conclusion of the war with Amalek at Rephidim. Moses is told to "Write this as a memorial in a book and recite it in the ears of Joshua, that I will utterly blot out the remembrance of Amalek from under heaven." This particular prophecy is not an oracle of victory in battle for a specific war with Amalek. It comes after a defeat of Amalek and appears to be inserted into the narrative, perhaps to justify continued enmity towards Amalek. Exod. 17:14-16 is commonly assigned to the E source in Pentateuchal criticism, though Eissfeldt assigned it to his source L and Lynn Clapham, in an unpublished Harvard seminar paper,[26] argued that it be-

---

[23]Albright, *Yahweh and the Gods of Canaan*, p. 15. [24]*Ibid.*, p. 16

[25]As observed by Aage Bentzen, *Introduction to the Old Testament*, Vol. I, 7th ed. (Copenhagen: G. E. C. Gad, 1967), pp. 141-42

[26]Lynn Clapham, "The Wandering in the Wilderness" (unpub. paper, OT Seminar, Harvard University, October, 1964), pp. 11-13.

longs to D. As it stands this oracle is not in poetic form and it is probably a secondary interpolation based, in part, on the fragment of an archaic war song preserved in Exod. 17:16 which mentions Amalek. This particular poetic fragment is discussed in greater detail below in the section on "War Songs and Holy War."

The second occurrence is more or less contemporary with the Balaam incident. In Num. 21:34 Moses is given an oracle of victory over Og of Bashan: "Do not fear him; for I have given him into your hand, and all his people, and his land; and you shall do to him as you did to Sihon king of the Amorites who dwelt at Heshbon." The oracle is in prose and is commonly attributed to the JE narrative tradition. No details are given as to how the oracle was received.

The third example of an oracle of victory in battle is preserved in Josh. 5:13-6:5 and is even more problematic than the two already mentioned. The "commander of Yahweh's hosts" (שר צבא יהוה) confronted Joshua. Like Moses before the burning bush, Joshua was told to remove his shoes, for he was standing on holy ground (cf. Exod. 3:5). Yahweh then addressed him with these words: "See, I have given into your hand Jericho, with its king and mighty men of valor. You shall march around the city, all the men of war going round the city. . . ." The narrative continues with the strange instructions for Yahweh's war of conquest to be waged against Jericho. This particular oracle appears to be a literary creation based, perhaps, on ancient cultic activity carried out at Gilgal in the premonarchical era.

The fourth such occurrence is also imbedded in a prose account, this time of the war against the Canaanites under Deborah and Barak. When Barak insisted on Deborah's presence with the troops, she uttered her prophecy: "Yahweh will sell Sisera into the hand of a woman" (Judg. 4:9). There is some ambiguity as to whether the woman in question is Deborah or Jael. Both women are praised in the "Song of Deborah," though it is Jael who actually slew Sisera (Judg. 4:21; 5:24-27). If the prophecy concerns Sisera alone, Jael is the woman. If, on the other hand, the reference to Sisera includes the Canaanite troops under him, Deborah could be the referent. The ambiguity is perhaps intentional as this enigmatic oracle of victory is probably secondary to the so-dalled "Song of Deborah" and the oral tradition concerning Jael the wife of Heber the Kenite.

It appears that the image of the prophet as Yahweh's messenger sent to deliver an oracle of victory or defeat in battle to the political-military leader in Israel is *not* at home in premonarchical Israel.[27] From the time

---

[27]Though the enigmatic Balaam is portrayed in the role of a prophet, it should be noted that he was later killed in battle by the Israelites and was remembered as a party in Israel's greatest apostasy of this early period

of Moses to David, the "Judges"[28] of Israel fulfilled the prophetic function as well as the political. As long as the leadership of the tribes was on a charismatic basis, individual judges, with their spontaneous gifts of morale-building and military direction, did most if not all of the specialized work of the first Israelite prophets.[29] Deborah was more than a mere prophetic counselor to Barak; she takes her place as one of the "Judges" in ancient Israel. It was not until the founding of the monarchy that true prophecy arose as an institutional office in Israel, set over against that of the king.[30]

The transition period from the Tribal League to the Davidic monarchy is plagued with historical difficulties. According to the received tradition, Samuel is credited with whipping up patriotic and religious fervor to the point of a successful rebellion against the Philistines (I Sam. 7:5-11).[31] He is said to have anointed both Saul and David as military commanders (*nāgîd*) over the Israelite tribal levy. It was during the preparation for battle against the Philistines, that Saul waited seven days for Samuel to appear at Gilgal and offer sacrifice with the troops to send them forth to battle (I Sam. 13:8). When his men began to desert him, Saul offered the sacrifice himself -- no doubt with the precedent of Gideon and others of the "Judges"

(cf. Num. 25:1-9,16-17; 31:1-8).

[28]The term judges (שפטים) in Old Testament usage is an arbitrary designation applied to the military leaders who delivered and governed Israel in the period between Joshua and David. According to a recent study by Wolfgang Richter ["Zu den 'Richtern Israels,'" *ZAW* 77 (1965), pp. 40-72], the primary function of the judges was not military and not only juristic, but to rule: i.e. government and legal justice. God himself is called a שפט who will "judge among the nations" (Isa. 2:4; cf. also Gen. 18:25; Pss. 50:6; 75:8; 82:8; 94:2; and Joel 4:12). The *imperium* of Yahweh was focused in "his servant" Moses who was the religious-military-political leader of Israel. The charismatic judges of early Israel continued the tradition of Moses and Joshua as the chief administrators of Yahweh's *imperium* until the time of Samuel. With the rise of the monarchy the administration of Yahweh's *imperium* in Israel was modified in such a manner as to mark the end of an era. In this study the term "Judges" is used to designate the continuity of succession in the charismatic office of religious-military-political leader in ancient Israel from Moses through Samuel.

[29]Cf. the discussion of Gottwald, *All the Kingdoms*, pp. 50-51.

[30]See W. F. Albright, *Samuel and the Beginnings of the Prophetic Movement* (Cincinnati: Hebrew Union College Press, the Goldenson Lecture for 1961), esp. pp. 14-18. See also the summary statement by G. Ernest Wright, "The Nations in Hebrew Prophecy," *Encounter* 26 (1965), pp. 229-30.

[31]See Albright, *Samuel*, p. 14.

in mind. Samuel then appeared immediately, almost as though he had waited all this time in order to provoke a clash with Saul. From this point on, Saul turned to oracular divination for his war oracles. It was not until after the death of Samuel and after Saul's failure to receive an oracle by the normal means of oracular divination -- dreams, the sacred lots, the court prophets (I Sam. 28:6) -- that Saul again turned to Samuel through the medium of Endor.

Samuel and Saul, then, mark the end of an era. With the institution of the monarchy war was secularized. It was not until after the breakup of the united monarchy (*ca.* 922 B.C.), and the bloody palace revolts of Baasha, Zimri and Omri (*ca.* 900-876) in the northern kingdom of Israel that the ancient institution of the "Judges", as charismatic leaders of Yahweh's holy wars, was revived under Elijah and Elisha. The political changes of the previous century and a half required that the role of the "Judge" be altered from what it had been in the era of the premonarchical Tribal League. The figure of Moses and Joshua, as leaders of Yahweh's holy wars, was wedded to that of Samuel, the king-maker and king-breaker, to produce the prophetic movement of the ninth century. By the time of Ahab (*ca.* 869-850), the prophet as Yahweh's spokesman in military situations was a political force which no king in either Israel or Judah could ignore.

During the reign of Ahab in Israel and his contemporary Jehoshaphat in Judah (*ca.* 873-849), a series of prophets appeared with specific oracles of victory or defeat in battle. Three such instances are recorded in I Kings 20, a peculiar chapter which appears in the middle of the stories of Elijah and his conflict with King Ahab (I Kings 17-21). As Montgomery put it, "This chapter with its sequel in 22:1-38 stands singularly alone in style and novelty of contents."[32] Much of the chapter has been judged as secondary intrusions from some prophetic source, written from a political rather than a religious point of view. Nonetheless, as Gray has argued, along with most contemporary critics, the so-called prophetic interpolations are "integral to the chapter and must be preserved."[33]

After Ben-hadad had provoked a military clash with Ahab and had assembled his troops against Samaria, a certain prophet came to Ahab, king of Israel, and said: "Thus says Yahweh, Have you seen all this great multitude? Look! I am giving it into your hand today, so that you will know I am Yahweh" (I Kings 20:13). This brief oracle is marked by the rubric forms of later prophetic oracles with its כה אמר יהוה and הנני, though its present

---

[32]James A. Montgomery, *A Critical and Exegetical Commentary on the Books of Kings*, ed. by Henry S. Gehman (ICC, Edinburgh: T. & T. Clark, 1951), p. 318.

[33]John Gray, *I & II Kings: A Commentary* (OTL, London: SCM Press, 1964), p. 376.

literary form preserves no trace of the poetic parallelism of the original utterance. In content the oracle is an announcement of victory in battle given to the king in a specific historical situation. After the oracle was given, Ahab posed the ancient military question: "Who shall begin the battle?" (cf. Judg. 1:1; 20:18). Without resorting to sacred lots or other means of divination, the prophet simply replied -- "You" (I Kings 20:14). Ahab then mustered his troops, including a levy of 7000 from "all the people of Israel," and defeated Ben-hadad during the great midday carousal in the Aramean military camp.

After the initial defeat of Aram, an unnamed "man of God" came to Ahab and said: "Thus says Yahweh, Because Aram has said, 'Yahweh is a god of the hills but he is not a god of the valleys;' therefore I will give all this great multitude into your hand, and you shall know that I am Yahweh" (I Kings 20:28). Though this oracle is clearly prose in its present form, it does preserve one bicolon with good poetic parallelism throughout:

Yahweh is a god of the hills;	אלהי הרים יהוה	7
He is not a god of the valleys.	לא אלהי עמקים הוא	8

The entire oracle was no doubt originally composed orally in poetic form. In terms of literary form the war oracle preserved here displays an almost identical pattern to that observed by Mays in his analysis of the OAN material in Amos 1-2.[34]

(a) *The messenger formula*: "This is what Yahweh has said . . ."

(b) *The indictment*: "Because Aram has said . . ."; to which compare, "Because of three crimes of Damascus . . ." (Amos 1:3).

(c) *The announcement of punishment*: "I will give them into your hand"; to which compare, "I will send fire . . ." (Amos 1:4-5).

By the ninth century the prophetic war oracle against a foreign nation was already in the form of a judgment speech. Yahweh, the Divine Warrior, declares that he will give Aram into the hand of Ahab because Aram has dared to challenge his universal suzerainty. The language used in verse 28b is taken from Israel's ancient traditions of holy war, as von Rad has observed.[35]

The nameless prophet of I Kings 20 has been the source of speculation in times past. Josephus identified him with Micaiah ben Imlah of I Kings 22, but on insufficient grounds.[36] Though he cannot be identified with a specific historical personage, his title in I Kings 20:28 does convey some information about him. Tsevat compares *'îš 'ĕlōhîm* to *ben 'ĕlōhîm* and concludes

---

[34]James L. Mays, *Amos: A Commentary* (OTL, Philadelphia: Westminster, 1969), p. 23.

[35]See von Rad, *Der Heilige Krieg*, p. 8.

[36]See the discussion of J. Gray, *I & II Kings*, p. 376.

that as the latter corresponds to a supernatural being belonging to the sphere of God, the former indicates a human being belonging to this same sphere.[37] The "man of God" of I Kings 20:28 was a prophet who, like Micaiah ben Imlah, had observed the proceedings within the divine council and, as Yahweh's messenger, was sent to deliver the indictment rendered by Yahweh the Judge. God was not through with Aram. There was to be yet another battle in the spring against Ben-hadad, and again Yahweh would deliver Aram into the hands of Ahab -- this time because of the hubris of the Arameans in exalting themselves against Yahweh.

After the second predicted victory over Aram, Ahab was again confronted by a "certain man of the sons of the prophets" (I Kings 20:35), but this time the scene was altogether different. Ahab was condemned for his leniency to Ben-hadad. Like Saul in his battle with the Amalekites (cf. I Sam. 15:1-21), Ahab had failed to carry out the provisions of Yahweh's holy war in destroying the enemy of Israel. And like Saul, he too was consequently rejected from being king over Israel: "This is what Yahweh has said: Because you have released the man I doomed to destruction, therefore your life shall be required for his life, and your people for his people" (I Kings 20:42). Again the oracle is in the form of a prophetic announcement of judgment. Yahweh's words, expressed in the first person, are introduced by the messenger formula כה אמר יהוה. The oracle itself consists of two parts: a specification of the crime of which the person concerned is guilty, and an announcement of the punishment which Yahweh has determined.[38] It should also be noted that once again an apparent poetic couplet has been preserved which witnesses to the original poetic composition of the oracle (I Kings 20:42b):

Your life (shall be required) for his life,	נפשך תחת נפשו	6
(And) your people for his people.	עמך תחת עמו	6

The prophecy of Micaiah ben Imlah in I Kings 22 is of particular interest because of the insight it provides into the nature of the prophetic office in the ninth century B.C. Israel and Aram were once again preparing for battle. Jehoshaphat, king of Judah, paid a visit to Ahab to form a military alliance; but before he would go to battle, he requested a war oracle from Yahweh. Ahab had some four hundred court prophets who answered the military question posed by the king of Israel with the words: "Go up to Ramoth-Gilead and triumph, for Yahweh will give it into your hand, O king" (I Kings 22:6). Jehoshaphat was not satisfied with this oracle of victory and asked if there was not a true prophet of Yahweh in Israel. Ahab reluctantly summoned Micaiah.

---

[37] Matitiahu Tsevat, "God and the Gods in Assembly," *HUCA* 40-41 (1969-70), pp. 126-27, n. 9; cf. also Frank M. Cross, Jr., "The Council of Yahweh in Second Isaiah," *JNES* 12 (1953), p. 274, n. 1.

[38] Cf. the discussion of Mays, *Amos*, pp. 22-23.

At first Micaiah mimicked the court prophets: "Go up and triumph! It (i.e. Aram) will be given into your hand" (I Kings 22:15).[39] Ahab was angered by Micaiah's reply and demanded that he speak the truth "in the name of Yahweh" (vs. 16). With the four hundred prophets the scene was one of oracular divination -- professional diviners uttered their war oracle proclaiming victory so as to embolden the king and his troops for the battle at hand; but with Micaiah something new entered the picture, something which Ahab described as speaking "the truth in the name of Yahweh." Micaiah stood before Ahab, not as a professional prophet who had mastered the technical skills of divination; but as one called by Yahweh himself to be an agent of Yahweh's *imperium*. Micaiah was not a cultic functionary so much as he was a political force set over against the king. He had perceived Yahweh's judgment regarding Ahab and his war with Aram. He stood before Ahab to proclaim the decree of the sovereign ruler of history who was about to mete out judgment to faithless Ahab.

Micaiah's message, though no doubt delivered originally in the poetic form of oral poetry, is a prose account of the proceedings which he had observed within the divine council. Micaiah maintained that it was Yahweh himself, through the agency of a "lying spirit (רוח שקר)," who had deceived Ahab in order to remove him from being king over Israel. In the subsequent battle at Ramoth-Gilead, Ahab disguised himself while Jehoshaphat appeared in his royal garments. Though Jehoshaphat was even mistaken for Ahab, and though the Aramean king had commanded the captains of his chariots to fight only with the king of Israel; it was Jehoshaphat who survived the battle, while Ahab died from the arrow of "a certain man (who) drew his bow at a venture" (vs. 34). There was no escape from the judgment of Yahweh.

Jehoshaphat, king of Judah, was the recipient of other war oracles prophesying victory over foreign nations. After Ahab's death, Jehoram, king of Israel (*ca.*849-842), proclaimed war against Mesha of Moab. Together with Jehoshaphat and the king of Edom, he marched against Moab. Again Jehoshaphat asked: "Is there no prophet of Yahweh here, through whom we may inquire of Yahweh?" (II Kings 3:11). This time it was Elisha who was summoned from within the war party itself, where he apparently was serving as a sort of war chaplain. Elisha would have little to do with Jehoram; but, because of his regard for Jehoshaphat, he requested a minstrel. As the minstrel played, the "hand" of Yahweh came upon him and he said (II Kings 3:16-19):

16 This is what Yahweh has said:	כה אמר יהוה	
This dry wadi shall be made	עשה [] נחל [] זה	8
full of cisterns --	גבים גבים [][a]	

[39]The text of I Kings 22:15 is reconstructed hrre on the basis of the parallel passage in II Chron. 18:14. For MT ונתן read ינתן and parse as a Niphal imperfect.

17	You shall not see wind,	לא תרוא רוח	4
	You shall not see rain;	[]לא תרוא גשם	4
	But that wadi will be filled with water.	ו[]נחל []הוא ימלא מים	7
	All of you will drink,	ושתיתם אתם	6
	Your armed host and your cattle.	⟨מחניכם⟩[b] ומקניכם [][b]	7
18	This is an easy thing in Yahweh's eyes;	[]נקל זאת בעיני יהוה	8
	He will also give the Moabites into your hand.	ונתן [] מואב בידכם	8
19	You shall conquer the fortified city,	והכיתם [][c] עיר מבצר [][d]	7
	And every good tree you shall fell;	וכל עץ טוב תפילו	7
	Every spring of water you shall stop up,	[]כל מעיני מים תסתמו	8
	Every good piece of land you shall ruin (with stones).	[]כל חלקה []טובה תכאבו [][e]	8

II Kings 3:16-19 in Outline

A. Promise of Water by Miraculous Means (vss. 16-17)
   - [1:b:b:1] The dry wadi shall be filled with water.
   - [b:b] You shall have water to drink.

B. Oracle of Victory in Battle (vss. 18-19)
   - [1:1] Yahweh will give Moab into your hands.
   - [1:1::1:1] You shall make Moab desolate.

Notes to the Text

[a]The second messenger formula is deleted in an attempt to restore the poetic structure of the original oracle.

[b]The Lucianic recension of LXX ($bgorc_2e_2$) reads παρεμβολαι which elsewhere renders מחניכם (in II Kings 3:9 where מחנה and בהמה appear together). The emendation improves the metrical balance of the bicolon and also the poetic assonance.

[c]Deleting כל to improve both meter and sense.

[d]Deleting כל עיר מבחור with LXX, codex Vaticanus and the Lucianic tradition (brc_2e_2). The phrase is a doublet or poetic variant to כל עיר מבצר.

[e]Deleting אבנים to obtain metrical balance in the final bicolon. The root *k'b* is used in the Hiphil in an OAN context in Ezek. 28:24 where it appears without an object -- קוץ מכאב = "a thorn to hurt them" (RSV) -- the object being understood from the context.

The poetic form of this oracle is more completely preserved than in any of the prophetic war oracles discussed so far. The text as reconstructed, however, is still rather prosaic and is no doubt little more than an approximation to the original prophetic utterance. Elisha was summoned before the three kings because there was no water for the army or their animals (II Kings

3:9). The prophet promised water by morning and pronounced an oracle of victory over Moab as well. The picture of Moab desolated and ruined in war is a popular image in subsequent OAN material.

The Chronicler recorded a further oracle of victory in battle given to Jehoshaphat by Jahaziel a Levite (II Chron. 20:1-37). The Moabites in league with the Ammonites and Meunites came against Jehoshaphat for battle. In fear Jehoshaphat "set himself to seek Yahweh" (vs. 3). He proclaimed a fast throughout Judah. After a lengthy prayer for deliverance which the Chronicler placed on the lips of Jehoshaphat, "the spirit of Yahweh came upon Jahaziel" who then delivered an oracle of victory in battle. Some of the older scholars (Wellhausen and Kautzsch) have seen this incident as a recasting of II Kings 3 on the part of the Chronicler. This view is now rejected by nearly all commentators. The essence of the story is not pure fabrication. Certain features have been magnified somewhat out of proportion (i.e. the great multitude in vs. 2), and there is literary expansion (i.e. the prayer for deliverance, vss. 6-12); but the historical kernal of the story remains -- an invasion of Judah from the south during the reign of Jehoshaphat.[40]

In literary form the oracle of Yahweh given by Jahaziel is a priestly salvation oracle,[41] introduced and concluded by the old formula, "Do not be afraid" (vss. 15 and 17). The coming battle is viewed as Yahweh's holy war.[42] The host was sent forth with an exhortation by the king and a religious procession. The people were to place their trust in Yahweh who would destroy their foe for them. As von Rad has pointed out,[43] cultic personnel accompanied the army in such battles and played a major role in the campaign. The victory celebration was marked by division of the booty and a service of thanksgiving in the field. Another religious service of thanksgiving apparently took place upon the return to Jerusalem of the king and his victorious army which presumably involved the entire populace.[44]

Elisha uttered prophetic war oracles on other occasions, though the historical situations as such are not always clear, nor are the oracles preserved in their original form. The king of Aram continued to wage war against

---

[40]Arguments are advanced below to date this battle early in the reign of King Jehoshaphat, before Omri's conquest of Moab; see pp. 117-18 and 140.

[41]See Joachim Begrich, "Das priestliche Heilsorakel," *ZAW* 52 (1934), p. 83; and A. R. Johnson, *The Cultic Prophet in Ancient Israel* (Cardiff: University of Wales Press Board, 1944), pp. 61-62. Cf. also Jacob M. Meyers, *II Chronicles* (AB 13, Garden City, New York: Doubleday & Company, 1965), pp. 115-16.

[42]See Meyers, *II Chronicles*, p. 116.

[43]See von Rad, *Heilige Krieg*, pp. 80-81.

[44]See Meyers, *II Chronicles*, p. 116.

Israel (II Kings 6:8). Elisha is said to have saved the king of Israel on more than one occasion with timely warnings (II Kings 6:9-10). The king of Israel in question is not named and there is disagreement as to the date of the events recorded in II Kings 6:8-7:20. Šanda dated the events soon after 797 B.C.,[45] whereas Asami, in a seminar paper at Harvard University (1960) and again in his doctoral dissertation (1964), suggests that at least part of this section reflects the Aramean oppression in the time of Jehu (*ca.* 842-814).[46] No attempt will be made here to unravel the historical difficulties. Elisha delivered an enigmatic prophecy of miraculous deliverance from the siege of Samaria (II Kings 7:1):

> This is what Yahweh has said:
> At this time tomorrow a measure of fine flour
> will be sold for a shekel, and two measures
> of barley for a shekel, at the gate of Samaria.

During the night Yahweh himself dispersed the Arameans and delivered Samaria out of their hands.

Elisha played an important political role in the last half of the ninth century. He instigated the revolutions of Hazael in Aram (II Kings 8:7-15) and Jehu in Israel (II Kings 9-10). He was deeply involved in military and diplomatic matters during the Aramean invasion recorded in II Kings 6:8-23. Even on his death bed he was a political force of such importance that Joash king of Israel came to him to seek an oracle; and Elisha's final recorded prophecy was one of limited victory over Aram on the part of Joash (II Kings 13:14-19).

Though little is known about him, the prophet Jonah ben Amittai should also be mentioned here. During the reign of Jeroboam II (*ca.* 783-748), the son of Joash king of Israel, Jonah is said to have prophesied the restoration of the borders of Israel (II Kings 14:25). Moreover, no matter how one interprets the delightful little book of Jonah, the tradition clearly links the prophet to international affairs.[47]

Oracles of victory or defeat in battle have a long and complex history in ancient Israel. Within the context of the Covenant League charismatic

---

[45]Albert Šanda, *Die bücher der Könige* (EH 9/II, Münster: Aschendorffsche Verlagsbuchhandlung, 1912), pp. 49-50.

[46]Sadao Asami, "The Elisha Pericope" (unpub. paper, OT Seminar, Harvard University, 1960-61); and "The Central Sanctuary," p. 341.

[47]See my paper, "The Figure of Jonah and the Servant of Yahweh" (unpub. paper, OT Seminar, Harvard University, Jan., 1967); where I have argued that the book of Jonah is to be classified as proto-midrash in literary form and reflects an historical kernal which can be reconstructed, at least in part.

"Judges" mediated the *imperium* of Yahweh, coming to the fore particularly in times of military conflict. Though prophetic oracles of victory or defeat in battle were no doubt uttered within the ancient institution of holy war, specific instances of such oracles are lacking in the received tradition. It is not until the ninth century revival of holy war traditions in the northern kingdom of Israel that such oracles make their appearance in the biblical text. In the ninth century oracle against Aram, as delivered by an unnamed "man of God" (I Kings 20:28), the outline of the OAN tradition of Amos 1-2 can already be discerned. With respect to literary form the war oracle had already become a judgment speech.

3. Summons to Battle

In his important study of the summons to battle (*Aufforderung zur Kampf*) and the summons to flight (*Aufforderung zur Flucht*) as forms of prophetic speech, R. Bach has argued that both literary forms have their roots in the ancient institution of holy war in premonarchical Israel.[48] He began with examples of these speech forms in the prophetic literature, particularly within the OAN material in Jeremiah, and worked back in time to reconstruct an original *Sitz im Leben*. The presentation here will not attempt to duplicate Bach's analysis, but will instead focus on the occurrences of these two particular speech forms prior to the time of Amos.

Bach argued for a close connection between the sacred lots, as used by Saul and David, and the emergence of the summons to battle as a form of prophetic speech.[49] He suggested that the older function of the charismatic leader in Israel split with the rise of the monarchy, the military part being taken over by the king, while the charismatic was first taken over by the sacred lots which, by the ninth century, gave way to the prophetic oracle, particularly in the northern kingdom of Israel.[50]

Bach has intuited the source and early development of the summons to battle as a speech form, but his own presuppositions have caused him to oversimplify the historical process. Dependent on von Rad's reconstruction of the institution of holy war, Bach has not projected his analysis back into the era of the Exodus-Conquest. Consequently he has had to condense too much historical development into too brief a span of time. He correctly observed that the rise of the monarchy is the critical factor in the development of the prophetic summons to battle. But his suggestion that the non-military function of the older charismatic leader was somehow taken over by the sacred lots is not correct. The use of the ephod, the teraphim and other means of

---

[48] R. Bach, *Aufforderungen*, pp. 92-101; cf. note 53 on p. 12 above.

[49] *Ibid.*, p. 107.

[50] *Ibid.*, pp. 110-112.

oracular divination have a long and complex history, one that goes back into the hoary reaches of the patriarchal period. By the time of Saul and David the sacred lots were very much part of Israel's cultic heritage but were rapidly being displaced by a new impulse from the religious reformation of the Samuel era. The rise of kingship in Israel not only marked the end of the Tribal League and the era of charismatic "Judges" -- it also marked the end of numerous pagan elements in Israel's worship, at least from an official point of view. It is interesting to note that in the Samuel tradition there is no reference to tabernacle, ark or priesthood after the death of Eli.[51] Moreover, one should also note that as official military leader in Israel (*nāgîd*), Saul made use of the sacred lots to obtain war oracles only after Samuel had rejected him from being ruler. Before that time it was Samuel who announced the word of Yahweh to Saul, in a manner not unlike the relationship between Deborah and Barak.

The split in the function of Israel's charismatic leaders is not between the military aspects, on the one hand, and the oracular, on the other. The split is between the king and the prophet, and even the restoration of the Tabernacle and the major priestly families under David was not enough to undo the achievement of Samuel. The king was never the sole administrator of Yahweh's *imperium* in ancient Israel, even in military matters. That task fell to the successors of Samuel, the prophets in Israel, who continued to interpret the religion of Moses and Samuel in a manner designed to hold the king in check. Even though David built a powerful professional army, it was the prophet who retained the authority to summon the levy of Israel's Covenant League in holy war. And it is this function that explains the origin of the summons to battle as a basic form of prophetic speech.

Apart from incidents where a war oracle is either explicitly or implicitly obtained by means of divination, there are two major groups of prophetic summons to battle in the literature of ancient Israel: those of the Exodus-Conquest period attributed to Moses or Joshua, and those of the Tribal League given by the charismatic judges or by the inter-tribal council. Within the second group of such oracles there are two divisions: summons to war in defense of the Tribal League against an external threat, and summons to war against a member of the league itself who has broken faith with the covenant terms of the tribal confederation.

a. Summons to Battle in Wars of the Exodus-Conquest

According to the Pentateuchal narrative the Israelites fought a battle with the Amalekites even before they had reached Mount Sinai. The brief account of this incident in Exod. 17:8-16 (E) contains legendary overtones

---

[51]See W. F. Albright, *Samuel*, p. 16.

and poses historical difficulties. Nonetheless, the tradition of a military conflict between Israel and Amalek is indeed ancient and, in all probability, reflects the first military activity of the recently freed Hebrews. In the narrative Moses presents the summons to battle to Joshua, who appears here for the first time in the biblical text (Exod. 17:9): "Choose for us (mighty) men and go to war against Amalek tomorrow; I will stand on the top of the hill with the rod of God (מטה אלהים) in my hand." Though the summons is in prose, the presence of a fragment of an ancient war song in verse 16 suggests that there was an earlier poetic account of this incident. The pericope as a whole forms a sort of perpetual summons to battle against Amalek.

Four other passages should be mentioned relative to Moses and the speech form in question. A summons *not* to fight is uttered by Moses in Num. 14:41-43 (JE) when the Israelites decided to storm Palestine from the south: "Do not go up lest you be struck down before your enemies, for Yahweh is not in your midst. For the Amalekites and Canaanites are before you, and you shall fall by the sword; because you have turned back from following Yahweh, Yahweh will not be with you." In a later battle with Sihon in Transjordan the Deuteronomist placed a specific summons to battle on the lips of Moses (Deut. 2:24-25): "Rise up, take your journey, and go over the valley of the Arnon; behold, I have given into your hand Sihon the Amorite . . . contend with him in battle." The oracle of victory in battle against Og of Bashan in Num. 21:34 (E) is in effect a summons to battle on the lips of Moses who has received the oracle of Yahweh. The Priestly account of the war with Midian contains two summons to battle, the first of which is addressed to Moses from Yahweh (Num. 31:2): "Avenge the people of Israel on the Midianites!" Moses then addressed the people of Israel (Num. 31:3-4): "Arm men from among you for the war that they may go against Midian, to execute Yahweh's vengeance on Midian. You shall send a thousand from each of the tribes of Israel to the war." Each of the occurrences of a summons to battle on the lips of Moses is plagued with historical difficulties. Either Deuteronomic language is dominant or the speech form is imbedded in Priestly narrative. In either case the evidence points toward relatively late composition which raises the question of authenticity.

As Moses' successor and the military leader in the wars of the Conquest, Joshua also is said to have uttered summons to battle on specific occasions. Before crossing the Jordan, Joshua told the people to "Sanctify yourselves; for tomorrow Yahweh will do wonders in your midst" (Josh. 3:5). The setting was that of holy war in which Joshua was to lead the people of Yahweh in a war of conquest to take possession of the land of promise. He summoned the Israelites to battle against Jericho (Josh. 6:2-5, 16-19) and Ai (Josh. 8:1-2,4-8,18), after receiving specific battle instructions from Yahweh -- perhaps by means of oracular divination. In the battle against the Canaanite confederacy at Gibeon and Jabin, king of Hazor, Joshua received battle instructions and assurance of victory from Yahweh (Josh. 10:8; 11:6), though no explicit summons to battle as such is placed on his lips.

As with the case of Moses, it is not possible to move from the narrative accounts of the wars of Joshua into history per se. The tradition as it stands has been rewritten and reflects relatively late composition. Nonetheless, one cannot simply dismiss the tradition of these wars of conquest as without historical basis whatsoever, with von Rad. The tradition of Yahweh's Holy War as reflected in the war songs of ancient Israel casts an independent light from the premonarchical era on the historicity of the Exodus-Conquest tradition. As is argued in greater detail below, one must distinguish between the institution of holy war as reconstructed by von Rad and Yahweh's Holy War as re-enacted in the cultus of the Tribal League at Gilgal.[52] The central theme of the ritual conquest tradition as celebrated in ancient Israel was Yahweh's glorious victory over his enemies, both earthly and cosmic, as he marched with his hosts from the mountains of southern Palestine to take possession of the land of promise. The details are beyond recovery, but the outline of Yahweh's Holy War is clear. It includes the conquest of Amalek, Sihon, Og, Midian and Canaan. Though the actual words of Moses and Joshua cannot be recovered, it is certainly plausible that later tradition is correct in placing summons to battle on their lips. The summons to battle as a prophetic form of speech has its origins in the wars of the Exodus-Conquest which constitute Yahweh's Holy War par excellence.

b. Summons to Battle in Defense of the Covenant League

One of the battles of conquest under Joshua is of particular importance because it introduced a new element to the traditions of holy war in ancient Israel. After the Gibeonites had succeeded in forming an alliance with Israel, they were in turn attacked by a Canaanite coalition (Josh. 9:3-10:5). The men of Gibeon turned to Joshua for help. Joshua then led the Israelite army in battle in defense of a political confederate. This was no longer strictly speaking a war of conquest, but rather a defensive battle against an external aggressor. The description of the ensuing battle is filled with holy war imagery, including a fragment of an ancient war song which is discussed in detail later.[53] Yahweh threw the enemy into a panic before Israel (Josh. 10:10). As the Canaanites fled, Yahweh threw down great stones from heaven upon them (vs. 11). The cosmic dimension of the battle is climaxed by the noted incident when the sun stood still at Gibeon (vss. 12-13). The traditional interpretation of the poetic fragment in this account was that the sun stood still in the heavens such that "there has been no day like it

---

[52]See p. 14, notes 62 and 63 above.

[53]See the discussion below, pp. 48-49.

before or since . . . for Yahweh fought for Israel" (vs. 14).

Three other battles are recorded in the book of Judges which are defensive in nature. Ehud "sounded the trumpet in the hill country of Ephraim" (Judg. 3:27) summoning Israel to battle against Moab. Deborah summoned Barak with a contingent of troops from Naphtali and Zebulun against Sisera, the general of the Canaanite forces (Judg. 4:6-7). From the "Song of Deborah" we find that the Israelite forces also included men from Ephraim, Benjamin, Machir and Issachar (Judg. 5:14-15); and perhaps from Reuben, Gilead, Dan and Asher as well.[54] No matter how one interprets the absence of Judah and Simeon in this particular battle, we have tribal confederates responding in joint military action to an external threat.[55] The third battle in defense of the Covenant League is that under Gideon who summoned all of Manasseh in addition to Asher, Zebulun and Naphtali against the Midianites (Judg. 6:34-35).

One could argue that joint military campaigns among the tribes of Israel against an external threat, even in the period of the judges, were not always defensive in nature. In Judg. 1:1-7 Judah requested Simeon's aid in battle against the mysterious Adonibezek, leader of the Canaanites and Perizzites. According to the tradition this particular war was offensive in nature as the tribes in question were seeking to possess the land allotted to them. The fact that Judah and Simeon were engaged in military struggles in southern

---

[54]In an exegetical seminar at Harvard University in 1961, Professor Cross suggested that the traditional interpretation of the list of tribes in Judges 5 is incorrect. He would see no sign of any failure to cooperate on the part of any of the tribes mentioned, but rather their full cooperation in the holy war against Sisera. Patrick Miller has worked out this idea in greater detail in *The Divine Warrior in Early Israel*, pp. 96-97. Miller interprets the למה of vs. 16 as originally an emphatic particle *lo-mi*, "indeed, surely," or the like, as Cross had already suggested. He also called attention to the close parallel between Judg. 5:16-17 and the blessings of Zebulun and Issachar in Gen. 49:13-15. Only the comment on Gilead does not relate to this particular section of Gen. 49. The poet in Judg. 5 has filled out the list of participating tribes with formulaic material taken from the context of tribal blessings. The only people cursed for failing to take part in the war were the inhabitants of Meroz (Judg. 5:23).

[55]See the discussion of Rudolf Smend, *Yahweh War & Tribal Confederation* (1970), pp. 16-18. Smend rejects the "ten-tribe theory" and assumes that Judah and Simeon did belong to the tribal confederation at this time. "That they do not appear in the song means with certainty that for participation in the battle they came so little into consideration that the poet did not consider it necessary to reprimand them for their absence" (p. 17).

Palestine may perhaps explain their absence from the struggle of the other tribes against Sisera and the Canaanites in northern Palestine.[56]

It is not until the time of Samuel and Saul that all twelve tribes in Israel are explicitly summoned to battle in response to an external threat. When Saul heard of the plight of Jabesh-Gilead at the hands of the Ammonites, he cut up a yoke of oxen and sent the pieces throughout "all the territory of Israel" with a summons to battle (I Sam. 11:7): "Whoever does not come out after Saul and Samuel, so shall it be done to his oxen!" According to the record some 330,000[57] men from Israel and Judah responded and Jabesh-Gilead was delivered from the Ammonites.

The summons to battle in defense of the Covenant League in ancient Israel had a long history, spanning the entire era of the judges. Joshua, Ehud, Deborah, Gideon and Saul are clearly linked to such tradition. In times of crisis when a member of the Covenant League was threatened by some external military force, a charismatic leader would emerge in Israel to summon the levy of the tribal confederation to holy war. Subsequent war oracles as delivered by the classical prophets stand within this tradition.

c. Summons to Battle Against Members of the League

On occasion civil war broke out within the Tribal League of ancient Israel. After Jephthah had delivered Gilead from the Ammonites, the men of Ephraim crossed the Jordan to wage war against Gilead. Jephthah gathered "all the men of Gilead" and defeated Ephraim, because they had said: "You are fugitives of Ephraim, you Gileadites, in the midst of Ephraim and Manasseh" (Judg. 12:4). The precise meaning of this charge is not clear. The Ephraimites appear contentious and jealous, upset because Jephthah had not asked them to join in the battle against the Ammonites. And yet the question remains: was there a deeper cause of this inter-tribal conflict? It should be noted that Gilead had turned outside the structures of the Tribal League to

---

[56]Cf. the discussion of W. F. Albright in the prolegomenon to the recent reprint of C. F. Burney, *The Book of Judges* in The Library of Biblical Studies, ed. by Harry M. Orlinsky (New York: KTAV Publishing House, 1970), p. 12. Albright suggests that these military struggles on the part of Judah and Simeon occurred a century or two before the time of Joshua.

[57]On the meaning of such large numbers in Israel's most ancient traditions see the discussion of George E. Mendenhall, "The Census Lists of Numbers 1 and 26," *JBL* 77 (1958), pp. 52-66. Hebrew *'elef* does not always designate the numeral "thousand"; it also referred to "some subsection of a tribe, though it is not now possible to identify it more closely especially since we have no extra-biblical parallels to this usage" (p. 61).

obtain the aid of Jephthah and his mercenary troops, instead of summoning the levy of all Israel to wage Yahweh's holy war against Ammon. Such behavior in itself was contrary to the terms of the ancient covenant treaties, where it was required of a vassal that he place his trust in his suzerain alone. Thus the action of the Ephraimites against Jephthah and the people of Gilead may have been in accord with legal stipulations of the tribal confederacy itself. At any rate, the men of Ephraim were defeated in the well-known Shibboleth-Sibboleth incident; and Jephthah, the Transjordanian war hero, became one of the so-called minor judges and judged Israel for six years (Judg. 12:7).

A clearer and much more instructive example of holy war declared against a member of the Tribal League for breach of the conditions of the confederation is that of the war against Benjamin in Judg. 19-20. The rape and murder of the Levite's concubine by certain men in Gibeah set the stage for war. The Levite cut up the body of his concubine into twelve pieces and sent her throughout all the land of Israel, thereby summoning the tribes to avenge the crime. The tribal council assembled at Mizpah with a levy of 400,000 armed men. The tribal council decided that the town of Gibeah should surrender the men who had committed the crime that they might be executed. When the men of Benjamin would not comply with the request of the council, war was declared; and the people of Israel went up to Bethel, where the ark of the covenant was located, to seek guidance in the coming battle. Twice they were defeated by the Benjaminites. Before the third and final encounter, an oracle of victory in battle was given by Phinehas the priest (Judg. 20:28): "Go up; for tomorrow I will give them into your hand." An ambush was successful and the men of Benjamin were decimated. The picture presented is that of the *ḥerem* of Yahweh's holy war (Judg. 20:48): ". . . the men of Israel . . . smote them with the edge of the sword, men and beasts and all that they found. And all the towns which they found they set on fire."

A further example of war on a member of the tribal confederation is found in the sequel to the war against Benjamin. No one had come from Jabesh-Gilead in response to the Levite's summons to a council of war. Failure to respond to such a summons was a grave offense and 12,000 choice warriors were sent with an explicit summons to devote the town to total destruction (Judg. 21:10-11): "Go and smite the inhabitants of Jabesh-Gilead with the edge of the sword; also the women and the little ones. This is what you shall do; every male and every woman that has lain with a male you shall utterly destroy." Only 400 young virgins were spared and brought to the camp at Mizpah where they were given as wives to the surviving Benjaminite warriors.

The concept of accountability to the covenant agreement of the tribal confederacy lived on into the monarchy. When Solomon died, his son Rehoboam refused to listen to the demands of the men of Israel at Shechem. The result was a spontaneous voicing of an age-old dismissal formula (I Kings 12:

16): "To your tents, O Israel!"[58] The men of Israel refused to recognize the political authority of Rehoboam who then assembled the armies of Judah and Benjamin to wage war against Israel, only to be thwarted by the prophet Shemaiah. According to the tradition, Shemaiah issued an oracle from Yahweh in the form of a summons *not* to fight (I Kings 12:24): "Do not go up! Do not wage war against your kinsmen, the children of Israel. Return every man to his home, for this thing is from me." Rehoboam and his hosts returned home and civil war was averted.

The situation under Rehoboam is different in several respects from that of the earlier confrontation between Benjamin and the other tribes. In the earlier conflict there was no mention of a charismatic figure as such. The tribal council deliberated the case and the priest Phinehas apparently made use of the sacred lots to obtain a war oracle. In the later conflict between the northern tribes and Rehoboam, a charismatic prophet appeared as the representative of Yahweh's *imperium*. The prophet Shemaiah confronted King Rehoboam and ordered him to give up the fight for control of the northern tribes. The war oracle as delivered by Shemaiah was of such force that Rehoboam deemed it politic to accept a major political setback and return to Jerusalem.

The summons to battle as a form of prophetic speech has its origin within the institution of holy war in ancient Israel. The wars of the Exodus-Conquest period are beyond the pale of history and are encrusted with layers of traditional interpretation. Within this tradition the figure of Moses embodies the ideal "Judge". As commander-in-chief both Moses and Joshua summoned the levy of proto-Israel to wage the wars of Yahweh against Amalek, the two Amorite kings of Transjordan, Midian and Canaan.

There has been much speculation about the nature of warfare during the period of the judges in ancient Israel. As Hayes has noted, it is probable that warfare in the era of the Tribal League was conducted under the leadership of a number of charismatic types.[59] Nonetheless, the detailed analyses of these charismatic types, as presented by Max Weber and others, should not be accepted uncritically. Weber found traces of both individual and collective warrior ecstasy during this era.[60] According to Weber, Samson represents

---

[58]Harold Forshey has called my attention to the fact that the phrase "To your tents!" is not a call to arms per se, but rather a dismissal or disavowal of legal obligations (cf. Judg. 7:8; 20:8; I Sam. 13:2 and II Sam. 20:1). See also the discussion of Albrecht Alt, "Zelte und Hütten," *Kleine Schriften zur Geschichte des Volkes Israel*, Vol. III, ed. by Martin Noth (München: C. H. Beck, 1959), pp. 233-42; and Abraham Malamat, "Organs of Statecraft in the Israelite Monarchy," *BA* 27 (1965), pp. 34-65.

[59]See J. Hayes, "The Oracles Against the Nations," p. 54.

[60]Max Weber, *Ancient Judaism*, tr. and ed. by Hans H. Gerth and Don Mar-

a type of individual ecstasy similar to the Nordic "berserks" who "plunge themselves into the midst of the enemy in a frenzy of blood-lust . . . half unconsciously slaughter(ing) whatever is around them."[61] The *tᵉrûʿāh* to Weber was "the war orgy of the Israelites" which he classified as "the acute collective ecstasy of the war dance."[62] He considered the Nazirites as the remnants of "a body of professional warriors" whose ascetic training produced war ecstasy.[63] In similar fashion he connected the origin of the *nᵉbîʾîm* with war prophets:[64]

> As war prophets the Yahwe Nebiim appeared in Northern Israel with the beginning of the National wars, actually religious wars, above all in the wars of liberation against the uncircumcised Philistines. Ecstatic prophecy obviously made its appearance then though probably not for the first time, but it appeared in all genuine wars of liberation. . . . This prophecy at first had nothing to do with any sort of "prediction" . . . its business was . . . the incitement to crusade, promise of victory, and ecstatic victory magic.

Most of these observations by Weber, and others who have made use of the comparative method in the historical analysis of early warfare, have merit and deserve serious consideration. At the same time, there is great distance, in every respect, between the "Nordic berserk" and the warrior Saul, who was "also among the prophets" in ancient Israel (cf. I Sam. 10:11-12). Nowhere, within the biblical text, is there a shred of unambiguous evidence for the individual and collective warrior ecstasy as presented by Weber. In particular it must be remembered that the legendary figure of Samson is by no means typical of the "Judges" of ancient Israel.

In premonarchical Israel the summons to battle as a speech form appears on the lips of Ehod, Deborah, Gideon and Saul. In each case the person in question was a charismatic war leader of at least part of the tribal confederation. In one instance there was no charismatic leader as such; and it was the inter-tribal council that declared war, summoning the levy of all Israel against rebellious Benjamin.

It is Samuel who forms a bridge between the various types of charismatic war prophecy of the premonarchical era and the emergence of the war oracle on the lips of the classical prophets. As Albright has shown, Samuel stands in "the closest possible relation to the ecstatic prophets . . . (he) not only encourages them but actually presides over their meetings (I Sam. 19:20)."[65]

---

tindale (New York: Free Press and London: Collier-Macmillan Ltd., 1952), p. 94.

[61] *Ibid.*, p. 94.

[62] *Loc. cit.*

[63] *Loc. cit.*

[64] *Ibid.*, p. 97.

[65] W. F. Albright, "Samuel," p. 9.

Samuel was a Nazirite, as witnessed by both Jewish tradition and the fragmentary Hebrew manuscript of Samuel found in Cave IV at Qumran: "he shall become a *nāzîr* forever" (I Sam. 1:22).[66] As leader and patron of the ecstatic prophets, who had carried on their ancient function as oracular diviners, Samuel was a *rō'ēh*, a "seer".[67] He was also a charismatic judge, that is, a recognized arbitrator because of his inter-tribal role in the ancient covenant confederation of Israel.[68] But even more important, he was a *nābî'*, "one called directly by God to his service, outside hereditary office and royal appointment.[69]

Herein lies the origin of the authority of the classical prophets who represent the *imperium* of Yahweh and constitute a political force over against the king in Israel and Judah. When, some four hundred years after Samuel, the prophet Jeremiah made use of the summons to battle as a form of prophetic speech, he stood within an ancient tradition in which, as Yahweh's herald, he had the authority to summon the levy of the Divine Warrior's hosts to holy war. He also stood within a literary tradition, at least as old as Amos, which saw foreign peoples as accountable to Yahweh, the suzerain of the nations.

4. Summons to Flight

The summons to flight, a speech form well attested in the OAN material in Jeremiah, is not common in pre-Amos tradition. Bach cites but one clear example from the period of the Tribal League and early monarchy, that of Saul addressed to the Kenites (I Sam. 15:6).[70] Samuel had sent Saul to destroy Amalek. After assembling his troops before the "city of Amalek," Saul issued a warning to the Kenites: "Come! Leave Amalek and withdraw, that I may not have to destroy you with them; for you were kind to the Israelites when they came up from Egypt." A further example of this speech form appears in I Sam. 22:5 where the prophet Gad urged David to flee from the refuge of Adullam: "Do not remain in the refuge. Leave, and go up to the land of Judah!"

The utterance in both cases is not a prophetic oracle as such, but rather a warning addressed to those in danger, to save their lives through flight from impending destruction. One is reminded of the warning given to Lot by the two messengers from Yahweh to flee from Sodom (Gen. 19:12-17).

---

[66]See 4 Q Sam[a] which Frank M. Cross, Jr. has utilized in his translation of I and II Samuel in the so-called Confraternity edition of *The Holy Bible*, Vol. II, *Samuel to Maccabees* (Paterson, New Jersey: St. Anthony Guild Press, 1969), pp. 4 and 738.

[67]Albright, "Samuel," p. 13.

[68]*Loc. cit.*

[69]*Loc. cit.*

[70]R. Bach, *Aufforderungen zur Flucht*, p. 48.

In the OAN tradition of Jeremiah and Second Isaiah this speech form was transformed, from a prophetic oracle of impending doom to an oracle of hope in a flight from Babylon, a "Second Exodus" for those in exile.[71]

War Songs and Holy War

Behind the major narrative strands of the Pentateuch stand original epic poems composed orally within the cultus of the Covenant League in ancient Israel. This poetic heritage lived on, even after the formation of the Davidic Empire and the construction of Solomon's Temple in Jerusalem, surfacing from time to time in some of the psalms and in certain prophetic oracles, particularly within the OAN tradition. Much of this epic poetry was apparently reduced to narrative prose in written form as early as the tenth century and consequently lost as far as its original form is concerned. The most important parts of this poetic tradition as far as our purposes are concerned are the remnants of Israel's ancient war songs. A few fragments have been retained imbedded within the narrative portions of the Pentateuch and in the work of the Deuteronomic historian. Other fragments can be recovered from later poetic contexts. These fragments, along with certain larger poetic works, form an important background for understanding the OAN tradition.

Exod. 17:16 contains a fragment of an archaic war poem appended to the narrative which may be reconstructed as follows:[72]

For the hand is on Yahweh's banner;	כי יד על נס[a] יה<ו>[b]	6
The battle belongs to Yahweh,	מלחמה ליהוה	6
Against Amalek from generation to generation.	בעמלק מדר דר	7

---

[71]John Mauchline has challenged this interpretation in his recent article, "Implicit Signs of a Persistent Belief in the Davidic Empire," *VT* 20 (1970), pp. 287-303. Note in particular his comment (p. 301): "The movement of the delivered Jews from Babylon to Judah is not described as a second exodus; it is a second movement from Babylon at the call of God, and now the land given of old to Abraham will be permanently possessed."

[72]Notes to the text of Exod. 17:16 -- a) The name of the altar in vs. 15, יהוה נסי, must also be reflected in the MT expression כסיה of vs. 16, as numerous translators and commentators have noted (cf. RSV and Jerusalem Bible). The confusion of *kaph* and *nun* is possible, as Professor Cross has noted [cf. in particular figs. 1 and 2 (pp. 175-76) of his article, "The Development of the Jewish Scripts," in *BANE* (1961), pp. 170-264]. The Vulgate reading *solium domini* supports the word division as read and suggests that these letters survive from a time before final vowels were indicated in the orthography. Lynn Clapham, in a Harvard seminar paper ["The Wandering in the Wilderness" (OT Seminar, Fall, 1964), pp. 12-13] suggested the reading

Both the name of the altar which Moses erected, יהוה נסי ("Yahweh is my battle rallying point"), and the poetic fragment in vs. 16 refer to the war against Amalek as Yahweh's war. In our historical reconstruction, the war with Amalek is the first of a series of wars which, together with the defeat of the Egyptians at the Reed Sea, constitute Yahweh's Holy War par excellence. The textual corruption in the poetic fragment was no doubt related to an alternate interpretation of the first colon which found the more familiar "throne of Yahweh" [כס(א) יהו(ה)] for the enigmatic "banner of Yahweh."[73]

The כסא יהוה was the ark of the covenant, the moveable throne upon which the invisible Yahweh was seated as he lead Israel forth to battle in cultic procession. The role of the ark in the holy wars of Yahweh during the Exodus-Conquest period is suggested in the archaic formula preserved in Num. 10:35-36.[74]

Arise, O Yahweh!	קומה יהוה	11
Let your enemies be scattered;	[] יפצו איביך	
Let your adversaries flee before you!	[] ינסו משנאיך מפניך	11
Return, O Yahweh, (with) the myriads;	שובה יהוה [בר]בות[a]	8/7
(O El, with) the "thousands" of Israel!	⟨אל ב⟩[b] אלפי ישראל	7

These two liturgical fragments are rooted in holy war ideology and are probably to be interpreted as *incipits* of longer liturgical pieces, the so-called "Song(s) to the Ark," which were originally used in the re-enactment of the wars of Yahweh within the cultus of the ritual conquest.[75]

Another fragment of an ancient war song dealing with events of the Exodus-Conquest period is found in Josh. 10:12-13.[76]

כס יה, "throne of Yahu." But as Cross has noted, the *'aleph* in כסא, "chair, throne," is consonantal, as witnessed by Ugaritic evidence, and would not have been omitted in the early orthography. b) The addition of the *waw* is to indicate that the pronunciation *Yahwe(h)* is preferred to *Yahū*, as suggested by Clapham. The final *he* would not have appeared on יהוה (or מלחמה) in the original orthography.

[73]Cf. SP, Vulgate and Syriac which read כסא יהוה.

[74]Notes to the text of Num. 10:35-36 -- a) A metathesis of the *resh* and *beth* is read, with Cross, to make sense of a "clearly corrupt" text [cf. his "Divine Warrior," pp. 24-25; and now *Canaanite Myth and Hebrew Epic*, p. 100]. Point the word as either *b*^{e}*ribb*^{e}*bōt* or *b*^{e}*rabbōt*. b) The emendation presented here was suggested by Professor Cross in private consultation and, among the various attempts to restore the text of this bicolon, does the least violence to the received text. Note that the confusion of *beth* and *pe* is a well attested scribal error in the early orthography.

[75]See Cross, "Divine Warrior," p. 25; and *Canaanite Myth*, pp. 99-105.

Sun, stand still in Gibeon!	שמש בגבעון דוֹמָ[a]	6
Moon, (stand still) in the valley of Aijalon!	[] ירח בעמק אילון	7
The Sun stood still, the Moon stayed;	[] ידם שמש [] ירח עמד	7
Until he had taken vengeance upon the nations of his enemies.	עד יקם גוי איביו	7

Patrick Miller cited this text as an *incipit* which may have been part of a longer poem now lost.[77] It should be noted that MT regards this poetic fragment as a piece from the "Book of Yashar," though LXX makes no mention of this fact. The poetic fragment is a summons to the divine bodies to aid in battle -- an important motif in the institution of holy war.[78]

Besides the so-called "Book of Yashar," the Pentateuch also cites the enigmatic "Book of the Wars of Yahweh" (Num. 21:14), a source whose very existence has been challenged by Tur-Sinai.[79] From the context of the citation, however, most scholars have assumed the work in question to be an anthology of old war poems dealing with the conflict of the invading Israelites with the original inhabitants of Canaan. The passage in Num. 21:14-15 attributed to this source presents major difficulties and was recently dismissed by the late W. F. Albright as beyond reconstruction.[80] The following reconstruction of this poetic fragment is therefore provisional in nature.[81]

The Benefactor has come in a storm;	אָתָ[a] והב[b] בסופה	7
Yes, He has come to the wadies of the Arnon.	ואָתָ [] נחלי-מ[c] ארנון	8
He marched through the wadies;	[] אש[ר][d] [] נחלים	5
He {marched / turned aside} to the seat of Ar	{אשר / נטה}[e] לשבת עד	5
He leaned toward the border of Moab;	[] נשען לגבול מואב	7
. . . . . .	. . .	(7)

[76]For a detailed analysis of this poetic fragment and a most provocative interpretation of its meaning, see John S. Holladay, "The Day(s) the Moon Stood Still," *JBL* 87 (1968), pp. 166-78. Note to the text of Josh. 10:12-13 -- a) Read the lengthened form of the imperative, as in Num. 10:35-36, to achieve better metrical balance. The final *he* would not have appeared in the earliest orthography.

[77]P. Miller, *The Divine Warrior*, pp. 123-28.

[78]See Miller, *ibid.*, pp. 124-26 and 239-40 for a discussion of the literature on the sun and moon as deities in the ancient Near East. See also J. S. Holladay, *op. cit.* The sun and moon were members of the divine council and were summoned to fight in Yahweh's behalf. Cf. Judg. 5:20 for a similar motif.

[79]N. H. Tur-Sinai, "Was There an Ancient 'Book of the Wars of the Lord?'" (Heb.), *BIES* 24 (1959/60), pp. 146-48.

[80]W. F. Albright, *Yahweh and the Gods of Canaan*, p. 44.

This brief poetic quotation was cited by the narrator in Numbers 21 primarily because it placed the boundary of Moab at the Arnon. The subsequent misreading of the verbal roots in question led to confusion in the versions and textual corruption in the transmission of MT. The picture presented here is that of the Divine Warrior poised on the edge of the promised land, before the most celebrated battles of the Exodus-Conquest. He has come in the whirl-wind with his hosts to the sources of the River Arnon in Transjordan. He marches through the wadies, turning aside to settle affairs with Moab before marching against the Amorite kings to the north, and then across the Jordan to Gilgal and the conquest of Canaan. If our reconstruction of Yahweh's Holy War is correct, the picture is indeed a fitting one for the *incipit* of a narrative poem entitled "The Book of the Wars of Yahweh."

Other fragments of ancient war songs are found imbedded in poetic contexts. In Ps. 68:8-9, as reconstructed by W. F. Albright, we read:[82]

O YHWH, when Thou didst go out	יהו בצאתך
In the van of Thy people,	לפנ עמך
When Thou didst march through the desert,	בצעדך בישמן
Then the earth quaked	ארץ רעש
Heaven also tossed,	אף-שמם נטפ
Before YHWH, God of Sinai,	מפנ יהו ז-סני
In the presence of YHWH Israel's God.	מפנ יהו אלה ישראל

---

[81]For an earlier attempt to reconstruct this fragment, see my article "Num 21:14-15 and the Book of the Wars of Yahweh," *CBQ* 36 (1974), pp. 359-60. The present attempt is based, in large measure, on suggestions made by Mitchell Dahood in a personal letter. Notes to the text of Num. 21:14-15 -- a) The direct object marker את is not found in ancient Hebrew poetry. Read instead the verbal root *'th*, "to come," which is frequently predicated of deity in both Ugaritic and Hebrew poetry (cf. Deut. 33:2; Ps. 68:32 and Isa. 21:12). b) Following the suggestion of Dahood, the והב of MT is here pointed *wōhēb*, a participial form which preserves the *prima waw*. For a parallel see the יהבך of Ps. 55:23 which Dahood has rendered, "your Provider" [*Psalms II*, p. 37]. c) Reading enclitic *mem* in the middle of a construct chain, with Albright [*Yahweh and the Gods of Canaan*, p. 44]. Cf. *hararê-m Śē'îr*, "mountains of Seir," in Gen. 14:6. d) Reading *resh* for *daleth* with SP to form the verbal root *'šr*, "to come, proceed, march." Cf. Deut. 33:2 where the roots *'šr* and *'th* occur in parallel, and note the discussion of F. M. Cross and D. N. Freedman, "The Blessing of Moses," *JBL* 67 (1948), pp. 193, 199, n. 11. e) The relative particle אשר of MT is inappropriate for old Hebrew poetry. Either delete with LXX and the Old Latin versions or take it as a variant form as in the previous note.

And again in Ps. 68:18, as rendered by Cross, we find:[83]

The chariots of God are two myriads,	רכב אלהם רבתם	7
Two thousand the bowmen of Yahweh,	אלפ שנב [יהו]	6
When he came from Sinai with the Holy Ones.	ב⟨בא⟩ מסני בקדש	7

As Albright has argued, these passages are probably *incipits* of independent war songs which unfortunately have not been preserved in their entirety.

The introduction to the "Song of Moses" (Deut. 33:2-3) presents the same picture:[84]

Yahweh from Sinai came,	יהו מסני בא	6
He beamed forth from Seir upon us,	[ ]זרח משער למ	7
He shone from Mount Paran.	הפע מהר פרן	6
With him were myriads of holy ones,	את-מ רבבת קדש	6
At his right hand marched the divine ones,	מימנ אש[ר] [א]לם	7
Yea, the purified of the peoples.	אף חבב עמם	5

A larger section of an ancient war song is preserved in the "Song of Habakkuk" (Hab. 3:3-15) where, as Albright has shown, ancient material has been reused in a new context.[85] This particular passage is discussed in greater detail in Chapter IV below.

In addition to isolated poetic fragments and the reuse of archaic material in later poetic compositions, the Old Testament also contains a few ancient war songs preserved in their entirety. The most important such poem is the so-called "Song of the Sea" in Exod. 15:1-18 which Cross has subjected to detailed textual, prosodic and historical analysis.[86] This hymn may be divided into two main parts, the first of which describes the combat of Yahweh, the Divine Warrior, in which his enemies, the Egyptians, are defeated at the Reed Sea (vss. 1-12). The second part of the hymn presents the possession of the land of promise along with the dismay of its former inhabitants. As Cross has shown, the final strophe of the hymn reflects an ancient mythic pattern: the building of a sanctuary on the mount of inheritance, and the god's mani-

---

[82] W. F. Albright, "A Catalogue of Early Hebrew Lyric Poems (Psalm LXVIII)," *HUCA* 23 (1950/51), p. 37.

[83] F. M. Cross, Jr., *Canaanite Myth and Hebrew Epic*, p. 102.

[84] *Ibid.*, p. 101; cf. also *JBL* 67 (1948), pp. 193, 197-202.

[85] W. F. Albright, "The Psalm of Habakkuk," in *Studies in Old Testament Prophecy*, ed. H. H. Rowley (T. H. Robinson Festschrift, Edinburgh: T. & T. Clark, 1950), pp. 1-18.

[86] F. M. Cross, Jr., "The Song of Miriam," *JNES* 14 (1955), pp. 237-50; "The Song of the Sea," *JThC* 5 (1968), pp. 1-25; and *Canaanite Myth and Hebrew Epic* (1973), pp. 121-44.

festation of "eternal kingship."[87] The imagery of the hymn as a whole, then, reveals a dialectic in the evolution of Israelite religion and religious institutions. Historical memory of events experienced by proto-Israel in the Exodus-Conquest is dominant; yet these very events are imposed on a matrix of mythopoeic patterns of West Semitic, especially Canaanite, myth. The "Song of the Sea" is a hymn of praise to the Divine Warrior who led his hosts from slavery in Egypt to establish them in the land of promise. Its central theme is Yahweh's Holy War which comprises the events of the Exodus-Conquest taken as a whole.

As suggested earlier, the Oracles of Balaam reflect a similar hymnic background. The first three oracles in particular are hymns of praise to Yahweh and his people Israel. Though Yahweh is not explicitly designated a warrior, he is said to have caused his people to "storm like a wild bull" (Num. 23:22 and 24:8) and "attack like a lion" (Num. 23:24 and 24:9). No foe is able to stand before Yahweh and his people (Num. 23:23). Israel shall "devour the people who resist, and the bones of them will he crush" (Num. 24:6). The events of the Exodus-Conquest are fused in this poetic tradition, though the picture is by no means as explicit as that presented in the "Song of the Sea." It should also be noted that in Num. 24:7 the poet exclaims: "may (Israel's) kingdom/royalty be exalted." This reference, together with the comment that Yahweh has clothed Israel with royal majesty (Num. 23:21), need not be interpreted as reflecting the later Davidic monarchy, as many commentators have argued, but rather should be understood in connection with early mythopoeic patterns of West Semitic thought concerning kingship and the gods and, in particular, the *imperium* of Yahweh.

Another archaic war song, the so-called "Song of Heshbon" (Num. 21:27-30), has been subjected to a detailed prosodic-textual analysis by Paul Hanson who argues that the poem is "an Amorite Victory Song celebrating the victory of their hero Sihon over the Moabites."[88] The oracle against Moab in Jeremiah 48 shows direct literary dependence on Num. 21:28-29, at least in MT (Jer. 48:45-46). Haran has argued that the OAN tradition concerning Moab in Isaiah 15-16 and Jeremiah 48 are both dependent on what he calls the "Song of the Mošlîm" (Num. 21:27-30).[89] Albright is no doubt much nearer the truth in his suggestion, based on stylistic criteria, of a ninth-century prototype behind Isaiah 15-16 and Jeremiah 48.[90] It will be argued in Chapter V below

---

[87]F. M. Cross, Jr., "Song of the Sea," p. 24.

[88]Paul D. Hanson, "The Song of Heshbon and David's Nîr," *HTR* 61 (1968), pp. 297-320.

[89]M. Diman-Haran, "An Archaic Remnant in Prophetic Literature" (Heb.), *BIES* 13 (1946/47), pp. 7-15.

[90]W. F. Albright, *Yahweh and the Gods of Canaan*, pp. 23-24, n. 57.

that Jer. 48:45-46 is apparently not original to the OAN tradition of Jeremiah and should probably be deleted with LXX as a scribal gloss, based in part on Num. 21:28-29 but also on Num. 24:17 in the Oracles of Balaam.

One other victory song ought to be at least mentioned in connection with the institution of holy war. Von Rad begins his analysis of holy war with a discussion of the "Song of Deborah" as preserved in Judges 5. This particular poem has been studied in detail by Albright (1922, 1936),[91] Cross (1950)[92] and P. Miller (1963, 1973).[93] Albright has dated the poem to *ca.* 1150 B.C.[94] and, as von Rad has shown, it is the most important witness to the institution of holy war during the period of the judges. In form the poem is a victory song celebrating the defeat of Sisera and the Canaanites at the hands of Deborah and Barak. Much has been made of the list of ten confederates singled out for blessing or "critical derision"[95] for their participation or failure to participate in the battle. The suggestion made by Cross, which is developed in greater detail by Miller, that the only curse as such uttered in this poem is that directed against Meroz in vs. 23 is persuasive. The so-called curses or "critical derision" directed against Reuben, Gilead, Dan and Asher show literary dependence on the tribal blessings directed to members of the tribal confederacy in Genesis 49 and Deuteronomy 33. The list of tribes presented in the Song of Deborah is the list of actual participants in the battle, together with appropriate tribal blessings which are formulaic in nature.[96]

The institution of holy war during the period of the judges should be distinguished from Yahweh's Holy War par excellence as celebrated in the cultus of a ritual conquest. Yahweh's Holy War is the ritual fusing of the events of the Exodus-Conquest into one great cultic event. In Yahweh's Holy War the Divine Warrior marched with his hosts from Sinai to Shittim and then across the Jordan to Gilgal, the battle camp for the conquest of Canaan. The institution of holy war as reflected in the Song of Deborah had its historical roots in this "pre-Settlement" era among the tribal groups which constituted proto-Israel under Moses and Joshua. The nature of the institution of holy war before the time of Deborah can be reconstructed, at least in part, from an analysis of Yahweh's Holy War as celebrated in the ritual conquest

---

[91]Albright, *JPOS* 2 (1922), pp. 69-86 and 284-85; and "The Song of Deborah in the Light of Archaeology," *BASOR* 62 (1936), pp. 26-31.

[92]F. M. Cross, Jr., *Yahwistic Poetry*, pp. 27-42.

[93]P. D. Miller, Jr., "Holy War and Cosmic War," pp. 195-210 and *The Divine Warrior in Early Israel*, pp. 87-102.

[94]W. F. Albright, *Yahweh and the Gods of Canaan*, p. 13.

[95]R. Smend, *Yahweh War & Tribal Confederation*, p. 14.

[96]See p. 41, n. 54 above.

tradition. The ark of the covenant was a battle palladium. The tribal groups had designated positions within the battle camp under priestly organization. Moses and Joshua, as "Judges" over Israel filled the role later assumed by the prophets in delivering war oracles to inspire the troops in battle.

The Davidic League --"A Covenant of Brotherhood"

The establishment of the Davidic monarchy and the centralization of Israel's worship in Jerusalem introduced a powerful impulse to the developing religion of ancient Israel which tended to reshape earlier tradition. The cultus of the premonarchic Covenant League was retained but was subordinated to a royal cultus administered by dominant priestly families under the control of the king. Yahweh's Holy War, as a cultic re-enactment of the Exodus-Conquest, was no longer climaxed by mere possession of the land of promise. The ark of the covenant was carried in ritual procession to its "eternal resting place" on Mount Zion in Jerusalem. The climax of the Royal Festival became the enthronement of the Davidic monarch in dynastic covenant.[97] The ark of the covenant was subsequently housed in an elaborate temple, constructed under Solomon, which became the center of Israelite worship until its destruction by Nebuchadnezzar in 587 B.C.

Under David, Israel as a political entity was no longer a loosely federated tribal league, but rapidly became the center of an international empire. After defeating the Philistines (II Sam. 5:17-25; I Chron. 18:1), David first turned his attention to Moab. He defeated Moab, ruthlessly punished their army, laid Moab under tribute and became their overlord. Their kingdom as such remained intact as a vassal to Israel.

The conquests of the Arameans and the Ammonites were next and are associated, at least in part. After humiliating David's delegation and thus provoking war with Israel, Hanun king of Ammon summoned his Aramean allies to aid him in battle. The Arameans were roundly defeated and a treaty of peace was drawn which made of the Aramean states a kind of province whose administrative seat was Damascus. In addition to the more or less organized coalition of Aramean states which were defeated in battle, the kingdom of Hamath under King Toi (תעי) concluded a "treaty of frendship" with David, thus assuming vassal status within the emerging Davidic Empire (cf. II Sam. 8:9-10). The Ammonite campaign continued under Joab, David's general. When finally forced to capitulate, Ammon became Davidic territory with David ostensibly as king (II Sam. 12:26-31 and I Chron. 20:1).

---

[97]See the discussion of William R. Millar, "Isaiah 24-27 and the Origin of Apocalyptic" (unpub. Ph.D. thesis, Harvard University, 1970), pp. 167-71. This work is being revised for publication by Harvard University Press.

After the Aramean campaign, Edom was attacked and ravaged with dreadful cruelty by Joab and his troops (cf. II Sam. 8:13-14; I Kings 11:15-17). David was then the undisputed master from Egypt to the Euphrates. The Philistines were reduced to their pentapolis and immediate coastal area. David was king of Judah, Israel, Jerusalem, Ammon and the Canaanite city-states incorporated into Judah and Israel. He ruled through provincial governors or vassal chiefs in Aram, Edom and Moab. He had established treaty relationships with Tyre and Hamath. David had thus become the most powerful ruler in the world of his day, and Israel was transformed from a tribal confederation to suzerain of a league of nations.

The phrase "covenant of brotherhood" (ברית אחים) is used by Amos to describe the relationship between Tyre, Edom and Israel (Amos 1:9). Priest has argued that this phrase refers to a treaty first made in the days of Hiram and David, a treaty which was retained by Solomon and which "may even have weathered the chauvinism of Elijah and Elisha."[98] Gerstenberger has collected data from the Hittite treaties to demonstrate that the concept of "brotherhood" (*aḫḫūtu*) played a prominant role in international treaties, not only among equally high- or low-ranking potentates but also among partners of unequal status.[99] Even inimical nations with no blood relationship whatever could, by virtue of such a treaty effected between them, be brought into a relationship of "brotherhood."[100] Fishbane, in his recent article on Amos 1:11, which was dependent in part on an earlier article by Professor Moran, confirmed the work of Gerstenberger and renders the term אחיו as used in connection with Edom in Amos' oracle as "his vassal."[101]

In the case of the Davidic Empire we have an extension of the earlier Covenant League of tribal groups around a central sanctuary to a league of nations centered in Jerusalem under Yahweh, God of Israel, and David his chosen monarch. The Davidic Empire later became an ideal type which was persistent, particularly within prophetic circles, long after the disintegration of the actual empire as such. Mauchline, in his recent discussion of Amos 1-2, argues that the crimes for which Israel's neighbors were condemned were not crimes against Israel and Judah, but crimes committed between members of an association of peoples, against what Amos specifically termed "brotherly obligation."[102]

---

[98]J. Priest, "The Covenant of Brothers," *JBL* 84 (1965), pp. 400-406.

[99]Erhard Gerstenberger, "Covenant and Commandment," *JBL* 84 (1965), pp. 38-51.

[100]*Ibid.*, pp. 40-42.

[101]Michael Fishbane, "The Treaty Background of Amos 1:11 and Related Matters," *JBL* 89 (1970), p. 315.

[102]John Mauchline, "Implicit Signs of a Persistent Belief in the Davi-

> Amos believed that these people had a bond of association which they had treated with contempt, a bond in the name of Yahweh which meant that, in spite of their political separation from Israel now, they were still a spiritual unity.

Ivan Kaufman, in a Harvard seminar paper (1962),[103] presented a similar argument. Noting that the nations whom Yahweh addressed in Amos 1-2 were considered to be violators of some standard of behavior, Kaufman posited the "Empire of David and Solomon" as the proper legal background for understanding this particular tradition.[104]

> It would be reasonable to assume that Amos' oracles concerning the nations between Assyria and Egypt reflect a sense of the suzerainty of Israel over the nations around her. It is suggestive that one of the primary stipulations in the Hittite suzerainty treaty is that vassal countries are prohibited from hostility among themselves. . . . The nations represented in this Empire are a more or less homogeneous unit between two large and different units namely Assyria and Egypt.

Cross has expanded Kaufman's thesis to explain subsequent development of the OAN tradition in Isaiah, Jeremiah and Ezekiel where the legal background is greatly extended. The prophets interpreted the system of treaties which constituted the Davidic Empire, and later the Assyrian and Babylonian empires, as sanctioned by the *imperium* of Yahweh. In the developing OAN tradition, the prophets condemned the various member nations of the political system in question for acts of violence against one another in violation of the established order.

Amos 1-2 and Divine Judgment

The series of oracles against foreign nations in Amos 1-2 has drawn considerable comment by biblical interpreters.[105] The elaborate, almost mono-

---

dic Empire," *VT* 20 (1970), p. 289.

[103] Ivan T. Kaufman, "The Significance of Oracles Concerning Foreign Nations in Jeremiah" (unpub. paper, OT Seminar, Harvard University, Fall, 1962).

[104] *Ibid.*, p. 4.

[105] In addition to the commentaries, the OT introductions, and the literature cited in the following discussion, other recent works of importance should be noted: A. S. Kapelrud, "God as Destroyer in the Preaching of Amos and in the Ancient Near East," *JBL* 71 (1952), pp. 33-38; J. Morgenstern, "The Universalism of Amos," *Essays Presented to L. Baeck* (London: East & West Library, 1954), pp. 106-26; Robert Bach, "Gottesrecht und Weltliches Recht in der Verkündigung des Propheten Amos," *Festschrift G. Dehn* (Neukir-

tonous structure of the framework of the oracles, the order of the nations treated, and the climax of the series with its more detailed indictment of Israel led Bentzen (1950) to posit a "ritual background" in the form of a New Year's Festival curse upon foreign nations, analagous to the Egyptian execration texts from the Middle Kingdom.[106] Strong opposition was soon voiced against this view from certain quarters, while others accepted Bentzen's view with various modifications. Reventlow (1962) accepted the "ritual background" but understood it in terms of a *Völkerritual* at a Covenant-renewal Festival.[107] Gottwald (1964) accepted the execration pattern as the proper background but turned his attention to the more general fact that the oracles in question "have a previous history."[108] Basing his case in large part on arguments presented by Y. Kaufmann and M. Haran, Gottwald asserted that where the oracles can be approximately dated they appear to be pre-Amosean.[109] He noted in passing that the historical argument as such "is not decisive in itself for it is always possible that Amos selected well-known instances of national wrong-doing without respect to their modernity."[110] Nonetheless, when the historical argument is joined to an analysis of the literary character of the oracles, Gottwald was convinced "that the probability of a pre-Amosean prototype for the foreign oracles becomes very strong."[111] It should be noted, however, that the only specific argument advanced by Gottwald to support this conclusion is the apparent "discrepancy between the framework and the indictment:"[112]

> There is really little logical point to speaking of a plentitude of national wrongs, as the "three . . . four" formula certainly does,

---

chen: Neukirchener Verlag, 1957), pp. 23-24; B. K. Soper, "For Three Transgressions and for Four: A New Interpretation of Amos i 3," *ET* 71 (1959/60), pp. 86-87; S. Cohen, "The Political Background of the Words of Amos," *HUCA* 36 (1965), pp. 153-60; L. M. Muntingh, " Political and International Relations of Israel's Neighbouring Peoples according to the Oracles of Amos," *OuTWP* 7 (1966), pp. 134-42; M. Haran, "Some Problems of the Historical Background of 'Prophecies of the Nations' in the Book of Amos" (Heb.), *Yediot* 30 (1966), pp. 56-69; and M. Weiss, "For Three Transgressions and for Four" (Heb.), *Tarbiẓ* 36 (1966), pp. 307-18.

[106] Aage Bentzen, "The Ritual Background of Amos i 2 - ii 16," *OTS* 8 (1950), pp. 85-99.

[107] H. G. Reventlow, *Das Amt des Propheten bei Amos* (FRLANT 80, 1962).

[108] N. K. Gottwald, *All the Kingdoms of the Earth* (New York: Harper & Row, 1964), pp. 103-112.

[109] *Ibid.*, pp. 103-105.

[110] *Ibid.*, p. 105.

[111] *Loc. cit.*

[112] *Ibid.*, p. 106.

> only to mention a single wrong in each instance. . . . In the citation of only one crime for each nation, even in logical defiance of the traditional execration pattern, Amos gave just enough to show that the foreign nations are culpable while at the same time throwing the weight of his indictment upon Israel.

Gottwald's argument is not convincing as the parallelism of numbers is a stylistic device in archaic poetry and need not be taken literally.

Even if one accepts the possibility of a pre-Amosean prototype for the OAN material, it would still appear that the oracles in question, with the exception of the oracle against Judah in Amos 2:4-5, contain genuine material from a single composition, represented as uttered by Yahweh in Jerusalem.[113] This OAN tradition (Amos 1:3-2:16) may be reconstructed as follows:[114]

1:3	Because of three crimes of Damascus,	על שלשה פשעי דמשק	8
	Because of four I will not turn back;	[]על ארבעה לא אשובן[][a]	8
	Because they threshed Gilead with threshers.	על דושם בחרצות [][b] גלעד	9
4	I will send fire on the house of Hazael;	ושלחתי אש בבית חזאל	10
	It will consume the strongholds of Ben-hadad.	ואכלה ארמנות בן הדד	10
	I will cut off the enthroned in Beth-eden,	והכרתי ירשב [מבית עדן][c]	9
	And he who wields the scepter in the Valley of Aven.	ותומך שבט [מבקעת ארן]	8
5	I will break the bar of Damascus' gate;	[ושברתי בריח דמשק][d]	8
	The people of Aram shall go in exile to Kir.	וגלו עם ארם קירה	8
6	Because of three crimes of Gaza,	על שלשה פשעי עזה	8
	Because of four I will not turn back;	[]על ארבעה לא אשובן[]	8
	Because they exiled an ally.	על הגלתם גלות שְׁלֵמָה[e] [][f]	9
7	I will send fire in the walls of Gaza;	ושלחתי אש בחומת עזה	10
	It will consume her strongholds.	ואכלה ארמנתיה	9
8	I will cut off the enthroned in Ashdod,	והכרתי יושב מאשדוד	9
	And he who wields the scepter in Ashkelon.	ותומך שבט מאשקלון	8
	I will turn my hand against Ekron;	והשיבותי ידי על עקרון	10
	The last man of the Philistines will perish.	ואבדו שארית פלשתים	10

---

[113] See the discussion of G. Ernest Wright, "The Nations in Hebrew Prophecy," *Encounter* 26 (1965), p. 236.

[114] For a detailed discussion of this material see my article, "The Prosodic Structure of Amos 1-2," *HTR* 67 (1974), pp. 427-36.

9	Because of three crimes of Tyre,	על שלשה פשעי צר	7
	Because of four I will not turn back;	[]על ארבעה לא אשובן[]	8
	Because they delivered up captives to Edom;	על הסגירם גלות [][g] לאדום	9
	They did not remember the covenant of brothers.	ולא זכרו ברית אחים	9
10	I will send fire in the walls of Tyre;	ושלחתי אש בחומת צר	9
	It will consume her strongholds.	ואכלה ארמנותיה	9
11	Because of three crimes of Edom,	על שלשה פשעי אדום	8
	Because of four I will not turn back;	[]על ארבעה לא אשובן[]	8
	Because he chased his brother with the sword;	על רדפו בחרב אחיו	7
	⟨Edom⟩ violated his obligations of kinship.	ושחת ⟨אדם⟩[h] רחמיו [][i]	7
12	I will send fire on Teman;	ושלחתי אש בתימן	8
	It will consume the strongholds of Bozrah.	ואכלה ארמנות בצרה	9
13	Because of three crimes of Ammon,	על שלשה פשעי [][j] עמון	8
	Because of four I will not turn back;	[]על ארבעה לא אשובן[]	8
	Because they ripped open pregnant women of Gilead.	על בקעם הרות [] גלעד [][k]	7
14	I will kindle a fire in the walls of Rabbah;	והצתי אש בחומת רבה	10
	It will consume her strongholds.	ואכלה ארמנותיה	9
	With a war-cry in the day of battle,	בתרועה ביום מלחמה	9
	With a tempest in the day of the storm-wind;	בסער[l] ביום סופה	8
15	Milcom will go into exile,	והלך מלכם[m] בגולה	8
	Together with ⟨his priests⟩ and his nobles.	⟨כהניו⟩[n] ושריו יחדו	8
2:1	Because of three crimes of Moab,	על שלשה פשעי מואב	8
	Because of four I will not turn back;	[]על ארבעה לא אשובן[]	8
	Because he burned a human sacrifice to a demon.	על שרפו [][o] מלך אד[]ם לש[]ד[p]	8
2	I will send fire on ⟨the cities⟩ of Moab;	ושלחתי אש ב⟨ערי⟩[q] מואב	10
	It will consume the strongholds of Kerioth.	ואכלה ארמנות []קריות	10
	Moab shall die with tumult,	ומת בשאון מואב[r]	7
	With a war-cry, with trumpet blast --	בתרועה בקול שופר	8
3	I will cut off the ruler from his midst;	והכרתי שופט מקרבה[s]	9
	All his nobles I will slay with him.	וכל שרי⟨ו⟩[t] אהרוג עמו [][u]	8

6	Because of three crimes of Israel,	על שלשה פשעי ישראל	9
	Because of four I will not turn back;	[]על ארבעה לא אשובן[]	8
	Because they sold the innocent for silver,	על מכרם בכסף צדיק	7
	The poor for a pair of sandals.	[]אביון בעבור נעלים[v]	7
7	They trample on the head of the helpless;	[]שאפים [][w] בראש דלים	6
	The way of the afflicted they pervert.	[]דרך ענוים יטו	6
	[A man and his father go in to the same maid,		
	so that my holy name is profaned.]		
8	Pledged garments they spread out beside the altar;	בגדים חבלים יטו אצל [][x] מזבח	11
	Forfeited wine they drink in the house of their God.	יין ענושים ישתו בית אלהיהו	11
9	I destroyed the Amorites --	אנכי השמדתי [] אמרי [][y]	9
	Whose height was like the height of cedars,	[]כגבה ארזים גבהו	9
	Who were strong like the oaks.	וחסן הוא כאלונים	8
	I destroyed his fruit above,	ואשמיד פריו ממעל	7
	And his roots below.	ושרשיו מתחת	6
10	[I brought you up from the land of Egypt.		
	I led you in the wilderness for forty years		
	to possess the land of the Amorites.]		
11	I made some of your sons prophets,	ואקים מבניכם לנביאים	11
	And some of your young men Nazirites.	ומבחוריכם לנזרים	10
	[Is that not so, O people of Israel?]		
12	But you made the Nazirites drink wine;	ותשקו [] נזרים יין	7
	You commanded the prophets	[]על []נביאים צויתם	7
	Saying: "You shall not prophesy!"	לאמר לא תנבאו	7
13	Behold, I will make a shaking,	הנה אנכי מעיק[z]	7
	As a wagon shakes	כאשר תעיק []עגלה	7
	When it is full of sheaves.	[]מלאה לה עמיר	6
14	Flight shall fail the swift;	ואבד מנוס מקל	7
	The strong shall lose his strength;	[]חזק לא יאמץ כחו	8
	The warrior shall not save his life.	[]גבור לא ימלט נפשו	8

15	The bowman will be unable to stand;	[]תפש []קשת לא יעמד	6
	The swift of foot will be unable to flee;	[]קל ברגליו לא ⟨ינוס⟩[aa]	7
	The horseman will be unable to escape.	[]רכב סוס לא ימלט [][bb]	7
16	[The bravest among the warriors	[]אמיץ לבו בגבורים	(8)
	shall flee naked in that day.]	ערום ינוס ביום []הוא	(7)

Notes to the Text of Amos 1:3-2:16

[a]This reading was suggested by Professor Cross in consulation to improve the metrical balance in the various strophes (Amos 1:3,6,9,11; 2:1,4,6). The suffixed particle may originally have been *-a/en(nu)*, which functioned as a sort of ballast variant over against the various place names of the previous colon which varied in length.

[b]Deleting הברזל of MT *metri causa*. This particular element in the oracles against Damascus, Gaza, Ammon and Moab has suffered considerable textual expansion and conflation.

[c]The two place names are interchanged to achieve closer metrical balance. The confusion of paired words in poetic transmission is strikingly illustrated in a recent release of a recording by the popular singer Jack Jones. In his rendition of the song "Everybody's Beautiful" he sings the following line: "We shouldn't care about the *color* of his hair / or the *length* of his skin" (emphasis mine). The exchange of the paired words "color/length" yields nonsense, and still it got through to final publication in 1971. When the sense of the poem is not impaired and when the metrical balance of the spoken (or sung) word is no longer operative, paired words are frequently displaced in the transmission of poetry.

[d]This colon has been relocated to achieve poetic balance within this strophe and to balance the structure observed in the following strophe (Amos 1:6-8) where the line in question corresponds to the first half of the final bicolon.

[e]Jean Nougayrol [*Iraq* 25 (1963), p. 110] remarked that for the Hittites in particular the word *sulummû* had the double value of "peace" and "treaty". Albright [*BASOR* 163 (1961), p. 52, n. 75] in a discussion of Genesis 14 translated *šelôm(ōh)* as "(a king) allied to him." Other parallels cited by Albright include Ps. 41:10; Ob. 7; Jer. 20:10 and Isa. 54:10. Dahood [*Psalms I*, p. 42] gives further parallels and suggests the reading of a Qal passive participle, *šᵉlūmāyw*, in Ps. 7:5. BDB (p. 1023) lists שֶׁלֶם as a "sacrifice for alliance or friendship." The failure to understand this particular meaning of the term in Amos 1:6 may have led to expansion of the text in MT.

[f]Deleting להסגיר לאדום of MT *metri causa*. There is textual interdependence between Amos 1:6 (oracle against Philistia) and Amos 1:9 (oracle against Tyre). It is generally assumed that the oracle against Tyre is secondary and

dependent on the earlier oracle against Philistia. The textual relationship reflected in MT seems to indicate mutual dependence. Both poetic lines have suffered expansion from the parallel text in the course of textual transmission.

[g]Deleting שלמה of MT *metri causa*. There is textual conflation here; see note f above.

[h]The colon in MT is too short. LXX adds ἐπι γης; the Lucianic tradition reads ἐπι της γης. Elsewhere in Amos בארץ, לארץ and על ארץ are rendered by ἐπι της γης or its grammatical equivalent. A possible restoration is to read ארצה and to compare the idiom in Gen. 38:9. In the story of Onan where he refused to fulfill his kinship obligation to Tamar the text reads: ושחת ארצה לבלתי נתן זרע לאחיו. Here in Amos 1:11 Edom refuses to fulfill his covenant obligation to his brother (אחיו). The reading אדם was suggested by Professor Cross and is to be preferred. The consonants would render both the place name Edom and the idiom, "to the ground," *'ădāmā(h)*. The deletion of the word "Edom" in MT is then understandable as the word is redundant as far as sense is concerned.

[i]The following bicolon of MT is deleted in order to achieve structural balance with the following strophe:

He kept his wrath continually;	ויטר פ-לעד אפו	8
His anger he maintained relentlessly.	ועברתו שמרה נצח	8

Cf. Dahood [*Psalms II* (1968), p. 201] who cites W. L. Moran on the conjunction p^e in the first colon. The couplet appears in slightly different form in Jer. 3:5. For a similar rejection of the authenticity of this bicolon, on different grounds, see the recent article by W. Rudolph, "Die angefochtenen Völkersprüche in Amos 1 und 2," *Schalom* (Arbeiten zur Theologie I/46; Stuttgart, 1971), pp. 47-49.

[j]Deleting the בני of MT *metri causa*.

[k]Deleting למען הרחיב את-גבולם of MT as an expansionary gloss.

[l]The pointing of MT *b^esa'ar* results in metrical imbalance. The longer term *s^e'ārāh* gives better assonance in parallel with *t^eru'āh* and is found with סופה in Isa. 29:6.

[m]Repointing MT *malkām* with a number of commentators. Cf. Jer. 49:1,3 and Zeph. 1:5.

[n]The colon as it stands in MT is too short. LXX adds οἱ ἱερεις αὐτων and the parallel bicolon in Jer. 49:3 supports the emendation.

[o]Deleting עצמות of MT *metri causa*. This particular poetic element in the oracles against Damascus, Philistia, Ammon and Moab has suffered textual expansion and conflation.

[p]Following the suggestion of Albright [*Yahweh and the Gods of Canaan* (1968), p. 240] which is in turn based on the earlier work of Tur-Sinai [*LS*

1 (1948), pp. 64ff.]. By changing the pointing to read *mōlek 'ādām laš-šēd* instead of *mélek 'Edōm laš-šid*, one obtains a perfectly satisfactory text, parallel to that of Ps. 106:37. Either reading renders the same syllable count as far as prosodic analysis is concerned.

[q]The colon is too short as it stands in MT. Elliger [*BHS* 10 (1970), p. 27] proposes the insertion of קיר here and the substitution of ארמנותיה for ארמנות הקריות. Th. H. Robinson also has suggested Kir-Moab as the city in question [HAT 14 (1964), p. 76]. One can also read Ar-Moab (cf. Isa. 15:1 where Kir-Moab and Ar-Moab appear as poetic variants). The emendation proposed here involves only one change in the text and attains poetic balance, both in syllable count and in plurality (cities of Moab / strongholds of Kerioth).

[r]If we are correct in reading the name of the god Milcom in vs. 15 above (see note m), the name of the god Chemosh may originally have appeared here. Note the manner in which Moab is personified in the present quatrain as preserved in MT. His ruler (שופט) and his nobles (שריו) will be slain with him. The picture is that of Ps. 82:6-7 where the gods of the nations are to die like men.

[s]Following the Lucianic recension of LXX and numerous commentators who read the masculine suffix here. No change is required in the consonantal text.

[t]Emending the pronominal suffix with various commentators, as the antecedent (שופט) is masculine.

[u]The Judah oracle (Amos 2:4-5) is omitted as a secondary addition to the text. See the discussion in the main body of this study.

[v]Mays [*Amos* (1969), pp. 45-46] suggests that the reference here to "a pair of sandals" is probably an idiom for the legal transfer of land. The point here is that the *ṣaddiq* are sold into slavery. In the ancient Near East men were sold into slavery either for money or land. Footgear was used as a probative instrument in the transfer of real property [cf. R. de Vaux, *Ancient Israel* (New York: McGraw-Hill, 1961), p. 169; E. A. Speiser, *BASOR* 77 (1940), pp. 15ff.; and R. Gordis, *JNES* 9 (1950), p. 45].

[w]Omitting על-עפר-ארץ as a secondary expansion with Procksch, Elliger and others. As Mays has noted, "The prepositional phrase disturbs metre and syntax" [*Amos* (1969), p. 42].

[x]Omitting כל as a secondary prosaic feature.

[y]Omitting מפנהם as a secondary prosaic addition to the text. Note that some MSS read מפניכם.

[z]Following Mays and KB for the hapax *'ūq*, the meaning of which is uncertain.

[aa]A conjectural emendation to avoid the repetition of the same verb in both cola (cf. vs. 14 where the verbal roots *nws*, *'mṣ*, and *mlṭ* appear in

parallel.

[bb]Omitting נפשו of MT *metri causa*. The text is conflate with vs. 14c.

Amos 1:3-2:16 in Outline

I

Oracle against Aram-Damascus (ch. 1:3-5)

[1:1:1] Indictment: "They threshed Gilead with threshers."

Announcement of Punishment:

[1:1] I will send fire to consume them.

[1:1] I will remove their rulers.

[1:1] I will return the people of Aram to Kir.

Oracle against Philistia (ch. 1:6-8)

[1:1:1] Indictment: "They exiled an ally."

Announcement of Punishment:

[1:1] I will send fire to consume them.

[1:1] I will remove their rulers.

[1:1] I will destroy what remains of Philistia.

II

Oracle against Tyre (ch. 1:9-10)

[1:1::1:1] Indictment: "They violated the 'covenant of brothers.'"

[1:1] Punishment: I will send fire to consume them.

Oracle against Edom (ch. 1:11-12)

[1:1::1:1] Indictment: "He violated his kinship obligations."

[1:1] Punishment: I will send fire to consume them.

III

Oracle against Ammon (ch. 1:13-15)

[1:1:1] Indictment: "They ripped open pregnant women of Gilead."

Announcement of Punishment:

[1:1] I will send fire to consume them.

[1:1::1:1] Ammon will be defeated and go into exile.

Oracle against Moab (ch. 2:1-3)

[1:1:1] Indictment: "He burned a human sacrifice to a demon."

Announcement of Punishment:

[1:1] I will send fire to consume them.

[1:1::1:1] Moab will be defeated and decimated.

IV

Oracle of Judgment against Israel (ch. 2:6-16)

1. Indictment (vss. 6-8): They have perverted justice by

[1:1::1:1/1:1]	Enslaving the poor.
[prose] ?	Committing promiscuous intercourse with bond servants.
[1:1]	Abusing the right of pledges and fines.

2. Recitation of *Magnalia Dei* (vss. 9-11)

[1:1:1::1:1]	The Conquest: I destroyed the Amorites.
[prose] ?	The Exodus: I brought you out of Egypt and through the wilderness.
[1:1]	The "Judges": I raised up prophets and Nazirites.
[rubric]	"Is that not so, O people of Israel?"

3. Indictment resumed (vs. 12): You have rejected the authority and power of Yahweh.

[1:1:1]	You corrupted the Nazirites and silenced the prophets.

4. Announcement of Judgment (vss. 13-16)

[1:1:1]	I will make a "shaking (?)".
[2(1:1:1)]	Israel will panic at the theophany of the Divine Warrior.
[prose] ?	"The bravest of her warriors will flee naked in that day."

Utilizing various means of prosodic analysis, scholars have long distinguished two types of oracles in Amos 1:3-2:5/ The oracles against Tyre, Edom and Judah are shorter and display a slightly different prosodic pattern from that observed in the oracles against Damascus, Philistia, Ammon and Moab. Most commentators have taken the latter four as the more original. Thus Mays, in his recent commentary on Amos, stands within distinguished company when he dismisses the oracles against Judah, Edom and Tyre as secondary additions to the text.[115]

The case against the authenticity of the Judah oracle is persuasive. Not only does it seem a bit strange to hear Yahweh "roaring from Zion / Jerusalem" against Judah (cf. Amos 1:2), the language utilized within the oracle is clearly Deuteronomic and prosaic. The תורת יהוה, "instruction of Yahweh," is used as a collective concept in parallel with חקים, "statutes." The reference implies a collection of law established as Yahweh's *Tōrāh*. The use of the verb שמר with the singular object תורה along with such plurals as חקים and מצות is a feature of Deuteronomic style, as Mays has noted.[116] The

[115] James L. Mays, *Amos: A Commentary* (OTL, Philadelphia: Westminster Press, 1969), pp. 25-42.

use of כזב in the sense of "false gods" or "idols" should be compared to the similar use of הבל in Jeremiah (2:5; 8:19; 14:22) and in Deuteronomic literature (Deut. 32:21; I Kings 16:13,26; II Kings 17:15). The idea of "following after other gods" is again a feature of Deuteronomic style (cf. Deut. 4:3; 6:14; 8:19; 11:28; etc.). As Mays put it, "not only the vocabulary, but the entire conception of rejecting Yahweh's law to follow other gods is a basic preoccupation of the Deuteronomic tradition."[117] Moreover, it should be noted that the prosaic line in verse 4c cannot be reduced to poetic balance without major emendation. It would appear that the Judah oracle was added to the series by the Deuteronomic editors of Amos.[118]

The fact that the Judah oracle must be dismissed as a secondary addition to the series does not mean, however, that the oracles against Tyre and Edom are also inauthentic. The mere fact that they share a similar prosodic structure is not sufficient argument, as a detailed prosodic-textual analysis of Amos 1-2 reveals. There is no *a priori* reason for making the OAN tradition here as banal and monotonous in structural form as many commentators have assumed it to be.

The historical arguments advanced relative to a post-Amos dating of the Edom oracle falter in the light of recent study of the treaty background reflected in Amos 1:11. Restating earlier arguments advanced by Kaufmann and Haran, Fishbane has shown that the legal background reflected in the first bicolon of this oracle is that of an international treaty relationship between Edom and Israel which was terminated *ca.* 850 B.C. in the reign of Jehoram, king of Judah (II Kings 8:20).[119] The key terms in his argument are אחיו and רחמיו for which he finds numerous parallels in the international treaty language of both biblical and extra-biblical materials. The correction of Fishbane's analysis by Coote[120] and the textual emendation suggested here would mean that the specific arguments should be modified somewhat. Nonetheless, Fishbane's central argument remains intact: "No other period is possible" for this oracle which has preserved the "precise diplomatic terminology" of its ninth century setting in history.[121]

The arguments advanced in the previous section of this study that the idealized Davidic Empire is the legal background against which the indictments of the OAN material in Amos 1-2 is to be understood is a strong argu-

---

[116] *Ibid.*, p. 41; cf. Deut. 4:40; 6:17; 7:11; 11:32; 16:12; 17:19; etc.

[117] *Ibid.*, pp. 41-42.

[118] See W. Schmidt, "Die deuteronomistische Redaktion des Amosbuches," *ZAW* 77 (1965), pp. 168-92.

[119] M. Fishbane, "The Treaty Background of Amos 1:11 and Related Matters," *JBL* 89 (1970), pp. 313-18.

[120] R. B. Coote, "Amos 1:11: TḤMYW," *JBL* 90 (1971), pp. 206-208.

[121] Fishbane, *op. cit.*, p. 317.

ment for including oracles against Edom and Tyre in the original composition. It is likely that "Israel" here is the old sacral league of the United Monarchy under David (cf. Amos 7:8,15; 8:2; 3:1; 4:12; 9:7). Amos has uttered judgment oracles against each of the member nations of the "Davidic Empire" in order to set the stage for the judgment facing Israel, which is his central concern.

Analysis of Amos 1:3-2:16 is made difficult by two important factors. If the Judah oracle is secondary, then the text of the material as a whole has been edited and reapplied to a later historical situation. This means that there may have been other additions as well.[122] The only possible means of determining such additions is a careful prosodic-textual analysis. Such an analysis, however, is confronted with a second factor of major importance: the original prosodic structure has been distorted by textual conflation and expansion. This fact is easily seen by noting the indictment in each oracle as preserved in MT. For the nations concerned the indictment is of the pattern: "For three crimes of (name) and for four I will not turn back, because they have (specification of one crime)." The specification of the crime as such appears in two different prosodic patterns as follows:

1)	ch. 1:3	על דושם בחרצות []ברזל []גלעד	11
	1:6	על חגלותם גלות שלמה להסגיר לאדום	15
	1:13	על בקעם הרות []גלעד למען הרחיב []גבולם	14
	2:1	על שרפו עצמות מלך אד[]ם לש[]ד	11
2)	ch. 1:9	על הסגירם גלות שלמה לאדום	12
		ולא זכרו ברית אחים	9
	1:11	על רדפו בחרב אחיו	7
		ושחת רחמיו	5
	2:4	על מאסם []תורת יהוה	7
		וחקיו לא שמרו	7
	2:6	על מכרם בכסף צדיק	7
		ואביון בעבור נעלים	8

In the first group the indictment is run-on in nature, whereas it takes the form of a balanced bicolon in the second. Textual corruption has distorted the picture at several points. Assuming poetic balance, the bicola of the second group may be reconstructed as follows:[123]

---

[122]On the basis of the prosodic-textual analysis presented here the bicolon in Amos 1:11c of the Edom oracle is deleted as secondary.

[123]For detailed discussion of the individual changes in the text see the Notes to the Text of Amos 1:3-2:16 above.

ch. 1:9	על הסגירם גלות [] לאדום	9
	ולא זכרו ברית אחים	9
1:11	על רדפו בחרב אחיו	7
	ושחת ⟨אדם⟩ רחמין	7
2:4	על מאסם תורת יהוה	7
	וחקיו לא שמלו	7
2:6	על מכרם בכסף צדיק	7
	[]אביון בעבור נעלים	7

The poetic element in question is much more difficult to reconstruct for the first group. Since the form of the oracles is so highly stylized elsewhere, it would seem likely that this element was originally uniform in structure, at least within this group of four oracles. In all four cases the element is run-on in nature and cannot be made into a balanced bicolon as in group two. It would appear that MT represents an expanded text and that the poetic line in question originally was structurally united with the formulaic framework to form the third part of a tricolon. If this is the case, the poetic structure of the entire series of oracles was more complex than commonly assumed. The analysis presented here is an attempt to recover that prosodic structure.

From a prosodic point of view the first six oracles (excluding the Judah oracle) fall into three pairs. In the oracles against Damascus and Philistia the indictment is expressed in the form of a tricolon followed by a three-part announcement of judgment. As Talmon has noted, the pairing of Aram and Philistia here may also reflect historical reality, for Isa. 9:12 describes Philistia as an ally of Damascus in an attack on Israel.[124] Of greater interest from a prosodic point of view is the geographical chiasm which this pair of nations forms with the next pair. In the oracles against Tyre and Edom the indictment is in the form of a quatrain followed by a much abbreviated announcement of judgment.[125] Only the formulaic couplet announcing the coming of Yahweh's destroying fire is included. Once more it should be noted that the prosodic structure may in fact reflect historical reality in the sense that Tyre and Edom were the least threatened as far as the expanding might of Assyria was concerned. Their judgment is coming, but it is less imminent and hence less developed within the poem itself.

---

[124] See Gottwald, *All the Kingdoms*, p. 106, n. 23.

[125] As it stands in MT the oracle against Edom has an additional bicolon which is here taken as a secondary addition to the text. As both of the other pairs of nations display identical prosodic patterns within each pair, the oracles against Tyre and Edom were probably also identical in their original prosodic structure.

In the third pair the concern of the poet is much nearer home, as reflected both in the prosodic structure and the specificity of imagery. Though these two oracles are similar in structure to the oracles against Damascus and Philistia, important differences should also be noted. The indictment in the form of a tricolon is identical in form to that of the first pair. Ammon, like Damascus, has committed atrocities against Gilead; but the indictment against Moab is unique in content and is to be understood over against the final indictment of Israel (Amos 2:12). By offering a human sacrifice to a false god (cf. II Kings 3:26-27), Moab has rejected the authority and power of Yahweh. Moab's rebellion is against Yahweh himself, though by implication the ninth century military clash with Israel and Judah is probably in view.

Though the presence of three bicola in the announcement of punishment in the oracles against Ammon and Moab is superficially the same as that of the first pair, there is an important distinction. After the formulaic bicolon of Yahweh's consuming fire, which incidently appears in all six of these oracles, the imagery and form of the announcement shifts. The second and third bicola stand together as a quatrain and present explicit battle imagery reminiscent of Israel's holy war traditions. The תרועה, "battle cry," appears in both oracles, along with such terms as סער ("tempest"), סופה ("storm-wind"), שאון ("tumult") and קול שופר ("trumpet blast"). The battle portrayed has cosmic dimensions as Milcom, god of Ammon, will go into exile together with his priests and nobles (Amos 1:15). In similar fashion Moab is personified in a manner that makes one wonder whether Chemosh might not have originally stood in the text of Amos 2:2. It is interesting to note that Milcom was distorted in MT to render "their king," and it is easy to understand why later scribes would be offended with the "polytheistic" implications in a reference to these two deities. The poetic imagery presented here has its ultimate source in Israel's ancient war songs. Yahweh, the Divine Warrior, will once again vent his wrath against his ancient foes whom he defeated long ago in the traditions of the Exodus-Conquest. This holy war imagery is to be understood over against the following announcement of judgment against Israel (Amos 2:13-16). Yahweh's holy war is directed not only against Israel's ancient foes, but against Israel as well.

The third pair of oracles displays another prosodic feature which set them off as distinct from the first. The balancing of the first person personal pronoun over against the third person is dominant throughout all six oracles, but it is treated differently here. Unlike the oracles against Damascus and Philistia, the second part of the announcement of punishment against Ammon is in the third person throughout, while the same element in the oracle against Moab sets the two bicola over against each other in reverse order. The presence of the first person declaration of warfare against Moab in the concluding bicolon sets the stage for the oracle against Israel.

The oracle of judgment against Israel is prosaic at points; but since there is no structural pair to compare at each point, secondary additions cannot be determined with any degree of certainty. The most convincing case for secondary expansion can be made for Amos 2:10 where the inclusion of a reference to the Exodus and the Wilderness Wandering after the discussion of the Conquest has disturbed a good many commentators.

Though the oracle against Israel departs from the pattern of the six previous oracles in dramatic fashion, structural ties with the earlier oracles are still evident. As with the previous oracles, the indictment begins with the condemnation of Israel for a single crime -- they have perverted the justice due to the poor in his legal suit (cf. Exod. 23:6). This crime is expanded, however, by the enumeration of three separate examples: 1) they have enslaved the poor (vss. 6-7a), 2) they have committed promiscuous intercourse with bond servants (vs. 7b); and 3) they have abused the right of pledges and fines (vs. 8). The pattern is then interrupted with a recitation of the mighty acts of Yahweh in Israel's behalf (vss. 9-11). This prosodic interlude is actually part of the indictment, as Mays has observed.[126] It serves to separate the three examples of Israel's "rebellion" (פשע) from the fourth and final sin against Yahweh (vs. 12). In rejecting the prophets and Nazirites, Israel, like Moab, has rejected the authority of Yahweh and consequently faces the wrath of the Divine Warrior, who will wage his holy war against his own people (vss. 13-16). This final indictment is further set off from all that precedes it by the use of the second person of direct address. Yahweh's patience has run out for Israel. His people have committed not three, but all four offences, and hence their judgment is certain.

In this composition Amos has made an important contribution to the developing OAN tradition. He has taken the earlier speech form of a war oracle, in the form of a judgment speech against a specific nation or people (cf. I Kings 20:28), and transformed it into a judgment speech against Israel. The so-called prehistory of the OAN material of Amos 1-2, as noted by Kaufmann, Gottwald and others, is simply the reflection of this earlier speech form. The war oracle as a judgment speech against a foreign nation was an important form of prophetic speech in the resurgence of prophecy in the northern kingdom of Israel during the ninth century. In composing his judgment speech against Israel, Amos has made use of this prophetic heritage. He has molded older historical and literary tradition into a new literary form.

Taking the Davidic Empire as an ideal type, Amos composed an oracle of judgment against each of its member nations, including Israel. Yahweh, the Divine Warrior, was about to punish each of these nations for breach of covenant. Yahweh, the suzerain of these nations, will punish his disobedient

---

[126] Mays, *op. cit.*, pp. 49-50.

vassals through military defeat, no doubt at the hands of resurgent Assyria. As Amos saw so clearly, the "Day of Yahweh" would be a day of darkness and destruction for Israel, not a day of deliverance from her foes (cf. Amos 5: 18-20). The fire of Yahweh's vengeance will consume the very strongholds of David's former empire.

CHAPTER THREE

JUDAH AND THE NATIONS FROM AMOS TO JEREMIAH

A discussion of the war oracle in ancient Israel presupposes military conflict. Individual prophetic war oracles must be understood over against international political developments and specific wars. In many instances it is not possible to determine the precise battle that occasioned a given war oracle. Nonetheless, the general political and military background must be drawn into focus if one is to determine the meaning of individual war oracles and trace the historical development of this particular form of prophetic speech. This chapter will attempt to trace the shifting political alliances and resultant military clashes, from *ca.* 750 to 580 B.C., involving the nations which the various prophets addressed in the OAN tradition. Against this background the historical use of the war oracle within the classical OAN tradition will be examined.

Though the Davidic Empire as a political reality did not survive the breakup of the United Monarchy in 922 B.C., the ideal extent of Israel's suzerainty under David lived on in prophetic circles. Mauchline has demonstrated this persistent belief in the Davidic Empire in the 8th and 7th centuries, particularly in the writings of Amos, Isaiah and Jeremiah.[1] The emergence of both the Assyrian and the Neo-Babylonian empires did not obliterate the prophetic vision of Israel as the Kingdom of David at its height in the first half of the tenth century B.C. In fact, this political ideal played a formative role in the shaping of the messianic hope of ancient Israel.

At the mid-point of the 8th century Egypt was divided with numerous petty dynasts competing for the political authority of the decadent Dynasty XXII. Egypt seemed to be moving relentlessly down the road toward disaster and eclipse while Assyria was once again on the rise. From 801 to 746 the Assyrian kings were occupied with difficulties closer to home -- north, east and south of Assyria -- and consequently left the West relatively undisturbed.[2] Jeroboam II of Israel was thus able to conquer Damascus and to restore the old Davidic border on the north in eastern Syria (cf. II Kings 14: 23-25); while his younger contemporary, Uzziah king of Judah, regained control of the southern desert, the land of Edom, and its sea trade routes to

---

[1]J. Mauchline, *VT* 20 (1970), pp. 287-303.

[2]William W. Hallo, "From Qarqar to Carchemish: Assyria and Israel in the Light of New Discoveries," in *BAR II* (1964), pp. 165-69.

the south (II Chron. 26:1-15). As Hallo put it:[3]

> Summarizing the first half of the 8th century, it may thus be said that Assyrians, Arameans and Urarteans fought each other to a standstill in Mesopotamia and Syria. Given the internal stability that chanced to prevail in Judah and Israel at the same time, it is no wonder that the divided kingdom briefly regained the economic strength and territorial extent of the Solomonic empire.

The long respite on the part of Assyria caused the people of Israel to forget how much the conquests and splendor of Jeroboam's reign were due to Assyria who had maimed Israel's more immediate oppressors. With the rise of Tiglath-pileser III in 745, after the death of Jeroboam II in Israel, things changed. Assyria was now bent on conquest and Syria-Palestine was a prime target in her march toward Egypt and control of the Near East.

The OAN tradition of the prophets Amos and Isaiah is to be be understood against the shifting political situation in the ancient Near East which saw Assyria emerge as a dominant world power during the second half of the eighth century. Writing before the emergence of Tiglath-pileser III and his successors, Amos addressed the nations in terms of ancient political structures stemming ultimately from Israel's Covenant League. He was aware of Assyria, Egypt and Ethiopia, but saw these nations in terms of Yahweh's sovereign power in history (cf. Amos 3:9-11; 6:2,14; 9:7). From a political point of view these powers were beyond the scope of his immediate concern. For the moment they were but potential agents of Yahweh's chastening wrath against his rebellious vassals within the so-called Davidic League of nations.

The shifting political scene that saw the encroachment of Assyrian might in the north and the Ethiopian triumph over the petty dynasts of the Egyptian Delta to the south, had its effect on the developing OAN tradition within Hebrew prophecy. Isaiah found occasion to direct oracles against Assyria, Egypt and Ethiopia as well as the member nations of the "Davidic Empire." In so doing he recognized the political realities of his day and incorporated them into his understanding of the universal sovereignty of Yahweh.[4]

---

[3] *Ibid.*, p. 167.

[4] The maps on the next two pages are adaptations of maps included in the book by Yohanan Aharoni and Michael Avi-Yonah, *The Macmillan Bible Atlas* (London: Collier-Macmillan Ltd., 1968), pp. 68 and 91.

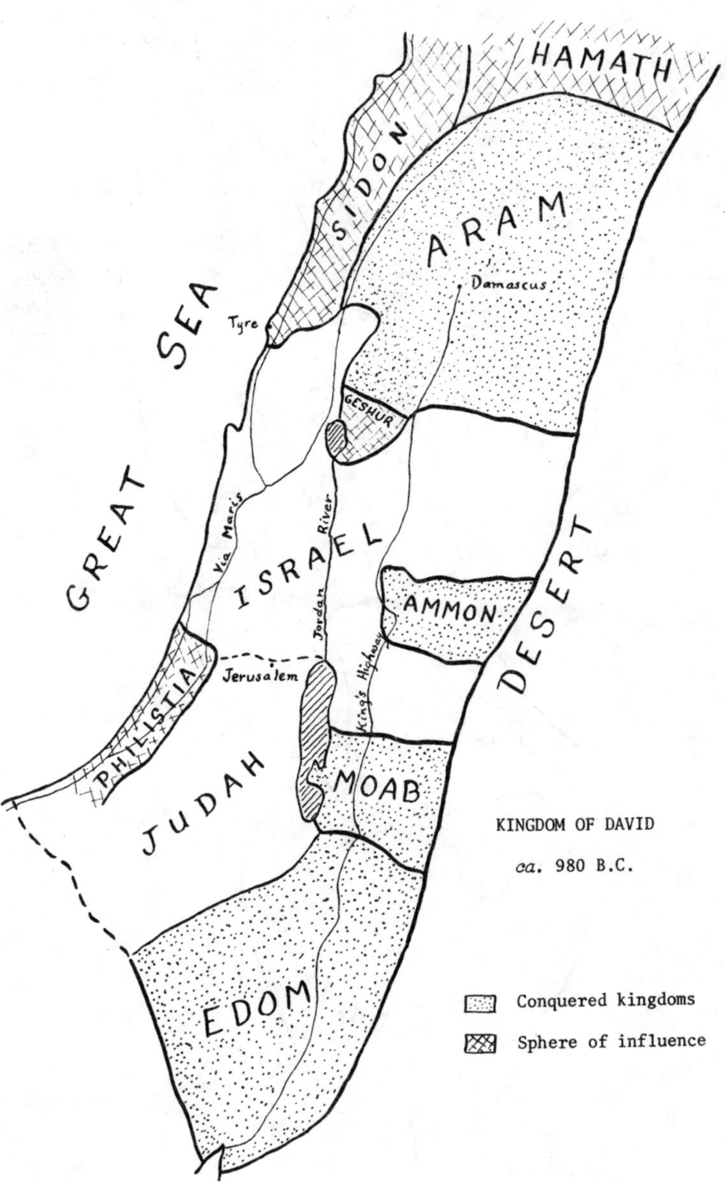

KINGDOM OF DAVID

ca. 980 B.C.

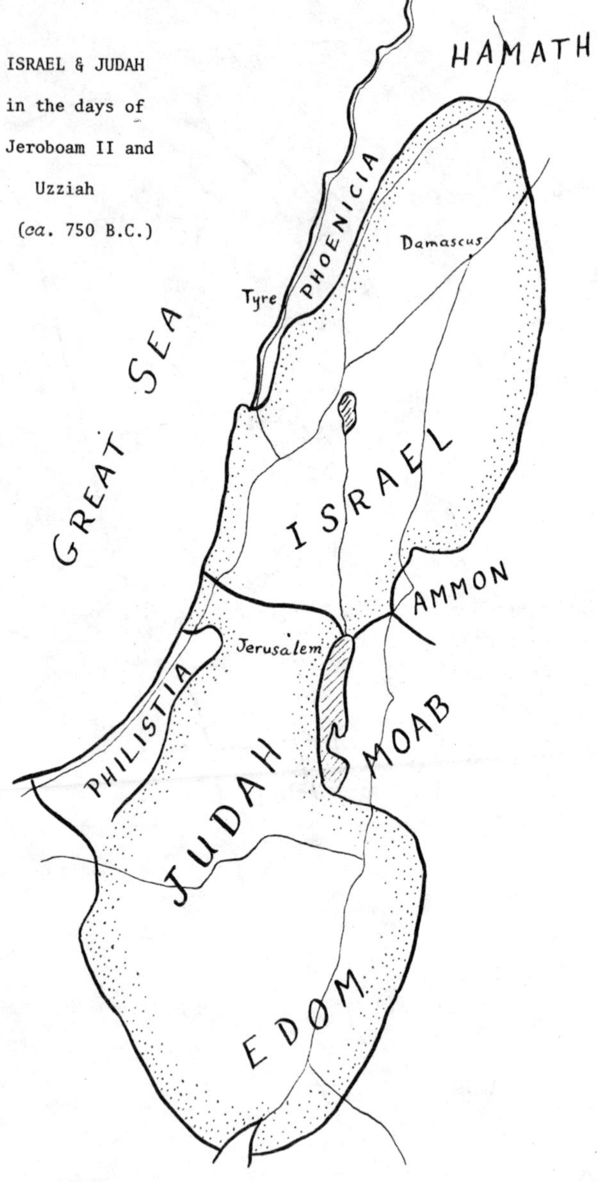
ISRAEL & JUDAH
in the days of
Jeroboam II and
Uzziah
(ca. 750 B.C.)
HAMATH
PHOENICIA
Damascus
Tyre
GREAT SEA
ISRAEL
AMMON
Jerusalem
PHILISTIA
MOAB
JUDAH
EDOM

An Era of Transition (ca. 750 - 700 B.C.)

The accession of the usurper Tiglath-pileser III (745-727) to the throne in Assyria marks the beginning of a new era in Assyrian history; for he and his two successors changed the entire balance of power in the ancient Near East. In 745 Tiglath-pileser found Assyria "in a difficult, even desperate, military and economic situation," but "the next forty years saw Assyria recover and consolidate control of all its old territories and re-establish itself as the pre-eminent military and economic power of the Middle East."[5]

The exact course of Tiglath-pileser's first great campaign in the West (743-738) is somewhat difficult to follow. The new publication of the annals of Tiglath-pileser III by Hayim Tadmor will no doubt shed further light on matters of detail.[6] For our purposes it is sufficient to note that Tiglath-pileser reorganized the nearer Syrian provinces under direct Assyrian rule, dividing the former provinces into smaller prefectures so as to secure centralized domination of the entire empire.[7] At the same time he regulated the succession to political power in the middle tier of states, including Israel, and waged war against the more distant ones.[8]

Israel was soon beset with internal crises brought on by the new Assyrian policy and political prominence in Syria-Palestine apparently passed to Judah. The inscriptions of Tiglath-pileser for 738 mention the fact that he fought in northern Syria against a large league of states headed by Azariah (Uzziah) of Judah.[9] Uzziah's daring attempt to halt the expansion of Assyria failed. The league dissolved and by 738 Tiglath-pileser had already reached the mountains of Lebanon, founding Assyrian provinces in the former territory of the kingdom of Hamath. The list of kings paying tribute to Assyria at this time includes the kings of Byblos, Tyre, Aram (Rezin), Samaria (Menahem), and even a certain queen of Arabia.[10]

Uzziah died in 735 or 734 and was succeeded by his son Jotham, who had apparently shared a lengthy coregency with his father.[11] Jotham died in 734

---

[5]H. W. F. Saggs, "The Nimrud Letters," *Iraq* 21 (1959), p. 176.

[6]See Hayim Tadmor, "Introductory Remarks to a New Edition of the Annals of Tiglath-Pileser III," *Israel Academy of Sciences and Humanities* II/9 (1967), pp. 168-86.

[7]Cf. Abraham Malamat, "Amos 1:5 in the Light of the Til Barsip Inscriptions," *BASOR* 129 (1953), p. 25.

[8]Cf. Hallo, "Qarqar to Carchemish," p. 170.

[9]Cf. James B. Pritchard, ed., *Ancient Near Eastern Texts*, 2nd ed. (Princeton, New Jersey: Princeton University, 1955), pp. 282-83. See also the discussion of Hayim Tadmor, "Azriyau of Yaudi," *Scripta Hierosolymitana* 8 (1961), pp. 232-71.

[10]See Aharoni and Avi-Yonah, *Macmillan Bible Atlas*, p. 92.

and was succeeded by Ahaz who was immediately confronted with a political crisis of major proportions. Pekah had usurped the throne in Samaria and, together with Rezin king of Aram, apparently began preparing a new league against Assyria. When Ahaz refused to join this league, the two kings marched against Jerusalem in an attempt to dethrone Ahaz and replace him with a certain "son of Tabeel" (Isa. 7:6).[12] During the campaign of Rezin and Pekah against Ahaz, the Edomites asserted their independence and invaded Judah from the south (II Kings 16:6; II Chron. 28:17). The people of Philistia also took the opportunity to overcome the cities of the Negeb and the Shephelah of Judah (II Chron. 28:18). If the reconstruction of Aharoni and Avi-Yonah is correct, Rezin king of Aram either neutralized Ammon and Moab or engaged their assistance against Judah at this time.[13] Ahaz, then, in spite of the warnings of Isaiah (Isa. 7:4), turned to Assyria for aid.

Tiglath-pileser's actions were swift and decisive. From Assyrian inscriptions it is known that he had already set out on a campaign to Philistia in 734 conquering Gaza. Hanun king of Gaza took refuge in Egypt and Tiglath-pileser left troops on the Egyptian border thus cutting the kings of Palestine off from Egyptian aid. In response to the appeal of King Ahaz of Judah, Tiglath-pileser marched against Israel and Aram-Damascus. Though there is still some doubt in matters of detail, the reconstruction of Aharoni and Avi-Yona is probably correct:[14]

> . . . in 733 . . . the Assyrian army came from the Valley of Lebanon, conquering the outlying fortresses of Israel in the northern Jordan Valley and then split up into several columns to spread out over the various regions of the Holy Land. The Galilee, Jezreel, Sharon, and Gilead were all conquered; only Mount Ephraim remained untouched. Traces of the fire and destruction were found in excavations at Hazor (stratum V) and Megiddo (straturm IV). . . . Following this defeat, Pekah the son of Remaliah was killed, and Hoshea the son of Elah, the last king of Israel, saved the remnant of his kingdom

---

[11]Following the chronology as worked out by Joe Seger and Frank M. Cross, Jr. at Harvard University (unpub.). Seger and Cross see a coregency of approximately 16 years (*ca.* 749-734) with both Jotham and his father Uzziah dying in the same year. Edwin R. Thiele [*The Mysterious Numbers of the Hebrew Kings*, rev. ed. (Grand Rapids, Mich.: William B. Eerdmans Publishing Co., 1965), p. 205] sees a coregency of at least ten years (750-740/39).

[12]Hallo ["Qarqar to Carchemish," p. 173] suggests that "the Ben-tab'al of Isaiah 7:6 may well have been a son of Azariah or Jotham by a princess from Tab-el."

[13]*Macmillan Bible Atlas*, pp. 94-95.

[14]*Ibid.*, p. 95.

by raising heavy tribute for payment to Assyria.

In the years 734-733 the plains of Esdraelon and Sharon, the region around Mount Carmel and Gilead in Transjordan were incorporated into the Assyrian provincial system, leaving the city-state of Samaria with but a measure of independence. In 732 the Assyrian victory was complete with the conquest of Damascus and the incorporation of its territory into the Assyrian empire (II Kings 16:9). Tiglath-pileser's second western campaign (734-732) was thus far more decisive in its effect than the first, for "from the Taurus mountains in the north to the river of Egypt in the south, the entire Mediterranean littoral now paid him homage, whether as province or as vassal kingdom."[15] In 731 Tiglath-pileser's attention was again diverted to other regions with a rebellion in Babylonia which was settled in 729 when he set himself up as Pulu, king of Babylon.[16]

In 727 Tiglath-pileser III died and his successor Shalmaneser V (727-722) was apparently occupied elsewhere for some time securing his throne. Consequently Israel was not hard-pressed by Assyria for some time, though Hoshea continued to pay tribute. Then in 726 an event to the south altered the situation.

II Kings 17:4 records the fact that Hoshea king of Israel appealed to an Egyptian king "So" for aid against Assyria. In the past there has been wide agreement to identify So with a certain "Sib'u, *turtan* of Egypt," mentioned in the annals of Sargon II in connection with an unsuccessful attack against the Assyrian king in 720.[17] Borger has since demonstrated on linguistic grounds that the accepted reading *sib/p* in Sargon's annals is highly improbable. The name should be transcribed *Re'u* and thus the proposed identification is no longer feasible.[18] Goedicke has since shown that King So is in fact Tefnakhte of Sais.[19] Albright has confirmed this identification on textual and linguistic grounds.[20]

---

[15]Hallo, "Qarqar to Carchemish," p. 174.

[16]Cf. II Kings 15:19 and I Chron. 5:26. See also H. W. F. Saggs, "The Nimrud Letters," *Iraq* 17 (1955), pp. 44-50.

[17]Cf. L. Oppenheim in J. B. Pritchard, ed., *ANET*[2], p. 285 and Hans Goedicke, "The End of 'So, King of Egypt,'" *BASOR* 171 (1963), pp. 64-66.

[18]R. Borger, "Das Ende des ägyptischen Feldherrn Sib'e Sô'," *JNES* 19 (1960), pp. 49ff.

[19]Goedicke, *BASOR* 171 (1963), pp. 64-66.

[20]W. F. Albright, "The Elimination of King 'So,'" *BASOR* 171 (1963), p. 66. Originally the text of II Kings probably read: *'el Sô'* ⟨*'el*⟩ *melek Miṣraim* -- "to Sais, to the king of Egypt." The preposition *'el* is used indifferently of motion to a place or person; and thus its repetition in different senses offers no difficulty. The loss of the second *'el* by haplography re-

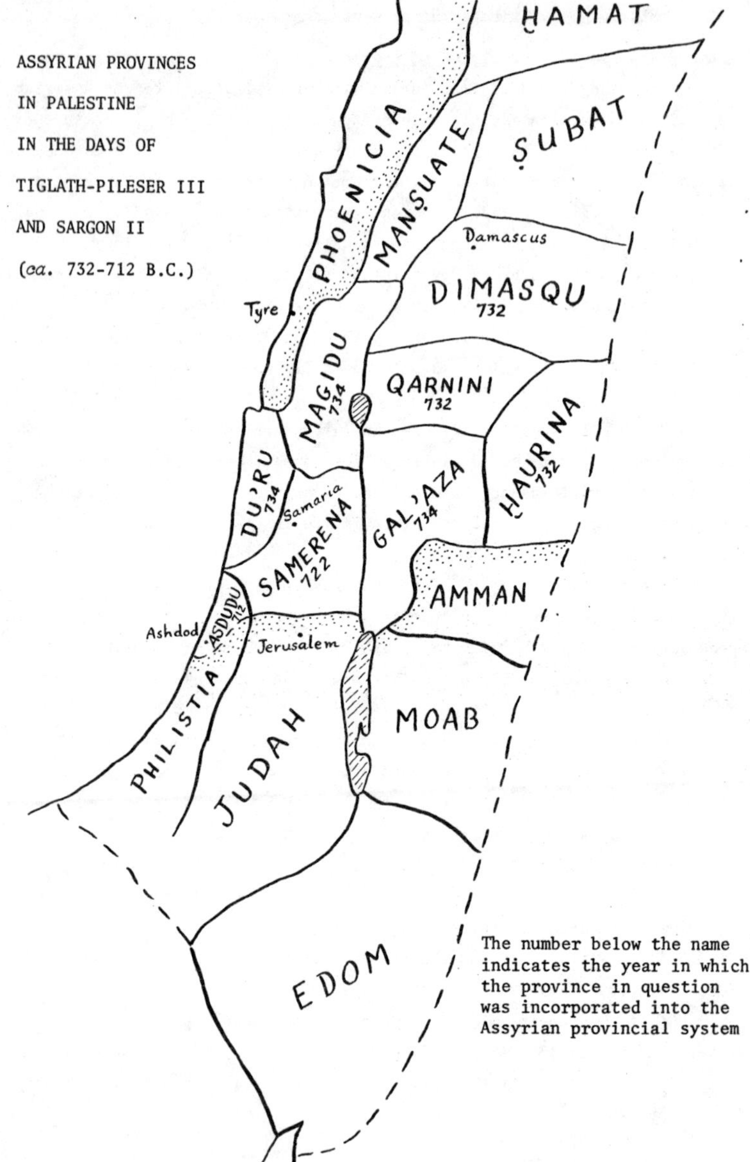

quires no explanation. The vocalization also makes good sense. The final "s" was not on the word in Egyptian and thus the phonetic representation in Hebrew would have been: **Saī* > *Sā'* > *Sô'* (the ā going to ô by analogy: cf. *dagan* > *dāgān* > *dāgôn*, the Phoenician deity).

Hoshea, who evidently was no longer as pro-Assyrian as he had been in 732, welcomed the news from Egypt. A great new dynasty was emerging in the Delta which promised to unite a badly divided Egypt and return her to her legendary greatness. Reports evidently confirmed the news as Tefnakhte rapidly gained the supremacy of the Delta area and began to move south with his troops. At last the time was right and Hoshea withheld tribute from Assyria, apparently convinced that Tefnakhte would come to his aid. Goedicke has pointed out that it is doubtful if Tefnakhte ever sent aid to Hoshea and, even if he had, he certainly would not have prevented Assyria from incorporating Palestine into its provincial system.[21] As it turned out Shalmaneser V besieged Samaria in 724 and in 722 Israel fell to his successor Sargon II (722-705). It is probable that Tefnakhte did not go to Hoshea's aid because his power in Egypt disappeared even more quickly than it had risen.

By a curious quirk in history Tefnakhte's rise to power in the Delta had been preceded in Upper Egypt by the emergence of an even more capable leader in the person of Pi'ankhi, a Cushite ruler, whose brother later became the first pharaoh of the Ethiopian Dynasty XXV in Egypt. Pi'ankhi had been king of Nubia for about twenty years and apparently was already making a bid for monarchic universal power in the Nile Valley and the restoration of a unified Egypt, when he received news of Tefnakhte's sudden rise to power in the North.[22] He did not go immediately against Tefnakhte but waited until his rival had moved most of his forces out of the Delta into the lower part of Upper Egypt. He then ordered his troops which were already in Upper Egypt,[23] northward to besiege Hermopolis which had just submitted to Tefnakhte. Meanwhile he dispatched a second army which defeated Tefnakhte's fleet on the Nile and continued on its way to oppose Tefnakhte's troops at Heracleopolis, the last major city in the Delta which was still holding out against Tefnakhte. Pi'ankhi's troops were victorious both by land and sea and Tefnakhte saw his empire crumbling even more quickly than it had taken form.[24] Pi'ankhi apparently conquered at least three other cities in the Delta without a major battle on his way to Memphis.[25] Memphis, though strongly fortified, was stormed in a most ingenious manner.[26] Tefnakhte had fled but was now in desperate straits. Burning his remaining ships and supplies which he could not save, he took refuge on one of the remote islands in the western mouths of the Nile. He then submitted to Pi'ankhi in a clever move to save his own life.[27] While he had nominally submitted to Pi'ankhi, he only awaited the withdrawal

---

[21]See Goedicke, *op. cit.*, p. 66.

[22]See James H. Breasted, *Ancient Records of Egypt*, Vol. IV (Chicago: University of Chicago Press, 1906), Piankhi Stela, lines 1-5.

[23]*Ibid.*, line 8. [24]*Ibid.*, lines 9-76. [25]*Ibid.*, lines 77-84.

[26]*Ibid.*, lines 89-98. [27]*Ibid.*, lines 127-144.

of the Ethiopian to resume his plans.[28] Following Pi'ankhi's invasion, however, his plans were vastly different from what they had been nine months earlier when he stood on the threshhold of establishing a new and powerful dynasty in Egypt.

The dating of Pi'ankhi's incursion into Egypt is a much disputed matter and to the writer's knowledge he is alone in dating it to 723/22. Albright in 1956 dated the invasion to the winter of 716/15, putting it at the end of Tefnakhte's reign and the beginning of Dynasty XXIV.[29] Drioton and Vandier had dated the event to *ca.* 720,[30] as did Breasted over sixty years ago.[31] Hall, writing in 1929, placed Pi'ankhi's incursion in 721, the year before Sargon's victory at Raphia.[32] Goedicke preferred to place the event during the years of Tefnakhte's reign, i.e. 726-716, but maintained that, "we lack evidence for a more specific dating."[33] The writer feels that there is evidence for a more specific date. The invasion must have come after Hoshea's appeal for aid in 724 and, as Hall has observed, before the defeat of Pi'ankhi's forces at Raphia by Assyria in 720.[34] Hoshea's appeal probably coincided with the height of Tefnakhte's power, and since the invasion itself lasted almost a year, the actual fall of Memphis took place no earlier than 723 and probably not later than 722.

When Pi'ankhi left the Delta to return south, he apparently left the various petty dynasts in their individual cities as vassals.[35] In Upper Egypt his rule continued for an uncertain but brief period. Meanwhile in 722 Sargon II (722-705) had assumed the throne in Assyria during the siege of Samaria. In his first campaigns following the fall of Israel, he was defeated near Der by Merodach-baladen, then king of the small kingdom of Bit-

---

[28]See Breasted, *Ancient Records*, IV, p. 414.

[29]W. F. Albright, "Further Light on Synchronisms between Egypt and Asia in the Period 935-685 B.C.," *BASOR* 141 (1956), p. 25.

[30]According to Goedicke, *op. cit.*, p. 65.

[31]See Breasted, *op. cit.*, p. 416.

[32]H. R. Hall, *Cambridge Ancient History*, III (Cambridge: Cambridge University Press, 1929), p. 274.

[33]Goedicke, *op. cit.*, p. 65.

[34]See the discussion on p. 82 below in support of these Egyptian troops, mentioned in Sargon's annals (cf. *ANET*^{2}, p. 285), as those of Pi'ankhi; and of Re'u (Sib'u) as one of Pi'ankhi's generals.

[35]Cf. Piankhi Stela, lines 154ff. All the kings and princes of the Delta came "to see the beauty of his majesty (Pi'ankhi)." They brought tribute and took an oath of allegiance; but there is no mention of Pi'ankhi attempting to occupy the territory through subordinate officers. He apparently was satisfied with establishing his suzerainty.

Yakin, who had the assistance of the Elamite king Humbanigash.[36] He then turned against Syria where, following the death of his brother, Shalmaneser V, the Assyrian rule had collapsed, at least as far north as Hamath. Apparently Pi'ankhi deemed the time a propitious one to deal a vital blow to Assyria,[37] for on the historic battlefields of Qarqar on the Orontes Sargon met the kings of Hamath and Damascus and others whom the Egyptian general Sib'u (Re'u) had been able to muster. Though the fact that this Egyptian was indeed Pi'ankhi's general cannot be demonstrated, it appears to be rather likely that such was the case. A direct reference to Pi'ankhi would not be expected; for the Ethiopian monarch normally did not lead his army, but rather delegated this task to his generals whom he invested with considerable authority.[38] Moreover, none of the petty dynasts of the Delta would have been in a position to undertake such a campaign so soon after Pi'ankhi's invasion and conquest. At any rate the defeat of the allies was complete and in 720 Sargon pursued the Egyptian contingent as far as Raphia, from where the Egyptian general fled home -- presumably to Ethiopia, for Sargon did not cross the Egyptian border. A further indication that this was indeed a defeat of Pi'ankhi's forces by Assyria is the fact that Tefnakhte emerged from his obscurity in 720 as king again in the Delta;[39] a rather daring deed if Pi'ankhi's power had not been curbed. It may well be that the wily Tefnakhte was again master of a difficult situation by shrewd maneuvering, for Sargon records the fact that he received tribute from a *Pir'u*, or Pharaoh of Egypt.[40] It is not at all beyond the realm of possibility that Tefnakhte allied himself with Assyria so as to make a new bid for control of Egypt and to keep the Assyrian forces out of the Delta. It is most interesting to note that only two years later (718) Tefnakhte erected a stela which he dated as his eighth year as Pharaoh; evidently con-

---

[36]See A. L. Oppenheim, *IDB*, IV, p. 223.

[37]Cf. Sargon's annals [*ANET*², p. 285] where Sargon interprets the Egyptian's motives: "Sib'e, the *turtan* of Egypt set out from Rapihu against me to deliver a decisive battle."

[38]Cf. Piankhi Stela, lines 8ff and especially 24ff where, "enraged like a panther" Pi'ankhi decided to go northward himself and *personally* direct the battle against Tefnakhte (emphasis mine).

[39]See H. R. Hall, *op. cit.*, p. 275.

[40]Cf. *ANET*², p. 285. Note that Tadmor [*JCS* 12 (1958), p. 78] identifies this Pir'u king of Egypt as a general title of Šilkanni-Osorkon IV of the prism of Aššur. He feels that "the Khorsabad scribes misplaced a passage and connected it with the campaigns of 715." On previous attempts to identify this Pharaoh see E. F. Weidner, *AfO* 14 (1941), p. 45 and H. von Zeissl, "Aethiopen und Assyrer in Aegypten," *Beiträge zur Geschichte der ägyptischen "Spätzeit"* (Aegyptologische Forschungen, Heft 14, 1944), pp. 21ff.

sidering his reign from his first rise to power in 726.[41] Moreover, Tefnakhte's son Bocchoris in 716/15 was recognized by all as a Pharaoh of Dynasty XXIV. Bocchoris left a monument dated to his sixth year and reigned until 710/09 when Shabaka, Pi'ankhi's brother, founded the Ethiopian Dynasty XXV which was involved in so much of the diplomatic intrigue in Palestine in the following decades.

A respite followed Sargon's first campaign in the West, but it lasted only two years (719-718), during which time Sargon was engaged in the far north.[42] In 717 Carchemish conspired against Assyria and Sargon unleashed a two-year show of strength in the West (717-716). Carchemish was defeated and incorporated into the empire. Sargon then marched south to the Egyptian border, where, according to a fragment of a clay prism published in 1941, he received tribute from king Shilkanni (Osorkon IV) of Bubastis, the last king of the so-called Dynasty XXIII in Egypt.[43] It is perhaps significant that Osorkon (^{m}*Ši-il-kan-ni*) is called king (*LUGAL*) and not Pharaoh (^{m}*Pi-ir-ʾu*) in this inscription. According to Albright the *Pirʾu* (Pharaoh) who was king of Egypt in 715, according to the annals of Sargon II, was probably Bocchoris (whom Albright dates to 715-709).[44] Osorkon was a king of Egypt in the western Delta in 716, but Tefnakhte of Sais (in 720) and his son Bocchoris (in 715) apparently were recognized as Pharaoh by the Assyrians.[45]

In the midst of these events on the Egyptian border, Ahaz of Judah died and was succeeded by Hezekiah (715-687). Sargon was probably already on his way back to Assyria. Under the influence of the prophet Isaiah, Hezekiah inaugurated not only a great religious reform but also an anti-Assyrian policy, both of which, as resumed later by Josiah, ultimately enabled Judah to survive Assyria.

Sargon was again occupied on his northern frontier until 712, when Pal-

---

[41]For this stela see H. Gauthier, *Livre des Rois d'Égypte*, III in Mémoires publiés par les Membres de l'Institut Français d'Archéologie Orientale, Tome 19 (1913), p. 409.

[42]See Hallo, "Qarqar to Carchemish," pp. 179-80.

[43]This inscription was first published by Ernst Weidner, "Šilkan(he)ni, König von Muṣri, ein Zeitgenosse Sargons II," *AfO* 14 (1941), pp. 44-45. See also H. Tadmor, "The Campaigns of Sargon II of Assur," *JCS* 12 (1958), pp. 22-40, 77-100.

[44]W. F. Albright, "Further Light on . . . 935-685 B.C.," *BASOR* 141 (1956), p. 25; cf. also A. Alt, "Neue assyrische Nachrichten über Palästina und Syrien," *ZDPV* 67 (1945), pp. 128-58.

[45]It is interesting to note that a half century later in the struggles between Asshurbanapal and the Ethiopian Dynasty XXV, Assyria continued to recognize the royal house at Sais as the legitimate rulers of Lower Egypt.

estine once more felt the full impact of the Assyrian arms. The provocation for Sargon's third and last western campaign came from Ashdod, where a certain Yamani had usurped the throne.[46] According to Sargon's account, he made contact with his neighbors -- the other Philistine cities, Judah, Edom, Moab and Egypt -- in an attempt to stir up a rebellion.[47] Anticipating an Assyrian attack he fortified Ashdod against siege. When news of Ashdod's revolt reached Sargon, he dispatched his army under a commander-in-chief who "came to Ashdod and fought it and took it" (Isa. 20:1). Ashdod and her surrounding territory were organized as a new Assyrian province ruled by a governor. According to Tadmor, the political status of Ashdod from 712 to the middle of the seventh century poses a problem, as local kings (Mitinti in 701 and Ahimilki in 677 and 667) are known alongside the Assyrian governors.[48] Esarhaddon later made a similar arrangement in Lower Egypt, where, in 671, after organizing it as an Assyrian province, he allowed local princes to retain their status side by side with the Assyrian governors.[49]

For the rest of his reign (710-705) Sargon was occupied elsewhere in Mesopotamia and Anatolia. His death on a battlefield in Anatolia in 705 triggered widespread rebellion, beginning with Babylonia but involving most of the western vassal states as well. Ashkelon and Ekron took an active part in this rebellion, probably because of the ominous proximity of Assyrian authority in the province of Ashdod.[50] Hezekiah intervened in Ekron deposing the loyal Assyrian vassal, Padi, taking him captive to Jerusalem. The growing aggressive policy of the Ethiopian dynasty in Egypt was no doubt an important factor in the anti-Assyrian stand of Ashkelon and Ekron. For four years Sennacherib (705-681), Sargon's successor in Assyria, took no steps to quell the rebellion. Finally in 701, after settling affairs in Babylon, he marched against Philistia and Judah.

Sennacherib's campaign against Judah in 701 is well known, though still the subject of sharp debate among scholars. The records present an unusually complete account from both sides. The problem rises over the very different interpretations given to the biblical and Assyrian evidence. Albright, Bright and others have argued that there were actually two contests between Sennacherib and Hezekiah and that the Assyrians won the first but lost the second.[51]

---

[46] Yamani was a Philistine and not a Greek or Cypriot adventurer as is sometimes surmised; cf. Tadmor, *JCS* 12 (1958), p. 80, n. 217.

[47] See *ANET*², pp. 286-87; cf. also *ARAB*, II, par. 30, pp. 13-14.

[48] See H. Tadmor, "Philistia Under Assyrian Rule," *BA* 29 (1966), p. 95.

[49] See *ANET*², p. 213.

[50] See Tadmor, *op. cit.*, p. 96.

[51] The most complete statement of this position is that of John Bright, *A History of Israel* (Philadelphia: Westminster, 1959), pp. 282-87.

Hallo, Tadmor and others reject the two-campaign theory.[52] It is sufficient here to note, with Hallo, that the accession of Sennacherib in 705 "symbolized in many ways the start of a new phase in the Assyrian impact on western Asia." Hallo designates this period (705-648) as "Pax Assyriaca" and maintains that:

> Although the warlike ideals of their forebears continued to color the records of the later Sargonids, the impression of sustained militarism that they create is an exaggerated one. The real spirit of the time is revealed . . . (by) marvels of civil engineering . . . (and) greatly increased attention to administrative matters. . . . The new "Pax Assyriaca" stabilized the relations of Assyria and her western vassals to some extent. Where we have outlined no less than six major Assyrian campaigns to the west in the preceding forty years, there were only three of comparable magnitude in the nearly sixty years here under review, namely, Sennacherib's invasion of Judah in 701, Esarhaddon's capture of Sidon in 677, and the more or less continuous decade of warfare against Egypt by Esarhaddon and Ashurbanipal (673-663).[53]

Pax Assyriaca (ca. 700 - 640 B.C.)

The triumph of Assyria and the subsequent "Pax Assyriaca" brought an apparent eclipse to the developing OAN tradition in Old Testement prophecy, for no OAN material as such can be dated to this period with any degree of confidence. During the first half of the seventh century Judah, Moab, Ammon, Edom and Philistia remained subservient to Assyria as vassal kingdoms or nominal Assyrian provinces. The other nations addressed in subsequent OAN material of the second half of the seventh century show a more stormy history throughout the so-called "Pax Assyriaca." Only the broad outline of events in the historical development of these peoples -- Phoenicia (especially Tyre), Egypt, Elam and Qedar -- will be traced here, as the specific oracles against these nations are to be understood against the background of the final third of the seventh century and the opening of the sixth.

The conquest of Phoenicia by Assyria was a drawn-out affair which met continued opposition, particularly on the part of Tyre. In 701 Sennacherib marched against Phoenicia and Luli, "king of Sidon" (*ca.* 730-701), fled to Cyprus where he died.[54] The Assyrians installed Ittobaʿal II as king in Sidon who was in turn succeeded by ʿAbdmilkot. Allying himself with Cilicia, ʿAbdmilkot revolted against Assyria; and this time the Assyrian conquest of the rebel cities was followed by destruction and exile of the population.[55]

---

[52]See Hallo, "Qarqar to Carchemish," p. 183, n. 144.

[53]*Ibid.*, p. 182.

[54]See *ANET*^{2}, pp. 287-88.

[55]*ANET*^{2}, p. 291; see also Sabatino Moscati, *The World of the Phoenicians* (New York: Frederick A. Praeger, 1968), pp. 20-21.

In 677 Sidon was razed to the ground and replaced by the new city of Kar-Esarhaddon. Tyre was spared and a treaty was drawn up which set up an Assyrian governor alongside king Ba'al.[56] Six years later (671) Tyre revolted, in league with Taharqo king of Egypt.[57] Though Esarhaddon's reign (681-669) in Assyria marked continued decline in Phoenician independence, Tyre still appears to have been autonomous and under the rule of Ba'al during the reign of Asshurbanapal (669-*ca.* 630).[58] Sometime after the sack of Thebes (663) Ba'al rebelled again; and though the revolt was quelled, Tyre was not occupied and merely had to send homage and tribute as a nominal vassal to Assyria.[59]

The emergence of the Ethiopian Dynasty XXV (*ca.* 710-664) in Egypt set the stage for one of the great power struggles in antiquity. With a direct clash of interest in Lower Egypt and southern Palestine an eventual confrontation with Assyria was inevitable. As Gardiner has noted:[60]

> It had long become clear that a decision between the equally pertinacious Assyrian and Ethiopian rules would have to be reached, but in point of fact there was a third party to the dispute and it was with this that the ultimate victory was destined to lie. As in the time of Pi'ankhy Lower Egypt and a part of Middle Egypt had disintegrated into a number of petty princedoms always ready to side with whichever of the two great powers would be the more likely to leave them their independence. One of these was to prevail before long, but for the moment it was Assyria which held the upper hand.

The third party to which Gardiner makes reference is the royal house at Sais which, under Psammetichus (Psamtek) I (663-609), produced the Saite Dynasty XXVI. The campaigns of Esarhaddon and Asshurbanapal from 675 to 663, climaxed by the sack of Thebes, marks the crest of Assyrian expansion. To defeat the Ethiopians Asshurbanapal apparently used the royal house in Sais to unify Lower Egypt against the Ethiopian king.[61] In so doing the Assyrians set the stage for a second phase in the power struggle.

The so-called Saite revival in art, painting and architecture, literature and religion -- a nostalgic attempt to recreate the forms and styles of

---

[56]Cf. *ARAB*, II, pp. 587-91 and R. Borger, *Die Inschriften Asarhaddons Königs von Assyrien* (Graz, 1956), p. 69.

[57]Cf. *ARAB*, II, p. 556.

[58]Cf. *ARAB*, II, p. 547 and R. Borger, *op. cit.*, p. 71. See also S. Moscati, *op. cit.*, p. 22.

[59]See *ANET*^{2}, p. 295.

[60]Sir Alan Gardiner, *Egypt of the Pharaohs*, A Galaxy Book (New York: Oxford University Press, 1966), pp. 345-46.

[61]See *ANET*^{2}, pp. 294-95.

the Old Kingdom in Egypt -- reached its heights during the 54 year reign of Psammeticus I. After about a decade on the throne Psammeticus shook off the restraint and supervision of the resident Assyrian officials and allied himself with Gyges of Lydia in a successful revolt against Assyria. When Asshurbanapal had finally settled affairs with Elam and the Arab tribes (Qedar) around 640, the independence movement of Psammeticus had gone so far that the Assyrian monarch did not care to risk opposing it.

The history of Elam from *ca.* 700 to 639 is marked by conspiracy, revolt and factional strife. Seven times in six decades Elam rebelled against Assyria. It is quite possible that Egypt (or Ethiopia) was involved in most, if not all, of these revolts; and Judah may have been a party in as many as four of the widespread conspiracies associated with them. In the widespread rebellion of 703-701, Shutruk-nahunte II (717-699) of Elam is singled out as the most prominant ally of Merodach-baladan of Babylon.[62] Sennacherib put down the revolt, routing the Elamite forces in 703 and again in 700. Between these two conquests of Elam, Sennacherib defeated a coalition of western states including "Hezekiah the Jew," the princes of Egypt, and the "king of Ethiopia."[63] From 694 to 689 the bitter struggle between Elam and Assyria was resumed, no doubt precipitating revolt in the West again as had occurred earlier in the Elamite revolts of 721-720 and 703-700. The involvement of Egypt in such a revolt is reflected in the biblical reference to Taharqo (Terhakah) in II Kings 19:9. Unfortunately the Assyrian records are incomplete for the years immediately following the sack of Babylon in 689. A second campaign in southern Palestine on the part of Sennacherib to quell a revolt in *ca.* 688 is certainly possible, if not probable.

The defeat of Elam in *ca.* 689 marked the end of political unity and the beginning of an era of factionalism there. As Cameron put it:[64]

> . . . it is clear that henceforth there was no single ruler of great importance in Elam. On the contrary, there were many kings, rulers in Susa, in Madaktu, in Hidalu, and probably in other cities as well. The great days of Elam as an international power were gone. Internecine warfare was rampant, and Assyria wisely played one sovereign off against another.

Nonetheless, the embers of revolt continued to smolder and burst forth in

---

[62]See D. D. Luckenbill, *The Annals of Sennacherib* (Chicago: University of Chicago Press, 1924), pp. 48-49.

[63]See *ANET*^{2}, p. 287.

[64]G. G. Cameron, *History of Early Iran* (Chicago: University of Chicago Press, 1936), p. 168; cf. also F. W. König, *Geschichte Elams* (Leipzig: J. C. Hinrichs, 1931), pp. 19ff.

flames of open rebellion twice in connection with the Assyrian conquest of Egypt (*ca.*675-663). In 675 Elam launched a sudden raid into Babylonia entering Sippar and carrying off Ishtar and other gods to Elam. Sidney Smith has made an interesting observation about this incident:[65]

> It may seem fanciful to suppose that this raid was inspired from Egypt, and yet it is not altogether impossible, seeing that the Pharaoh of this period was especially active in intrigues against the Assyrians; and a connection is certainly suggested in the Babylonian chronicle.

Shortly after this raid Umman-haldash II, king of Elam, "died without falling ill" and was replaced by his brother Urtaku (674-664).[66] The gods of Akkad were returned in 673 without a struggle and Elam apparently abandoned interference in Babylonia, at least for the time being.[67] A decade later, while Asshurbanapal was fighting in Egypt, Urtaku dispatched a raiding expedition across the Tigris into Babylonia. After preliminary success due to surprise, the Elamites were defeated and driven back.

Shortly after the return from this unsuccessful expedition Urtaku died and Elam was plunged into civil strife. Three sons of Urtaku and two sons of his brother Umman-haldash II sought refuge in Nineveh while Teumann (664-655), the "brother" of Urtaku by diplomatic marriage, assumed the throne in Susa.[68] Teumann then turned eastward to form an alliance with various states, including Anshan and Persia (Parashu), against Assyria. He may have formed a military alliance with Ethiopia as well, for a fragmentary Assyrian epigraph, intended to accompany a missing sculpture, lists Tanuatamun of Ethiopia together with Teumann and two members of the rival royal Elamite family, Tammaritu and Paru.[69] By 655 Teumann had turned to thoughts of conquest in Mesopotamia but was forced to retreat to Susa before the Assyrian might. Both Teumann and his son were killed as they fled the scene of battle, and the Elamite resistance was crushed. Assyria then installed Ummanigash (655-651), the eldest son of Urtaku, as vassal king of Elam. Ummanigash took up resi-

---

[65]Sidney Smith, *The Cambridge Ancient History*, III (Cambridge: Cambridge University Press, 1929), pp. 80-81.

[66]*Ibid.*, p. 80. Though Esarhaddon seems to have been involved in the choice of the new king of Elam, he was still suspicious of Urtaku's loyalty; cf. Esarhaddon Chronicle, obv. 16-18 in Sidney Smith, *Babylonian Historical Texts* (London, 1924), pp. 12ff.

[67]Cf. Babylonian Chronicle B, iv, lines 17ff. and Esarhaddon Chronicle, obv. 21-23 in Sidney Smith, *op. cit.*

[68]See Cameron, *op. cit.*, p. 186.

[69]See *ANET*^{2}, p. 297; and *ARAB*, II, par. 1117, p. 405.

dence in Madaktu and apparently had but little authority in Susa where Undasi, the son of Teumann, succeeded his father.

When revolt broke out in Babylon in 652 under Shamashshumukin, the brother of Asshurbanapal, Ummanigash was a party in the widespread conspiracy which included numerous petty states in Syria-Palestine and Psammetichus, the pharaoh of the Saite Dynasty XXVI, who had already freed Egypt from Assyrian rule. If any credance is given the Chronicler's account of the Babylonian captivity of King Manasseh (cf. II Chron. 33:10-17), it would appear that Judah was once again a member of a widespread conspiracy against Assyria, as was the case earlier in 701 and probably in *ca.* 688.

The Babylonian revolt led to civil war in Elam and Asshurbanapal, taking full advantage of the situation, played one Elamite faction off against another. Once the revolt of Shamashshumukin of Babylon was finally put down, Asshurbanapal turned his full attention to Elam which he attacked from both the north and south.[70] By 646 Elam was once more under Assyrian control, at least for the moment. Six years later the stage was set for a final coup which once and for all put an end to an independent Elamite kingdom.[71] In 639 Susa was taken by Assyria and utterly destroyed. The wily Umman-haldash III once again escaped capture, retiring to inaccessible mountain regions. Asshurbanapal pursued the Elamite "to the very gateway to the land Parsumash" where Kurash (Cyrus I) met the Assyrians and submitted to Asshurbanapal, offering his eldest son, Arukku, as hostage to Assyria.[72] Some time after the destruction of Susa internal troubles again drove Umman-haldash III from his diminished kingdom. He fled north only to fall into the hands of Assyrian troops who brought him to Nineveh. There, according to the great Rassam Cylinder, he joined other defeated monarchs, including the king of Qedar, in the harness of Asshurbanapal's chariot.[73] After 639 Elam was abandoned by the Assyrians to be occupied by Persian tribes.

In his recent study William Dumbrell has shown that the Qedarites emerged as the dominant power of the desert league of Arab tribes in Syria-Palestine during the closing years of the reign of Sennacherib (*ca.* 690-688).[74] The years up to the Babylonian revolt in 652 seem to have been ones of relative tranquility for Assyria in the Qedarite controlled area of Syria-Palestine, though Dumbrell has cited evidence for certain "incidents" requiring Assyrian

---

[70]See Cameron, *History of Early Iran*, p. 198.

[71]*Ibid.*, p. 202. [72]*Ibid.*, p. 204.

[73]See Maximilian Streck, *Assurbanipal und die letzten assyrischen Könige bis zum untergange Ninevehs* (Leipzig: J. C. Hinrichs, 1916), pp. 82f. and 836f. Cf. also S. Smith, *Cambridge Ancient History*, III, p. 126.

[74]William J. Dumbrell, "The Midianites and Their Transjordanian Successors" (unpub. Th.D. thesis, Harvard University, 1970).

forrays against Qedar in this period.[75]

> One can well understand that such a potentially explosive situation as that which existed in the Syrian desert and to the south needed only a little spark to ignite it, and it is therefore readily conceivable that the Arabs were more than willing to take advantage of Shamashshumukin's revolt which began in 652.

Qedar joined in the revolt against Assyria sending troops under Abiyate (*ᵐA-bi-ia-te-ʾ*) and his brother Aamu (*ᵐA-a-mu*) to assist Shamashshumukin in Babylon. They also launched a series of raids against border states in Palestine from Zobah to Edom.[76] The Arab reinforcements sent to Babylon under Abiyate and Aamu were defeated as they were about to enter Babylon, though some portion of the Arab force did manage to enter the beleaguered city.[77] The Arabs attempted to break out of Babylon but were again defeated, though both leaders managed to escape. Abiyate then went to Nineveh where he submitted to Asshurbanapal and was appointed king of the Arabs.[78] Some time prior to Abiyate's return to his people, a certain Uaiteʾ [*ᵐU-a-ate-ʾ mār(DUMU) bir-dadda(ᵈIM)*] "made himself king of Arabia," thus claiming leadership of the Arab confederacy.[79] The result was a split among the Arab tribes, some following Abiyate and others Uaiteʾ. Around 640 Abiyate apparently deemed it politic to renounce his fealty to Assyria and to join with Natnu of Nabate and with Uaiteʾ in revolt again.[80] Asshurbanapal's second campaign against the Arabs (*ca.* 639-637) was directed against this revolt. Uaiteʾ and Abiyate were captured in separate battles and taken to Assyria. It is interesting to note that after humiliating Uaiteʾ, Asshurbanapal apparently had mercy on him as he did earlier with Necho I of Egypt, Tammaritu of Elam, and perhaps Manasseh of Judah, whom he restored as vassal kings after subjecting them to an humiliating ceremony of submission. That this was the case is suggested by the fact that a later inscription makes reference to Nuhur (*ᵐNu-ḫu-ru*), the son of Uaiteʾ, who came in submission to Asshurbanapal and was granted his father's throne.[81]

Though the details are not certain, it would seem likely that the assassination of King Amon in Judah in *ca.* 640 (cf. II Kings 21:23-24) was in some way related to the simultaneous revolt against Assyria on the part of Elam, Qedar and Tyre. Realizing full well that the time was not yet right for such

---

[75] *Ibid.*, p. 198.

[76] See *ANET*², p. 298 (cols. 7.82ff. of the Rassam Cylinder).

[77] See Dumbrell, *op. cit.*, pp. 206-208.

[78] *Ibid.*, p. 206. [79] *Ibid.*, p. 207.

[80] See *ANET*², p. 299.

[81] Cf. Dumbrell, *op. cit.*, p. 213; see also R. C. Thompson, "The British Museum Excavations at Nineveh, 1931-32," *AAA* 20 (1933), p. 96, lines 127-29.

drastic action, the "people of the land" put the murderers to death and placed the boy Josiah on the throne. This action forestalled Assyrian intervention and gave Judah the opportunity to revolt at a more opportune moment.

Regnum Davidicum Redivivum (ca. 640 - 609 B.C.)

1. Decline of Assyria

Throughout the Neo-Assyrian period the kings in Nineveh faced what has been aptly called "the Babylonian Problem."[82] As early as 689 Sennacherib found it necessary to destroy the rebellious city of Babylon and to install his son Esarhaddon there as vicegerent. On ascending the Assyrian throne in 681, Esarhaddon continued a pro-Babylonian policy.[83] In 672 he designated his sons Asshurbanapal and Shamashshumukin to succeed him as kings of Assyria and Babylon respectively. His intention seems to have been to create a double line of kings with a fully independent unity in Babylonia under an Assyrian line of kings.

Esarhaddon's plan, like that of the anomalous Ausgleich compromise in the Dual Monarchy of Austria-Hungary, was doomed to failure. As von Voigtlander put it:[84]

> Assurbanipal . . . retained military control of Nippur, probably on advice of councilors who had distrusted the "brother kings" arrangement from the first. He also retained the prerogative of placing his name as king of Assyria on the temple restorations and religious dedications of the period.

After a period of amicable relations the experiment came to its predictable end. Stung by increasing encroachments on his autonomy, Shamashshumukin formed a widespread alliance with Elam, the Chaldeans and Arameans, Qedar and distant Egypt in revolt against his brother. In three years of bitterly fought campaigns, Asshurbanapal regained control of Babylonia. His brother, Shamashshumukin, died in the conflagration which marked the end of the siege of Babylon in 648. Asshurbanapal then installed Kandalanu who ruled as nominal king of Babylon for at least twenty years.

In the past a number of scholars conjectured that Kandalanu was, in fact, Asshurbanapal ruling under a Babylonian throne name in the tradition of his

---

[82] See Elizabeth von Voigtlander, "A Survey of Neo-Babylonian History" (unpub. Ph.D. dissertation, University of Michigan, 1963), p. 2.

[83] *Ibid.*, p. 3; cf. also A. T. Olmstead, *History of Assyria* (New York: Scribner's, 1923), pp. 347-50, 352 to substantiate the pro-Babylonian policy of Esarhaddon.

[84] See von Voigtlander, *op. cit.*, p. 4, n. 8.

predecessors Tiglath-pileser III (Pulu) and Shalmaneser V (Ululaia).[85] Von Voigtlander has presented a more convincing case for the identity of Kandalanu with Asshuretililani, the son and successor of Asshurbanapal.[86]

> The experience of the early Sargonids had shown that an empty throne in Babylon created a political vacuum destined to be filled by a local aspirant inimical to Assyrian interests. The Assyrians had tried the solution of nominating and supporting a local puppet only to discover that weaklings were frequently faithless. The most satisfactory solution yet found had been the later policy of Sennacherib, who had placed his son, Assur-eṭil-ilani, who was probably still a minor, was therefore nominated to the Babylonian throne, reigning under his by-name, Kandalanu.

It is possible that in the early years of his kingship, Kandalanu remained in Assyria, exercising only nominal kingship in Babylon. Two letters, however, both demonstrably addressed to a son of Asshurbanapal ruling in Babylon, give evidence that at some subsequent time Kandalanu/Asshuretililani was actively engaged in administration in Babylon.[87]

Little is known concerning the history of Babylon and Assyria for the decade from 640 to 630 B.C.[88] A number of indications, however, suggest that

---

[85]*Ibid.*, p. 5; cf. Babylonian King List A in *ANET*², p. 272.

[86]*Ibid.*, pp. 7-8 and p. 27, n. 20 for a discussion of the name Kandalanu.

[87]See Leroy Waterman, *Royal Correspondence of the Assyrian Empire* (Ann Arbor: University of Michigan Press, 1930-36). Both letters (H 469 and H 793) were recognized by Waterman to have been addressed to Asshuretililani. The first is a report on affairs in Uruk and contains a reference (rev. 1) to "Asshurbanapal, your father." The second, written by Belibni, by its invocation of Nabu and Marduk shows that it was written to a king in Babylon. It begs Asshuretililani's intercession with his father during a period when Belibni found himself out of favor. It was also recognized as addressed to Asshuretililani by E. Klauber, *Assyrische Beamtentum nach Briefen aus der Sargonidenzeit* (Leipzig, 1910), p. 26. Von Voigtlander cited the works mentioned here in her cogent discussion of the issue in question, *op. cit.*, pp. 27-28, n. 22.

[88]The eponym (*limmu*) lists run only until 648. After that date it is necessary to reconstruct a chronological list from the *limmu* as they appear on documents. This has been attempted by M. Falkner in her "Die Eponymen der spätassyrischen Zeit," *AfO* 17 (1954-55), pp. 100-120. The annals of Asshurbanapal cease after 639. Cf. also H. Tadmor, "The Last Three Decades of Assyria," 25th International Congress of Orientalists, *Trudi* I (Moscow, 1960), pp. 240-241.

the last years of Asshurbanapal were troubled ones. By the end of the decade the growing weakness of Assyria was clearly evident in the West, as shown by Josiah's reform movement in Jerusalem which had its inception in 632.

The chronology of the transition between the end of Assyrian rule in Babylon and the rise of Nabopolassar to power in 626 is a vexed problem. The latest tablet known from Asshurbanapal's reign comes form Nippur and is dated in his 38th year, third month (June 631).[89] The so-called Harran inscriptions of Nabonidus' mother, discovered in 1956, gives 42 years to Asshurbanapal.[90] In this inscription the mother of Nabonidus named the seven kings under whom she lived out her 104 years, carefully counting the years of each king. In a Harvard seminar paper in 1962, Carl Graesser noted that the 45 year total from the accession of Asshurbanapal to that of Nabopolassar as reported in this inscription cannot be reconciled with the 43 years which other data make available for this period.[91] Von Voigtlander has carried the argument further in a careful analysis of the inscription in question in which she concludes:[92]

> It is useless to approach the above statements from the view of absolute chronology. Let us instead consider that they report what a very aged woman believed to be her birthdate and her, and probably her son's, statement of her age. Superimposed on this is the effort of the redactor to correlate these statements with his understanding of Assyro-Babylonian chronology.

Asshurbanapal probably died in or about 630 and was succeeded by his son Asshuretililani, whose latest document is from Nippur, dated 4/VII/1 (October 627).[93] Asshuretililani's rule as king of Assyria was challenged early. In 629 Sinsharishkun, another son of Asshurbanapal, was recognized as king in Sippar and Uruk.[94] A certain Sinshumlishir, commandant of the

---

[89]Cf. von Voigtlander, *op. cit.*, p. 10; see also A. J. Sachs *apud* D. J. Wiseman, *Chronicles of Chaldean Kings (626 - 556 B.C.)* (London: British Museum, 1956), p. 92.

[90]Published by C. J. Gadd, "The Harran Inscriptions of Nabonidus," *Anatolian Studies* 8 (1958), pp. 35-92.

[91]Carl Graesser, "Josiah's Imperial Program" (unpub. paper, OT Seminar, Harvard University, Fall, 1962), pp. 3-4.

[92]See von Voigtlander, *op. cit.*, pp. 226-27.

[93]*Ibid.*, see Chart A, p. 244. Cf. also Johann Schaumberger's tables in R. A. Parker and W. H. Dubberstein, *Babylonian Chronology 626 B.C. -- A. D. 75*, 3rd ed. (Providence, Rhode Island: Brown University Press, 1956).

[94]A list of tablets from Babylonia dated in the reign of Sinsharishkun is found in M. Falkner, "Neue Inschriften aus der Zeit Sin-šarru-iškuns,"

Nippur garrison, laid claim to the throne of Assyria in 627/26.[95] The year 627/26 has also been described as "the year in which there was no king in the land."[96] In the year 626 the diadem of Babylon passed from the hands of Assyria to the Chaldean Nabopolassar (626-605) who organized a new dynasty in Babylon. The death throes of the mighty Assyrian Empire were near at hand.

2. Resurgence of Judah

With the decline of Assyria after the middle of the seventh century B.C., the stage was set for the restoration of Judah among the nations. With the outbreak of hostilities in Syria and Mesopotamia from 652 to 648, pressure no doubt mounted on Manasseh to bring Judah into the widespread revolt. As G. Ernest Wright has noted: "This would have been the most natural occasion for the revolt of Manasseh as described in II Chron. 33:11."[97] If, indeed, Manasseh was taken by the commanders of the army of the king of Assyria with hooks and bound with fetters of bronze and brought to Babylon, he was subsequently restored to his throne as an Assyrian vassal.[98]

From 648 to his death in 642 Manasseh remained a loyal vassal to Assyria; and his son Amon (642-640) apparently continued his father's policy. When Elam, the Arab confederacy and Tyre were again in revolt against Assyria in 640, pressure was again exerted on Judah to join in as well. The assassina-

---

AfO 16 (1952-53), pp. 308-309. To these should be added the nine Nippur tablets from his third year published by A. L. Oppenheim, "'Siege Documents' from Nippur," *Iraq* 17 (1955), pp. 87-89; and four unpublished tablets from Uruk, W 20032, 9-12 (UVB XVIII 41) dated in his fifth and sixth years. Sinsharishkun's claim to the Assyrian throne, stated repeatedly in his Assyrian inscriptions (*ARAB*, II, pars. 1138, 1143, 1146, 1147, 1150 and 1157) is in the stereotyped formula used by usurpers. Von Voigtlander concluded that the insurrection of Sinsharishkun/Sinshumlishir began in Assyria and spread to Babylonia (*op. cit.*, pp. 13-15). By 627 Sinsharishkun had eliminated his brother Asshuretililani.

[95] See von Voigtlander, *op. cit.*, p. 16 and p. 30, n. 40. She has raised the possibility that Sinsharishkun and Sinshumlishir are in fact two names for the same individual, the latter being a throne name.

[96] *Ibid.*, p. 14.

[97] G. Ernest Wright, *Biblical Archaeology* (Philadelphia: Westminster Press and London: Gerald Duckworth & Co., 1957), p. 176.

[98] The Chronicler interpreted the restoration of Manasseh as the result of his repentance and turning again to Yahweh. It is likely that he submitted again to Assyria and was restored as vassal king according to Assyrian policy, as earlier with Necho I in Egypt and later with the royal families of Elam and Qedar.

tion of Amon was probably an attempt on the part of rebel extremists to force Judah to throw off the Assyrian yoke.[99] Instead, a more moderate group, the *ʿam hā-ʾāreṣ* ("people of the land"), regained control in Judah, executed the king's murderers, and installed the eight year old Josiah (640-609) as king of Judah. This action apparently staved off Assyrian intervention in Judah, though it seems that the advisors to the young king were merely seeking a more opportune time to restore the "kingdom of David."

According to II Chron. 34:3, in the eighth year of his reign Josiah "began to seek the God of David his father." In other words, as early as 632 Josiah repudiated the gods of his Assyrian overlords.[100] Four years later he annexed the Assyrian provinces to the north -- Samaria, Megiddo, and probably Gilead. According to Ginsberg:[101]

> Josiah, then, reconquered even Israelite Transjordan, or part of it, and in so doing came into conflict with the children of Ammon. . . . It is, moreover, not out of the question that Josiah, in restoring the ancient empire of king David, brought not only practically all of the former territories of Judah and Israel under his direct rule but also the three Transjordan states (minus such territories) under his suzerainty.

Of the three Transjordan states only Moab, which was but a shadow of her former self, escaped direct territorial incursion on the part of Judah. The Negeb in particular was wrested from Edomite control.

Basing his argument primarily on Isaiah 15-16 and Jeremiah 48 which he dated to *ca.* 650 with Albright, Landes argued that Arab incursions in the mid-seventh century virtually brought the Moabite kingdom to an end with only the strong border fortresses enabling Ammon to survive.[102]

> . . . although the Moabites were able to resist the Arab invaders with some success at this point, it seems likely that the whole force of the Arab inundation marked the end of Moab as a strong autonomous state. It continued to exist for another generation or two, but in a much weakened condition.

---

[99] See G. Ernest Wright, *Biblical Archaeology*, p. 176.

[100] Cf. Frank M. Cross, Jr. and David N. Freedman, "Josiah's Revolt Against Assyria," *JNES* 12 (1953), p. 57.

[101] H. L. Ginsberg, "Judah and the Transjordan States from 734 to 582 B.C.E.," *Alexander Marx Jubilee Volume* (New York: Jewish Theological Seminary of America, 1950), pp. 347-68.

[102] George Landis, "A History of the Ammonites" (unpub. Ph.D. dissertation, Johns Hopkins University, 1956), pp. 297-98; cf. W. F. Albright, *The Biblical Period from Abraham to Ezra* (New York: Harper & Row, 1963), p. 79.

Ginsberg,[103] van Zyl[104] and Dumbrell[105] have argued that this conclusion overstates the case. The defeat of the Qedarite forces under Ammuladin by Kamashhalta of Moab suggests that Moab was still viable at that time. With Albright's retraction of a mid-seventh century date for the OAN tradition in Isaiah 15-16 and Jeremiah 48, the case for the virtual destruction of the Transjordan states in *ca.* 650 is greatly weakened.[106] The Arab incursions certainly did weaken Ammon, Moab and Edom in the second half of the seventh century B.C., but one must not dismiss the role played by Judah as well. In the reign of Josiah the kingdom of David was reborn.[107]

---

[103] H. L. Ginsberg, *op. cit.*, p. 362, n. 43.

[104] A. H. van Zyl, *The Moabites* (Pretoria Oriental Series 3, Leiden: E. J. Brill, 1960), pp. 153-57.

[105] W. Dumbrell, "The Midianites and Their Transjordanian Successors" (unpub. Th.D. thesis, Harvard Univ., 1970), pp. 243, n. 156 and 277, n. 32.

[106] W. F. Albright, *Yahweh and the Gods of Canaan* (Garden City, New York: Doubleday & Company, 1968), pp. 23-24, n. 57.

[107] The map on p. 98 is taken in part from Aharoni and Avi-Yonah, *The Macmillan Bible Atlas* (1968), p. 102.

KINGDOM OF JOSIAH

(*ca.* 628-609)

Unfortunately for Judah the international situation in the Levant in the seventh century was only superficially similar to that of the tenth century, such that it was quite impossible to restore the empire of David for any length of time. Egypt was again seeking an Asian empire of her own, and the temporary vacuum formed by the demise of Assyria was soon to be filled by another great power in Mesopotamia -- the Neo-Assyrian Empire. Josiah met his death at Megiddo in battle against the Egyptian forces of Necho II (609-594) who was on his way north to Harran to check the progress of the Medo-Babylonian alliance against Assyria. Malamat has gone so far as to suggest that by 609 Judah had formed an actual military alliance with Babylon against Egypt and Assyria.[108]

The death of Josiah in 609 marked the beginning of the end for the kingdom of Judah and for the former members of the Davidic League as well. Judah, Moab, Ammon, Edom, Aram and Phoenicia were soon to be swallowed up by the military might of Nebuchadrezzar (II) the Great (605-561). Philistia, Egypt, Qedar and distant Elam (Persia) were to share the same fate.

Imperium Babylonicum (ca. 626 - 582 B.C.)

1. Babylon and Egypt

The accession of Nabopolassar to the Babylonian throne in 626 marks the beginning of a new era in the history of the ancient Near East. Portrayed as an Assyrian commander, perhaps by birth a Chaldean, Nabopolassar took advantage of the Assyrian dynastic troubles to set up a Babylonian state.[109] The Babylonian Chronicle for 626 begins with a revolt in Babylon in which Nabopolassar routed the Assyrian garrison established by Sinsharishkun. The insurrection gained momentum and by the end of 626 Nabopolassar also held Uruk.[110] On the 26th day of Arahsamnu (Nov. 23, 626) Nabopolassar was formally seated as king in Babylon.[111] As his first official act in the chronicle was to

---

[108]Abraham Malamat, "The Last Wars of the Kingdom of Judah," *JNES* 9 (1950), p. 219; cf. also David N. Freedman, "The Babylonian Chronicle," *BAR I*, Anchor Books (Garden City, New York: Doubleday & Co., 1960), p. 116, n. 10. Von Voigtlander rejects the thesis "that Josiah was allied with Babylon and was fighting a delaying action at this point to prevent the Egyptians from reaching Harran before the garrison there could be reinforced" (*op. cit.*, p. 88). She argues that "the situation in Harran was not as desperate as that."

[109]See von Voigtlander, *op. cit.*, pp. 17-18.

[110]*Ibid.*, p. 19.

[111]See BM 25127, 14-15; published by Donald J. Wiseman, *Chronicles of Chaldean Kings (626-556 B.C.)* (London: British Museum, 1956). Subsequent citations of texts from the British Museum (BM) are taken from this volume

return to Susa the gods carried off to Uruk by the Assyrians some twenty years earlier, it is clear that he either had or hoped to have Elamite (or Persian) support in his struggle against Assyria.

Despite the testimony of the king list which gives Nabopolassar an uninterrupted twenty-one year reign, possession of Babylon was in dispute for some time. By November 624 Uruk was retaken by the Assyrian forces of Sinsharishkun.[112] In 623 the Assyrians extended their military operations still further to deal with a revolt in Der, a key city east of the Tigris.[113] Sinc Der controlled one of the main routes into Elam, it seems likely that Elam was in league with Babylon in revolt against Assyria. Later in 623 Sinsharishkun, with his army finally appeared in Babylonia. Though the chronicle account unfortunately breaks off at this point, there seems little reason to doubt von Voigtlander's conclusion that Nabopolassar's hold on Babylon was secure by the end of 623.[114] By midsummer of 621, Nabopolassar was again recognized in Uruk. Nippur probably also succumbed to the overwhelming Babylonian pressure at this time.[115]

After the fall of Nippur, Nabopolassar turned his attention to the middle and upper Euphrates in an attempt to force a passage through to the Mediterranean. As von Voigtlander noted: "It can scarcely be supposed that Nabu-apal-uṣur expected to carry out this project without a major engagement with the Assyrian army."[116] Moving up the Euphrates, Nabopolassar engaged the Assyrians on July 23, 616.[117] The Assyrian forces fled in disorder after the initial attack. In a second encounter in September the "army of Egypt" appeared along with the Assyrians in opposition to Nabopolassar.[118] As Egyptian

---

which is hereafter designated by the abbreviation *CCK*.

[112] See von Voigtlander, *op. cit.*, p. 20.

[113] At this point in the account of the Babylonian Chronicle about half the normal writing surface of the tablet has been broken away, taking with it about 10-12 signs at the beginning of lines 29-37. There are consequently serious problems in interpretation of the text. The subject nouns with the exception of the "king of Assyria and his army" (line 30) have been lost. Up to this point it has been possible to distinguish Assyrians from Babylonians by the verbal forms, the Assyrian army taking plural forms while the phrase "Nabopolassar and his army" is treated as singular. In the third year both kings took the field with their armies, and hence all the verbs are singular.

[114] See von Voigtlander, *op. cit.*, p. 22.

[115] *Ibid.*, pp. 23 and 68.

[116] *Ibid.*, p. 69

[117] *Ibid.*, p. 71.

[118] See BM 21901, 10-11 in *CCK* and *ARAB*, II, par. 1171, p. 417.

forces had not appeared in Syria since the conspiracy against Sargon on the part of the Egyptian (or Ethiopian) general Re'u a century earlier (in 720), this reference to the "army of Egypt" has invited speculation. Assyrian domination in Egypt had been terminated at least by 653 by the energetic policies of Psammeticus I.[119] The penetration of an Egyptian force so far into Syria in 616 can only mean that the Egyptians were aware of the growing weakness of Assyria and perhaps also of Nabopolassar's intention to establish Babylonian control there. As von Voigtlander has argued:[120]

> It is not necessary to suppose that the Egyptians and Assyrians were allies at this time. Following this, there is no mention of the presence of Egyptian forces in the area for six years. . . . It is difficult to believe that the fate of Assyria itself concerned the Egyptians directly. Their interest lay in control of the provinces between Egypt and Assyria.

At this point Egypt was probably nothing more than an interested neutral party in the power struggle to the north.

However one interprets the Egyptian presence in Syria in 616, it is clearly evident that a noteable weakening of Assyria had occurred. The following year a third power, the Medes, was to join Babylon and Egypt in the power struggle to succeed decadent Assyria. Von Voigtlander has argued that this weakening of Assyria was not due to Babylonian pressure alone.[121] Warfare between factions within Assyria itself apparently contributed to Assyrian decline. Sinsharishkun's belated foray into Babylonia in 623 appears to be the action "of a man, hard pressed elsewhere, who snatches time for temporary measures to control a local insurrection."[122] It is also probable that the Medes had already begun their series of incursions into Assyrian territory.[123]

Aware that the Egyptians were now potential enemies to any force pushing into Syria, Nabopolassar decided to ally himself with the Medes in order to destroy the great citadels of Assyria along the Tigris. The Medes may not have welcomed Nabopolassar's intrusion into Assyria with much enthusiasm as they had their own plans of conquest and expansion. Nonetheless the threat of a possible alliance between Assyria and Babylon against them was adequate reason to convince the Medes to go along with the Babylonian venture.

---

[119] See Étienne Drioton and Jacques Vandier, *L'Egypte*, 3rd ed. (Paris: Presses Universitaires de France, 1952), p. 576.

[120] Von Voigtlander, *op. cit.*, p. 72.

[121] *Loc. cit.*

[122] *Ibid.*, p. 73.

[123] Cf. Herodotus (book I, par. 102) in *Herodotus I*, tr. by A. D. Godley (4 vols.; The Loeb Classical Library, London: William Heineman and New York: G. P. Putnam's Sons, 1921), p. 133. All citations from the Greek classics hereafter are to the pertinent volume of the Loeb Classical Library.

In May 615 Nabopolassar laid siege to Asshur but was forced to retreat before the Assyrian forces of Sinsharishkun. By midsummer of 614 an army of Medes was advancing toward Nineveh.[124] Again Sinsharishkun repelled the invaders, at least from Nineveh. Turning downstream along the bank of the Tigris, the Medes attacked Asshur which was poorly defended, since Sinsharishkun had gone to the defense of Nineveh. The city was sacked and its inhabitants massacred. The destruction of Asshur was such a shocking violation of international practice of the time, which usually permitted a city to ransom itself unless it could be termed "rebellious," that even the Babylonian chonicler took pains to dissociate Nabopolassar from this act of savagery. The chronicler specificially stated that although Nabopolassar was coming to assist the Medes, he did not arrive until after the sack.[125] Nabopolassar and Umakishtar, king of the Medes, then concluded an alliance of "peace and cordial relations" which apparently remained in effect through the major campaigns against Nineveh (612) and Harran (610). After 609 the Medes disappear from the extant chronicles.

After two unsuccessful assaults on Nineveh in 612, the wall of the city was finally breached and the Medes and Babylonians poured into the city. Sinsharishkun died, as Shamashshumukin before him, in the ruins of the city.[126] Though Nineveh was utterly destroyed, Sinsharishkun's son Asshuruballit II (611-609) did manage to escape and made his way to Harran, the final bastion of Assyria.[127] Between 612 and 610 Egypt formed an alliance with the badly shattered Assyrians at Harran. Egypt had no intention of restoring the

---

[124]See BM 21901, 24-25 in *CCK* and read with von Voigtlander (*op. cit.*, p. 76): . . . *māt ma-da-ai̯a-ana muḫḫi ninua*[KI] *ki-i* [*pani-šu iš-ta-kan šarru* [KUR]*assur u ummani-šu ana ri-ṣu-ut-su*] *i-ḫi-šam-ma* ("When the Medes set their face toward Nineveh, the king of Assyria and his army hurried to its aid."

[125]See von Voigtlander, *op. cit.*, p. 76 and cf. BM 21901, 26-28 as restored by Wiseman in *CCK*.

[126]See von Voigtlander, *op. cit.*, p. 85, n. 43. She notes that: "It has been frequently suggested that his death in the flames of Nineveh is recalled in the Sardanapalus legend. After his name there is a gap in the text (BM 21901, 44) where his fate was no doubt stated.

[127]Although the name is lost in the chronicle account, there is little doubt as to the identity of the escapee. Von Voigtlander has restored the text as follows (BM 21901, 45): [[md]*HI ú-bal-liṭ mār*] ⌜*šarri*⌝, translating "[Asshuruballit, the son] ⌜of the king⌝ of Assur escaped from the king." The beginning of line 46 *ša* [KUR]*assur* supports her restoration. The verb *išhitamma* is singular, indicating that an individual and not the army is the subject. For *šht* with the meaning "to escape" see *CCK*, BM 21946, obv. 6.

Assyrian Empire as such; rather the object was to keep Syria and the Mediterranean littoral from falling into Babylonian hands. In 610 the combined armies of Babylonia and the Medes marched against the Assyrians and an Egyptian contingent at Harran. The Egyptian force was a garrison awaiting reinforcements from Pharaoh Necho's army which was apparently delayed by Josiah's fateful battle at Megiddo in 609. The Assyrians and Egyptians fled from Harran, apparently without a struggle, and the city was taken. A vain attempt on the part of Asshuruballit to retake Harran in 609 with Egyptian help failed.[128] The final curtain had fallen on Assyrian power in the ancient Near East.

In March 609 the victorious armies of the Medes and Babylonians returned to their own lands. Sometime later, according to tradition, a covenant of friendship between Babylonia and the Medes was sealed by the marriage of Nabopolassar's son Nebuchadrezzar to Umakishtar's daughter Amyntas.[129] With their eastern frontier secured by treaty, the Babylonians were free to give their full attention to affairs in the West.

Nebuchadrezzar appears for the first time in the chronicles when he accompanied his father on a mountain campaign in May 607.[130] When Nabopolassar returned to Babylon the next month, he left the young prince Nebuchadrezzar to complete the military devastation. On Nebuchadrezzar's return to Babylon in August or September, Nabopolassar set out on an expedition to the upper Euphrates designed to establish a base at Kimuḫu against the Egyptian forces in Syria.[131] Kimuḫu was taken by the Babylonians in November 607 only to fall again to the Egyptians in the summer of 606.[132] In the fall of that year Nabopolassar made his last expedition establishing a base at Quramati on the eastern side of the Euphrates.[133] In the spring of 605 Nabopolassar turned

---

[128]Cf. *ARAB*, II, par. 1182.

[129]See Berossus *apud* Josephus, *Contra Apionem*, I, 19.

[130]See BM 22047, 6-11. The mountains of *Za*[. . .] cannot be identified. Albright has suggested that the place in question be read *Za*[*mani*] and that this was an expedition into southern Armenia to secure his right flank "against both his Egyptian foes and his Median allies" -- "The Nebuchadnezzar and Neriglissar Chronicles," *BASOR* 143 (1956), p. 29.

[131]See BM 22047, 12-15. The location of Kimuḫu is not known. Albright (*ibid.*, pp. 29-30) argued for a location north of Carchemish in the neighborhood of Samosata. The purpose of Nabopolassar's expedition was apparently to establish a base for operations against Carchemish which by this time was held by the Egyptians.

[132]See BM 22047, 16-18 and von Voigtlander, *op. cit.*, p. 90.

[133]See BM 22047, 19-26. The location of Quramati is also in doubt. Wiseman's location downstream from Meskeneh (*CCK*, pp. 22-23) was rejected by Albright [*BASOR* 143 (1956), pp. 30-31] who locates it much farther north, at

over command of the army to Nebuchadrezzar who, in his first major campaign, took the Egyptians by surprise and soundly defeated them at Carchemish. The Egyptians who did manage to escape from the first battle were overtaken and defeated near Hamath.[134]

Though the defeat of the Egyptians at Carchemish in 605 marked the beginning of Babylonian dominance in Syria-Palestine, the struggle was by no means over. The entries in the Babylonian Chronicle for the next four years show repeated military expeditions in the West.

On August 15, 605 Nabopolassar died, and Nebuchadrezzar returned in haste to Babylon to secure his throne. After the ceremonies of accession, he returned to Syria to continue his military exploits. In February 604 he returned to Babylon for the New Year's festival. Later that year Nebuchadrezzar was again in Palestine where he destroyed Ashkelon, which had apparently turned in vain to Egypt for help.[135] Further campaigns in Palestine in 603 and 602 were designed "to eliminate the Egyptian sphere of influence from Gaza north and to force the states of the area to become tributary to Babylon."[136] In December 601, having already reduced most of Syria and Palestine, Nebuchadrezzar launched a campaign against the borders of Egypt. In the ensuing battle, which took place early in 600, the Egyptian forces were again crippled, but at great cost to Nebuchadrezzar. Both sides sustained heavy casualties. Nebuchadrezzar was forced to withdraw and his next year was spent in Babylon rebuilding his army.[137] Egypt, on the other hand, was so seriously weakened that, for the moment, she was reduced to virtual parity with the lesser states of southern Palestine.

2. Judah and Her Neighbors

From the death of Josiah at the hands of Pharaoh Necho in 609 to the second fall of Jerusalem in 587, the kings of Judah and the other Palestinian states held their thrones at the pleasure of Egypt or Babylon. Foreign policy in Jerusalem and other major cities of the area was determined by which of these two powers seemed stronger or more menacing. The end of an era was at

---

or near Apamea opposite Zeugma.

[134]See BM 21946, 1-7; published for the first time by Wiseman, *CCK*, pp. 66-71, 84-86; pl. 5, pp. 14-16.

[135]See BM 21946, 12-20. Note also Saqqara papyrus 86984 (Cairo), restored text and translation by H. L. Ginsberg, "An Aramaic Contemporary of the Lachish Letters," *BASOR* 111 (1948), pp. 24-27. Albright, Ginsberg and others have argued that the letter is from Adon king of Ashkelon who is desperately seeking aid against an impending invasion of Nebuchadrezzar.

[136]See von Voigtlander, *op. cit.*, p. 93.

[137]See BM 21946, rev. 8.

hand as far as the small states of Palestine were concerned. In fact, the Babylonian Chronicle no longer concerned itself with separate states in Syria and Palestine but simply designated the entire area as Ḫatti, with Jerusalem known simply as "the city of Iaḫudu."[138]

After the death of Josiah, Judah became an Egyptian vassal. Jehoahaz, a son and successor of Josiah, was deposed after reigning only three months, when Necho returned from his expedition to Harran. Necho then installed Eliakim, another son of Josiah,[139] with the crown name Jehoiakim (609/8-597). From 609 to 605 he faithfully paid the tribute imposed by Necho.[140] Though positive evidence is lacking, it seems likely that Edom may also have been subjected at least to nominal Egyptian vassalage at this time. Ammon and Moab apparently retained their independence or perhaps a pro-Babylonian stance as they were more exposed to Babylonian pressure and were also pressed by the expanding threat of the Qedarite dominated league of Arab tribes.

After the defeat of Egypt at Carchemish in 605, Nebuchadrezzar placed the area as far south as Riblah under tribute.[141] In 604 he extended his exactions to "all the kings of Ḫatti land," though Jehoiakim, along with Adon king of Ashkelon (?), and perhaps others, held out for a time.[142] Sometime in 603, probably after the fall of Ashkelon, Judah also became tributary to the Babylonians. This relationship stood until 601.

The indecisive battle between the forces of Nebuchadrezzar and Necho at "the borders of Egypt" in 601/600 was a blow to the pro-Babylonian faction in Jerusalem. Jehoiakim withheld tribute in a vain attempt to reassert Judean independence. In 599/98 Nebuchadrezzar sent out raiding parties from his Syrian bases to plunder the Arabs.[143] Landes has argued that the Ammonites and Moabites were among those induced to cooperate with the Babylonian troops at this time in making raids on other rebellious states including Judah (cf. II Kings 24:2).[144] In return for protection against the ever-threatening

---

[138]See von Voigtlander, *op. cit.*, p. 95 and BM 21946, obv. 12.

[139]See W. F. Albright, "The Seal of Eliakim and the Latest Preëxilic History of Judah, with some Observations on Ezekiel," *JBL* 51 (1932), p. 92; who argues that Jehoiakim was a younger brother of Jehoahaz whom the people regarded as regent until the death of Jehoahaz in Egypt.

[140]A sum of 100 talents of silver and one of gold; cf. II Kings 23:23-24 and II Chron. 36:1-4.

[141]See BM 21946, obv. 12-13.

[142]See BM 21946, obv. 17; on King Adon see note 135 above.

[143]He may have needed their support for his invasion of Egypt; cf. W. F. Albright, *The Biblical Period from Abraham to Ezra* (New York: Harper & Row, 1963), p. 81 and p. 109, n. 162.

[144]See G. Landes, "A History of the Ammonites," p. 310.

Arabs, the Ammonites and Moabites had again submitted themselves to a foreign suzerain, at least for the moment. The Babylonians sent raiding bands of Syrians, Moabites and Ammonites against Judah as well, as late as 598.[145] Josephus has reconstructed this raid, perhaps with the aid of additional sources since lost.[146]

Late in November 598 a mixed force of Chaldeans, Syrians, Moabites and Ammonites appeared before Jerusalem. Albright has argued that the death of Jehoiakim at this time was probably the result of a palace revolt in Jerusalem, and that "his body was thrown outside of the gates of Jerusalem, and left there, like the body of an ass," as reflected in Jer. 22:19 and 36:30.[147] Jehoiakim was succeeded by his eighteen year old son, Jehoiachin. On March 16, 597, after a reign of only three months and ten days, Jehoiachin was carried into exile by the Babylonians and his uncle Mattaniah was placed on the throne with the throne name of Zedekiah (II Kings 24:17). The treasuries of the palace and temple were looted by the Babylonians, and the royal family, members of the court, soldiers, and artisans were deported to Babylon (II Kgs. 24:13-16). In Babylon Jehoiachin was maintained in nominal captivity along with a group of kings from other lands. In Jerusalem Zedekiah was regarded as regent for the exiled king of Judah.

Although the Babylonian Chronicle continues through Nebuchadrezzar's tenth year (595/94) the text is badly damaged and details are not altogether clear. Some scholars have restored Elam to the text for a campaign in Nebuchadrezzar's ninth year (596/95).[148] In the winter of 595/94 the Babylonian monarch made a belated trip to Ḫatti to receive tribute.[149] With this expedition the account of the Babylonian Chronicle breaks off.

---

[145]Cf. II Kings 24:2 and II Chron. 36:5-7. See also E. Vogt, "Die neubabylonische Chronic über die Einnahme von Jerusalem," *SVT* 4 (1957), p. 92; who places this invasion in 599/98 with Martin Noth.

[146]In both Josephus and the Babylonian Chronicle Nebuchadrezzar is said to have accompanied the first expedition but not the second. See *Antiq.*X, vi, 3 in *Jewish Antiquities, Books IX-XI*, tr. by Ralph Marcus (9 vols.; The Loeb Classical Library, London: William Heineman, 1958), pp. 209-211.

[147]W. F. Albright, "Seal of Eliakim," *JBL* 51 (1932), pp. 90-91. Josephus (*Antiq.* X, vi, 3) adds the note that upon entering Jerusalem, Nebuchadrezzar killed Jehoiakim and ordered his body "to be cast outside unburied before the walls, and appointed his son Jōachimos as king of the country."

[148]See BM 21946, rev. 14-15. Von Voigtlander accepts the restoration of Elam here and cites the dating of Jeremiah's oracle against Elam to "the beginning of the reign of Zedekiah" (Jer. 49:34) as confirmation (*op. cit.*, p. 109, n. 82).

[149]See BM 21946, rev. 21-24.

Meanwhile in Egypt Necho II (609-594) was pursuing a policy which focused on maritime power. Necho built two naval fleets, one to ply the Red Sea and the other the Mediterranean.[150] He also vainly pursued the gradiose scheme of digging a canal connecting the Egyptian Delta with the Red Sea through the Wadi Tumilat.[151] If successful, such a venture would have diverted South Arabian traffic from the caravan routes terminating in Syria and Lower Palestine, thus posing a grave threat to the Babylonian economy. Egyptian ambitions for political dominance in the Near East were by no means destroyed by the Babylonian advances in Syria-Palestine from 605 to 594.

Jerusalem was the focus of an anti-Babylonian coalition in *ca.* 594 when envoys from Edom, Moab, Ammon, Tyre and Sidon conspired against Babylon (Jer. 27:3). This revolt was probably stimulated by the promise of Egyptian support. For some reason the revolt did not materialize.[152] Some three years later, in 591, Psammeticus II (594-588) made a trip through *Khurru* (Phoenicia) which may have had as its purpose the inciting of rebellion in Palestine.[153] Though evidence for subversion from the other Palestinian states is lacking, in Jerusalem Zedekiah foolishly decided to withhold, or perhaps to reduce, the amount of tribute paid to Babylon in 590 or 589.[154] In January 588 Babylonian troops appeared before the walls of Jerusalem.[155] The Babylonians may not have

---

[150]See E. Drioton, *L'Egypt pharaonique* (Paris: A. Colin, 1959), p. 178; and F. K. Kienitz, *Die politische Geschichte Ägyptens vom 7. bis zum 4. Jahrhundert vor der Zeitwende* (Berlin: Akademie Verlag, 1953), pp. 25, 154-58. Herodotus (II, 159) discusses Egypt's naval enterprises. Cf. also R. D. Barnett, "Early Shipping in the Near East," *Antiquity* 32 (1958), p. 229.

[151]See Herman de Meulenaere, *Herodotos over de 26ste Dynastie (II,147 - III,15)* (Louvain:Leuvense Universitaire Uitgaven, 1951), pp. 50-54; with references to earlier literature.

[152]Cf. Jer. 27:4-22; 51:29. A number of reasons have been suggested: 1) Jeremiah's influence, 2) Egypt would not join in, 3) Nebuchadrezzar took prompt action to forestall the revolt (so Oesterly and Robinson), and 4) perhaps the conspirators could not agree.

[153]See F. Kienitz, *op. cit.*, p. 25; and H. de Meulenaere, *op. cit.*, p. 70.

[154]Josephus (*Antiq.* X, vii, 3) states that Zedekiah was faithful to Babylon for eight years and then shifted his allegiance to Egypt. Albright has argued persuasively that the chronological statement in Jer. 52:28-30 is correct and is an interpolation from Babylonian records. Accordingly he dates the second fall of Jerusalem to the 18th year of Nebuchadrezzar in 587 ["The Nebuchadnezzar and Neriglissar Chronicles," *BASOR* 143 (1956), p. 32]. For a discussion of the vexed question of Tishri regnal years in Jerusalem for this period see D. N. Freedman, "The Babylonian Chronicle," *BA* 19 (1956), pp. 56-8.

[155]Cf. II Kings 25:1 and Jer. 39:1. See also Josephus (*Antiq.* X, vii, 4)

placed the city under close siege until after they had systematically reduced the other strongholds of Judah.[156] An Egyptian army under a new pharaoh, Apries (Hophra) (588-568), came to the aid of Jerusalem causing the siege to be lifted temporarily; but the Egyptians were routed and the siege was resumed. Finally in the summer of 587, weakened by siegeworks, famine and plague, Jerusalem was stormed and methodically destroyed (cf. II Kings 25:8-21 and Jer. 52:12-27). Booty and prisoners were transported to Mesopotamia.

The catastrophe which struck Judah in 587 did not immediately affect Ammon, Moab and Edom. Landes has argued that by the beginning of the last decade of the seventh century Ammon had asserted its complete independence and rapidly became the dominant state of southern Transjordan, expanding as far west as the Jordan Valley.[157] Nebuchadrezzar's victory at Carchemish in 605 posed a new threat to the petty states of Palestine, and it is indeed probable that the king of Ammon was among the "kings of Ḫatti" who paid homage to the Babylonian monarch in 604.[158] After three years Jehoiakim of Judah revolted, though Ammon and Moab remained loyal and fought with the Babylonian raiding parties dispatched from Syria against Judah (II Kings 24:2). If Jehoiakim had been successful in 598 in his attempt to overthrow Babylonian domination, he would probably have asserted his rights to the territory of Josiah's kingdom which had been regained by Ammon and Moab after 609.

The Ammonites and Moabites probably remained loyal to Babylon in order to secure protection against the Qedarite dominated Arab confederation which was encroaching upon the borders of all the states in Transjordan. It was not until *ca.* 594 -- after the first fall of Jerusalem -- that Ammon and Moab were induced to join with Edom, Tyre and Sidon in a conspiracy against Babylon.[159]

Though the widespread revolt against Babylon did not materialize, Ammon,

---

who dated this event to the 9th year on the 10th day of the 10th month of the reign of Zedekiah.

[156]Josephus (*Antiq.* X, vii, 3) places the ravaging of Judah and the Egyptian relief expedition before the official beginning of the siege which took place in Zedekiah's 9th year. But as von Voigtlander has shown (*op. cit.*, p. 133, n. 9): "there is no space in (Josephus') timetable for these activities if Zedekiah's revolt did not take place before the end of his 8th or the beginning of his 9th year."

[157]George M. Landes, "Ammon, Ammonites," *IDB*, I, p. 112; cf. also H. L. Ginsberg, *Alexander Marx Jubilee Volume* (1950), pp. 362-63.

[158]See van Zyl, *The Moabites*, p. 155; cf. also II Kings 24:1-2.

[159]On the reasons for this shift in foreign policy among the Transjordan states between 598 and 594 see H. L. Ginsberg, *Alexander Marx Jubilee Volume*, pp. 363-65; A. H. van Zyl, *The Moabites*, pp. 155-56; and B. Meissner, *Könige Babyloniens und Assyriens*, pp. 265-72.

like Judah, remained in open rebellion, even to the point of interference in the internal affairs of the remnant of Judah after 587.[160] King Baalis of Ammon was involved in the plot to assassinate Gedaliah, the governor of Judah (Jer. 40:14). Apparently the Ammonite king was trying to gain control of Judah, possibly in the hope of restoring the kingdom of Josiah, this time under Ammonite rule. Though the subsequent political events in Transjordan from *ca.* 586 to 582 are obscure, it seems probable that punitive measures were undertaken by Nebuchadrezzar. Josephus records a Babylonian campaign in Coele-Syria against Ammon and Moab "in the fifth year after the sacking of Jerusalem, which was the twenty-third year of the reign of Nebuchadrezzar."[161] The biblical account in Jer. 52:30 apparently describes the same event, noting that some 745 Jews were included in the deportation of 582 which was carried out by Nebuzaradan, the doughty Babylonian general who had also executed the deportation of 587. The devastating punitive action of 582 created a politivacuum in Transjordan into which poured the *Bᵉnê Qedem*, the Arab invaders of the Qedarite League, who destroyed all organized political activity in this area (cf. Ezek. 25:4-5, 8-9). By the middle of the sixth century the Ammonite state had collapsed, as witnessed by archaeological explorations in Transjordan which indicate that sedentary occupation of Ammon ceased almost completely until the early third century.[162]

The situation in Moab was similar to that in Ammon. In 604 the Moabite king submitted to Nebuchadrezzar and remained loyal to Babylon in the revolt of *ca.* 600-597. As van Zyl put it, "Because Moab repeatedly collaborated with the enemy of Judah, the flame of hatred between these two nations, which had been kindled long ago, blazed up higher during this period."[163] Though Moab did send envoys to Jerusalem in the conspiracy of 594, it would appear that she withdrew and returned to nominal vassalage to Babylon. Though Judah was devastated in 587, Moab was not entered by the Babylonians at that time.[164] Fugitives who fled from Judah were scorned by the Moabites who, according to the prophet Jeremiah, rejoiced in the fate that had befallen Judah and proclaimed their own country to be an impregnable fortress (Jer. 48:26-30). The

---

[160]Cf. G. Landes, "Ammon, Ammonites," *IDB*, I, p. 112; and H. L. Ginsberg, *ibid.*, pp. 365-66.

[161]See *Antiq*. X, ix, 7. But cf. also von Voigtlander, *op. cit.*, p. 133, n. 16; who notes that Josephus' account that Nebuchadrezzar not only invaded Egypt but killed its king is demonstrably false and casts doubt on the other activities related here.

[162]See Nelson Glueck, "Explorations in Eastern Palestine III," *AASOR*, vols. 18-19 (1937-39), p. 269.

[163]A. H. van Zyl, *The Moabites*, p. 155.

[164]*Ibid.*, p. 156.

haughtiness of Moab produced a flood of condemnation from the prophets of Judah. In the Babylonian campaign of 582 the voice of Moab, like that of Ammon, was silenced. Some of the Moabites were exiled to Babylonia, while others fled to Egypt.[165] The destruction of the line of Moabite fortresses in the first quarter of the sixth century meant the end of Moab. Subsequent Arab encroachment destroyed any surviving sedentary Moabite culture in Transjordan.

The kingdom of Edom somehow managed to survive the devastations of 587 and 582 in Palestine. Along with the other petty states of the area, Edom submitted quietly to the Babylonian yoke in 604. Though envoys from Edom were present in Jerusalem in the conspiracy a decade later, Edom apparently withdrew. When the Babylonian forces besieged and captured Jerusalem in 587, the Edomites joined the forces of Nebuchadrezzar and exulted over the destruction of their ancient enemy (cf. Ps. 137:7; Lam. 4:21-22 and Obad. 10-16).[166] After the deportation of the people of Judah to Babylon in 587 and 582, the Edomites moved northward into southern Judah making Hebron the capital of a kingdom which eventually came to be known as Idumea. Behind them the Nabateans, part of the larger Arab movement, pressed into former Edomite territory and established a kingdom with Petra as their capital.

The fate of Philistia and Phoenicia at the hands of Nebuchadrezzar is not altogether clear, at least in detail. Only the fall of Ashkelon in 604 can be dated. Gaza, which had fallen into Egyptian hands in the reign of Necho II (609-594), is later cited as a Babylonian dependency along with Tyre, Sidon, Arvad and Ashdod.[167] Josephus cites an earlier source by Philostratos concerning a thirteen year siege of Tyre.[168] The siege was apparently begun in 587, the year Jerusalem fell, and terminated in 573, when Tyre surrendered.[169]

---

[165] Cf. Jer. 48:7. In the 6th year of Cambyses a certain Kamushusharuṣur is mentioned (see van Zyl, *The Moabites*, p. 157, n. 6). This may be an indication of the fact that some Moabites were taken to Babylonia into exile along with the 745 Jews in 582 (cf. Jer. 52:30). Van Zyl discusses the names כמשיחי, כמשצדק and כמשפלט in texts discovered at Sakkara in 1926, published by Aimé-Giron, *Textes araméens d'Egypte* (Kairo, 1931).

[166] See Bruce C. Cresson, "Israel and Edom: A Study of the Anti-Edom Bias in Old Testament Religion" (unpub. Ph.D. thesis, Duke University, 1963), p. 142. For the most part Cresson's conclusions overstate the case and have forced him to date some of the Edomite OAN material much too late.

[167] Cf. Arthur Unger, *Babylon, die heilige Stadt nach der Beschriebung der Babylonier* (Berlin: W. de Gruyter, 1931), p. 286.

[168] See Josephus (*Antiq*. X, xi, 1).

[169] Cf. Josephus (*Contra Apionem* I, 21). Subsequent administrative documents dated to Nebuchadrezzar's 40th to 42nd years show that in 565-63 Tyre was under Babylonian administration (cf. von Voigtlander, *op. cit.*, p. 123).

CHAPTER FOUR

THE PROPHETIC WAR ORACLE FROM AMOS TO JEREMIAH

A study of the war oracle in ancient Israel is, by its very nature, a study of the prophetic tradition. Since classical prophecy as such had its beginning in the mid-eighth century with Amos and Hosea, projection prior to that time is dependent on historical and legal sources which, strictly speaking, are not prophetic literature. There is little objection to use of Deuteronomy and the work of the Deuteronomic Historian (Joshua through II Kings) and, to some extent, the work of the Chronicler in this regard. Prophetic sources were used in the compilation of these works and careful study of this material has revealed much about the phenomenon of prophecy in ancient Israel beyond what could be learned from analysis of the books of the classical prophets alone.

The use of the Psalms in studies of prophecy in ancient Israel, however, is problematic to say the least. The individual psalms are much more difficult to date and to control in historical analysis. Moreover, the Psalms represent the legacy of the priestly cult of the Jerusalem temple; and the apparent tension between prophet and priest in ancient Israel has produced a sizeable literature and unresolved dispute in academic circles.[1] Nonetheless, the Psalms cannot be ignored in a discussion of literary forms in Old Testament prophecy. As Bentzen has argued:[2]

> . . . the Book of Psalms contains types which are not proper psalms, but are e.g. more or less related to *prophetic* or . . . *oracular* literature, and also with incantation, such as *cultic benedictions and curses* and cultic *oracles*, sometimes combined in the complex compositions consisting of different types, the so-called *liturgies*.

---

[1]For a discussion of the pertinent literature see Richard Hentschke, *Die Stellung der vorexilischen Schriftpropheten zum Kultus* (BZAW 75, Berlin: Verlag Alfred Töpelmann, 1957); Aubrey Johnson, *The Cultic Prophet in Ancient Israel*, 2nd ed. (Cardiff: University of Wales Press, 1962); and Ernst Würthwein, "Kultpolemik or Kultbescheid? Beobachtungen zu den Thema 'Prophetie und Kult,'" *Tradition und Situation* (Festschrift A. Weiser, Göttingen: Vandenhoeck & Ruprecht, 1963), pp. 115-131.

[2]Aage Bentzen, *Introduction to the Old Testament*, I, 7th ed. (Copenhagen: G. E. C. Gad Publisher, 1967), p. 147; emphasis is his.

Not only are the so-called prophetic types of literature found in the Psalms, the prophetic literature is in turn influenced by the psalmic. To quote Bentzen again: "The great prophets are not prior to the psalms, but the psalms are prior to the great prophets. And, besides the psalms, the forms inherited from cultic (priestly) prophets have framed the style of the great prophets."[3] In light of the close relationship between the psalms and the prophetic tradition, it is necessary to consider the Book of Psalms in a discussion of the war oracle and the OAN tradition in ancient Israel.

The War Oracle and the Psalms

Many of the Psalms reflect a military background. The national psalms of lamentation (Pss. 12, 58?, 60, 74, 79, 80, 83, 85, 90, 94:1-11, 123, 126, and 137)[4] were composed as prayers for deliverance of Israel from her adversaries. Others of the Psalms are even more explicitly military. Dahood argues that Psalm 110, a royal psalm, was "probably composed to celebrate a military victory."[5] Mowinckel has argued that Psalms 20 and 21 were probably uttered before a military expedition promising to the king Yahweh's help and victory over his enemies.[6] Psalm 149 is interpreted in a similar manner by Dahood who sees it as "a hymn sung and performed in the religious assembly on the eve of a battle against the heathen nations."[7]

No attempt is made here to undertake an exhaustive study of warfare and the prophetic war oracle within the Psalms. But since aspects of the royal cult of the Jerusalem temple become important in understanding the transformation of the war oracle in early apocalyptic, two representative psalms have been selected for detailed analysis. Psalm 83 is included because of its treatment of the various nations and the probability of a ninth or eighth century date which makes it a helpful point of departure for historical analysis. Psalm 60 contains the clearest example of an explicit war oracle against the nations, introduced by "Yahweh spoke from his sanctuary" -- the cultic counterpart to the prophetic "Thus saith Yahweh."

---

[3] *Ibid.*, p. 160, n. 5.

[4] On the classification of national psalms of lamentation see Sigmund Mowinckel, *The Psalms in Israel's Worship*, tr. by D. R. Ap-Thomas (2 vols.; New York and Nashville: Abingdon Press, 1962), I, pp. 193-246; and Georg Fohrer, *Introduction to the Old Testament*, tr. by D. E. Green (New York and Nashville: Abingdon Press, 1968), pp. 281-93.

[5] Mitchell Dahood, S. J., *Psalms III, 101-150* (AB 17A; Garden City, New York: Doubleday & Company, 1970), p. 112.

[6] Mowinckel, *op. cit.*, II, p. 62.

[7] Dahood, *op. cit.*, p. 356.

Psalm 83

2	Yahweh, what god is like you?	⟨יהוה⟩[a] מ⟨י⟩[b] אל דמי לך	7
	Be not silent! Be not still, O El!	אל תחרש [ ]אל תשקט אל	7
3	Look! Your enemies raise a tumult;	[ ][c] הנה אויביך יהמיון	9
	Your foes lift their head.	ומשנאיך נשאו ראש	9
4	Against your people they weave a plot;	על⟨י⟩[d] עמך יערימו סוד	9
	They conspire against your treasure.	[ ]יתיעצו על צְפוּנֶיךָ[e]	9
5	They say: "Come, let us obliterate them as a nation;	אמרו לכו ונכחידם מגוי	10
	Let the name of Israel be remembered no more."	ולא יזכר שם ישראל עוד	10
6	Indeed, they consult together with singleness of purpose;	כי נועצו לב יחדו	7
	Your assailants make an alliance:	עֹלֶיךָ[f] ברית יכרתו	8
7	The tents of Moab and the Hagrites,	אהלי[g] [מואב והגרים][h]	7
	Edom and the Ishmaelites;	[אדום וישמעאלים]	7
8	Byblos along with Amalek,	גבל [ ]עמ[ ]ך[i] [ ]עמלק	7
	Philistia with the inhabitants of Tyre.	פלשת עם ישבי צור	7
9	Yea, Assyria has joined them;	גם אשור נלוה עמם	7
	They are the strong arm of Lot's children.	היו זרוע לבני לוט	8
	Selah.	סלה	
10	Treat them like Midian,	עשה להם כמדין [ ][j]	7
	Like Jabin at the river Kishon --	כיבין בנחל קישון	7
11	Wiped off the face of the earth,	נשמדו בעין דאר[k]	6
	They served to dung the ground.	היו דמן לאדמה	7
12	Make their nobles like Oreb;	שית-מ[ ][l] נדיבמו כערב	9
	Like Zeeb (make) all their chiefs.	וכזאב [ ][m] כל נסיכמו	9
13	[Those who said: "Let us seize for ourselves the habitation of Yahweh."]		
14	My God, make them like chaff,	אלהי שיתמ[ ][n] כ[קש][o]	7
	Like tumbleweed before the wind.	כ[גלגל] לפני רוח	7
15	As a flame consumes the forest,	כ[להבה][p] תבער יער	7
	As fire sets the mountains ablaze --	כ[אש] תלהט הרים	7
16	So pursue them with your tempest;	כן תרדפם[q] בסערך	8
	With your storm-wind discomfit them.	[ ]בסופתך תבהלם[q]	8
17	Fill their faces with shame;	מלא פניהם קלון	7
	Let your name, Yahweh, avenge itself.	[ ]יְבַקֵּשׁ[ ][r] שמך יהוה	7
18	May they be humiliated and discomfited for ever and ever;	בשו ויבהלו	8
		עדי עד[s]	3

May they perish in utter disgrace. ויחפרו ויאבדו 8
19 Let them know that your name is Yahweh; ידעו כי {שמך / אתה}[t] יהוה 9
That you alone are the Most High
over all the earth. לבדך עליון על כל []ארץ 9

Notes to the Text of Psalm 83

[a]Psalm 83 is the concluding psalm of the so-called Elohistic Psalter. As Dahood has noted (*Psalms II*, p. 273), the LXX, Vulg., and Syr. all read *ʾelōhîm mî yidmeh lāk* (cf. Ps. 89:7), or its equivalent, "Who shall be like you?" MT as it stands reflects the substitution of אלהים for יהוה and the loss of one *mem* by haplography with the subsequent misreading of the negative *ʾal* for *ʾēl*, "god."

[b]The vowel letter would not have appeared in the earliest consonantal text.

[c]The כי is omitted as a secondary expansion.

[d]The ballast variant of the preposition achieves better metrical balance in this bicolon.

[e]Vocalizing *ṣepûnîkā* (MT *ṣepûneykā*), a singular noun with the genitive ending, with Dahood (*Psalms II*, p. 274). Some of the ancient versions read a singular noun here which makes a better parallel to singular *ʿammekā*, "your people."

[f]Again following Dahood who notes that *kārat berît ʿal* is not attested elsewhere. The term is parsed as a participle *ʿōlekā* from the root *ʿlh*, "to rise up against, attack." In meaning the term is synonymous to "your enemies" and "your foes" of vs. 3. The poet considered Israel's attackers as the assailants of Yahweh.

[g]Note the interesting variant in the fragments of the Psalms scroll discovered at Masada which reads: אלהי אדום, "the gods of Edom." See Yigael Yadin, "The Excavation of Masada -- 1963/64," *IEJ* 15 (1965), p. 104.

[h]MT as it stands yields poor metrical balance in this bicolon. In his recent dissertation ["The Midianites and Their Transjordanian Successors" (Harvard Th.D. thesis, 1970), p. 189] Dumbrell paired Edom and Moab in the first colon and the Ishmaelites and Hagrites in the second to achieve an 8:7 syllable count. It is preferable to exchange the two pairs of terms noting the poetic relation to the following bicolon (see next note) and the concluding colon of this strophe (vs. 9b), where "Lot's children" must refer back to Moab which then should come first so as to form a poetic inclusion.

[i]This colon has produced much comment in the literature. Dumbrell (*op. cit.*, p. 189) read "Gebal, Ammon and Ammalek" with MT, LXX and Vulg. The Syr. (*tḥwmʾ dʿmwn*) interprets גבל as the "region, border" of Ammon. Dahood is nearer the truth in his rendition: "Byblos and with it Amalek," though his

attempt to explain the form is unduly complex. It is sufficient to note that *ʿmn* appears as a ballast variant or emphatic form of the preposition *ʿm* in UT:ʿnt:III:21-22, *tant šmm ʿm arṣ / thmt ʿmn kbkbm*, "the meeting of heaven with the nether world, of the deep with the stars" (Dahood, *Psalms II*, p. 275). Cf. also UT:1083:3-5. Ugaritic preserves a series of paired prepositions: *b/bn, bʿd/bʿdn, l/ln* as well as *ʿm/ʿmn*. Charles Krahmalkov ["Studies in Amorite Grammar" (Harvard Ph.D. thesis, 1965), pp. 58-61] has discussed *ʿmn* at length, which he vocalized **ʿimmun*. The key to the translation here is to note the chiastic arrangement within this strophe. A listing of three successive place names in this colon would destroy the poetic balance and the geographic chiasm. Beginning east of the Jordan, the poet looked first north to Moab and the Hagrites and then south to Edom and the Ishmaelites. Then turning to Cis-Jordan, the poet paired Byblos and Tyre (as Ezekiel does in ch. 27: 8-9) and Amalek and Philistia in poetic chiasm, moving from north to south and then south to north. The more traditional pairing of Philistia and Tyre is also retained in the second bicolon. Amalek is also parallel to the Hagrites and the Ishmaelites in the previous two cola and hence ties together the two bicola.

[j]The term כסיסרא is omitted as a secondary gloss which destroys the poetic balance of this bicolon. If retained, the verse would be scanned as 7:4:7 with the omitted phrase connecting both cola (cf. vs. 18 below). However, such a possibility is not likely here as the term does not fit equally well with either colon.

[k]The traditional interpretation of בעין דאר, "at En-dor," has little "historical or geographical propriety," to use the words of Dahood (*Psalms II*, p. 275). One can press the fact that traditional En-dor is at least in the geographical vicinity of the rout of Jabin and Sisera (Judg. 4-5) and of Gideon's decisive victory over the Midianites (Judg. 6-7). But nowhere is En-dor in anyway associated with these two events. Dahood's attempt to explain the term here as a parallel to עין אדם, "surface of the earth," in Zech. 9:1 is accepted with some hesitation [see M. Dahood, "Zacharia 9,1, *ʿên ʾĀdām*," *CBQ* 25 (1963), pp. 123-24].

[l]Reading enclitic *mem* for grammatically dubious pointing of MT, with Dahood (*Psalms II*, p. 276).

[m]Omitting וכזבח וכצלמנע as a secondary gloss or possibly a poetic doublet which disturbs the metrical balance of the bicolon.

[n]Repointing the grammatically dubious pointing of MT as the imperative with the third person masculine plural suffix.

[o]MT as it stands gives poor poetic balance yielding an 8:6 syllable count. Exchanging the two words yields better metrical balance and improves the poetic image as well. The "tumbleweed" is associated with the "wind" (cf. Isa. 17:13) whereas the "chaff" is not only driven by the wind (cf. Isa. 40:24;

41:2; Jer. 13:24), but also as "stubble" is burned (cf. Exod. 15:7; Isa. 5:24; 47:14; Nah. 1:10; Joel 2:5; so in metaphor in Isa. 33:11; Obad. 18; Nah. 3:19). Both aspects, destruction by wind and fire, are expanded in the remaining cola of this strophe.

[p]Again the metrical balance is improved by exchanging the paired words. For an interesting example of such confusion of paired words in poetic transmission see p. 61, n. c above.

[q]Taking the *tqtl* verbal forms in a jussive sense with Dahood (*Psalms II*, p. 276-77) and noting that the t-form of the verb is used here in a stylistic manner for emphasis.

[r]Repointing MT *wîbaqq*^{e}*šû šim*^{e}*kā* as a singular verbal form taken in a jussive sense. Dahood (*Psalms II*, p. 277) has noted that the root *bqš* denotes "to exact penalty, avenge" in Gen. 31:39; Isa. 1:12 and Josh. 22:23 [where it is used absolutely, as in the present context, with Yahweh the subject: *yhwh hûʾ y*^{e}*baqqēš*, "May the LORD himself take vengeance" (RSV)].

[s]As noted by Freedman (see Dahood, *Psalms II*, p. 277), the phrase עדי עד connects with both cola to form a poetic unit of 8:3:8 syllable count. For a discussion and list of texts exhibiting this prosodic pattern see Dahood, *Psalms II*, pp. 51-52.

[t]Taking שמך and אתה as poetic variants both of which are included in MT.

Psalm 83 in Outline

A. The Complaint: Israel is Threatened (vss. 2-9)

1. Your enemies have conspired to destroy Israel. (vss. 2-5)

[1:1] O Yahweh, vindicate yourself!
[1:1::1:1] Your enemies have conspired against your people.
[1:1] They have agreed to destroy Israel.

2. They have assembled in force. (vss. 6-9)

[1:1] They have formed a military alliance.
[1:1::1:1] From north to south they have assembled.
[1:1] Assyria, too, has joined them.

B. The Prayer: A Plea to the Divine Warrior (vss. 10-19)

[1:1::1:1::1:1] Destroy them as you did Midian! (vss. 10-12)
[1:1::1:1::1:1] Consume them with your fury! (vss. 14-16)
[1:1::1:b:1::1:1] Wreak vengeance upon them, O Yahweh! (vss. 17-19)

The poetic structure of Psalm 83, as revealed by the above prosodic-textual analysis, is indeed striking. The poem falls into two major divisions which display carefully balanced internal structure. The first division (vss. 2-9) portrays the complaint -- Israel's very existence is threatened by a military coalition. Two carefully balanced strophes present the nature of the conspiracy, introduced by a plea to Yahweh to vindicate himself.

The rhetorical device known as poetic inclusion (*inclusio*), in which the first concept in a series of poetic concepts or units is restated in the final poetic unit, is used throughout the poem. In the third strophe (vss. 10-12) Midian is mentioned in the first line referring to Gideon's battle as recorded in Judges 6-7. In parallel with Gideon is Jabin, a reference to Deborah's battle against the Canaanites in Judges 4-5. The reference to Oreb and Zeeb in the final bicolon (vs. 12) picks up the reference to Midian of the first colon to form an inclusion. The fourth strophe (vss. 14-16) is similar in structure with the wind of judgment in the first bicolon appearing again in the third. The final strophe (vss. 17-19) continues and expands the same poetic feature. The opening bicolon (vs. 17) is not the normal *parallelismus membrorum* with two balanced cola. Instead the first colon is expanded in the second bicolon (vs. 18), while the second colon is expanded in the third bicolon (vs. 19) to form, not only an *inclusio* within the poetic strophe, but for the entire poem as well -- for the final colon (vs. 19b) is parallel to the opening colon of the entire poem in verse 2a.

On the basis of the observed use of the phenomenon of poetic inclusion, one can conclude that the dominant party in the conspiracy is Moab, which, in the inclusion of the second strophe (vs. 9b), is designated one of "Lot's children." Dahood's statement that Moab and Edom constitute "Lot's children" is not entirely correct.[8] Moab and Ammon are the traditional children of Lot; and nowhere is Edom so designated. In league with Moab is Edom and various Arab tribal groups (Hagrites, Ishmaelites and Amalekites) of the east and south. Philistia and Phoenicia are also involved in the conspiracy; whereas the shadow of Assyrian might, the real threat, darkens the plot still further.

It is not possible to date the historical situation recalled in this poem with any degree of certainty. Suggested dates range from the time of Samuel to the Maccabean wars. Mazar has argued the "Psalm 83 (is) one of the earliest psalms, which can be assigned to the end of the period of the Judges, in any event to a time prior to the westward expansion of the Arameans."[9] The absence of Aram from the list of nations, however, must be balanced over against the reference to Assyria. As Dumbrell has noted: "the mention of Assyria as a foe could not be consonant with such an early dating, while friendly relations with Tyre seem to have been maintained until the Amos period."[10] Basing his argument primarily on the Arab groups mentioned, Dumbrell

---

[8] M. Dahood, *Psalms II, 51-100* (AB 17; Garden City, New York: Doubleday & Company, 1968), p. 275.

[9] B. Mazar, "The Historical Background of the Book of Genesis," *JNES* 28 (1969), pp. 79-80.

[10] W. Dumbrell, "The Midianites," p. 190.

posits a date of *ca.* 750-722, "the Amos period."[11] Landes in his discussion of Ammon and Moab also dated this psalm to the 8th century, though a 9th century date is also possible.[12]

If the lament over Moab preserved in Isaiah 15-16 was originally composed in the 9th century,[13] then it may be that the Chronicler's account of Jehoshaphat's war against Moab and her allies (II Chron. 20:1-30) must be taken seriously. Most commentators today reject the older view advanced by Wellhausen, Kautzsch and others that this story is merely a recasting of II Kings 3.[14] Since the latter battle took place in *ca.* 849, the battle recorded by the Chronicler must be placed earlier in the reign of Jehoshaphat (*ca.* 873-849). According to the Mesha stela: "Omri . . . humbled Moab many years, for Chemosh was angry at his land. And his son followed him and he also said, 'I will humble Moab.' . . . but I have triumphed over him and over his house."[15] Mesha then recounts the reconquest of Transjordan north of the Arnon. It should be noted that the only mention of southern Moab on the Mesha stela is is at the very end of the inscription which concerns a war against Horonaim which, according to Aharoni and Avi-Yonah, "is probably the war mentioned in 2 Kings 3."[16] It is certainly possible to place the destruction of southern Moab, as reflected in Isaiah 15-16, early in the reign of Jehoshaphat, i.e. *ca.* 870, before Omri's conquest of Transjordan north of the Arnon.

Psalm 83 may reflect this same historical situation (*ca.* 870). The coalition of nations opposing Judah/Israel is dominated by Moab and is made up primarily of southern peoples (Edomites, Hagrites, Ishmaelites and Amalekites). According to the Chronicler, the coalition included "Moabites and Ammonites, with some of the Meunites" (II Chron. 20:1) who are also called "the mountain folk of Seir" (II Chron. 20:10,22). As the former kingdom of Edom was still considered a province of Judah in the time of Jehoshaphat (I Kings 22:47) and did not achieve its independence until the reign of Jehoram (*ca.* 849-842),[17] the mention of "mountain folk of Seir" and the apparent breakup of the coalition (II Chron. 20:23) in which the "Edomites" destroyed Moab and Ammon, becomes understandable. At least for the moment "Edom" remained in the Judean fold.

---

[11] *Ibid.*, pp. 190 and 221, n. 45.

[12] G. Landes, " A History of the Ammonites" (1956), pp. 349-61.

[13] As Albright has suggested in *Yahweh and the Gods of Canaan* (1968), pp. 23-24, n. 57.

[14] See Jacob M. Myers, *II Chronicles* (AB 13; Garden City, New York: Doubleday & Company, 1965), p. 114.

[15] See *ANET*^{2}, p. 320.

[16] Y. Aharoni and M. Avi-Yonah, *The Macmillan Bible Atlas*, p. 84.

[17] Cf. II Kings 8:20-22.

One further bit of information completes the picture. According to the annals of Ashurnasirpal II (883-859) the Assyrians marched west to the Mediterranean Sea ("the Great Sea of the Amurru country").[18] Among those presenting tribute to the Assyrian king were Tyre, Sidon and Byblos. Aram-Damascus, Israel and Judah were not mentioned as Ashurnasirpal had "seized the entire extent of the Lebanon mountain" leaving the rest of Palestine to subsequent campaigns. It is already known that Omri, king of Israel (*ca.* 876-869), after four years of bitter civil war, became a vigorous and capable ruler and must be regarded as one of the greatest kings of Israel. He established friendly relations with Judah, cemented by a marriage between the two royal houses, and may well have achieved some success against Aram.[19] In this regard it should be noted that a few years earlier Ben-hadad I had hearkened to the appeal of Asa king of Judah in a border conflict between Judah and Israel. At any rate, in the face of external threat on the part of Assyria; Israel, Judah and Aram apparently stood together in *ca.* 870, foreshadowing the larger Palestinian coalition that was to meet Shalmaneser III at Qarqar in 853. If Assyria wished to prevent such a coalition from taking shape, the natural course would have been for her to use her own allies in an attempt to remove Judah from the incipient coalition. In this regard the Assyrian monarch was apparently successful. Neither Judah nor the peoples mentioned in the coalition of Psalm 83 are included in the list of allied kings at Qarqar in the Assyrian records, even though contingents came from Israel, Ammon, Gindibu of Arabia, and possibly from Egypt (*Muṣri*).[20]

Psalm 83 is important because it illustrates one of the cultic settings which produced poetry in ancient Israel which was concerned with foreign nations. Israel was threatened by a league of nations which had formed a military alliance against her. Most of these nations were once part of the "Davidic League" and hence their action against Judah could be seen as a covenant violation and thus subject to divine judgment.[21] Nonetheless, it should be

---

[18]See *ANET*^{2}, p. 276.

[19]So argues H. B. MacLean, "King Omri," *IDB* (1962), III, p. 601.

[20]See Aharoni and Avi-Yonah, *The Macmillan Bible Atlas*, p. 81.

[21]Cf. Howard Macy, "The Legal Metaphor in Oracles Against Foreign Nations" (see p. 14, n. 60 above), who has shown that the theme of covenant violation as cause for judgment on foreign nations can be traced within the OAN tradition. See also Delbert R. Hillers, *Treaty-Curses and the Old Testament Prophets* (Biblica et Orientalia 16; Rome: Pontifical Biblical Institute, 1964); who demonstrated the linguistic affinity between treaty curses in the ancient Near East and the OAN corpus. Violation of international treaty relationships, whether real or idealized, did form a legal basis for oracles against foreign nations.

noted that the dominant motifs of Psalm 83 are not so much rooted in legal traditions as they are in the literary traditions of holy warware as celebrated in the pre-monarchical cultus of the Covenant League of ancient Israel.

Gideon's battle against the Midianites is cited in parallel with the war against the Canaanites of the time of Deborah. In both cases the focus is on Yahweh, the Divine Warrior, who consumed his enemies with the fire of his wrath (Ps. 83:15) and pursued them with the devastating might of the storm-wind (סופה/סער; Ps. 83:16). The motifs of fire and the storm-wind as agents of Yahweh's consuming wrath stem originally from the most ancient Israelite war poetry where the Divine Warrior destroyed his enemies as he led his people from his holy mountain in southern Palestine to possess the land of promise in the Exodus-Conquest.[22]

Traditions of holy war were preserved within the Jerusalem temple cult as well as in various prophetic circles in ancient Israel. One of the major carriers of holy war traditions in the period of the monarchy was the Royal Fall Festival. William Millar has reconstructed, in broad outline, this ancient annual festival as follows:[23]

1) A ritual conquest in which the Divine Warrior defeated the forces of Chaos.
2) A procession of the Ark to the temple in Jerusalem as Yahweh returned from battle as the victorious king.
3) A victory feast on Mount Zion consisting of sacrifices and ritual banqueting.

War songs and laments were used particularly in the first aspect of this cultic celebration -- the ritual conquest. As both the institution of kingship and the temple cultus itself were of Canaanite origin, ancient mythic language and concepts found entrance into Israel's worship in the Royal Fall Festival, along with the epic traditions from Israel's Covenant League. In the Royal Fall Festival as celebrated in Jerusalem, the ancient celebration of Yahweh's Holy War of the Exodus-Conquest was reshaped to incorporate the institutions of kingship and temple.

Psalm 83, though originally composed for an *ad hoc* cultic ceremony in time of war, is in the literary form of a community lament. As such it also reflects, in part, some of the major themes incorporated into the cultic celebration of the Royal Fall Festival in ancient Israel. Yahweh is portrayed, on the one hand, as the Divine Warrior of the Exodus-Conquest (Ps. 83:10-16);

---

[22]On the motif of fire in ancient war poetry see Patrick D. Miller, Jr., "Fire in the Mythology of Canaan and Israel," *CBQ* 27 (1965), pp. 256-61.

[23]William R. Millar, "Isaiah 24-27 and the Origin of Apocalyptic" (unpub. Ph.D. thesis, Harvard University, 1970), pp. 174-76.

but he is also El Elyon (Ps. 83:2,19), the Exalted One, the Most High, the father of all gods and lord of heaven and storm -- the king of the gods. In this regard it is interesting to note the textual variant of the manuscript from Masada where אהלי ("tents") of MT is rendered אלהי ("gods" of Edom, Moab, etc.).[24] A simple metathesis is no doubt the mechanical reason for the variant reading; but it should be noted that either reading makes sense within the context of the ancient Royal Fall Festival. The king of Israel is Yahweh's representative among the nations who, in this instance, have joined forces to destroy Israel. The Divine Warrior is summoned to battle, as in times past, that his name might be vindicated and his enemies destroyed, whether these enemies are understood in the concrete sense as the nations mentioned, or in the abstract sense as personified in their gods.

In some respects Psalm 60 is of even greater importance than Psalm 83 in the study of the war oracle and the development of the OAN tradition in ancient Israel. It not only contains a specific war oracle against Moab, Edom and Philistia (Ps. 60:8-10 = 108:8-10); it also introduces the concept of the "cup of Yahweh's wrath" which becomes an important feature of the OAN tradition of Jeremiah and other prophets in the late 7th and 6th centuries B.C.

Psalm 60:3-14 (cf. Psalm 108:6-13)

3	O God --	אלהים	
	You have rejected us, you broke forth upon us;	זנחתנו פרצתנו[a]	8
	You were wrathful, you turned away from us.	אנפת תשובב לנו	8
4	You shook the land and destroyed it;	הרעשתה ארץ פ-צָמַתָּה[b]	8
	. . . . . ? . . it tottered.	רפה שבריה [][c] מטה	8
5	You made your people drain the chalice;	הר<ו>יתה[d] עמך קשה[e]	8
	You made us drink wine that dazed us.	השקיתנו יין תרעלה	8
6	You have given a banner for those who fear you,	נתתה[f] ליראיך נס	9
	To which to rally at the presence of the bowmen.	להתנוסס מפני קשט[g]	9/8
	Selah.	סלה	
7	That your beloved may be delivered,	למען יחלצון ידידך[h]	10
	Save with your right hand! Grant us triumph!	הרשיעה ימינך []ענגו[i]	10
8	Yahweh spoke from his sanctuary:	<יהוה>[j] דבר בקדשו	7
	With exultation I will divide up Shechem;	אעלזה אחלקה שכם	7
	The Valley of Succoth I will measure off.	ועמק סכות אמדד	7
9	Gilead is mine, Manasseh is mine,	לי גלעד []לי[k] מנשה	7
	And Ephraim is my helmet;	ואפרים מעוז ראשי	7
	Judah is my commander's staff.	יהודה מחקקי	7

[24] See Y. Yadin, "The Excavation of Masada," *IEJ* 15 (1965), p. 104.

10	Moab will be my wash pot;	מואב סיר רחצי ⟨יהיה⟩[l]	7
	Upon Edom I will cast my sandal;	על אדום אשליך נעלי[m]	7
	Over Philistia I will give a cry of conquest.	עלי פלשת ⟨א⟩תרעע[n]	7
11	Would that he would bring me to the citadel of Tyre!	מי יבלני עיר-מ[o] צור	8
	Would that he would lead me as far as Aram!	מי ⟨י⟩נחני[p] עד א[ר]ם[q]	8
12	Will you still spurn us?	הלא אתה [][r] זנחתנו	8
	Will you go forth no more with our armies?	[]לא תצא [][r] בצבאותינו	8
13	Grant us help against the adversary,	הב[][s] לנו עזרת מצר	7
	For futile is the victory of man.	ושוא תשועת אדם	7
14	With Yahweh we will achieve might;	ב⟨יהוה⟩[j] נעשה חיל	6
	He himself will trample on our adversaries.	[]הוא יבוס צרינו	6

<u>Notes to the Text of Psalm 60:3-14</u>

[a]Dahood (*Psalms II*, p. 75) renders *znḥ*, "to be angry," in parallel with *ʾnp*, "to be wrathful," in the following colon. This interpretation is based, in part, on his rendition of פרצתנו as the conjuntion p^e followed by רצתנו, "you ran from us," in parallel with תשובב לנו, "you turned away from us." This interpretation is indeed ingenius and has some external support. In Job 16:14 the root *rwṣ*, "to run," is predicated to God who "rushes . . . like a warrior" [so M. Pope, *Job* (AB 15, 1965), p. 115]. Nonetheless, one should note that in this particular passage, as elsewhere, the Divine Warrior is "charging . . . like a warrior" in battle [so A. Blommerde, *Northwest Semitic Grammar and Job* (Rome, 1969), p. 78], not fleeing from the scene of battle. It is preferable to see a poetic chiasm here with *znḥ* in parallel with *šwb* and *prṣ* with *ʾnp*. One should also note that זנחתנו occurs again in vs. 12 where it is in parallel with the Divine Warrior absenting himself from the armies of Israel. The phrase תשובב לנו has an apt parallel in UT:2 Aqht:VI: 42, *t̲b ly*, "Turn away from me," as translated by W. F. Albright in *BASOR* 94 (1944), p. 34, n. 22. The intransitive use of Polel שבב appears also in Jer. 8:5, "Why does this people turn away?"

[b]Dahood's reconstruction of פצמתה, a hapax legomenon in MT of uncertain meaning, as the verbal root *ṣmt*, "to destroy, annihilate," preceded by the conjunction p^e is persuasive (cf. Ugar. where *ṣmt* is used in parallel with *mhṣ*).

[c]Dahood (*Psalms II*, p. 78) argues that רפה שבריה should be rendered "weak from its fractures." Such a reading is problematic in that the construct state would be expected, reading perhaps רפת for רפה. It seems best to stress the uncertainty in the interpretation of the first two words. The כי is omitted as a prosaic addition to the text perhaps resulting from an

early misreading of the feminine substantive רפה as the imp rative *rᵉpāʾ*, "Heal!"

[d]The emendation suggested does not indicate scribal confusion between *ʾaleph* and *waw* but rather the variant usage of internal vowel letters. The confusion of the roots *rʾh* and *rwh*, found elsewhere in the OAN material, served to complicate the picture even more (cf. Job 21:20). Dahood suggests the root *yrʾ* II, "to drink deeply," but the existence of this root is problematic. The root *rwh*, "to be saturated, drink one's fill," is clearly attested and is preferred here.

[e]MT *qāšāh* is interpreted, with Dahood (*Psalms II*, p. 78), as the accusative of *qš*, "chalice," found in UT:ʿnt:V:41-42, *klnyy qšh nbln / klnyy nbl ksh*, "All of us carry his chalice, all of us carry his cup." The uncommon poetic equivalent of *ks*, "cup," was apparently used here to form poetic assonance with the following verb *hišqîtānû*, "You made us drink." The motif of the "cup of Yahweh's wrath" proffered to the nations in judgment is an important motif in the OAN tradition of Jeremiah.

[f]Dahood reads a precative perfect, with full writing of the final syllable *-āh* which he suggests may correspond to the energic ending of the imperative (cf. *Psalms II*, p. 79 and *Psalms I*, p. 26). Kraus (BK 15/1, p. 426), Bardtke (*BHS* 11, p. 55) and others suggest that the text be emended to read either *tᵉnāh* or *tēnāh* with imperative force. Interpreting the *nēs* as an object by which Yahweh has proven his might in times past, a symbol of the presence of the Divine Warrior in battle which was to be erected within the institution of holy war, it seems preferable to render the verbal force as perfect, with the recent translation of the Bible made under the auspices of the Catholic Biblical Association (the so-called Confraternity Bible). On the meaning of the term *nēs* see Tur-Sinai, "Lachish Letter IV," *JQR* 39 N.S. (1948-49), p. 367. For a detailed discussion of banners and their uses in the Qumran texts see Y. Yadin, *The Scroll of the War of the Sons of Light* (Oxford, 1962), pp. 38-64.

[g]Dahood (*Psalms II*, p. 79) reads the hapax legomenon *qōšeṭ* as an abstract form, "archery," here understood concretely. It is also possible to repoint the word as an agent noun, reading *qāššaṭ* (cf. *qāššat* in Gen. 21:20) or perhaps *qōšeṭ*. The additional syllable in these latter alternatives would strengthen the metrical balance of the bicolon. The final *ṭ* may have resulted from the partial assimilation to emphatic *qoph* [cf. the partial assimilation in UT:1005:4; 1010:14, *ṣṭq* (=*ṣdq*) *šlm*] or it may be explained as an Aramaic back-formation (cf. Syr. *qaššātâ*, "archer, bowman").

[h]The term *ydd* occurs in the Ugaritic literature in the phrase *ydd il ġzr*, "beloved of ʾEl, the hero" (UT:49:VI:30-31; 51:VII:46-47 and elsewhere) and as an epithet of the god Mot (UT:67:III:10). Professor Cross has called my attention to an unpublished Ugaritic text now in the possession of Patrick

Miller where *ydd* is used of a dead man who is honored in a cultic banquet. There is no need to see an allusion here to King Solomon, as Dahood has suggested (*Psalms II*, p. 76).

[i]The *waw* is dropped to improve metrical balance. The root *ʿnw*, "to triimph," is attested in Phoenician Karatepe 1:18, *wʿn ʾnk ʾrṣt ʿzt*, "And I conquered powerful lands," and in several biblical occurrences. See Dahood (*Psalms I*, p. 116) for examples and references to literature.

[j]Psalm 60 appears in the Elohistic section of the Psalter. The substitution of the more original term Yahweh improves the metrical balance.

[k]The *waw* is omitted with the parallel passage in Ps. 108:9 and a few Hebrew MSS of the psalm in question.

[l]The line is too short. Kraus [BK 15/1 (1960), p. 427] has suggested an haplography from either מחקקי ⟨ים⟩ מואב or ⟨מי⟩ מואב. Professor Cross, in private consultation, argued that neither emendation is satisfactory. It is Moab, not the waters or sea of Moab, that is the focus of attention. Cross suggested the possibility of a vertical haplography due to the similarity between יהודה and יהיה. It seems preferable to follow the word order of a parallel passage in Zeph. 2:9, where the verb *tihyeh* occurs with Moab in order to form a balanced poetic bicolon. The verb is understood in the two previous cola and its omission here gave a superficial formal balance between three successive lines beginning with Ephraim, Judah and Moab respectively.

[m]The image here is apparently that of taking legal possession of the land of Edom. R. de Vaux argued that: "The shoe seems to have served as a probative instrument in transfers of land: in Ps 60:10=108:10, the phrase 'over Edom I cast my sandal' implies taking possession" [*Ancient Israel* (New York: McGraw-Hill, 1961), p. 169]. See also E. A. Speiser, "Of Shoes and Shekels," *BASOR* 77 (1940), pp. 15-20; who follows Koschaker in regarding shoes as token payment to validate special transactions in the Nuzi texts.

[n]Following the parallel passage in Ps. 108:10 which renders better metrical balance.

[o]Reading *mem* enclitic with Dahood (*Psalms II*, p. 81) but interpreting צור as Tyre, rather than the dubious "Rock City" (=Sela/Petra).

[p]Dahood, citing literature from 1879 through 1967, argues that it is not necessary to assume the haplography of a *yodh*, "because there is ample evidence that two like consonants were sometimes written as one, that is, when the same consonant ended one word and began the next, it was sometimes written but once" (*Psalms II*, p. 81). See also W. Watson, "Shared Consonants in Northwest Semitic," *Bib* 50 (1969), pp. 525-33; and "More on Shared Consonants," *Bib* 52 (1971), pp. 44-50. As this circumstance is perhaps the most likely situation for an haplography to cccur and since there is no way to determine that a scribal haplography did not in fact occur, it seems rather presumptuous to formulate a grammatical rule with J. O. Lehman [*JNES* 26 (1967), p. 93]

who describes this phenomenon as "the textual ambivalence of Hebrew consonants." It is preferable to reconstruct the text in the manner in which scholarly consensus agrees it must be understood when that reconstruction involves the most elementary of scribal errors of transmission.

[q]Reading ארם for אדום. A reference to Edom here makes little sense after vs. 10 where Edom is listed with Moab and Philistia in the war oracle proper. The reading of Tyre and Aram in this verse fills out the roll call of the member nations of David's empire. The confusion of Aram/Edom occurs elsewhere in the biblical text (cf. II Sam. 8:13; II Chron. 20:2 and Ps. 60:2, at least according to BDB, p. 10b).

[r]The divine name אלהים has been added to the text, perhaps by the Elohistic editor of this section of the Psalter, to specify the identity of the person addressed.

[s]The shorter form of the verbal imperative is used to improve the metrical balance at the suggestion of Professor Cross.

Psalm 60:3-14 in Outline

A. The Complaint: You have forsaken your people. (vss. 3-5)
  [1:1] You have turned from us in anger.
  [1:1] You destroyed the land.
  [1:1] You made us drink the "Cup of Wrath."

B. The Request: Return to us as in times past. (vss. 6-7)
  [1:1] You have given us a rallying signal for battle.
  [1:1] Now fight for us!

C. The Divine Oracle (vss. 8-10)
  [1:1:1] I will reapportion Shechem/Succoth.
  [1:1:1] All of "Israel" belongs to me.
  [1:1:1] Moab, Edom and Philistia will fall again.

D. The Request Continued (vs. 11)
  [1:1] Would that Tyre and Aram would be included as well!

E. Summation (vss. 12-14)
  [1:1] Complaint: Will you continue to absent yourself?
  [1:1] Request: Deliver us from our enemies!
  [1:1] Oracle: Yahweh will vanquish our foes.

In its present form Psalm 60 is a national lament in which the community prays for deliverance from its adversaries. It may well be that the psalm is composite as suggested by Briggs who argued that the war oracle in vss. 8-10 "is undoubtedly ancient and might go back to the time of David."[25] Perhaps

[25]See Charles A. Briggs and Emilie G. Briggs, *A Critical and Exegetical*

the strongest argument for an early dating of this oracle is its content. The picture presented is that of the Exodus-Conquest or of the United Monarchy. In vs. 8 Shechem stands for Israel west of the Jordan and the Valley of Succoth for Israelite territory in Transjordan. Yahweh will apportion all of Israel among his people. Transjordan is then broken down further into Gilead and Manasseh (vs. 9a) and Cisjordan into Ephraim and Judah (vs. 9bc), while Judah is given the position of prominance. The picture is not the Davidic Empire in its entirety, however, for Moab, Edom and Philistia are yet to be subdued and there is no mention of Aram, Hamath, Tyre and Ammon.[26]

When the psalm as a whole is analyzed, other archaic features become evident. The *pᵉ* conjunction (vs. 4) and the enclitic *mem* (vs. 11) are early grammatical features which led to subsequent misunderstanding of the text. The usage of the temms *yᵉdîdekā,* "your beloved" (vs. 7), and *qš(h)*, "chalice" (vs. 5) have their clearest parallels in Ugaritic material and hence suggest either an early date or perhaps the time of the recrudescence of Canaanite mythological terminology in the 7th or 6th centuries.[27]

The dominant motifs of the psalm reflect the institution of holy warfare in ancient Israel. The complaint voiced by the community is that the Divine Warrior who led the armies of Israel in the battles of the Exodus-Conquest has now forsaken his people; and, in fact, has turned in wrath on them. The portrayal of Israel's defeat in vs. 4 is almost apocalyptic in nature,[28] but one should not jump to conclusions of late date on this score alone. The shaking of the land in a violent earthquake is a motif much at home in the war songs of the Exodus-Conquest and premonarchical Covenant League. The banner (*nēs*) of Yahweh, the symbol par excellence of the Divine Warrior in holy warfare in times past,[29] is now impotent. Israel has drunk the wine offered her and is staggering, helpless before her foes. It is this motif of the "cup of Yahweh's wrath" which provides the most helpful clue for the dating of this poem.

Commentary on the Book of Psalms, vol. II (ICC; New York: Charles Scribner's Sons, 1907), p. 59. Note the superscription in Ps. 60:1-2 which ascribes this poem to a specific battle setting in the Davidic period and the fact that the oracle displays poetic features that set it off as distinct from the series of bicola which precede and follow it.

[26]Unless Moab subsumes Ammon as well, as is sometimes the case elsewhere in the OAN tradition.

[27]Cf. notes e and h on pp. 122-23 above.

[28]As noted in *The Jerusalem Bible* (Garden City, New York: Doubleday & Company, 1966), p. 841.

[29]Cf. the phrase יהוה נסי, "Yahweh is my battle rallying point" (Exod. 17:15), regardless of what this cryptic expression had meant in its original usage; see the discussion above, pp. 47-48.

As a motif within the prophetic OAN tradition the cup of Yahweh's wrath, proffered to the nations in judgment, cannot be traced back earlier than the closing decades of the 7th century. The resurgence of Judah under King Josiah (*ca.* 640/39-609/8) may well be the historical setting which produced this important literary motif. If our reconstruction of Ps. 60:11 is correct with its reference to Tyre and Aram, this poem probably reflects the era of political expansion in Judah under Josiah, *ca.* 630-620. The war oracle as such in vss. 8-10 may be the reuse of earlier material. In its present setting the roll call of nations is filled out in terms of the idealized Davidic Empire. The assured victory over Moab, Edom and Philistia formed the heart of Josiah's political expansion. His dream, however, was the full restoration of David's empire with political suzerainty over Tyre and Aram as well.

The War Oracle in Pre-Exilic OAN Tradition

The formal collections of OAN material in Amos 1-2 and Jeremiah 46-51 are the natural foci in any analysis of prophetic oracles against foreign nations in the Old Testament. These two collections are relatively easy to control in respect to historical setting and textual reconstruction. Moreover, they constitute the two central poles in the development of prophecy itself as an historical phenomenon in ancient Israel. Amos was the first of the classical "writing prophets" whereas Jeremiah witnessed the destruction of both the institutions of temple and kingship in Jerusalem and hence reflects the transitional period from classical prophecy to what eventually became apocalyptic.

The century from the Syro-Ephraimite crisis in 734-733 to the resurgence of Judah under Josiah saw many profound changes in ancient Israel, changes which in part are reflected in the use of the prophetic war oracle. An attempt will be made here to trace the prophetic war oracle from the confrontation of Isaiah and Ahaz in 734 to the last quarter of the 7th century which saw the fall of Assyria before the emergent Neo-Babylonian Empire.

1. Isaiah

When Ahaz of Judah faced the coalition of Aram-Damascus and Israel, who were intent on forcing Judah to join with them against Assyria, Isaiah confronted the king with an oracle which may be reconstructed as follows (Isa. 7:7-9):

7	Thus saith the Lord Yahweh:		כה אמר אדני יהוה
	It shall not stand;	3	לא תקום
	It shall not come to pass.	3	[ ]לא תהיה
8	Indeed, the head of Aram is Damascus,	6	כי ראש ארם דמשק
	And the head of Damascus is Rezin.	6	וראש דמשק רצין

[Within 65 years Ephraim will be broken to pieces so that it will no longer be a people.]

9 The head of Ephraim is Samaria, — []ראש אפרים שמרון 6

And the head of Samaria is ⟨Pekah⟩.[30] — וראש שמרון ⟨פקח⟩ 6

[If you will not believe, surely you shall not be established.]

In its present form the oracle is but a torso of the original oral composition. As some scholars have noted, the climax of the oracle should focus on Judah and Jerusalem and, perhaps, can be reconstructed as follows:[31]

The head of Judah is Jerusalem; — ראש יהודה ירושלים 8

Indeed, the head of Jerusalem is Yahweh. — כי ראש ירושלים יהוה 8

The inference is that Aram-Damascus and Ephraim are but human foe who have dared to oppose Yahweh, the Divine Warrior.

The prose setting which introduces the oracle contains several terms which reflect traditions of holy warfare in ancient Israel. Ahaz is portrayed in terms which in times past were used to describe the panic experienced by the foes of the Divine Warrior (vs. 2b): "his heart and the heart of his people shook as the trees of the forest shake before the wind." Ahaz was told to "Take heed, be quiet, do not fear (אל תירא), and do not let your heart be faint" (vs. 4). As Hayes has noted: "Is. 7:4 reflects the older Holy War attitudes of faith in the divine assurance of victory."[32]

In this instance the prophet Isaiah stands within the ancient tradition of prophetic responsibility in warfare. He gives the king assurance of Yahweh's presence and Israel's triumph in battle. It would appear that the prose setting as delineated in Isa. 7:1-6 is dependent on the earlier poetic oracle which was perhaps uttered before a larger audience, perhaps within the Jerusalem temple cult. The plural verbal forms in vs. 9b have sometimes been noted by scholars who argue that they "do not fit the context unless Isaiah is here addressing the house of David instead of Ahaz as an individual Davidic person."[33] The peculiar phrase, "When the house of David was told . . ." (Isa. 7:2), lends substance to this suggestion.

A further oracle against Aram-Damascus which can be dated to the early ministry of Isaiah appears in Isa. 17:1-6 and may be reconstructed as follows:

---

[30]Cf. Isa. 7:1. The emendation improves the metrical balance and forms a better parallel to the name Rezin in the previous bicolon.

[31]Cf. Herbert Donner, *Israel unter den Völkern* (SVT 11; Leiden: E. J. Brill, 1964), p. 14; and John Hayes, "Oracles Against the Nations," pp. 77-79, 195-96.

[32]J. Hayes, *op. cit.*, p. 77, n. 88.

[33]*Ibid.*, pp. 78-79, n. 92.

1	An oracle concerning Damascus:	משא דמשק	
	Look! Damascus is no longer a city!	הנה דמשק מוּסָר[a] מעיר	9
	She will become a heap of ruins;	והיתה מעי מפלה	9
2	Her cities are deserted forever.	עזבות עדי<ה>[b] ע[ד]<י> ע[ד][c]	9
	They shall be for flocks,	לעדרים תהיינה	7
	Which will lie down undisturbed.	ורבצו []אין מחריד	7
3	The fortress will disappear from Ephraim,	ונשבת מבצר מאפרים	8
	And the kingdom from Damascus.	וממלכה מדמשק	7
	[And the remnant of Aram will be	ושאר ארם [יהיו][d]	(7)
	like the glory of the children of Israel.]	ככבוד בני ישראל	(8)
	Utterance of Yahweh of hosts.	נאם יהוה צבאות	-
4	In that day the glory of Jacob will be brought low,	[][e] ביום []הוא ידל כבוד יעקב	9
	And the fat of his flesh will grow lean;	ומשמן בשרו ירזה	9
5	It will be as when the reaper gathers standing grain.	[י]היה[f] כאסף קצ[]ר[g] קמה	9
	His arm will harvest the ears,	[]זרעו שבלים יקצור	8
	As when one gleans the ears of grain.	[][h] כמלקט שבלים	7
	The Valley of Rephaim (will be) as when an olive tree is beaten;	[]עמק[i] רפאים [כנקף זית][j]	7
6	Gleanings will be left in it.	ונשאר בו עוללת	7
	Two or three pieces of fruit on the top-most branches;	שנים שלשה גרגרים בראש אמיר	12
	Four or five on the fruitful boughs.	ארבעה חמשה בסעפי[][k] פריה	13
	Utterance of Yahweh the God of Israel.	נאם יהוה אלהי ישראל	-

Notes to the Text of Isaiah 17:1-6

[a]Reading the feminine form מוסרה for מוסר with H. Donner, SVT 11 (1964), p. 39; who cites Duhm and Marti. The final *he* would not necessarily have appeared in the earliest orthography. The reading improves the meter as well.

[b]The passage is so interpreted in a number of modern translations; cf. RSV and Jerusalem Bible. Among the ancient versions cf. Targ.

[c]Reading with LXX εἰς τον αἰῶνα for the dubious עדי ערער of MT. Cf. also the Syriac which reads the place name Adoer.

[d]If this prosaic line is to be read as poetry, the verb should be placed here so as to achieve at least a semblance of poetic balance.

[e]Deleting והיה *metri causa*.

[f]Reading the imperfect *yihyeh* for MT *w*[e]*hāyāh* to improve the meter.

[g]Reading the agent noun *qōṣēr*, "reaper," for *qāṣîr*, "harvesting, harvest," as sense requires.

[h]Deleting והיה *metri causa*.

[i]Deleting the *beth* with the relocation of כנקף זית in this line.

[j]This phrase apparently dropped out of the text and was incorrectly restored. The relocation has been suggested by a number of scholars and improves both the prosodic structure and meaning.

[k]Following 1QIsa[a] which reads בסעפי הפריה. The article would not have appeared in the original poetic composition.

<u>Isaiah 17:1-6 in Outline</u>

A. Oracle Against Aram-Damascus (vss. 1-3)

[1:1:1] Damascus will become a deserted ruin.
[1:1] Her cities will be the abode of shepherds.
[1:1] Fortress and kingdom shall fall.
[1:1] ? Aram will be no better off than Israel.

B. Oracle Against Israel (vss. 4-6)

[1:1:1] The glory of Jacob shall be brought low.
[1:1] The grim reaper stands ready.
[1:1] Only gleanings will remain in the Valley of Rephaim.
[1:1] The decimation will be complete.

The oracle consists of two fairly well balanced strophes which, in their present form, constitute an oracle of judgment directed against both Aram-Damascus and Jacob/Israel. No reason for the judgment is given. Damascus, perhaps already destroyed, will become the habitation of shepherds and their flocks -- deserted forever. Israel is like standing grain awaiting harvest, and the grim reaper stands ready. When he is finished only sparce gleanings will remain. The glory of Jacob -- here signifying what remains of Israel and perhaps Judah as well -- will be diminished even further. The Valley of Rephaim (vs. 5), the border region between Jerusalem and the northern kingdom, shall have but gleanings left in it (vs. 6). The historical situation reflected here is that of *ca.* 733-32, the destruction of Damascus at the hands of Tiglath-pileser III and all that that event portends for Israel.

In the present arrangement of the biblical text, the oracle against Damascus and Ephraim (Isa. 17:1-6) is grouped with two other fragmentary oracles, one of which is of interest for the present study. The "woe oracle" of Isa. 17:12-14 is sometimes entitled "The Roaring of the Nations."[34] Motifs and terminology from Israel's ancient holy war traditions are here directed against the nations who roar against Judah "like the roaring of many waters" (vs. 13). The Divine Warrior will rebuke them, he will chase them

---

[34]See G. Ernest Wright, *The Book of Isaiah* (LBC 11; Richmond, Virginia: John Knox Press, 1968), p. 58.

like chaff (מץ) before the wind (רוח), like tumbleweed (גלגל) before the storm-wind (סופה). Possible affinities with Canaanite mythology have been noted in this passage.[35] One should also note the affinities to Ps. 83:14-16, where much of the same imagery and terminology appears, and the dependence of both poems on the ancient war songs of Israel's Covenant League.

The rise of Assyria under Tiglath-pileser III presented a new impulse to the developing prophetic tradition in ancient Israel. John Holladay has argued that the change in international policy on the part of the Assyrians, beginning toward the end of the 9th century and culminating in the reign of Tiglath-pileser III, is paralleled by the rise of popular prophecy in ancient Israel.[36] Just as the Assyrian ambassadors shifted the focus of their concern from the individual rulers to the populace at large in their diplomatic relations with subject peoples, so the prophets in Israel changed their stance. No longer did the prophet address himself primarily to the king as such; his concern was now the entire populace -- the people of Israel.

In his presentation of "popular prophecy" Holladay has drawn too sharp a distinction between the pre-classical and classical prophets. He maintained that:[37]

> . . . with the lone exception of the most legendary sections of the Elijah-Elisha cycles, there is not one single indication of a prophetic oracle being delivered to anyone outside of the royal court prior to the time of Amos. Nor is there any indication that any of the pre-classical prophets uttered even one oracle against the whole nation or individual non-royal groups within the nation.

This is a bold statement and one that should not go unchallenged. Our study of the war oracle in ancient Israel reveals one example which does not fit Holladay's analysis, at least without some modification. When Rehoboam I marched north with the levy of the tribes of Judah and Benjamin against the northern tribes, he was confronted by the prophet Shemaiah who delivered an oracle "to Rehoboam . . . *and to the rest of the people*" (I Kings 12:23 -- emphasis mine). The oracle itself utilizes plural verbal forms and is clearly addressed to the troops under Rehoboam's command (cf. vs. 24). Shemaiah was challenging the king's right to summon the tribal levy to battle. It was the prophet alone who had the authority to summon the levy of all Israel in holy war. King Rehoboam had overstepped the bounds of his authority and was successfully checked by a prophet who clearly represented the *imperium* of

---

[35]See H. G. May, "Some Cosmic Connotations of MAYIM RABBIM, 'Many Waters,'" *JBL* 74 (1955), pp. 9-21.

[36]John S. Holladay, Jr., "Assyrian Statecraft and the Prophets of Israel," *HTR* 63 (1970), pp. 29-51.

[37]*Ibid.*, p. 35.

Yahweh in the eyes of the 180,000 warriors assembled from "all the house of Judah, and the tribe of Benjamin . . . to fight against the house of Israel" (I Kings 12:21).

It is hard to imagine that the prophets at any time in ancient Israel limited themselves only to the king in their administration of Yahweh's *imperium*. If war oracles could be uttered against foreign nations during the monarchy, they could also be uttered against Judah and Isael, just as in the premonarchical period war oracles were directed against the tribe of Benjamin (Judg. 19-20) and against Jabesh-gilead (Judg. 21:10-11), when these members of the Covenant League had violated the terms of the tribal confederation.[38]

With the rise of the monarchy in Israel the concept of the Covenant League was extended to embrace the member nations of David's empire. The legal backdrop of the idealized Davidic Empire as the basis for judging nations was still operative in Amos 1-2. There each nation was judged for its individual violation of the "covenant of brotherhood" (Amos 1:9). But with the rise of Assyria in the 8th century and the subsequent challenge from Egypt for political dominance in the ancient Near East, this model was no longer viable without modification. A new model was needed to form the legal basis for prophetic oracles against foreign nations. The Davidic ideal lived on, however, especially within the cultus of the Royal Fall Festival in Jerusalem and was to surface again in the time of Hezekiah (715-687) and especially Josiah (*ca*. 640-609) as the theological basis for the political expansion of Judah. The destruction of both kingship and temple at the hands of the Neo-Babylonian Empire in the 6th century served to transform this Davidic ideal into the messianic hope of the Exilic and post-Exilic eras.

The important contribution of Isaiah with respect to the developing OAN tradition was the incorporation of Assyria and Egypt/Ethiopia into the traditional roll call of the nations. The oracle against Arabia (Isa. 21:13-17) does not necessarily move beyond the Davidic ideal, as witnessed by the inclusion of Arab tribes within the roll call of nations in Psalm 83. These Arab groups in some cases were occupying land within the idealized boundaries of the Davidic Empire. Moreover, the agreements formulated between the Queen of Sheba and Solomon clearly placed Arabia within the sphere of influence of the United Monarchy. With Assyria and Egypt/Ethiopia no such rationalization was possible. A new model was needed and was found within the holy war traditions of ancient Israel, especially the war songs from the premonarchical era. The Divine Warrior was seen as the suzerain of all nations, the Lord of history, whose dominion knew no geographical bounds. Even mighty Assyria was but the "rod of Yahweh's anger" (שבט אפי) as the Divine Warrior chastened his people.

---

[38]Cf. also the battle curse directed against Meroz in the Song of Deborah (Judg. 5:23).

Once he was through using his unwitting servant, the Divine Warrior would vent his wrath against Assyria and punish "the arrogant boasting of the king of Assyria and his haughty pride" (Isa. 10:5-12).

The resurgence of Assyria in the last half of the 8th century was paralleled by a dramatic recovery on the part of Egypt (*ca.* 726-710) which eventually succumbed to invasion from the south and political subjugation to Ethiopia. Though these events in Egypt did not immediately threaten Judah, Isaiah incorporated them within his model of the nations under the suzerainty of Yahweh in a series of oracles (see Isa. 18-20; 30:1-17; 31:1-3). Yahweh, the Divine Warrior, comes riding upon the storm cloud to Egypt where the gods of Egypt tremble before him (ch. 19:1). It is Yahweh who stirs up Egyptians against Egyptians in the civil struggle (ch. 19:2). It is Yahweh who confounds their plans (19:3) and gives the Egyptians over into the hand of a hard master, a fierce king who will rule over them -- Pi'ankhi or perhaps his brother Shabaka who founded the Ethiopian Dynasty XXV in *ca.* 710. The judgment upon Egypt is portrayed in apocalyptic fashion as the Nile is dried up (19:5-10) and the traditional wisdom of Egypt's sages is turned into confusion such that Egypt staggers "as a drunken man staggers in his vomit" (19:11-15).

The oracle against Egypt in Isa. 19:1-15 was expanded in subsequent usage among the followers of the prophet. Already possessing trans-historical elements it was but a short step to lift the oracle to the realm of eschatology within the apocalyptic communities of the Exilic and post-Exilic eras. An altar (מזבח) and a pillar (מצבה) were to be erected in Egypt to Yahweh as a sign (אות) and witness (עד) to Yahweh's presence in Egypt. When Egypt cries to Yahweh for deliverance from her oppressors, Yahweh will send a savior (מושיע) who "will defend and deliver them" (Isa. 19:19-20). The picture presented here is indeed remarkable. Yahweh will one day send a Moses *redivivus* to deliver Egypt from bondage! Yahweh will reveal himself to the Egyptians who in turn will worship him (Isa. 19:22). Yahweh will build a highway from Egypt to Assyria and both the Egyptians and the Assyrians will be one with Israel in their worship of Yahweh in the restored land of promise (19:23-25). The climax of this apocalyptic vision is presented in a remarkable tricolon (Isa. 19:25):

Blessed be my people Egypt;	ברוך עמי מצרים	6
The work of my hands is Assyria;	[]מעשה ידי אשור	6
My heritage is Israel.	[]נחלתי ישראל	6

Themes from the visionary circles of proto-apocalyptic thought are brought together in these additions to Isaiah's oracle against Egypt -- in particular the new Exodus and the restoration of the land of promise for all nations under Yahweh, the Lord of history. The presence of these additions to the text in Isaiah 19 illustrates the difficulty in utilizing the OAN material within the Isaianic corpus in historical analysis.

Though the traditional roll call of nations was expanded by Isaiah and his followers to include Arabia, Assyria, Egypt/Ethiopia and eventually Babylon; OAN material in Isaiah also includes the traditional components of the Davidic Empire. Ammon alone is missing though she is probably included in the prophet's mind in the majestic lament over Moab in Isaiah 15-16, to which is appended a prophecy of destruction within three years (Isa. 16:13-14).[39] Fragmentary oracles against Edom (Isa. 21:11-12) and Arabia (21:13-15) appear together, to which is appended a prophecy of destruction "within a year" for Qedar (21:16-17). A brief oracle against Philistia is dated to the year King Ahaz died (*ca.* 715) but is problematic in its interpretation. This particular oracle may be reconstructed as follows (Isa. 14:28-32):

28	In the year that King Ahaz died came this oracle:		
29	Rejoice not completely, O Philistia,	אל תשמחי פלשת כל[][a]	7
	That the rod which smote you is broken.	כי נשבר שבט מככָ[b]	7
	For from the root of the serpent shall come a basilisk;	כי משרש נחש יצא צפע	8
	His offspring shall be a flying seraph.	ופריו שרף מעופף	8
30	The first-born of the poor will graze;	ורעו בכורי דלים	8
	The needy will lie down in safety.	[]אביונים לבטח ירבצו	8
	He will slay your root with hunger;	והמ[ית][c] ברעב שרשך	8
	Your remnant he will slay.	ושאריתך יהרג	7
31	Wail, O gate!	הילילי שער	4
	Cry out, O city!	זעקי עיר	3
	Melt in fear, O Philistia, all of you!	נמוג פלשת כלכָ[d]	7
	For out of the north comes a cloud of smoke;	כי מצפון עשן בא	7
	His troops cannot be numbered.	[]אין ⟨מ⟩ודד[e] במועדיו	7
32	What will the messengers of the nation answer?	[]מה יענ⟨ו⟩[f] מלאכי גוי	7
	That Yahweh has founded Zion;	כי יהוה יסד ציון	7
	In her the afflicted of his people find refuge.	[]בה יחסו עניי עמו	8

Notes to the Text of Isaiah 14:28-32

[a]On this use of כל cf. Exod. 15:15. See also vs. 31b below for the source of this expansion in MT. The mechanical explanation is probably a simple dittography with the following *kaph*.

[b]Cf. 1QIsa[a] which reads מכבה here.

[c]Leveling through the third person in this bicolon, with H. Donner, SVT 11 (1964), p. 111. 1QIsa[a] follows MT here but reads אהרוג for יהרג. MT re-

---

[39]Cf. Isa. 11:14 where Ammon is used in poetic parallelism to Edom and Moab.

presents a more difficult reading which is probably the result of a simple metathesis.

[d]Reading the longer form of the pronominal suffix, as with מככה in vs. 29, to achieve closer metrical balance (4+3:7).

[e]Emending with 1QIsa[a] for MT בודד to achieve closer parallelism in thought. The MT reading would translate, "There is no straggler in his ranks." The cloud of smoke from the north is taken as a conceptual representative of the vastness of the military contingent.

[f]The subject of the verb is plural. The final *he* of MT may have been used as a marker for the *û* vowel.

Isaiah 14:28-32 in Outline

A. Announcement of Judgment against Philistia (vss. 29-30)

[1:1] Do not rejoice over your enemy's fall.

[1:1] The worst is yet to come.

[1:1] The "poor" will pasture their flocks (in Philistia).

[1:1] He will slay your remnant.

B. Summons to Mourn (vs. 31)

[b:b:1] Weep, O Philistia!

[1:1] For the Destroyer comes from the north.

C. Report of the Messengers (vs. 32)

[1:1:1] The only refuge is Zion.

This poem is probably but a torso of the original composition and presents major difficulties in interpretation. In its original form the poem may have made reference to a defeat of Assyria or the death of the Assyrian king which produced rejoicing in Philistia. The precise date of the historical allusion in vs. 29, however, is by no means certain. In his recent study of this poem, Donner has posited a date of *ca*. 722-720 and sees the death of Shalmaneser V as the rod which is now broken.[40] Professor Wright has suggested a connection with the anti-Assyrian coalition which was led by the city of Ashdod against Sargon II which was crushed by Assyria in 712/11.[41] The prophet warned Philistia that the situation was but temporary. It was rather Philistia who would be destroyed, apparently by Assyria, the unwitting servant of Yahweh. The reference to "smoke com(ing) out of the north" (מצפון) is probably a reference to Assyria, the basilisk of flying seraph of vs. 29.

---

[40]H. Donner, *Israel unter den Völkern* (SVT 11; Leiden: E. J. Brill, 1964), pp. 111-12. Donner notes other possible dates: 727, 719, 716, 705 and 333 and lists various proponents of the different alternatives.

[41]See G. Ernest Wright, *The Book of Isaiah* (1968), p. 56.

The cryptic language of this oracle lent itself to reinterpretation and adaptation within the so-called school of Isaiah. In its present form the oracle is ambiguous. The superscription which dates the oracle to the death of Ahaz clearly implies some connection with that king. If, indeed, the broken rod of vs. 29 was originally Assyria, it was certainly understood differently in some circles. Some interpreters saw the broken rod as Ahaz and the offspring of the serpent to be Hezekiah, the son of Ahaz, and the descendant (צפע) of Hezekiah to be David *redivivus*. A fascinating result of this line of interpretation is preserved in the Targum of Isaiah which reads:[42]

> . . . for from the sons of the sons of Jesse shall the Anointed One (or, Messiah) come forth, and his deeds shall be among you as a deadly serpent. And the needy of the people shall be nourished, and the meek in his days shall dwell in safety; but thy sons will he slay with hunger . . . the Lord hath founded Zion, and the needy of his people shall trust and rejoice in her.

The reference to the poor (דלים), the needy (אביונים) and the afflicted (עניים), who will pasture their flocks in Philistia (vs. 30) and find rest and security in Zion (vs. 32), apparently refer to the rural peasants as a social class in Palestine.[43] The various terms for the "poor" in Israel take on a specialized meaning with respect to Judah in the Exilic period.[44]

The expansionary reuse of earlier oracles against foreign nations is further illustrated in the oracle against Tyre (Isa. 23:1-12). The difficult vs. 13, which immediately follows this oracle in MT, seems to call attention to the Chaldeans, asserting that it is they, not the Assyrians, who will fulfill this prophecy against Tyre. In vs. 14 the opening line of the earlier poem is cited, in a manner reminiscent of the citation of the "Song of Miriam" in Exod. 15:21. An older oracle delivered almost a century before is reapplied to Nebuchadnezzar's siege and subsequent subjugation of Tyre. Verses 15 to 18 expand the oracle further by lifting it out of history per se into the eschatological world of apocalyptic thought with its prediction of a 70 year decline for Tyre, after which her commerce is to be dedicated to Yahweh.

The oracles against foreign nations in Isaiah reflect layers of inter-

---

[42]J. F. Stenning, *The Targum of Isaiah* (Oxford: Clarendon Press, 1949), p. 50.

[43]Cf. the usage of the first two of these terms in poetic parallelism in the Song of Hannah (I Sam. 2:8), which Marvin Chaney dates to the 10th century (see his forthcoming Harvard doctoral dissertation).

[44]Peter Miscall has discussed the historical development of these terms in his recent study, "The Concept of the Poor in the Old Testament" (unpub. Ph.D. thesis, Harvard University, 1972).

pretation and reuse within the so-called school of Isaiah. The oracles against Philistia (14:28-31), Aram-Damascus and Ephraim (17:1-6), Edom (21:11-12), Phoenicia (23:1-12)[45] and even Moab (16:13-14) tend to be either fragmentary or display traces of being expanded to fit new situations. In particular there is evidence for an Exilic or post-Exilic editing of some of these oracles, along with those against Egypt (18:1-6 and 19:1-15), within a visionary community that tended to interpret the oracles in an eschatological manner. At times it is difficult, if not impossible, to separate the original oracle from its subsequent expansion.

It is this reinterpretation and updating of Isaiah's oracles within the school of Isaiah that makes the Isaianic OAN material so difficult to control in historical analysis. All that can be said, with confidence, about the OAN tradition in the second half of the 8th century is that Isaiah continued and expanded the received prophetic tradition. He confronted Ahaz and Hezekiah in time of war with oracles of deliverance from military foes. Like Amos he delivered judgment oracles against the member nations of the idealized Davidic Empire. The basis for such judgment on the part of Yahweh, however, was no longer primarily set within a legal context of covenant violation among "brothers." The nations were judged for their pride in exalting themselves over against Yahweh. It is the arrogance (גאון), the pride (גאה), the insolence (גאוה) of Moab that is cited as cause for judgment (Isa. 16:6,12). Yahweh stretched out his hand in judgment over Tyre to bring to naught her pride (גאון; Isa. 23:9). Assyria is to be punished for the "arrogant boasting" of Sargon her king whose "haughty pride" is spelled out in detail (Isa. 10:8-14). It is because "the axe has magnified itself against him who wields it," that the Divine Warrior will consume the armies of Assyria with sickness and fire (10:13-19). The fire of Yahweh's wrath is summoned to destroy those who have set themselves up against the sovereign Lord of the nations.

In addressing the foreign ruler, Isaiah has drawn on ancient political mocking poetry to create a vigorous form of prophetic literature destined to produce some of the most notable poetic masterpieces in the literature of the Old Testament.[46] Margulis has described this body of literature as the OAFR tradition, "Oracles Against Foreign Rulers."[47] The most noted example of this literary type is Isaiah 14, a mocking dirge addressed to the king of Babylon, which Eissfeldt has described as: "The most powerful prophetic dirge

---

[45]Isa. 23:1-12 is often interpreted as an earlier oracle against Sidon (vss. 1-4, 12-14) which is combined with a later oracle against Tyre (vss. 5-11, 15-18).

[46]This literary type stems originally from mocking songs of the Covenant League, such as the "Song of Heshbon" (Num. 21:27-30).

[47]B. Margulis, "Studies in the Oracles Against the Nations," p. 276.

we possess in the Old Testament, . . . and indeed one of the most precious of all Old Testament poems."[48] The Book of Ezekiel is particularly rich in prophetic mocking dirges which were hurled at "the prince/king of Tyre" (ch. 28; two separate oracles) and "Pharaoh king of Egypt (chs. 29, 31 and 32). Besides their high literary quality, these poems abound in mythological themes and allusions, being part and parcel of the so-called recrudescence of Canaanite mythology within prophetic circles in the 7th and 6th centuries.

In addition to an oracle against Sargon, Isaiah also composed a taunt against Sennacherib which is preserved in both Isa. 37:22-29 and II Kings 19: 21-28. In this particular instance Hezekiah is said to have gone to the temple where he spread out before Yahweh a threatening letter he had received from the Assyrian general, and prayed for deliverance (Isa. 37:14-20). In response to Hezekiah's plea, Isaiah delivered an oracle against the insolent Assyrian monarch who in fact had mocked Yahweh, "the Holy One of Israel" (37: 23-24). The oracle concludes with a prophecy of defeat in battle at the hands of Yahweh (37:28-29):[49]

Your rising up and sitting down is before me;	לפני קמ<ך>[a] ושבתך	10
I know your going out and coming in.	[]צאתך ובאך ידעתי []	10
Your raging is against me;	התרגזך אלי [][b]	7
Your roaring is in my ears.	שְׁאֹנְ[]ךָ[c] [][d] באזני	7
I place my hook in your nose,	[]שמתי חחי באפך	8
And my bit in your mouth.	ומתגי בשפתיך	8
[I will turn you back on the way by which you came.]		

The imagery here has cosmic overtones and is to be compared to Job 40:25-26 (Heb.):

Can you draw out Leviathan with a hook,	תמשך לויתן בחכה	8
Press down his tongue with a cord?	ובחבל תשקיע לשנו	8
Can you put a cord through his nose,	התשים אגמון באפו	8
Pierce his jaw with a hook?	ובחוח תקוב לחיו	8

The Divine Warrior will indeed subdue the proud emperor, as *Ba'l* annihilated *Yamm* and muzzled *Lôtān* in Canaanite mythology (cf. Ps. 74:12-14 and the mythic

---

[48]Otto Eissfeldt, *The Old Testament: An Introduction*, tr. by Peter R. Ackroyd (New York and Evanston: Harper and Row, 1965), p. 97.

[49]Notes to the text (Isa. 37:28-29): a) Following 1QIsa[a] which reads קומכה. MT takes this phrase with the previous verse. b) With 1QIsa[a] which omits יען התרגזך אלי. MT apparently reflects an early dittography with subsequent expansion in order to make sense of the text. c) Delete the second *nun* as dittography; cf. LXX ἡ πικρια σου and Vulg., Targ., and Syr., all of which are easier to derive from the emended text than from MT. d) Delete עלה *metri causa*.

cycle of *Ba'l* and *'Anat* in the Ugaritic texts).

Mocking dirges introduce an element into the discussion of the developing OAN tradition which merits further comment -- the context of lamentation. G. Ernest Wright has drawn attention to the prominence of lament forms within the OAN tradition in pre-Exilic prophecy, particularly within the so-called *hôy* pericopes, or prophetic "woes."[50] He also noted "a second class of lamentation which does not use *hôy*," citing the lament over the fall of Moab in Isaiah 15-16 as a prime example.[51]

Waldemar Janzen has made a detailed analysis of the occurrences of the term *hôy* in the biblical text. He summarized his study with a note of humor: "If a metaphorical conclusion be allowed, we have written the story of the heroic but unsuccessful attempt of a brave little interjection to become a big word."[52] Beginning as an interjection at home in the context of funerary lament, the term took on a specialized meaning within classical prophecy. As Janzen put it:[53]

> We conclude, then, that the lamentation-vengeance pattern, a pattern widely attested in various cultures, forms a context within which the woe-cry can undergo a metamorphosis from grief and mourning to accusation, threat, and even curse. Moreover, this metamorphosis is discernible within the Old Testament itself, so that we are able to trace an unbroken continuum in the function of the woe-cry. . .

The problem of the origin of this specialized usage of *hôy* is a vexed one. Janzen concluded that:[54]

> It is impossible to say whether the two *hôi*-occurrences in Amos represent the introduction of *hôi* into the service of the prophets, or whether they are merely our earliest evidence of an already existing tradition. Their living ties with funerary lament, as well as the fact that the Day of the Lord, a theme with which *hôi* was subsequently to be closely associated, is presented here with an aspect new and surprising to Amos' hearers may speak for their originality here, or at least for the assumption that we are close to the source of the *hôi*-tradition in prophecy.

---

[50] G. Ernest Wright, "The Nations in Hebrew Prophecy," *Encounter* 26 (1965), p. 233.

[51] *Ibid.*, p. 234.

[52] Waldemar Janzen, "'Ašrê and Hôi in the Old Testament" (Ph.D. thesis, Harvard University, 1969), p. 268; published now as, *Mourning Cry and Woe Oracle* (BZAW 125; Berlin and New York: Walter de Gruyter, 1972).

[53] *Ibid.*, p. 181.

[54] *Ibid.*, p. 256.

Though arguments from silence are always precarious, it should be noted that the term *hôy*, or its equivalent, does not appear in Isaiah 15-16, even though Jeremiah inserted the term in his reuse of this material (cf. Jer. 48:1).[55] It may well be that this lament over Moab was written before the emergence of the *hôy*-genre and related terms in prophetic speech.

For many years Albright dated the lament over Moab in Isaiah 15-16 to *ca.* 650, when Moab was devastated by Arab tribes of the Syrian desert.[56] Recently Albright has withdrawn the 7th century date in favor of a date in the 9th century.[57] Some scholars have pressed for a date as early as the 11th century, but the emerging relative chronology of Hebrew prosody makes this position rather tenuous. As Albright put it, "the style is entirely different from that of Hebrew poems of the thirteenth-eleventh centuries B.C."[58]

It should be noted that Isaiah 15-16 is not only "the most remarkable and beautiful of all" the laments which do not use *hôy*, as Wright has noted;[59] it is the only one of its kind within the OAN tradition of pre-Exilic prophecy. It is certainly true that:[60]

> . . . in any occasion of threat of destruction, suffering, death, or actual catastrophe, it was considered the thing to do to compose and to utter a lament. The famous Sumerian Lament over the Fall of Ur is one example; the biblical Book of Lamentations over the fall of Jerusalem is another.

Nonetheless, it should be noted that Isaiah 15-16 is without parallel within the formal collections of OAN material in Amos, Isaiah and Jeremiah. The closest comparison would be that of the OAFR material, the mocking dirges directed against foreign rulers who will be felled by the axe of the Divine Warrior because of their insolence in challenging the suzerainty of Yahweh.

If Isaiah 15-16 finds its closest parallel in the Book of Lamentations, it may also reflect a similar *Sitz im Leben* -- a specific cultic setting. In Isa. 16:13 the prophet describes the preceding lament as "the word which Yahweh spoke concerning Moab in the past," calling attention to the fact that this poem was part of the received tradition and not his own composition. The poem obviously was not a part of any annual rite of mourning as the Book of Lamentations became within early Judaism. Like other biblical laments of the pre-Exilic period, such as David's lament over Saul and Jonathan (II Sam. 1:19-27), the lament over Moab was composed to meet the need of a specific cultic occasion. To use Mowinckel's terminology, it was composed for a "casual" or *ad hoc* cultic festival.[61]

---

[55] Cf. also the use of אוי in Jer. 48:46.

[56] See *Biblical Period*, p. 79, n. 154; and discussion above, pp. 95-96.

[57] See p. 96, n. 106 above. [58] See *Biblical Period*, p. 108, n. 154.

59 [59] Wright, "The Nations in Hebrew Prophecy," p. 234. [60] *Ibid.*, pp. 233-34.

The historical occasion which best fits the composition of this lament is the victory over Moab, Ammon and the Meunites under Jehoshaphat as recorded in II Chron. 20:1-30. When Jehoshaphat learned of the invasion he "proclaimed a fast throughout all Judah" (vs. 3) in which every man, woman, and child participated (vs. 13; cf. Joel 2:15-16). The king then offered a solemn prayer to Yahweh before the assembled congregation (vss. 15-17) couched in motifs from the traditions of holy war. The assembled people responded to the oracle with worship and praise (vss. 18-19). The next morning the army set out to meet the invading forces. Myers has described the cultic situation:[62]

> Apparently the writer viewed the expedition as a holy war, since cultic personnel accompanied the army and played a major role in the campaign . . . The victory celebration was marked by the claiming of the booty and a service of thanksgiving in the field. Another one, presumably involving all segments of the population took place upon the return to Jerusalem of the victorious king and his army.

However one evaluates the historicity of this event in matters of detail, it is clear that the Chronicler has used holy war traditions preserved among the priests of the Jerusalem temple to reconstruct this story. If such a battle and cultic celebration did take place, a lament was composed for the occasion. That lament may in fact be preserved, at least in part, in Isaiah 15-16.

Most of the prophecies against foreign nations, as noted by Wright, are not laments:[63]

> They are simply declarative statements, which are essentially descriptive of what will happen, or else they portray events of destruction in all of their terror and horror as having happened. That is, the prophet as party to the decisions of what went on in the heavenly government may announce the decree of that government and describe it as already carried out (the "prophetic perfect").

In other words the prophet is the announcer of historical decisions of the *imperium* of the Divine Suzerain. These decisions may evoke expressions of mourning over the nation concerned, but there is often a quality of irony present in the lament language and forms as such. The expression of mourning is in fact an announcement of doom, especially in the later Isaianic oracles in

---

[61]See Sigmund Mowinckel, *The Psalms in Israel's Worship*, tr. by D. R. Ap-Thomas (New York and Nashville: Abingdon Press, 1962), I, p. 193.

[62]Jacob M. Myers, *II Chronicles* (AB 13; Garden City, New York: Doubleday & Company, 1965), p. 116.

[63]G. E. Wright, "The Nations in Hebrew Prophecy," p. 234.

which the woes are addressed to nations and individual rulers who have defied the Holy One of Israel by not acknowledging Yahweh's *imperium*.[64] In such instances the *Umkehrung* of the punishment becomes the reversion of Yahweh's holy war.[65]

An excellent illustration of this reversion of Yahweh's holy war is preserved in an enigmatic war oracle preserved in Isa. 10:27c-34, which may be reconstructed as follows:[66]

27c	He has gone up from before the wasteland,	עָלָ[a] מפני <י>שמן[b]	8
28	he has come to Aiath.	בא על עית	4
	He has passed through to Migron;	עבר במגרון	5
	at Michmash he places his baggage.	למכמש יפקיד כליו	7
29	He has crossed the pass,	עָבְרוֹ[c] מעברה	6
	making Geba his night quarters.	גבע מלונ[]ו[d]	5
	Ramah trembles;	חרדה הרמה	6
	Gibeah of Saul has fled.	גבעת שאול נסה	6
30	Cry aloud, O Laisha!	צהלי קולך [לישה][e]	6
	Hearken, O daughter Gallim!	הקשיבי [בת גלים][e]	6
	Anathoth is afflicted;	עניה ענתות	6
31	Madmena is in flight.	נדדה מדמנה	6
	The inhabitants of Gebim seek refuge still,	ישבי גבים העיזו עוד	9
32	(for) today verily he stands at Nob;	היום בנב ל-עמד[f]	7
	He shakes his fist at the mount of daughter Zion,[g]	ינפף ידו הר ב[]ת ציון	9
	the hill of Jerusalem.	גבעת ירושלם	6
33	Behold, the ark of Yahweh of hosts,	הנה []א[ר]ון[h] יהוה צבאות	9
	Who lops off boughs with terrifying power.	מסעף פארה במערצה	9
	The great in height are hewed down;	[]רמי []קומה גדועים	7
	The lofty are brought low.	ו[]גבהים ישפלו	7

---

[64]Cf. Wright, *ibid.*, p. 234; and W. Janzen, "'Ašrê and Hôi in the Old Testament," pp. 44 and 257.

[65]As Janzen put it: "The nations become the instruments of Yahweh, in such a case, but meet the same fate if they in turn, act in self-styled sovereignty" (*ibid.*, p. 261).

[66]The following reconstruction of the text of this poem is dependent on the article by W. F. Albright, "The Assyrian March on Jerusalem," *AASOR* 4 (1922-23), pp. 134-40; though it differs from that of Albright both in matters of detail and in general interpretation. See also the recent reconstruction of this poem and discussion of the pertinent literature by H. Donner, *Israel unter den Völkern* (SVT 11; Leiden, 1964), pp. 30-38 and 181.

34 He will cut down the thickets of the forest with an axe; ונקף סבכי [] יער בברזל 9

Lebanon with its majestic cedar shall fall. []לבנון ב⟨ארז⟩[i] אדיר יפול 9

Notes to the Text of Isaiah 10:27c-34

[a]The problem of where the poem actually begins is a vexed one. Duhm suggested, and most commentators have adopted his view, that the last three words of vs. 27 do not belong with the preceding, but with what follows. Duhm would change ש to ר, reading על(ה) מפני רמ(ו)ן. But as Albright has pointed out (*op. cit.*, p. 135), "There is not a rarer corruption in the whole gamut of possibilities than of *reš* to *šin*." Albright connected the words with the preceding fragment, vss. 24-27, reading וחבל לעלם מנשמתי, "And he shall be destroyed forever in my wrath." A closer prosodic-textual analysis makes this reconstruction tenuous at best. Vs. 27ab scans as a poetic bicolon of long meter in chiastic form:

His burden shall depart from your shoulder; יסור סבלו מעל שכמך 10

His yoke will be destroyed from your neck. []עלו מעל צוארך [י]חבל 10

In content this bicolon forms a fitting conclusion to the prose fragment preserved in vss. 24-26. The phrase in question, then, must be taken as part of the following poem; and the *ʿōl* of MT is repointed as the verb *ʿālā(h)*.

[b]This word is the crux as far as the interpretation of the poem is concerned. Seeing the Assyrian invasion of Sennacherib, or perhaps the Aramean-Israelite coalition in 734, in this passage, most commentators have looked north of Ai for the site in question (hence Rimmon of RSV, Jerusalem Bible, etc.). It is better to take MT as it stands and seek to make sense out of it. The reading ישמן, "wasteland, wilderness," is reasonable from a textual point of view and has been suggested by some scholars in the past (cf. *BHS* 7, p. 17). But such a reading is indeed difficult to explain in terms of the traditional understanding of this passage as the march of the Assyrian forces against Jerusalem in 701 (or the Aramean-Israelite forces in 734). If one sees here, not only the movement of troops, but a reflection of a cultic procession from Gilgal to Jerusalem, which has been changed by Isaiah into Yahweh's march of judgment and triumph to Zion in the van of the Assyrian troops, the reference makes good sense. The term appears in the phrase על פני הישימן in Num. 21:20 and 23:28 where it refers to the end-point of the wilderness wandering, the site of the encampment of Israel in the region of Moab which can be seen from the top of Pisgah and Peor. In I Sam. 23:19,24 and 26:1,3 the term refers to some part of the wilderness of Judah bordering on the Dead Sea, perhaps Province XII of the Judahite provincial list preserved in Josh. 15:21-62 [see F. M. Cross and G. E. Wright, "The Boundary and Province Lists of the Kingdom of Judah," *JBL* 75 (1956), pp. 213, 223-24].

[c]1QIsa[a], LXX and Syr. read the singular verbal form עבר. The more difficult reading of MT is retained here but repointed as a Qal infinitive with a third person singular pronominal suffix; cf. Isa. 28:19.

[d]Interpreting MT as a dittography, מלב לב, with Gray (ICC, p. 210).

[e]As Albright has noted: "Transpositions of the type illustrated (here) are nearly always found in fragments of this sort, where a complicated succession of phrases containing many proper names has been subjected to the caprice of oral transmission for decades or even generations before being included in the literary corpus" (*op. cit.*, p. 136). Albright would see much greater confusion of place names in vss. 28-32 than that proposed here. The transposition improves the metrical balance and the assonance of vs. 30a. On the confusion of paired words in poetic transmission see p. 61, n. c above.

[f]Interpreting the *lamed* as the asseverative particle (probably *la*) at the suggestion of Phyllis Bird. Cf. W. L. Moran in *BANE*, p. 68 who cites both biblical and Amorite evidence for this particle (see also Dahood, *Psalms III*, pp. 406-407).

[g]The *Qerê* reading is taken here with 1QIsa[a], LXX, Syr. and Vulg. It is possible to take הר and בת as variant readings, both of which were incorporated into the text of MT. Albright dropped the phrase גבעת ירושלם as an explanatory gloss (*op. cit.*, p. 137, n. 8).

[h]The emendation here was suggested by Kyle McCarter (private communication) and adds substance to the interpretation of this poem as the reversion of Yahweh's holy war. The reading of *resh* as *daleth* in MT is easily understood as both scribes and interpreters later misread the text.

[i]The text is corrected on the basis of parallel readings in Zech. 11:2 and Ezek. 17:23. The missing word can be explained as a simple haplography as the reference here is clearly to the cedars of Lebanon in a metaphorical sense. An alternate possibility is to read באדיר⟨ו⟩ with numerous scholars. Dahood has called my attention to possible parallels in the Ugaritic texts (2 Aqht:V:6-7 and VI:20-23) which might make it possible to retain MT without emendation.

Isaiah 10:27c-34 in Outline

A. The Destroyer's Approach (vss. 27c-32)

[l:b::b:l]	He has come up from Yeshimon to Michmash.
[b:b::b:b]?	From Geba he spreads panic.
[b:b::b:b]?	Summons to mourn: Your cities are being desolated.
[l:b::l:b]	The Destroyer shakes his fist at Zion.

B. Announcement of Judgment (vss. 33-34)

[l:l]	The Destroyer is Yahweh.
[l:l]	He cuts down those who exalt themselves.
[l:l]	He will hew down the forest with an axe.

Interest in topography and historical geography has led to careful study of the various lists of place names in the Old Testament, and the list here (vss. 28-32) is no exception. The first modern topographer to trace in detail the ancient track from Geba to Jerusalem, as reflected here, was L. Féderlin who published his conclusions in 1906.[67] F. Hagemeyer carried the discussion further in 1909 in his study of Gibeah.[68] G. Dalman followed in 1916 with an important work, based in part on his earlier studies of the Michmash pass and the Wadi eṣ-Ṣwēnīt, which remains the standard topographical study of the passage in question.[69] Dalman attempted to locate the place names cited here and to reconstruct in some detail the precise route taken. His map is still in use, having been reproduced by Otto Kaiser in his commentary in *Das Alte Testament Deutsch* (1960).[70] The Swedish scholar Sven Linder carried the topographical analysis still further in his study of Gibeah published in 1922.[71]

In 1924 W. F. Albright went a step beyond his predecessors in his attempt to reconstruct the text of Isa. 10:28-32 on the basis of prosodic structure as well as topographical detail.[72] Albright's treatment of the Hebrew text was rather arbitrary involving several relocations and minor emendations. Nonetheless, it is his use of Hebrew prosody as an analytical tool which forms the basis of the present study.

The most important of recent studies of the passage in question are those of H. Donner who has refined the earlier work of Dalman in light of more recent archaeological information.[73] Donner has challenged the traditional interpretation of the poem preferring to see it against the events of the Syro-Ephraimite war of 734-32 rather than an Assyrian invasion. It should be noted, however, that his attempt to reconstruct the prosodic structure of the poem in terms of the accentual pattern of the so-called Ley-Sievers system of poetic scansion is almost as arbitrary as that of Albright.

---

[67] L. Féderlin, "A propos d'Isaie X, 29-31," *RB* N.S. 3 (1906), pp. 266-73.

[68] Franz Hagemeyer, "Gibea, die Stadt Sauls," *ZDPV* 32 (1909), pp. 1-37.

[69] G. Dalman, "Palästinische Wege und die Bedrohung Jerusalems nach Jesaja 10," *PJB* 12 (1916), pp. 34-57. Cf. also "Der Pass von Michmas," *ZDPV* 27 (1904), pp. 161-73; "Das Wādi eṣ-Ṣwēnīt," *ZDPV* 28 (1905), pp. 161-75; and "Die Nordstrasse Jerusalems," *PJB* 21 (1925), pp. 58-89.

[70] Otto Kaiser, *Der Prophet Jesaja, Kap. 1-12* (ATD 17; Göttingen: Vandenhoeck & Ruprecht, 1960), p. 113.

[71] Svend Linder, *Sauls Gibea* (Uppsala: Almqvist & Wiksells Boktrycker, 1922), pp. 90-106 and 232 (map).

[72] W. F. Albright, "The Assyrian March on Jerusalem, Isa. X, 28-32," *AASOR* 4 (1924), pp. 134-40.

[73] H. Donner, *Israel unter den Völkern* (SVT 11; Leiden: E. J. Brill, 1964), pp. 30-38, 181; and "Der Feind aus dem Norden," *ZDPV* 84 (1968), pp. 46-54.

Most scholars have interpreted the passage in question as a poetic description of the rapid progress of Assyrian troops, probably those of Sennacherib in 701, advancing from the north through Judah to the very gates of Jerusalem. James Moffat went so far as to insert Assyria directly into the text of his translation: "Assyria is on the march from Rimmon."[74] It should be noted that neither Assyria nor Rimmon appears in the MT as such, and consequently recent translators are content to place explicit reference to Assyria either in an explanatory note or a title of the section as a whole.[75] A number of older scholars interpreted the text in terms of an invasion of Sargon II in 715,[76] while among recent discussions there is a tendancy to place it still earlier within the context of the Syro-Ephraimite war of 734-32.[77]

The precise route of the invader as set forth in this passage does not coincide with what we know of the Assyrian invasions, especially that of Sennacherib in 701. According to both the Assyrian records and the biblical reference in Isa. 36:2 (= II Kings 18:17), Sennacherib's troops marched against Jerusalem from the southwest, coming from Lachish. Avi-Yonah, Aharoni and others have consequently reconstructed a more complex plan of invasion in which a second contingent of Assyrian troops marched south from Samaria, taking the route described in our text.[78] But the only evidence for such a strategy on the part of the Assyrians is the passage in question. Moreover, the route itself raises some difficulty for the careful student. As Dalman noted, it is not altogether clear why the Assyrians would turn eastward from Bethel rather than take the easier route directly south along the main road past Mizpah and Gibeah.[79] The distance from Bethel to Jerusalem is about twelve miles and even with primitive means of communication it hardly seems possible that the curious route which exposed the Assyrian army unnecessarily in the Michmash pass and the crossing of the deep Wādi eṣ-Ṣwēnīt would have gone unnoticed in Jerusalem. As Skinner noted in 1896, "The road from Michmash crosses the valley in a south-westerly direction, and about midway between Michmash and Geba (the whole distance is about two miles) traverses an extremely narrow defile, where a large army might easily be checked by a handful of resolute defenders."[80] It was this very place where Jonathan's famous

---

[74]James Moffatt, *A New Translation of the Bible* (New York: Harper & Row, 1922), p. 760.

[75]So *Jerusalem Bible*, *New English Bible*, *New American Bible*, etc.

[76]So Procksch, Cheyne, Sayce, and others.

[77]See in particular R. B. Y. Scott (*IB* 5, 1956), H. Donner (SVT 11, 1964), and G. E. Wright (LBC 11, 1968); among others.

[78]See *The Macmillan Bible Atlas* (1968), p. 99, map 154.

[79]See *PJB* 12 (1916), pp. 41ff.

exploit against the Philistines took place in an earlier era (I Sam. 14). Moreover, it should be noted that the enemy did not capitalize on the element of surprise by advancing the remaining six miles to Jerusalem, but rather camped for the night at Geba thus spreading terror throughout the region.

Numerous commentators have been so bothered by various details in this account that they have argued that the prophet is not describing any historical event at all, but rather presents a vision of what is to come, though of course it never really happens in precisely the manner described. As J. Alexander put it in 1846, "We may conceive the prophet standing in vision on the walls of Jerusalem, and looking toward the quarter from which the invasion was to come, numerating certain intervening points, without intending to predict that he would really pass through them."[81] Thus numerous scholars have insisted that we are not to understand Isaiah as seeking to delineate the actual route by which the Assyrians would come, but rather we must see here an ideal picture, designed to express the thought that the enemy, when he comes, will take over the whole land.[82]

Still other options in interpretation are possible and have been advanced in times past. G. Beer insisted that this passage belongs among the "future expectations" (*Zukunftserwartung*) of Isaiah and in fact was written much later than the time of Isaiah in reference to the Seleucid era.[83] To him Isa. 10:27 points to the deliverance from Seleucid Syria whereas 10:28-34 refers to the eschatological battle with Judah against the pagan nations. Though the substance of Beer's analysis must be rejected, the interpretation of the poem within the context of Hebrew eschatology deserves careful consideration.

The prosodic-textual analysis presented here reveals a rather startling picture -- the march of the Divine Warrior from the desert wasteland, near Jericho, to Jerusalem. Yahweh has come to wage his holy war, not against foreign peoples, but against Zion itself. Since the agent of Yahweh's wrath is the unwitting foe of Judah, it is still possible to see the movement of real troops within this poem; but of greater importance is the fact that it is the Divine Warrior himself who is leading the enemy force. The march of conquest, as reconstructed here, follows essentially the route of the traditional Conquest under Joshua, which was the climax of Yahweh's Holy War par excellence.

---

[80] J. Skinner, *The Book of the Prophet Isaiah, Chapters I-XXXIX* (Camb.-B; Cambridge: At the University Press, 1905), p. 92.

[81] Quoted by Edward J. Young, *The Book of Isaiah*, vol. 1 (Grand Rapids, Michigan: William B. Eerdmans, 1965), p. 374.

[82] *Loc. cit.*

[83] Georg Beer, "Zur Zukunftserwartung Jesajas," BZAW 27 (1914), pp. 26-33.

THE CAMPAIGN OF SENNACHERIB IN 701 B.C. IN JUDAH AND ALTERNATE INTERPRETATIONS OF THE ROUTE OF CONQUEST IN ISAIAH 10:27c-34[84]

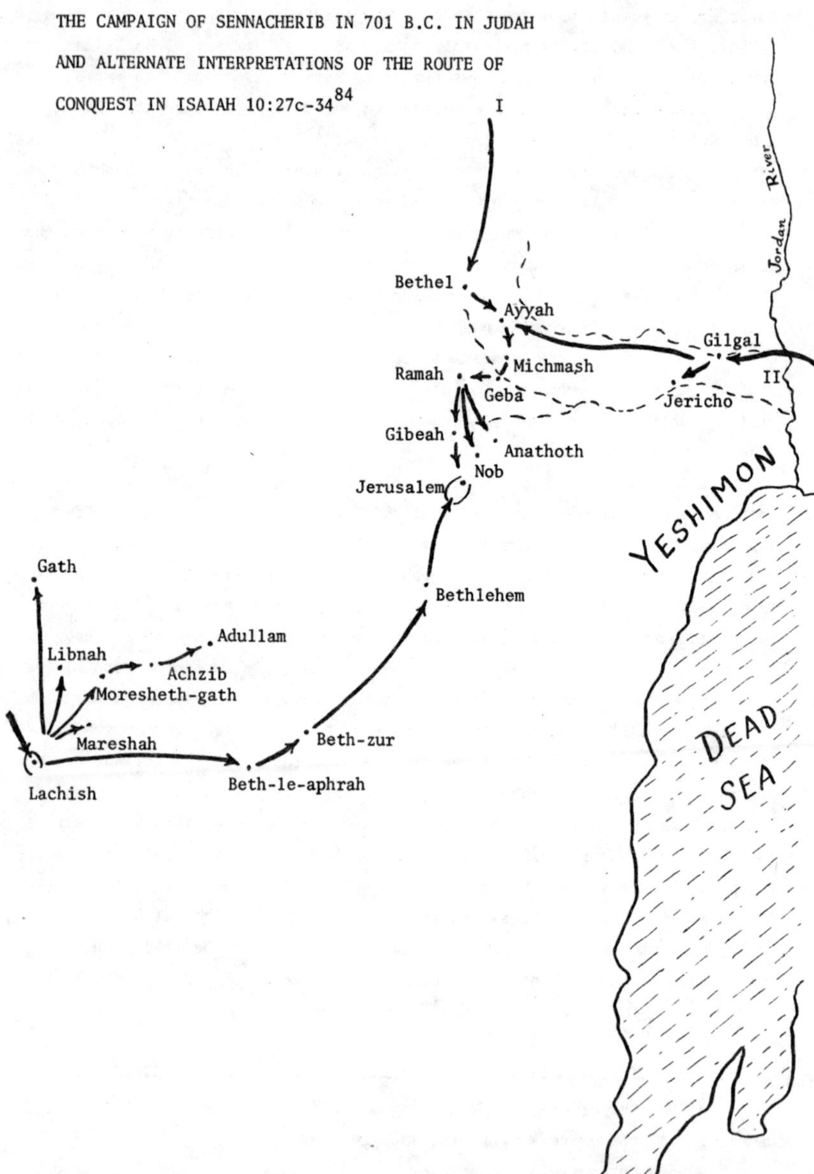

[84]The map shown here is taken from maps #54 (p. 43) and #154 (p. 99) of *The Macmillan Bible Atlas* (London: Collier-Macmillan Ltd., 1968) by Yohanan Aharoni and Michael Avi-Yonah.

The prosodic analysis reveals a poem of two rather distinct strophic units with a major change in metrical structure between verses 32 and 33. The approach of the Destroyer is presented in four quatrains, the first and last of which are clearly in the /l:b/ or "kinah" meter. In this particular pattern the metrical balance is between pairs of bicola in which one element of each bicolon is long and the other short, the total number of syllables in each balanced pair of bicola being constant.

The second and third quatrains of the first strophe can be read in the "kinah" meter, though they also present a staccato-like effect, reminiscent of certain elements in the mixed metrical patterns of Israel's most ancient war songs. A helpful comparison is that of the death of Sisera at the hands of Jael in the Song of Deborah (Judg. 5:26-28) which, as reconstructed by Albright displays a somewhat similar staccato effect in a series of short cola.[85] These two quatrains clearly belong together as evidenced by the fact that the final bicolon in each unit is virtually identical in both form and meaning. The summons to mourn as a form of prophetic speech appears as a structural segment of other war oracles in Isa. 14:31 and four times within Jeremiah's oracles agiinst foreign nations (Jer. 25:34-35; 48:17-19; 49:3 and 51:7-8).

The fourth quatrain presents a sort of poetic *inclusio* with the first, not only in terms of metrical pattern but also in terms of content. This /l:b/ quatrain concludes the march of conquest as such, as the Destroyer who began his journey in a similar quatrain which took him from Yeshimon to Michmash, stands now at Nob, the site from which the city of Jerusalem is first visible from the north. Here before Zion itself the Destroyer raises a clenched fist in threatening gesture.

Though there is clearly a break in the metrical pattern after vs. 32, it does not appear that this is the limit of the poem as such, as so many scholars have assumed. Up to this point the Destroyer has not been clearly identified. His route from Yeshimon to Mount Zion parallels the transfer of the cultic center in ancient Israel from Gilgal to Jerusalem, and hence the person of Yahweh or his cultic representatives is perhaps implied. But here in this second strophe all doubt is removed -- the Destroyer is the Divine Warrior himself who has come to cut down those who have exalted themselves.

It is not altogether clear whether the limit of the poem as such is reached in vs. 34 in spite of the chapter division in the received textual tradition. For in both content and prosodic form the picture continues to unfold. As a forester with an axe, Yahweh hews down great trees, even the "thickets of the forest" in the sanctuary of his holy city. Nonetheless,

---

[85]W. F. Albright, "The Earliest Forms of Hebrew Verse," *JPOS* 2 (1922), p. 80.

Yahweh is not through with Jerusalem; for a root shall sprout from the stump of Jesse on whom the Spirit of Yahweh shall rest (Isa. 11:1-5). In its present form the poem continues still further to present a remarkable eschatological vision of Yahweh's day of vindication (Isa. 11:6-9). The disorder of nature will be restored to pristine harmony and Jerusalem will be exalted such that the whole earth is filled with the knowledge of Yahweh. This eschatological vision of paradise regained and Jerusalem exalted is followed by a graphic description of a second march of conquest in which Yahweh "will raise an ensign for the nations" from whence he shall summon his people "from the four corners of the earth" to crush Philistia, Qedem, Edom, Moab and Ammon (Isa. 11:10-14). It is obvious that a number of the themes of proto-apocalyptic thought are present here and in what follows: a second Exodus (11:11), a reconstitution of united Israel (11:12-13), a second Conquest of the land of promise which will extend from Egypt to the Euphrates (11:14-15), the crossing of waters "dryshod" (11:15b), a processional highway in the desert and the pronouncement of faith through the singing of "a new song" (12:1-6). The material here is close to that of Second Isaiah in many ways and probably reflects an updating of earlier oracles against Assyria (Isa. 10:5-34) within a visionary community of the Exilic period.[86]

In its present context the march of conquest in Isa. 10:27c-34 is an integral part of a larger poetic unit, a unit which may be designated "an eschatological war oracle." It is a war oracle in that it presents a scene of battle -- the Destroyer has come up from the wilderness to wage war against Jerusalem. But the focus of interest is in the distant future; for even though the Destroyer has assembled his hosts against Jerusalem, there is yet hope. Yes, Yahweh will hew down those who exalt themselves -- even his own people. Nonetheless, a root shall sprout from the stump of Jesse as Yahweh shall yet work a new creation in his day of ultimate vindication. The curious reference to the "stump of Jesse" suggests that the prophecy will be fulfilled in a "Regnum Davidicum Redivivum." That is, a new David will appear who will delight in the fear of Yahweh and through whom Yahweh will accomplish his purposes among the nations. The thrust of the oracle as a whole, at least in its present expanded form, is clearly into the distant future in an eschatological sense. Nonetheless, this does not rule out the possibility that the march of conquest itself, as presented in Isa. 10:27c-34, may have had a prehistory.

It should be noted that to the prophet Isaiah the wicked Assyrians are but "the rod of Yahweh's anger, the staff of his fury" (10:8). Yahweh's hosts

---

[86]See Paul D. Hanson, *The Dawn of Apocalyptic: The Historical and Sociological Roots of Jewish Apocalyptic Eschatology* (Philadelphia: Fortress Press, 1975) for a discussion of this visionary community and its literary activity.

assembled here against Jerusalem may have been the unwitting troops of Assyria or even those of the Aramean-Israelite coalition. What is more important, as far as the prophet is concerned, is the fact that it was the Divine Warrior himself who was marching in the van of these troops, and he has come to wage holy war against his own people.

The route itself is not an impossible one from a military point of view. In fact the Tenth Legion of Titus marched against Jerusalem from Jericho to converge with two other legions from Caesarea which approached Jerusalem from the north, establishing camp at Nob (Mt. Scopus), in 70 A.D.[87] And the route of the Israelite conquest of Jericho and Ai, as reconstructed by Aharoni and Avi-Yonah, follows the route suggested here.[88] Though it is possible to see a specific military engagement as the occasion of this moving poetic portrayal of a march of conquest -- a journey from Jericho toward Ai, which then turned south at the Michmash pass on route to Jerusalem -- an alternate interpretation is possible, if not probable. As Ewald noted a century ago:[89]

> It is clear from the context that Ysayah is here describing a future march as his imagination depicts it; . . . But the fact that he could describe this future march with such particularity and accuracy, is fully explained only when we suppose that he had experienced similar marches in the past; the imagination is only able to expand and intensify what has already been presented to the mind.

Since the prophet Isaiah did not participate in such an invasion, the only way for us to suppose that he "experienced similar marches in the past" is to posit other occasions for such a march. A possible occasion would be a cultic procession from the wilderness encampment "before Yeshimon" to Ai and then south to Jerusalem.

This ritual procession from Yeshimon to Jerusalem may also be reflected in Ps. 68:8-9, one of the "Songs of the Wars of Yahweh," as Buttenweiser has described it,[90] which can be rendered as follows:

> ⟨Yahweh⟩, when thou didst go forth before thy people,
> When thou didst march *from Yeshimon* (בישימון) --
> The earth quaked, the heavens poured down rain,
> At the sight of God, the One of Sinai,
> At the sight of ⟨Yahweh⟩, the God of Israel.

---

[87] O. R. Sellers, "Nob," *IDB* III (1962), p. 557.

[88] *The Macmillan Bible Atlas* (1968), p. 43.

[89] Georg Heinrich August von Ewald, *Commentary on the Prophets of the Old Testament*, trans. by J. F. Smith, II (Theological Translation Fund Library 12; London and Edinburgh: Williams & Norgate, 1876), pp. 236-7.

[90] Moses Buttenwieser, *The Psalms: Chronologically Treated with a New Translation* (Chicago: University of Chicago Press, 1938), pp. 29-40.

That the preposition *b* sometimes has the meaning "from" has been recognized by several scholars who cite numerous examples.[91] In his translation of Psalm 68, Dahood so translates the preposition in vss. 6 and 25. A rather compelling argument for translating it in a similar fashion here as well is the parallel passage in the Song of Deborah (Judg. 5:4-5):

> Yahweh, when thou didst go forth *from* Seir (משעיר),
> When thou didst march *from* the region of Edom (משדה אדום);
> The earth quaked, the heavens poured down rain,
> Yea, the clouds dropped water.
> The mountains quaked at the sight of Yahweh, the One of Sinai,
> At the sight of Yahweh, the God of Israel.

Though the interpretation of Psalm 68 as a whole is problematic, to say the least, it does contain a clear description of a solemn processional march (vss. 25-28) which apparently has the temple in Jerusalem as its destination (cf. vss. 25 and 30). Moreover, its content reflects the Exodus-Conquest tradition, a tradition which was at home in Gilgal, a sanctuary in the vicinity of the Yeshimon.

It is clear that Gilgal was a cultic center of great importance in the cultus of the Israelite League before the monarchy and that whatever its specific location may have been, it was certainly near the Yeshimon. In his studies of the motif of the Divine Warrior in ancient Israel, Cross has reconstructed a "Ritual Conquest" tradition which stems from the Gilgal sanctuary.[92] The establishment of Zion as the cultic center under David resulted in a transformation of this "Ritual Conquest" tradition. As Cross has noted, the processional hymns and the proto-apocalyptic themes of the second Exodus-Conquest, the way through the desert to Zion, require the reconstruction of a processional march of the Divine Warrior in the royal cult.[93] Saul was made king before Yahweh in Gilgal (I Sam. 11:15); whereas with David the seat of Yahweh's kingship, the "Ark of the Covenant" of *Yahweh ṣ^{e}bāʾōt yōšēb k^{e}rūbīm* ("Yahweh of hosts who is enthroned on the cherubim"), was transferred to Jerusalem. The march of Conquest of Israel's earliest traditions no longer found its cultic fulfillment in the "crossing over" to the sanctuary at Gilgal. Yahweh's "holy encampment" was now established "in the mount of his heritage," in Zion. A ritual procession from the Yeshimon to Jerusalem may indeed have been a familiar experience to the prophet Isaiah.

---

[91]See the bibliography listed by Anton C. N. Blommerde, *Northwest Semitic Grammar and Job* (Biblica et Orientalia 22; Rome: Pontifical Biblical Institute, 1969), p. 19. See also Dahood, *Psalms III*, p. 397.

[92]Frank M. Cross, Jr., *Canaanite Myth and Hebrew Epic* (Cambridge: Harvard University Press, 1973), pp. 99-105.

[93]*Ibid.*, p. 106.

H. Donner titled his recent study of Isa. 10:27c-34, "Der Feind aus dem Norden."[94] Though he intended this terminology to suggest that the enemy in question here is not named and, in his opinion, is not Assyria; his choice of terms is a happy one in a manner perhaps not anticipated. The unnamed "foe from the north" is a familiar motif from the prophet Jeremiah. It has been noted that it is in these very poems that Jeremiah achieves the loftiest heights of lyrical expression. Speculation as to the identity of Jeremiah's anonymous destroyer from the north has focused on the Scythians, the Chaldeans and the Medes. It should be noted, however, that holy war motifs are dominant in these poems, as is also the case in the oracles against foreign nations in Jer. 25, 46-51. In some of the oracles against foreign nations in both Jeremiah and Isaiah an unnamed "Destroyer" appears who threatens the nations concerned. Though it is possible to interpret this "Destroyer" as an historical personage in keeping with the commonly accepted exegesis of Jeremiah's oracles concerning the enemy from the north, one can also argue, at least in some instances, that the "Destroyer" in question is the Divine Warrior himself. In Jer. 47:4-7 the "Destroyer" is presented as coming from the north to destroy the Philistines. The language of 47:2 suggests dependence on Jeremiah's poetry of the unnamed "foe from the north" (cf. Jer. 8:16) and it would appear that the "Destroyer" in this case is the Divine Warrior himself marching in the van of a vast military host, presumably the Babylonians; for vss. 5d-7 describe the "Destroyer" as the personified sword of Yahweh. The imagery is that of holy war with the Divine Warrior marching in battle against Philistia, a picture much in keeping with that which has been reconstructed here for Isa. 10:27c-34.

A further parallel usage of the unnamed foe from the north is found in Isa. 14:28-32, a brief oracle, also against Philistia, which is discussed in detail above.[95] It is the reinterpretation and updating of Isaiah's oracles within the so-called school of Isaiah that makes passages like Isa. 10:27c-12:6 and 14:28-32 so difficult to control in historical analysis. What was originally a war oracle pronouncing judgment upon Jerusalem, presumably at the hands of the Assyrians -- but not the total frustration of Yahweh's plans with his people -- has been updated into an eschatological war oracle which portrays the age to come.

---

[94]H. Donner, "Der Feind aus dem Norden," *ZDPV* 84 (1968), pp. 46-54.

[95]See pp. 133-36 above.

2. Zephaniah 2

Aside from Amos 1-2, Isaiah 13-23, Jeremiah 46-51 and Ezekiel 15-32 the next largest collection of OAN material in the Old Testament is that of Zephaniah 2. This collection of oracles which, according to tradition, is dated to "the days of Josiah the son of Amon, king of Judah" (Zeph. 1:1) involves the nations of Philistia, Moab, Ammon, Ethiopia and Assyria. Commentators have experienced much difficulty with these oracles, usually declaring them to be secondary in whole or in part because they could not fit them into the known historical conditions of the time of Josiah before 621. Basing his arguments largely on historical allusions in these foreign nation oracles, Hyatt redated the prophetic ministry of Zephaniah to the latter part of the reign of Jehoiakim (609/8-597).[96] Others have looked to the Exilic and post-Exilic eras for the historical setting of this material. The most extreme position is perhaps that of Louise Smith and Ernest Lacheman who argued for a date of *ca.* 200 largely on the basis of presumed apocalyptic elements, especially in the OAN material of chapter 2.[97] Smith and Lacheman did find the omission of an oracle against Edom peculiar and perhaps to be explained by the fact that "the apocalyptist used surviving pre-Exilic couplets as a basis" for his composition.[98]

During the past thirty years there have been a least two other attempts to date Zephaniah later than 609. In 1954 A. Edens, one of Hyatt's students, completed his doctoral dissertation at Vanderbilt University, "A Study of the Book of Zephaniah as to the Date, Extent and Significance of the Genuine Writings with a Translation." As is so often the case among doctoral dissertations, Edens demonstrated the conclusions of his faculty advisor in favor of a setting in *ca.* 600; though, it should be added, those conclusions have not found a wide following in the central stream of contemporary scholarship. In 1961, Donald L. Williams presented a somewhat similar dissertation at Duke University, "Zephaniah: A Re-interpretation," in which he argued that "the historical motivation of Zephaniah (is) the Babylonian advance in the reign of Jehoiakim."[99] In fact Williams identified the prophet Zephaniah with the so-called "second priest" of the same name in II Kings 25:18 and Jer. 52:24 who was killed by Nebuchadnezzar in 587. Zephaniah's ministry would then fall largely within the reign of Zedekiah during that fateful decade immediately prior to the Exile (597-587).

---

[96] J. Philip Hyatt, "The Date and Background of Zephaniah," *JNES* 7 (1948), pp. 25-29.

[97] Louise P. Smith and Ernest R. Lacheman, "The Authorship of the Book of Zephaniah," *JNES* 9 (1950), pp. 137-42.

[98] *Ibid.*, p. 141.

[99] Donald L. Williams, "The Date of Zephaniah," *JBL* 82 (1963), p. 83. This article summarizes the major conclusions of his doctoral dissertation.

The presence of apocalyptic features in the book of Zephaniah has exerted strong influence toward assigning a late date to this poetic material. But as Williams has noted, "to posit categorically an apocalyptic emphasis in the book of Zephaniah is to ignore Zephaniah's conceptual affinity with the great prophets, Amos and Isaiah."[100] The major themes of Zephaniah have their antecedents within the OAN tradition of the 8th century. Moreover, a prosodic-textual analysis of Zephaniah 2 makes the traditional date of *ca.* 640-609 plausible. The writer finds the arguments of Eissfeldt persuasive and would date most of the book of Zephaniah prior to the reform of Josiah which took place *ca.* 622/21.

<u>Zephaniah 2:1-15</u>[101]

4	For Gaza shall be deserted,	כי עזה עזובה תהיה	8
	And Ashkelon shall be a desolation.	ואשקלון לשממה	8
	In half a day they will be thrust out;	[][a] בצהרים []גְרוּשָׁה[b]	6
	Even Ekron shall be uprooted.	ועקרון תעקר	6
5	Alas, O inhabitants of the seacoast,	הוי ישבי חבל []ים	10
	O nation of the Cherethites!	גוי כרתים	
	Yahweh has spoken, O Canaan,	דבר יהוה [][c] כנען	10
	land of the Philistines:	ארץ פלשתים	
6	I will destroy you till no habitant is left;	והאבדתיך מאין יושב	8
	And you, O seacoast, shall be pastures,	והיתה[d] חבל []ים נות	8
	Hollows for shepherds and folds for flocks,	כרת[e] רעים וגדרות צאן	8
7	For the remnant of the house of Judah.	[][f] לשארית בית יהודה	8
	Their nurslings shall pasture	עליהם[g] ירעון	11
	in the estates of Ashkelon;	בבתי אשקלון	
	In the evening they shall lie down	בארב ירבצון	11
	for Yahweh will tend them.	כי יפקדם יהוה [][h]	

[100] *Ibid.*, p. 82.

[101] The opening strophe of this poem (Zeph. 2:1-3) is extremely difficult to reconstruct and interpret. The first two words (התקוששו וקושו) have driven virtually all commentators to despair or to radical emendation, while the text of vss. 2 and 3 has apparently suffered secondary expansion. It would appear that these three verses are addressed to the people of Judah, to judge by the phrase כל-ענוי הארץ ("all the humble of the land," vs. 3) who are urged to seek Yahweh by seeking after righteousness (צדק) and humility (ענוה) in order to be hidden on the day of Yahweh's wrath. Though these verses are omitted from the following prosodic-textual analysis, they are understood to be part of the original composition.

8	I have heard the taunts of Moab,	שמעתי חרפת מואב	7
	The insults of the Ammonites.	[]גדופי בני עמון	7
	For they have scorned my people;	⟨כי⟩[i] חרפו [] [על][j] עמי	7
	They have enlarged their territory.	ויגדילו גבולם	7
	[Therefore, as I live, says Yahweh of hosts, the God of Israel:]		
9	Indeed, Moab, you shall be like Sodom,	כי מואב כסדם תהיה[k]	8
	The Ammonites (shall be) like Gomorrah;	[]בני עמון כעמרה	8
	A patch of nettles and a pit of salt,	ממשק חרול ומכרה מלח[l]	8
	A desolation forever.	ושממה עד עולם	7
	The remnant of my people will plunder them;	שארית עמי יבזום	8
	The remainder of my nation will possess them.	ויתר גוִי ינחלום	7
10	This will be the price of their pride,	זאת להם תחת גאונם	7
	For they have taunted the people of Yahweh.	{כי חרפו / ויגדילו}[m] על עם יהוה [][n]	8
11	Terrifying is Yahweh against them;	נורא יהוה עליהם	7
	Yea, he will winnow the gods of the earth.	כי י[זר]ה[o] [] אלהי []ארץ	8
	They shall bow down before him;	[]ישתחוו לו	5
	Each in his own place,	איש ממקומו	5
	All the lands of the nations.	כל איי []גוים	5
12	You too, O Ethiopians, were slain	גם אתם כושים	12
	by his sword; look!	חללי חרבי המה[p]	
13	He will stretch out his hand against the north;	ויט ידו על צפון	7
	He will do away with Assyria.	ויאבד [] אשור	6
	He will make Nineveh a desolation,	וישם [] נינוה לשממה	10
	parched as the desert;	ציה כמדבר	5
14	Herds will lie down in her midst,	ורבצו בתוכה עדרים	10
	all the beasts of the field.	כל חיתו גי⟨א⟩[q]	5
	Both the screech owl and the hoot owl,	גם קאת גם קפד	3+3
	in her cornices will lodge;	בכפתריה ילינו	8
	Loudly demolition shall resound from the window,	קול ישורר בחלון חֹרֶב[r]	8
	From the sill up to the cedar beams he razes (her).	בסף כי ארזה ערה[s]	7
15	This exultant city,	[]זאת []עיר []עליזה	5
	The one who dwells secure;	היושבת לבטח	5
	Who says in her heart,	[]אמרה בלבבה	7
	I am and there is none beside (me).	אני ואפסי עוד	6

What a desolation she has become,	איך היתה לשמה	7
a lair for wild beasts;	מרבץ לחיה	5
Everyone who passes by hisses,	כל עובר עליה ישרק	8
he shakes his fist.	יניע ידו	4

Notes to the Text of Zephaniah 2:4-15

[a]This line is too long in MT and has probably suffered secondary expansion. The assonance of עזה-עזובה, אשקלון-לשממה and עקרון-תעקר would surely have been carried through with אשדוד if the term were original. At the time this oracle was written Ashdod had been under siege for several years and was destined to eventually fall to Psammeticus I (cf. Herodotus II, 157). On the meaning of בצהרים cf. lines 15-16 of the Mesha stela, where the king of Moab describes his campaign against Israelite-held Nebo (*ANET*^{2}, p. 320):

> So I went by night and fought against it from the break of dawn until noon (עד הצהרים), taking it and slaying all, seven thousand men, boys, women, girls and maid-servants, for I had devoted them to . . . Ashtar-Chemosh.

Cf. also Jer. 15:8 where the term is used in parallel with פתאם, "suddenly." See also the annals of Esarhaddon (*ANET*^{2}, p. 293): "I led siege to Memphis . . . and conquered it *in half a day*" (emphasis mine). The point is the rapidity of conquest and the contrast with the current predicament of Ashdod is obvious. The subsequent insertion of Ashdod to fill out the traditional list of Philistine cities is easy to understand.

[b]The deletion of Ashdod requires alteration of this verbal form. The word is parsed as a passive feminine participle; cf. Lev. 21:7 and note the assonance of the *-āh* sound in this verse.

[c]Deleting עליכם *metri causa*; דבר is repointed as a verb.

[d]The verbal form is pointed *w*^{e}*hāyîtāh* (MT *hāy*^{e}*tāh*) with John Kselman, "A Note on Jer 49,20 and Ze 2,6-7," *CBQ* 32 (1970), pp. 579-81.

[e]Following Kselman (*ibid.*, p. 581) who interprets *k*^{e}*rôt* to be the construct of **kārôt*, a feminine by-form of *kārîm*, "hollows."

[f]Deleting והיה חבל as an expansionary gloss.

[g]Reading *'ūlêhem* (MT *'*^{a}*lêhem*), "their nurslings," with Kselman (*ibid.*, p. 581). On the word *'ūl* cf. Jer. 49:20 = 50:45 and Job 24:9.

[h]Deleting אלהיהם ושב שבותם as an expansionary gloss which disturbs the metrical structure; cf. Jer. 48:47; 49:6,39 where similar expansions occur.

[i]The אשר of MT is a prosaic feature. The insertion of כי here is a conjecture to preserve the sense of MT and to achieve metrical balance.

[j]The על is relocated to improve the metrical balance of this bicolon. Cf. vs. 10 below where the על appears with עם.

[k]Reading the second person of direct address; the shifting of person is a prosodic feature of this poem. Note also that in Jeremiah's usage Moab is generally rendered as masculine; cf. Jer. 48:11-20, 35, 39.

[l]The translation of this line is dependent on Delbert R. Hillers, *Treaty-Curses and the Old Testament* (Rome, 1964), p. 76.

[m]Taking כי חרפו and ויגדלו as variant readings, both of which are incorporated into the expansionary text of MT.

[n]Deleting צבאות as an expansionary gloss.

[o]Reading a metathesis *y^ezāreh* (MT *rāzāh*) as suggested by O. Procksch in the apparatus of *BH*[3]. The root *zrh*, "to winnow," occurs elsewhere in OAN contexts (cf. Jer. 49:32, 36; 51:2: Ezek. 29:12; 30:23, 26) whereas the root *rzh*, "to grow lean," occurs in the Qal only here in MT. The appearance of the root *rzh* in vs. 14 below may have influenced the corruption here.

[p]The translation of this line is dependent on Liudger Sabottka, *Zephanja: Versuch einer Neuübersetzung mit philologischem Kommentar* (Biblica et Orientalia 25; Rome: Biblical Institute Press, 1972), pp. 91-94. Sabottka takes the suffix on *ḥarbî* as a third person singular form with numerous parallels. He takes *hēmmāh*, with Ugaritic *hm*, with essentially the same meaning as Hebrew *hēn/hinnēh*, "look! behold!" Cf. also Dahood, *Psalms III*, p. 400.

[q]LXX reads τῆς γῆς = גי(א)? Cf. also Targ. against the dubious reading of גוי, "nation," in MT. The term גי(א) appears elsewhere without the *'aleph*; cf. Josh. 15:8 and Deut. 34:6 in particular. The reading *gēwî*, "within" or the like, as proposed by Sabottka (*ibid.*, p. 96), is interesting but not persuasive.

[r]For a rather different interpretation of both the metrical structure and meaning of this difficult verse, see Sabottka (*ibid.*, pp. 91-98). His interpretation of *qôl* in an adverbial sense is accepted but his reading of the verb *y^ešorēr* in an intransitive sense is rejected.

[s]The reading of the enigmatic phrase בסף כי ארזה as the idiomatic equivalent of English "from top to bottom," as suggested by Dahood and adopted by Sabottka (*ibid.*, p. 98), is accepted here with some reservations. It is also possible to take the latter part of this phrase with what follows, with minor emandation, to read:

For I will winnow this city,	כי א[זר]ה עליאר []זאת	13
the exultant city who dwells secure;	עיר עליזה יושבת לבטח	
Who says in her heart,	[]אמרה בלבבה	13
I am and there is none beside.	אני ואפסי עוד	

But this reading creates problems for vs. 14 which would then be corrupt in MT as it stands.

Zephaniah 2:4-15 in Outline

A. Oracle against Philistia (vss. 4-7)

[1:1::1:1]	The cities of Philistia shall be desolated.
[1b:1b]	Alas, O Philistia, Yahweh has spoken.
[1:1::1:1]	I will reduce you to pastureland for Judah.

B. Oracle against Moab and Ammon (vss. 8-10)

1. Yahweh's Indictment:

[1:1::1:1]	I have heard their insults.

2. Yahweh's Sentence:

[rubric]	Oath formula -- As I live, saith Yahweh:
[1:1::1:1]	You shall be like Sodom and Gomorrah.
[1:1::1:1]	My people will despoil them because of their insolence.

C. Prophetic Vision: The Triumph of Yahweh (vs. 11)

[1:1::b:b:b]	Yahweh will winnow the gods of the earth.

D. Oracle against Assyria (vss. 12-15)

1. Prophetic Announcement:

[1:(b:b)]	Yahweh's sword extends from Ethiopia to Assyria.
[1:b::1:b::(b:b):1]	Nineveh shall be the habitation of desert animals.
[1:1]	The sound of her demolition shall resound.

2. Yahweh's Judgment/Lament:

[b:b::b:b]	She enjoys false security.
[1:b::1:b]	How desolate she has become!

Zephaniah 2 is generally understood as consisting of three or four separate oracles against the nations of Philistia, Moab and Ammon, Ethiopia/Egypt and Assyria. Generally the oracle against Moab and Ammon (vss. 8-10) is taken as a secondary addition, reflecting the attitude of these people to the fall of Jerusalem in 587. An analysis of the poetic structure, however, suggests that the individual oracles are part and parcel of a unified whole. There is logical development within the chapter; and, even more important, there is a single historical setting which makes good sense of the historical allusions in all three oracles.

The opening strophe (Zeph. 2:1-3) is apparently addressed to the "poor" of Judah announcing that Yahweh will vent his fierce wrath against his enemies . In particular the coastland of Philistia and the Transjordan lands of Moab and Ammon shall be destroyed. The focus of attention is apparently the Transjordan region, as Yahweh alone speaks in the oracle against Moab and Ammon, where he presents the basis for his judgment and swears an oath that that judgment will indeed be meted out. Because the peoples of Moab and Ammon have taunted Israel, they shall become spoil for Israel. The next verse (vs. 11) looks beyond the immediate historical situation in regards Judah's neighbors to set the stage for what follows. Yahweh will triumph over all the gods of the earth. This means that even mighty Assyria faces judgment. Assyria did not conquer Ethiopia on her own; the Ethiopians "were slain by Yahweh's sword" (vs. 12). And now that sword is stretched out against Assyria as well.

The OAN tradition of Zephaniah, like that of Amos 1-2, is set in a context of judgment leveled against the people of Israel -- in this case against Jerusalem (ch. 3:1-5). In his discussion of the "woe-oracles" in Zephaniah, Waldemar Janzen called attention to the fact that:[102]

> The woe of 3:1 represents the transition from the series of foreign nations oracles to prophecies concerning Jerusalem, but as Elliger notices correctly, a transition that links the two series more than it divides. . . . Jerusalem is not contrasted with the foreign nations, but is drawn perhaps editorially, into their list and threatened with the same prospect, namely the Day of the Lord.

There is an important difference, however, in the way Amos and Zephaniah have portrayed the Day of Yahweh.

For Amos the day of Yahweh's wrath is more firmly rooted in contemporary history. Yahweh will punish both Israel and her neighbors for violation of covenant obligations. Israel's punishment is couched in poetic language from ancient traditions of holy war. The earth will quake and terror will grip everyone in the day of the Divine Warrior's theophany (Amos 2:13-16). Nonetheless, Israel's punishment, like that of the other nations, is historical. The agent of Yahweh's wrath is Assyria and/or Egypt (cf. Amos 3:9-11) and the punishment is military conquest. For Zephaniah, on the other hand, the Day of Yahweh is trans-historical. The "gods of the earth" are opposed by Yahweh who will defeat them (2:11). The fire of Yahweh's wrath will consume "all the earth" (3:8). The speech of the various peoples of the earth will be changed "to a pure speech, that all of them may call on the name of Yahweh" (3:9).[103] The focus of attention in Zephaniah is not the judgment of Israel per se, but the vindication of Yahweh and the restoration of a righteous remnant as the true people of Yahweh (3:12-13). Zephaniah has moved beyond the events of history, in the sense of the here and now, to eschatology. The Divine Warrior and suzerain of all nations will accomplish his purposes through "a people humble and lowly, who seek refuge in the name of Yahweh" (3:12). Yahweh is again king in Jerusalem (3:15-16) and he will change

---

[102] Waldemar Janzen, "'Ašrê and Hôî in the Old Testament" (unpub. Ph.D. thesis, Harvard University, 1969), p. 234.

[103] This has sometimes been called the reversal of chaos motif.

Israel's shame into praise such that she is again "renowned and praised among all the peoples of the earth" (3:20).

The historical setting of Zephaniah 2-3 is the reign of Josiah (*ca.* 640-609), probably before or perhaps during the early stages of his great religious reform of 622/21. In its original form Zeph. 2:4-15 presents a theological basis for Josiah's program of political expansion at the expense of Assyria, particularly in Philistia and Transjordan.[104] Josiah annexed the Assyrian provinces to the north in *ca.* 628, as shown in the previous chapter. The historical allusions in Zeph. 2:4-15 fit this same period extremely well.

The oracle against Philistia prophesies the rapid destruction of Gaza, Ashkelon and Ekron (2:4). The emphasis is on rapidity of the conquest of the cities in question -- the battle will take but half a day.[105] If the original text of Zeph. 2:4 did not mention Ashdod, as argued above, the poet may be making implicit reference to the long siege of Ashdod still in progress. According to Herodotus (II, 157), Psammeticus I (663-609) took Ashdod after a siege of 29 years, said by some to be the longest military siege in history. If Herodotus is to be trusted here, this siege began *ca.* 640 and was still in progress when Zeph. 2:4-7 was written. The point the poet is making is that the coming destruction of Philistia at the hands of Yahweh is no uncertain, drawn-out matter. The Divine Warrior will destroy Philistia in short order, without lengthy siege. In passing, it should be noted that the presence of Egyptian troops in Philistia (*ca.* 640-628) would help to explain the absence of an oracle against Edom in Zephaniah 2. The focus of attention in *ca.* 628, as far as Josiah's foreign policy was concerned, was the annexation of the Assyrian provinces to the north, including the former province of Ashdod. Josiah is not in direct conflict with the Egyptians at this point. The success of Josiah's political expansion in northern Philistia is demonstrated by the so-called Yabneh Yam inscription which shows that a Judean governor resided at the fortress of Mesad Hashavyahu on the coast between Ashdod and Joppa in the reign of Josiah.[106]

The oracle against Moab and Ammon also makes good sense against the

---

[104] See the maps on pp. 79 and 97 above.

[105] See p. 156, note a above.

[106] See J. Naveh, "A Hebrew Letter from the Seventh Century B.C.," *IEJ* 10 (1960), pp. 129-39; F. M. Cross, Jr., "Epigraphic Notes on Hebrew Documents of the Eighth-Sixth Centuries B.C.: II. The Murabbaʿât Papyrus and the Letter Found Near Yabneh-Yam," *BASOR* 165 (1962), pp. 34-46; S. Talmon, "The New Hebrew Letter from the Seventh Century B.C. in Historical Perspective," *BASOR* 176 (1964), pp. 29-38; and W. F. Albright, "A Letter from the Time of Josiah," in *Supplement to Ancient Near Eastern Texts* (Princeton: Princeton University Press, 1969), p. 132.

historical background of *ca.* 650-628.[107] Kamashhalta, king of Moab, defeated the Qedarite forces under Ammuladin in *ca.* 650. The exaltation of Moab and Ammon against the people of Israel may reflect the events of *ca.* 650-640 under Kamashhalta who had regained hegemony in Transjordan, at least temporarily. The Qedarite resurgence under Abiyate and Uaite in *ca.* 640 was put down by Asshurbanapal. Subsequent Arab incursions in Transjordan after 640, together with the expansion of Judah under Josiah (*ca.* 628), seriously weakened Ammon and Moab making the reproach of Israel by the enlarging of their territory (Zeph. 2:8) rather improbable after *ca.* 630, unless one resorts to an Exilic or post-Exilic date for the oracle in question.[108]

The reference to the destruction of Ethiopia (vs. 12) no doubt recalls the campaigns of Esarhaddon and especially those of Asshurbanapal against the Ethiopian Dynasty XXV in Egypt which fell before Assyrian might in 663. The sack of Thebes in 663 marks the high point in Assyrian expansion and also the beginning of the Saite Dynasty XXVI under Psammeticus I (663-609). Zephaniah is stressing the fact that Assyria's greatest military achievements were attained under the providence of Yahweh. As Yahweh destroyed the great city of Thebes through his unwitting servant Assyria, so Nineveh too shall fall. The destruction of Nineveh is portrayed in the typical language of treaty curses, as noted by Hillers.[109] The same sort of language is used of Moab and Ammon in Zeph. 2:9. Moreover, the reason for Yahweh's judgment, as was the case with Moab and Ammon, is clearly stated. Assyria has exalted herself unwittingly against Yahweh, the suzerain of the nations (2:15a). For her insolence she will be decimated. As noted by virtually all commentators, this oracle against Assyria must be dated before the actual fall of Nineveh in 612. We would posit a date of *ca.* 628 with the rest of Zephaniah 2 and note that the nations judged in this chapter are the nations involved in the military-political expansion of Judah under Josiah.

The theme of Yahweh's sword stretched out against the nations can be traced back to Isaiah's oracle against the Assyrians who "shall fall by a sword, not of man; and a sword, not of man, shall devour him; and he shall

---

[107]See H. Cazelles, "Sophonie, Jérémie, et les Scythes en Palestine," *RB* 74 (1967), p. 43; who relates this oracle to the campaign of Asshurbanapal against "Uaite de Sumu-el" and Qedar in *ca.* 640.

[108]Cf. also A. H. van Zyl, *The Moabites*, p. 24; who finds no reason to doubt that Zeph. 2:8-11 is pre-Exilic. In particular he calls attention to the close resemblance of Zeph. 2:8 to Isa. 16:6. It should be noted that Isa. 16:6 is probably an Isaianic addition to the 9th century lament over Moab in Isaiah 15-16.

[109]See D. L. Hillers, *Treaty-Curses and the Old Testament Prophets* (Rome, 1964), pp. 53 and 77.

flee from the sword . . ." (Isa. 31:8).[110] The theme of Yahweh's triumph over the gods of the nations also has its antecedents in 8th century prophecy.[111] Amos declared that Milcom, the god of Ammon, "will go into exile together with his priests and his nobles" (Amos 1:15). The survival of the textual variant in Ps. 83:7, with the *gods* of the nations assembled against Yahweh who is entreated to vanquish his foes, illustrates the inchoate nature of this concept of a battle among the gods. By the time of Zephaniah, the concept had already emerged in apocalyptic fashion. In Zeph. 2:11 Yahweh is described as the Divine Warrior who "will winnow the gods of the earth." All the lands/gods[112] of the nations will bow down before him. The battle of the gods in Canaanite mythology thus finds its reflex in Hebrew poetry.

3. *Obadiah 1b-6a

In its present form the book of Obadiah is post-Exilic, probably reflecting the end of the 6th or the beginning of the 5th centuries.[113] Nonetheless, at least part of the book is certainly based on earlier tradition. The parallels between Obad. 1-10 and Jer. 49:7-16 are so close that literary dependence of some sort is obvious. On the basis of his analysis of this material Pfeiffer concluded that even if we allow for "wilful changes and

---

[110]The motif of Yahweh's sword extended in judgment stems ultimately from the ancient war poetry of Israel's Covenant League. See in particular Exod. 15:9, 12.

[111]Again note the earlier traces of the ultimate source of this motif in the Divine Warrior's deliverance of Israel at the Sea. Note in particular Exod. 15:11 -- "Who is like thee among the gods, Yahweh?"

[112]Note the double connotation of the term איים as used here in Zeph. 2:11. The normal translation of the term is "coast(land)" or "island" (cf. Isa. 20:6; 23:2, 6; Jer. 47:4 and Ezek. 27:6) and the term is sometimes used in parallel with ארץ, "land" (Ps. 72:10; Est. 10:1 and Dan. 11:18; cf. also Isa. 42:15, where Yahweh will turn the rivers (נהרות) into "habitable land" (איים). In the present context the term is used parallel to אלהי ארץ, "the gods of the earth." Cf. also Isa. 13:22; 34:14 and Jer. 50:39 (all OAN contexts) where the term is used of numinous desert creatures.

[113]So W. F. Albright, *Biblical Period*, p. 111, n. 182. Sellin sought to derive Obad. 1-10 from the period after the defection of Edom from Judah (II Kings 8:20-21), about 850 B.C. Kutal and Bič suggested an 8th century date. Wellhausen saw Obad. 2-9 as a description of Arab tribes invading Edom in the 5th century. Suggested dates for the origin of the book of Obadiah thus range from the 9th to the middle of the 4th century with no consensus of scholarly opinion.

accidental corruption, neither of the two texts, as we have them, could be derived from the other."[114] Apparently both writers made free use of a long-standing literary tradition concerning Edom. It is the writer's conviction that part of proto-Obadiah, the received poetic tradition behind Obad. 1-10 and Jer. 49:7-16, can be reconstructed and subjected to comparative prosodic analysis in an attempt to place it within the continuum of the historical development of both Hebrew prosody and the OAN tradition.

1b	We have heard a message from Yahweh;	שמועה שמענו מ[] יהוה	9
	A messenger has been sent among the nations.	[]ציר בגוים שלח	6
	Arise! Let us march against this people!	קומו ונקומה עליה	9
	Arise! To the battle!	⟨קומו⟩[a] למלחמה	6
2	Look!	הנה	-
	I have made you small among the nations;	קטן נתתיך בגוים	9
	You are wholly despised.	בזוי אתה מאד	5
3	The pride of your heart has led you astray;	זדון לבך השיאך	9
	The height is your dwelling place.	(מרום שבת⟨ך⟩)[b]	5
	O dwellers in the cleft of the rock,	שכני בחגוי סלע	7
	Who say in (your) heart:	אמר בלבו	5
	"Who can bring me down to the ground?	מי יורדני ארצָ[c]	7
4	I am exalted like an eagle!"	⟨כי⟩[d] אגביה[e] כנשר	5
	Even if you made your nest among the stars,	[]אם בין כוכבים שים קנך	9
	From thence I would fling you down, saith Yahweh.	משם אורידך [נאם יהוה]	10/6
5	When the thieves come to you,	אם גנבים באו לך	7
	They shall steal what they please.	([] יגנבו דים)[f]	5
	When the plunderers (come) by night,	אם שודדי⟨ם ב⟩לילה[g]	7
	How she is ruined!	איך נדמתה	4
	When the grape-gatherers come to you,	אם בצרים באו לך [][h]	7
6a	How Esau will be searched out!	איך נחפשו[][i] עשו	5

Notes to the Text of Obadiah 1b-6a

[a]Emending with Jer. 49:14 to improve the metrical structure.

[b]This colon is relocated in an attempt to restore the apparent prosodic structure. The relocation necessitates the change in the pronominal suffix.

[c]Reading the directional suffix *-ā(h)* to improve the meter.

---

[114]R. H. Pfeiffer, *Introduction to the Old Testament*, p. 585.

[d]Emending with Jer. 49:16.

[e]The verbal form is changed from third person to first which renders better sense in the prosodic context.

[f]Relocating this colon with the deletion of הלוא. The text of vss. 5 and 6 is difficult and has probably suffered secondary expansion or conflation; cf. Jer. 49:9.

[g]A conjectural emendation following the pattern of the parallel expression in Jer. 49:9, אם גנבים בלילה.

[h]The phrase הלוא ישאירו עללות is deleted as secondary; cf. Jer. 49:9 which represents an alternate form of this textual tradition.

*Obadiah 1b-6a in Outline

A. Summons to Battle

[l:b::l:b]	Yahweh has sent his message: March against Edom!

B. Judgment/Lament over Edom: Yahweh's Message

[l:b::l:b]	I destroy you because of your pride.
[lb:lb]	You have exalted yourself.
[l:l]	There is no escape -- I will humble you.
[lb:lb:lb]	How great is your desolation!

The /l:b/ and /lb/ metrical patterns observed here, and in Zeph. 2:13b-14, merit some comment. The so-called "qinah" meter, generally associated with contexts of lamentation, deserves detailed study in light of recent advancement in our knowledge of ancient Hebrew prosody. Professor Cross has listed the possible combinations of qinah meter as follows: /lb:lb/, /bl:lb/, /lb:bl/ and /bl:bl/.[115] In other words all permutations are possible and in fact can be mixed. Internal parallelism may occur between the long and short elements (thus /l:b/ in our notation), but the primary parallelism is between the larger two-part units.

Professor Cross has also called my attention to the presence of another reflex of the Canaanite battle of the gods here in this passage. The Edomites have dared to challenge the sovereign Lord of the nations with their boast: "Who can bring me down to the ground?" The Divine Warrior will fling them down from "among the stars." He will vanquish his foes, in both the human and cosmic spheres.

Both Jeremiah and Obadiah have made use of an already extant poetic tradition associated with Edom. The omission of an oracle against Edom in the book of Zephaniah, then, may simply reflect the fact that any such tradition found its way into the anti-Edom OAN tradition which eventually shaped

[115]Private communication.

the present book of Obadiah. At any rate, sometime after *ca.* 628 Josiah certainly saw fit to extend Judean control into the Negeb at the expense of Edom. If Zephaniah wrote any oracle in connection with this military-political expansion to the south, it was not retained within the formal collection of his oracles.

4. Nahum

The book of Nahum illustrates, even more explicitly than does Zephaniah, the impulse of liturgical usage within the OAN tradition. Whereas Zephaniah 2 seems to reflect ritual usage in connection with the political expansion of Judah under Josiah, the book of Nahum displays explicit liturgical influence, particularly in the opening verses (1:2-8) which comprise an acrostic hymn of theophany. As de Vries put it: "It is entirely likely that this hymn like others similar to it in the Psalter, had a place in the Jerusalem liturgy. One can say that it was at the very least inspired by it."[116] The appearance of a hymn in the poetic form of an acrostic is without parallel in the prophetic literature of the Old Testament. The book of Lamentations contains four complete acrostic poems (chs. 1-4) composed for liturgical usage within early Judaism to commemorate the destruction of Jerusalem and its temple in 587. Other Old Testament acrostics appear in the Wisdom literature.[117]

In the verses following the opening hymn (1:9 - 2:2), the book is arranged in a series of alternating addresses to Judah/Jerusalem, Nineveh and the king of Assyria. The change in addressee is marked only by the change in person and number within the pronominal affixes. Though this manner of composition as such does not necessarily indicate liturgical usage of a dramatic nature, it is easy to interpret it in such a manner. Consequently some scholars (Humbert, Lods and Sellin), though differing in matters of detail, have seen the book of Nahum as a prophetic liturgy composed after the fall of Nineveh (August 612) for the Royal Fall Festival in Jerusalem, which fell two months later. Bentzen also assumed a liturgical model for the book of Nahum but preferred to see the book as a real prophecy of doom against Nineveh in the form of "preparatory rites before a (military) campaign."[118] To Bentzen

---

[116] S. J. de Vries, "The Acrostic of Nahum in the Jerusalem Liturgy," *VT* 16 (1966), p. 479.

[117] See Pss. 9-10, 25, 34, 37, 111, 112, 119, 145; Prov. 31:10-31. See also the discussion of Norman K. Gottwald, *Studies in the Book of Lamentations* (SBT 14; London: SCM Press, 1962, rev. ed.), pp. 23-32; Max Löhr, "Alphabetische und Alphabetisierende Lieder im Alten Testament," *ZAW* 25 (1905), pp. 173-98; and F. Dornseiff, *Das Alphabet in Mystik und Magie* (Leipzig, 1922), p. 147.

the book is then an "imitation" of a liturgical form.

The book of Nahum was probably incorporated into liturgical usage, possibly as early as 612, but such usage alone does not explain the origin of the book. As de Vries has noted:[119]

> It is conceivable . . . that the elements composing the book of Nahum have all been employed in or associated with public worship. Very likely the prophetic oracles against the nations, to which *genre* the Nineveh poems belong, have their progenitor in the cultic curse of the enemy preparatory to battle. Together with the hymn of theophany and its parenetic expansion these poems have received their expansions . . . to widening cultic employment.

In this statement de Vries has posed the programmatic question of the relation of the book of Nahum to the developing OAN tradition in ancient Israel. Over forty years ago the same issue was put somewhat differently by Graham:[120]

> There is at least a possibility that (the book of Nahum) might have been motivated by political aims, that is to say, calculated to build up the view that Assyria's downfall was certain and that the part of wisdom lay in defiance of her and her ally Egypt.

Though the substance of Graham's arguments moves beyond the evidence at hand and his textual reconstruction of Nah. 1:9-2:3 must be rejected at numerous points, his intuition was correct. Liturgical elements, though present in the book, are of secondary importance. The book of Nahum stands within the developing OAN tradition and is to be understood over against the military-political events in Palestine between the fall of Thebes to Asshurbanapal in 663 (presupposed in Nah. 3:8) and the final destruction of Nineveh in 612.

Because of limitations in time and space the analysis here will focus on the hymn of theophany in 1:2-8 and a specific war oracle against Nineveh in 2:14-3:4. The evidence from this prosodic-textual analysis will be used in an attempt to date the book of Nahum more precisely within the developing OAN tradition.[121]

---

[118] A. Bentzen, *Introduction to the Old Testament* (1967^7), II, p. 151.

[119] S. J. de Vries, "The Acrostic of Nahum," *VT* 16 (1966), p. 481.

[120] W. C. Graham, "The Interpretation of Nah 1,9 - 2,3," *AJSL* 44 (1927/28), p. 40.

[121] For a more detailed discussion of Nah. 1:2-8 and the implications for dating the book of Nahum, see my article "The Acrostic of Nahum Reconsidered," *ZAW* 87 (1975), pp. 17-30.

Nahum 1:2-8 -- A Hymn of Theophany

2	A jealous and vengeful God (El) is Yahweh;	אל קנוא ונקם יהוה	8
	Yahweh takes vengeance, he is a Lord (Baal) of wrath.	נקם יהוה ובעל חמה	8
	Yahweh takes vengeance on his foes;	נקם יהוה לצריו	7
	He stores up fury for his enemies.	ונטר הוא לאיביו	8
3	Yahweh is slow to anger but immense in power;	יהוה ארך אפים וגדול כח	9
	Yahweh will surely not leave the guilty unpunished.	ונקה לא ינקה יהוה	9
	In the whirlwind and in the storm he makes his way;	[בסופה ו]בשערה[a] דרכו	10/6
	A cloud of dust is at his feet.	וענן אבק רגליו	7
4	He rebukes the sea so that it withers;	גוער בים ויבש[][b]	7
	All the rivers he dries up.	וכל []נהרות החריב	7
	Bashan and Carmel languish;	⟨דאב⟩[c] בשן וכרמל	7
	The green of Lebanon fades.	ופרח לבנון אמלל	7
5	The mountains quake before him;	הרים רעשו ממנו	8
	The hills melt away.	ו[]גבעות התמגגו	8
	Earth crashes in ruins before him,	ותִּשָּׁאֶה[d] ארץ מפניו	8
	The world and all that dwell therein.	ותבל וכל ישבי בה	8
6	His fury goes before him, who can stand?	זעמו לפנ[ו][e] מי יעמוד	8
	Who can endure his burning wrath?	ומי יקום בחרון אפו	9
	His anger is poured out like fire;	חמתו נתכה כאש	8
	The rocks are broken asunder by him.	ו[]צרים נתצו ממנו	9
7	Yahweh is good,	טוב יהוה	10
	yea, a stronghold in the day of trouble;	ל-מעוז[f] ביום צרה	
	He knows those who take refuge in him,	[]ידע[g] חסי בו	10
8	yea, those who pass through the flood.	ו-בשטף עבר[h]	
	He will utterly destroy those who defy him;	כלה יעשה מקמ⟨יו⟩[i]	7
	His enemies he will pursue into darkness.	ואיביו ירדף חשך	8

Notes to the Text of Nahum 1:2-8

[a]The metrical balance of this bicolon is easily restored by assuming the first two words to be variant readings. It should be noted, however, that this poem is remarkably well preserved with no evidence elsewhere of secondary expansion. The prosodic-textual analysis of the poem as a whole reveals

a carefully weighted internal structure which suggests that the anomalous poetic feature displayed in this bicolon is intentional.

[b]Deleting the pronominal suffix and repointing as *w^e^yābēš* (MT *wayyabb^e^-šēhû*) in order to improve the metrical balance; cf. Amos 1:2.

[c]This word apparently dropped out by haplography and its parallel אמלל was subsequently restored in its place. A *daleth*-word is required to fit the acrostic pattern.

[d]Taking the *he*-article with the previous word and repointing as *wattiš-šā'eh* from the root *š'h*, "crash into ruins," rather than the root *nś'* of MT; cf. Vulg. (*contremuit*, "to quake") and Syr. For parallel uses see Isa. 6:11; 17:12-13.

[e]This word is relocated so as to make the *zayin*-word appear in the initial position. The relocation requires that the *yodh* be read as *waw*.

[f]Taking the *lamedh* as asseverative; cf. W. L. Moran, *BANE*, p. 68 and M. Dahood, *Psalms III*, p. 406.

[g]The *waw* conjunction is omitted in order to preserve the acrostic pattern with *yodh* as the initial letter. The secondary insertion of the conjunction is easily explained by analogy in that *waw* appears in the second half of every other bicolon in vss. 3-8.

[h]Taking *waw* as emphatic (in parallel with the emphatic *lamedh* of the previous colon); cf. the use of emphatic *waw* in the Psalms as listed by M. Dahood (*Psalms III*, pp. 400-402. Note that עבר + ב = "pass through"; cf. Num. 20:21; 21:23; Josh. 18:9; etc.

[i]MT reads *m^e^qômāh*, "her place," which makes no sense in the present context. The parallel term is איביו, "his enemies," and some of the ancient versions render a synonym here; cf. LXX τους ἐπεγειρομενους, "those who rise up against him." See also Aquila απο ανισταμενων and Hieronymus *consurgentibus ei/illi*. Read קמיו and take the first *mem* as enclitic with the previous verb. Cf. Ps. 44:6 where קמינו is in parallel with צרינו with the same meaning. An alternate possibility is to read a derived conjugation of the root *qwm*, perhaps מקוממיו or the like. The reading which requires the minimum emendation is to take the first *mem* as the preposition (from מן) in the sense of "on account of" or "because"; cf. M. Dahood, *Psalms III*, p. 398 for parallels of this usage.

Nahum 1:2-8 in Outline

A. The Character of Yahweh (vss. 2-3a)

[1:1::1:1] He is a jealous God who will vent his wrath.

[1:1] He is slow to anger, but he will act.

B. The Arrival of the Divine Warrior (vs. 3b)

[1:b] ? He comes in the storm-wind.

C. The Reaction of the Cosmos (vss. 4-6)

1. Return to Chaos:

[1:1::1:1] Fertility becomes sterility.

[1:1::1:1] The world and its inhabitants collapse.

2. The Day of Yahweh's Wrath:

[1:1::1:1] None can withstand his fury.

D. Summary: The Two Sides of Yahweh (vss. 7-8)

[b1:1b] ? He is a refuge for those who trust him.

[1:1] He will destroy those who defy him.

The most obvious conclusion from this prosodic-textual analysis of Nah. 1:2-8 is that we are dealing here with archaizing poetry of the highest order. The oft-quoted applause of Bishop Robert Lowth is apropos: "Of all the minor prophets none seems to equal the sublimity, the order, the daring spirit of Nahum."[122] This brief poem is indeed a literary masterpiece. In addition to being an acrostic on the first half of the alphabet, it displays highly developed assonance, repetitive parallelism (vs. 2), eight instances of poetic chiasm, poetic inclusion, near perfect metrical balance between cola, and a studied internal balance within the poem as a whole which is indeed remarkable. The content of the theophany of the Divine Warrior who has come in the storm-wind to vindicate his name,[123] together with mythical allusions to cosmic entities are no less remarkable.

The poem consists of four strophes of unequal length. Within these strophes we find a carefully weighted structural pattern. The first strophe presents the character of the Divine Warrior with two bicola set over against one. The second strophe is a single bicolon which presents the arrival of the Divine Warrior in the whirlwind (סופה) of the storm (שערה). As it stands in MT this bicolon consists of a single /1:b/ unit with a syllable count of 10:7. This anomalous poetic feature, though easily explained as a secondary insertion of a variant reading, may in fact be original in light of the carefully worked out pattern of weighted prosodic units elsewhere in this poem. The third strophe presents the reaction of the cosmos to the arrival of the Divine Warrior, this time with two pairs of bicola set over against one pair. The final strophe carries through the same structural pattern in still a

---

[122]Cited by Walter A. Maier, *The Book of Nahum: A Commentary* (Saint Louis: Concordia Publishing House, 1959), p. 40.

[123]The name Yahweh is repeated four times in the three bicola of this strophe.

different way with an /lb/ bicolon set over against an /l/.[124]

It is interesting to note the distribution of the letters of the alphabetical acrostic within these four strophes, for the same weighted pattern prevails. The first strophe, though consisting of three bicola, presents only the first letter of the alphabet. The second strophe also presents only one letter but in a single bicolon. The third strophe presents the next six letters, while the final strophe presents three, this time as the first letter of each of the first three cola.

It is also of interest to note the phenomenon of inclusion as the final strophe restates the theme of the first -- the two sides of Yahweh's character. He is slow to anger but he will vent his wrath against those who defy him. It is obvious that we have here an intricately developed poetic whole. Attempts to reconstruct further elements of a presumed complete acrostic do violence not only to the text of the following verses but to the studied poetic effect of this remarkable hymn.

Thw question then arises, why just half the alphabet? Is this poem but the torso of an originally complete acrostic, as has been so often assumed? Gottwald has argued that the purpose of the acrostic as a literary form "is basically *conceptual* and not *sensual*" (emphasis his): "The function of the acrostic was to encourage completeness in the expression of grief, the confession of sin and the instilling of hope."[125] If an entire acrostic conveys completeness, half an acrostic may well be a prophetic way of indicating completeness with still more to come. Assyria faces imminent judgment, but only half of what is eventually in store for her. The normal application of the acrostic form to the expression of mourning, as in the book of Lamentations, may also be part of the prophet's reversal of imagery. Here the prophet has turned lament into bitter invective, and done so with a literary vengeance.

On first glance the metrical structure of Nah. 1:2-8 appears to be archaic. The most striking archaic feature is an instance of full repetitive parallelism carried through three successive cola:

> A vengeful God, *Yahweh takes vengeance*;
> *Yahweh takes vengeance*, he is full of wrath;
> *Yahweh takes vengeance* on his foes. (vs. 2)

This sequence of abc:bcd:bce is an apparent adaptation of ancient Canaanite repetitive style. The abc:abd pattern of the second two cola is in fact

---

[124]Again it should be noted that this /bl:lb/ bicolon can be read as an /l:l/ unit, though the fact that each of these cola introduces a separate letter of the acrostic suggests that, in the mind of the poet, they are not the same structurally as the following bicolon.

[125]N. K. Gottwald, *Studies in the Book of Lamentations*, p. 28.

paralleled in Exod. 15:6,11,16. It should be noted, however, that Nahum has not succeeded in this attempt to recreate the climactic parallelism of ancient Canaanite poetry. The chiastic relationship between the first two cola and the fact that the resultant unit is part of an /1:1::1:1/ quatrain, gives the poet away. What we have here is archaizing on the part of a 7th century poet, not the quotation of older material.

Examples of only partially successful attempts to imitate earlier forms of Hebrew poetry can be found elsewhere in the book of Nahum. In 2:2 we find a good example of mixed meter similar to that found in ancient war songs:

The Destroyer has come up against you.	עלה מפיץ על פניך	7
Man the ramparts!	נצור מצר[]	4
Watch the road!	.צפה דרך	3
Gird your loins!	חזק מתנים	4
Muster all your strength!	אמץ כח מאד	4

In terms of literary form this poetic unit is a summons to battle addressed to Nineveh. The Destroyer has come and Nineveh is to prepare herself for the coming conflict. The prophet is aware of the mixed metrical patterns of ancient Hebrew war poetry; but, at best, he is only partially successful in his attempt to recreate truly archaic features. Nowhere in the ancient war poetry do we find the pattern presented here with a long colon standing alone. The following short bicola balance each other in exact parallelism but are not in true parallelism with the opening colon.

A better example of mixed meter in the pattern of ancient war poetry is found in the war oracle against Nineveh in 2:14-3:4. The first section (2:14-3:1) of this oracle is an announcement of judgment against Assyria. Yahweh declares that he will destroy Nineveh because there is no end to her plundering. The battle scene is then portrayed (3:2-3) in the form of a prophetic vision, which is then interpreted (3:4). Nineveh is destroyed because of her "harlotry." The vivid portrayal of the battle charge and resultant carnage in verses 2-3 preserves archaic prosodic features:[126]

---

[126]Notes to the text of Nah. 3:2-3 -- a) This phrase is relocated to improve the parallelism in both meaning and prosodic structure. b) The final *mem* is deleted as an apparent dittography. The war oracle against Nineveh in Nah. 2:14-3:4 may be outlined as follows:

A. Announcement of Judgment/Lament over Assyria (2:14-3:1)

[1:1:1:1] Yahweh's sentence: I will destroy Nineveh.

[1:b:b] Yahweh's indictment: There is no end to her plundering.

B. Prophetic Vision: The Coming Battle (3:2-3)

[1:1::b:b::b:b] The battle charge

[b:b::1:1] The resultant carnage

The crack of a whip!	קול שוט	7
And the rumbling of wheels!	וקול רעש אופן	
A jolting chariot!	(מרכבה מרקדה)[a]	7
Galloping horses!	[]סוס דהב	3
Cavalry charging!	פרש מעלה	4
Flash of swords!	ולהב חרב	3
Glistening of spears!	ברק חנית	4
Hosts of slain!	[]רב חלל	3
Heaps of corpses!	וכבד פגר	3
There is no end to the dead bodies;	[]אין קצה לגויה	7
They stumble over the dead.	יכשלו בגוית[][b]	7

The resultant metrical pattern scans as 1:1::b:b::b:b / b:b::1:1.

The use of the short /b:b/ couplets here is indeed effective, sometimes balancing a longer colon (vs. 1b), but elsewhere simply adding to the emotion and vividness of the battle scene. One should compare the description of the death of Sisera at the hands of Jael in the Song of Deborah (Judg. 5:26-28) which, as reconstructed by Albright,[127] scans as 1:1::b:b::b:b::b:b / 1:1:: b:b::b:b. Nahum clearly has the characteristic mixed meter of the most ancient Hebrew poetry as his model in the construction of this war oracle and has come fairly close in his attempt to recover the ancient metrical pattern.

The war oracle in Nah. 2:14-3:4 is one of the so-called "woe-oracles." The context is one of judgment, followed by a vision of an imminent debacle for the Assyrian forces. The term הוי as used by Nahum has lost most of the overtones of lamentation conveyed in earlier prophetic usage. The metamorphosis from lamentation to vengeance is complete.

The book of Nahum must be dated in the half-century between 663 and 612 B.C. These dates are fixed by the reference in 3:8 to the fall of Thebes (663) and the fact that Nineveh was destroyed in 612. Though the general consensus of biblical scholarship is to date the book close to the actual fall of Nineveh, substantial arguments for an earlier date have been advanced by numerous scholars. Fohrer dates the book to the period "before the political successes of Josiah."[128] Friedrich König, almost 80 years ago, dated Nahum to *ca.* 648 and the Babylonian revolt against Assyria.[129] Stonehouse

---

C. The Vision Interpreted (3:4)

[1:1:1:1] Nineveh is destroyed because of her "harlotry."

[127] W. F. Albright, "The Earliest Forms of Hebrew Verse," *JPOS* 2 (1922), p. 80.

[128] Georg Fohrer, *Introduction to the Old Testament*, tr. by D. E. Green (New York and Nashville: Abingdon Press, 1968), p. 449.

[129] Friedrich Eduard König, *Einleitung in das Alte Testament* (Bonn:

posited *ca.* 626/25 and a supposed attack on Nineveh led by Cyaxares.[130] Herodotus, however, is the only authority for this invasion, and his account has been seriously questioned. A century ago Wellhausen, disturbed by Nahum's reference to Thebes, argued that "The event to which 3:8 refers cannot be decades old but must lie close to the present time of the prophet."[131] Having reached this conclusion, Wellhausen then proceeded to posit another later destruction of Thebes, of which secular history knows nothing. Schrader was also disturbed by this reference to Thebes.[132] The doubts of these and other scholars were forcefully summarized in a recent assessment by Maier:[133]

> The rhetorical question in the prophet's argument: "Art thou better than No of Amon?" would lose force if Nahum wrote about 616 B.C. . . . By that time No-Amon had thrown off the Assyrian yoke, had rebuilt itself, and could tauntingly proclaim that she, the ancient city on the Nile, had proved both her strength and Nineveh's weakness by casting off the Assyrian rule.

The description of Nineveh as presented in the book of Nahum does not seem to fit a date later than 626. Assyrian might is still unchecked (1:12); Assyria's prey "does not depart" (3:1); her merchants are multipled "more than the stars of the heaven" (3:16); Nineveh is still the harlot who "enslaves nations" (3:4). Though this is certainly poetic language and may look back on "the greatness that was Nineveh," it should be remembered that after the death of Asshurbanapal in *ca.* 630, the Assyrian empire succumbed rather quickly to dissension from within and wars of freedom from without.

In the book of Nahum, Judah is apparently under the Assyrian yoke, restrained by its bonds (1:13). As Maier put it, "Groaning under Ninevite tyranny, the Hebrews are in no mood to celebrate their festivals (2:1). Obviously Nahum must have written while Judah suffered the affliction of Assyrian rule."[134] Though Maier has overstated his case and his conclusion that the book of Nahum was written before 654 must surely be rejected, a number of his arguments do carry considerable weight.

In keeping with the OAN tradition elsewhere, the book of Nahum was probably motivated by political aims. As suggested by Graham, that purpose was

---

Eduard Weber's Verlag, 1893), p. 332.

[130]G. G. Stonehouse, *The Books of the Prophets Zephaniah and Nahum* (Westminster Commentaries; London: Methuen & Co., 1929).

[131]Cited by W. Maier, *The Book of Nahum*, p. 36.

[132]Eberhard Schrader, *The Cuneiform Inscriptions and the Old Testament*, tr. by Owen C. Whitehouse (London: Williams & Norgate, 1888), II, p. 152.

[133]W. Maier, *op. cit.*, p. 36.

[134]*Ibid.*, p. 30.

"to build up the view that Assyria's downfall was certain."[135] If so, any date after Asshurbanapal's final western campaign in *ca.* 639-637 could fit the occasion. The more probable date, however, is that of *ca.* 650. As argued above,[136] the revolt of Manasseh is not to be dismissed as a figment of the Chronicler's imagination. And if such a revolt did take place, the situation *ca.* 652-648 fits the occasion rather well. The only basis for such a revolt on Manasseh's part would have been the conviction that Assyria's days were numbered.[137] The book of Nahum presents the very message which would have been composed to persuade the Judean king to take part is such a revolt -- the assurance that Assyria's fall was certain, in fact that it was ordained of Yahweh the Divine Warrior. The book would then have taken on deeper meaning as part of the theological basis for the subsequent resurgence of Judean independence under Josiah, especially after the death of Asshurbanapal in *ca.* 630. The final destruction of Nineveh in 612 would have been the ultimate fulfillment of this prophecy, the completion of the other half of Yahweh's vengeance implied in the half-acrostic poem in Nah. 1:2-8. The reuse of the book of Nahum within a liturgical celebration of the fall of Nineveh in the Royal Fall Festival in Jerusalem in 612 would then make perfect sense.

5. Habakkuk

The book of Habakkuk poses difficult problems in the analysis of the historical development of the OAN tradition, as witnessed by the plethora of interpretations given to this brief work. The major problems center around the identity of the oppressor, the actual content of the oracle (משא) which the prophet "saw" (חזה), and the so-called *Sitz im Cultus*, or setting within the religious life of ancient Israel.

The book falls into three major divisions: 1) a dialogue between the prophet and Yahweh in which the prophet raises his complaint in the form of the individual song of lament (1:2-2:4); 2) a prophetic meditation on the fate of the "Wicked Man" (2:5-20; and 3) a hymn of theophany (3:1-19).

The first division is made up of two cycles, climaxed by the so-called "placarded revelation of Habakkuk."[138] In Hab. 1:2-4 the prophet raises his

---

[135] W. C. Graham, *op. cit.*, p. 40.

[136] See pp. 94-95 above.

[137] It should be noted that the coalition of nations opposing Assyria in the crisis of 652-648 extended from Elam to Egypt, including the Qedarite dominated Arab confederation, the Chaldeans and the Arameans. It took Asshurbanapal a full three years to regain control of Babylonia.

[138] See William H. Brownlee, "The Placarded Revelation of Habakkuk," *JBL* 82 (1963), pp. 319-25.

complaint which reaches its high point in the quatrain:

So the Torah is slacked,	על כן תפוג תורה	6
Justice never goes forth;	[]לא יצא לנצח משפט	7
For the wicked surround the righteous,	כי רשע מכתיר []צדיק	7
Justice goes forth perverted. (vs. 4)	[] יצא משפט מעקל	7

Yahweh responds by urging the prophet to look at international events. The Chaldeans, wicked as they are, are the instrument of his own choosing (vs. 6):

Look! I am raising up the Chaldeans,	[] הנני מקים [] כשדים	6
That nation -- bitter and violent,	הגוי []מר ו[]נמהר	6
Who marches through the breadth of the earth,	[]הולך למרחבי ארץ	7
To seize habitations not their own.	לרשת משכנות לא לו	7

It would appear that the "wicked" of verse 4 are the Assyrians who have oppressed the "righteous" of Israel. Yahweh has raised up the fierce Chaldeans to destroy Assyria (1:7-11).

The dialogue resumes with a prayer in which the prophet resumes his complaint (1:12-17). In verse 13 he declares:

Why do you look on faithless men	למה תביט בוגדים	10
and remain silent,	⟨ו⟩תחריש	
When the "Wicked Man" swallows up	בבלע רשע	10
the one more righteous than he?	צדיק ממנו	

The identity of the "Wicked Man" here is not entirely clear. Though he may be identified with the wicked one of verse 4, i.e. Assyria, it is also possible to see the Chaldeans as the "Wicked Man" here. They have destroyed wicked Assyria; but in retrospect Assyria was "righteous" in comparison to the new "oppressors." The prophet plaintively asks (vs. 17):

Is he then to keep on emptying his net forever,	העל כן יריק חרמו []תמיד	9
Slaying nations without mercy?	להרג גוים ⟨ו⟩לא יחמול	9

The prophet then takes his stance upon the watch-tower to await a further oracle from Yahweh (2:1-3). The long awaited oracle arrives, but its very brevity has lent a cryptic aura to its interpretation. With minimal emendation it may be reconstructed as follows:[139]

---

[139]Cf. W. H. Brownlee, *op. cit.*, p. 324; who resorts to more radical emendation, inserting a word presumably lost by haplography and relocating the second colon of this couplet after vs. 5a. Notes to the text of Hab. 2:4 -- a) This word may have been read originally as *'appîl* or perhaps *'uppāl* or *'appāl*. b) On this reading of נפש cf. BDB, p. 660a. See in particular Jer. 3:11; 26:19; 37:9; Isa. 43:4; 46:2; 51:23; Job 9:21; Song of S. 6:12; Pss. 25:13; 124:7; in older poetry cf. Gen. 49:6 and Num. 23:10.

Look!	הנה	-
The haughty man -- he himself shall not remain upright!	עפל[][a] לא ישרה נפשו[b] בו	9
The righteous man -- by his faithfulness he shall live!	צדיק[] באמונתו יחיה	9

The remaining two major divisions of the book of Habakkuk may be outlined as follows:[140]

A. A Meditation on the Wicked Man (Hab. 2:5-20)

1. Introduction (vss. 5-6a)

[1:1] Theme: Though he be as crafty as Hîyôn, he will not escape.

[1:1::1:1] The Wicked Man portrayed:
He is as greedy as Death.
He gathers for himself all nations.

[1:1] Against him the nations make their taunt:

2. The Taunt of the Nations (vss. 6b-17)

a. The first "woe" (vss. 6b-8)

[1:1] Alas for the cupidity of the conqueror.

[1:1:1::1:1] Those you have plundered will plunder you.

b. The second "woe" (vss. 9-11)

[1:1:1] Alas for the rapacious pride of the conqueror.

[1:1:1::1:1] Your schemes redound to shame.

c. The third "woe" (vss. 12-14)

[1:1] Alas for the violent rule of the conqueror.

[1:1:1] You have worn yourself out for naught.

[1:1:1] The earth shall be filled with the glory of Yahweh.

d. The fourth "woe" (vss. 15-17)

[1:1] Alas for the cynicism of the conqueror.

[1:1::1:1] The cup of wrath has come round to you.

[1:1::1:1] You shall be utterly destroyed for your wantonness.

3. Conclusion (vss. 18-20)

[1:1] Of what worth is an idol?

[1:1::1:1] The Wicked Man trusts vainly in his own creation.

[1:1] There is no life in his idols.

[1:1] But Yahweh is in his temple.

---

[140] Because of limitations in time and space, the Hebrew text and notes are not presented here for this material.

B. A Hymn of Theophany (Hab. 3:2-19)

1. A Request for a Theophany (vs. 2)

[1:1] Yahweh, I know your reputation.

[1:1:1] Reveal yourself anew, in our time.

2. The Theophany (vss. 3-6)

a. The appearance of the Divine Warrior (vss. 3-4)

[1:1] His triumphal march from the Southland.

[1:1::1:1:1] His blinding glory fills the earth.

b. The reaction of the cosmos (vss. 5-6)

[1:1] Pestilence and Plague go up before Him.

[1:1::1:1:1 The entire cosmos (the nations included) recoils before Him.

3. A Prophetic Vision (vss. 7-15)

a. Against whom has the Divine Warrior come? (vss. 7-8a)

[1:1] I saw Kushan/Midian in terror.

[1:1:1] Is your wrath, O Yahweh, directed against River/Sea?

b. The battle is cosmic in scope. (vss. 8b-11)

[1:1::1:1] Yahweh is prepared for battle.

2[1:1::1:1] The cosmos itself joins in the conflict.

c. Yahweh will destroy Death/Sea. (vss. 12-15)

[1:1::1:1] You are going forth, Yahweh, to save your people.

2[1:1::1:1] You are bent on destroying that wicked foe, Death/Sea.

4. The Prophet's Response (vss. 16-19)

[3(1:1)] I recoiled in distress on hearing the news.

[3(1:1)] The land will be decimated.

[1:1::1:1:1] Yet I will rejoice in Yahweh who gives victory.

The fourth "woe" (2:15-17) is of particular importance for its presentation of the motif of the cup of Yahweh's wrath proffered to the nations in judgment. These verses may be reconstructed as follows:

15 Alas for the one who makes his neighbor drink from the cup of fierce wrath; — הרי משקה רעהו מספ[][a] חמת[] []אף[b] — 11

He makes (them) drunk in order to look upon their nakedness. — שכר למען הביט על מעוריהם — 11

16 You are sated with contempt instead of glory. — שבעת קלון מכבוד — 8

Drink, yourself! Stagger! — שתה גם אתה []הרעל[c] — 8

It shall come round to you -- the cup of Yahweh's right hand; — תסוב עליך כוס ימין יהוה — 10

Foul shame will come upon your glory. — וקיקלון על<י>[d] כבודך — 10

17	The violence (done to) Lebanon will cover you;	[][e] חמס לבנון[f] יכסך	9
	The destruction of Behamot will terrify you,	ושד בהמות יחית⟨ך⟩[g]	9
	For the blood of men and the violence to the land,	מדמי אדם וחמס ארץ	9
	To the city and to all who dwell therein.	קריה וכל ישבי בה	8

Notes to the Text of Habakkuk 2:15-17

[a]Deleting the ת as a dittography. On the meaning of סף cf. Zech. 12:2 סף רעל, "cup of reeling."

[b]1QpHab reads חמתו אף. Delete the suffix altogether and cf. Zeph. 2:2 חרון אף יהוה, "the fierce wrath of Yahweh."

[c]Reading a metathesis with 1QpHab for MT והערל, "be uncircumcised" (?); cf. also LXX. On the root *rʿl*, "to reel, quiver, shake," cf. Nah. 2:4; Zech. 12:2 (סף רעל, "goblet of reeling" as a figure of Jerusalem); Isa. 51:17,22 (כוס תרעלה, "cup of reeling"); and Ps. 60:5 (יין תרעלה, "wine that dazed us" -- see p. 120 of this study).

[d]Reading the ballast variant of the preposition to improve the metrical balance.

[e]Deleting the כי to improve both the meter and the parallelism of this bicolon. The particle may have been introduced by dittography from the suffix of the previous word.

[f]Albright saw in this reference "the giant Lebanon (which) appears as a primordial monster of Syrian mythology" ["The Psalm of Habakkuk," (1950), p. 10, n. 32 (for complete reference see pp. 9-10, n. 46 above)]. W. Janzen has cited the suggestion of Cross of the possibility of reference to the deified giant Lebanon and to the ox of the wilderness of the Gilgamesh epic (*Gilgamesch Epos*, 5th Tafel), "ʾAšrê and Hôî in the Old Testament," p. 230, n. 100.

[g]Reading with LXX πτοησει σε; cf. also Syr. and Targ. 1QpHab reads יחתה (!).

Jer. 51:7, with its reference to Babylon as "a golden cup in Yahweh's right hand" is apparently dependent on Hab. 2:15-16 for it is the only other reference to the cup of wrath motif which clearly associates the cup with "Yahweh's right hand." It should also be noted that the collection of oracles against Babylon in Jeremiah 50-51 is concluded with the quotation of Hab. 2:13b (= Jer. 51:58b). It would appear that the "Wicked Man" of Hab. 2:5-19 was understood in subsequent OAN tradition to be the Chaldeans.

In its original form, however, the "Wicked Man" may have been the Assyrians as Brownlee suggests in his reconstruction of Hab. 2:5b, "*Assyria* has enlarged his appetite as Sheol, and *he* as death can not be sated" (empha-

---

[139]See W. H. Brownlee, *op. cit.*, p. 321.

sis his). This reading is certainly possible from a prosodic point of view, with a 9:8 couplet -- the only emendation being that of the substitution of *'Aššur* (אשור) for *'ašer* (אשר).

Albright has demonstrated the reuse of ancient material in the hymn of theophany of Habakkuk 3. In particular he argued that vs. 2 "must come from a very ancient prayer for the prolongation of (a king's) life, on the order of the hymn of Ishtar praying for the life of Ammiditana, *cir.* 1600 B.C."[140] In Albright's opinion vss. 3-7 were "probably taken with little alteration from a very early Israelite poem on the theophany of Yahweh as exhibited in the south-east storm."[141] Verses 8-15 appear to be "adapted from an early poem or poems of Canaanite origin, celebrating the triumph of Baal over Judge River, Prince Sea and Death, all apparently serving as variant names of a single primordial dragon of chaos."[142] In light of the observed phenomenon of archaic features in Habakkuk 2-3, Albright has concluded:[143]

> If we assume, as seems to me only reasonable, that the book of Habakkuk is substantially the work of a single author, it would appear that the latter was not an original spirit but that he possessed a considerable amount of literary appreciation and that he lived in a strongly archaizing period. The tradition that he was a prophet and a musician who flourished in the last years of the First Temple is thoroughly consonant with the literary picture as we have sketched it.

The book of Habakkuk, then, reflects a liturgical influence in the developing OAN tradition. The book was probably composed between 605 and 589, that is between Nebuchadnezzar's victory at Carchemish and the beginning of the last invasion of Jusah before the destruction of the first temple. Like the later oracles of Jeremiah and the OAN tradition of the Exilic period, the primary focus of the prophet appears to be on the preservation of the people of Israel. The OAN tradition in the hands of Habakkuk is not a political instrument designed to shape foreign policy in Israel/Judah. It has an introspective dimension that is eschatological in its orientation. Israel's only remaining hope lies in her faithfulness to Yahweh, the Divine Warrior, who will still triumph -- in his own time.

> For the fig tree will not yield;
> There is no harvest on the vines.
> The olive tree fails its task;
> The field produces no grain.

---

[140] See W. F. Albright, "The Psalm of Habakkuk," p. 8.

[141] *Loc. cit.*

[142] *Ibid.*, pp. 8-9.

[143] *Ibid.*, p. 9.

Cut off from the fold are the sheep;
There is no cattle in the pens.

Yet I will rejoice in Yahweh;
I will exult in the God of my help.
Yahweh is my lord and my might,
He will make my feet like the feet of hinds;
He will make me to tread on the back of Sea!

(Hab. 3:17-19)[144]

---

[144] Though differing in some matters of detail, this translation of the concluding three verses of the book of Habakkuk is largely that of W. F. Albright, *ibid.*, p. 13.

CHAPTER FIVE

JEREMIAH AND THE TRANSFORMATION OF THE WAR ORACLE

According to tradition Jeremiah began his career as a prophet in the 13th year of the reign of Josiah (Jer. 1:2), that is *ca.* 627/26. He lived to see the destruction of Jerusalem and its temple at the hands of Nebuchadnezzar, and apparently died in Egypt sometime after the assassination of Gedaliah (*ca.* 582; cf. Jer. 43:5-7). His ministry thus spanned the heights of political independence reached by Judah under Josiah and the depths of political subjugation under Jehoiakim (*ca.* 609-597) and Zedekiah (*ca.* 597-587).

In the account of his call to the prophetic office, Jeremiah is specifically designated נביא לגוים, "a prophet to the nations" (Jer. 1:5). His divine commission is specific (Jer. 1:9b-10):

Look! I have put my words in your mouth.
See! I have made you an overseer this day,
Over nations and kingdoms;
To uproot and tear down,
To destroy and to raze,
To build and to plant.

Nonetheless, scholars have had great difficulty accepting this account. In 1901 Duhm maintained that Jeremiah would not have considered himself sent to the nations before he had said anything to his own people.[1] He argued that Jeremiah appears in all his prophetic activity exclusively as an Israelite prophet. Even his advice to the ambassadors of the neighbor states in Jer. 27:1ff., and the statement of 28:8 that Jeremiah saw himself in the line of earlier prophets who had prophesied evil "over great kingdoms," at least for Duhm, did not make him a prophet to the nations. Stade, writing five years later, was even more forceful, arguing that it was impossible for an ancient prophet in Israel to see himself "als Propheten für die Heiden."[2] Stade considered it so unlikely that a prophet, who knew he was sent to his own people, would insert לגוים in the account of his call that it could only be explained as coming from some later reviser. Other references to the nations in Jer. 1:10; 28:8; 36:2 and elsewhere were secondary additions to the text, inserted

---

[1]See D. B. Duhm, *Das Buch Jeremia* (KHC 11; Tübingen: J. C. B. Mohr, 1901), p. 6.

[2]B. Stade, "Der 'Völkerprophet' Jeremiah und der jetzige Text von Jer. Kap. 1," *ZAW* 26 (1906), p. 102.

to bring the late collection of foreign oracles in chs. 46-51 into connection with Jeremiah's activity. For Stade even the fact that Jeremiah occasionally prophesied against other peoples does not prove "das er 'für die Heiden' bestellt ist."[3] Bruston agreed with Stade though he did resort to a different emendation of the text of Jer. 1:5.[4] As Hay has noted, "All of these objections are based fundamentally on the prejudice that Jeremiah could not have considered himself called to be a prophet to the foreign nations as well as to Judah."[5]

More recent studies in the prophetic literature have noted the political dimension that permeates Hebrew prophecy from the days of Samuel to the very end of the prophetic institution in post-Exilic Israel. Our study of the war oracle from the time of Amos to Habakkuk has confirmed the fact that, indeed, the typical prophet in pre-Exilic Israel was a "prophet to the nations." As Wright has put it, "prophecies *against* foreign nations . . . (are) such a constant feature in prophecy that we must assume (them) to be an integral part of the prophetic message and outlook" (emphasis his). When Jeremiah called attention to the prophets who had preceded him who had "prophesied war, famine, and pestilence against many countries and great kingdoms" (28:8), he placed himself squarely within Israel's most ancient traditions.

Jeremiah and Holy War

John Bright has called attention to Jeremiah's "profound feeling for Israel's ancient traditions."[7] The most basic of these traditions as far as understanding Jeremiah's use of the war oracle are the traditions of holy war. We have already noted that the Royal Fall Festival was an important carrier of holy war traditions in ancient Israel. War songs celebrating Yahweh's Holy War of the Exodus-Conquest were at home in the ritual conquest traditions, both in the premonarchical cult at Gilgal and in its subsequent adaptation to the cultic celebration of Yahweh's enthronement in Jerusalem. Isaiah, who was strongly influenced by the royal theology of the Jerusalem priesthood, has preserved reflections of this tradition. Jeremiah rejected much of the so-called royal theology, particularly the inviolability of Zion.

---

[3]*Ibid.*, p. 103.

[4]Ch. Bruston, "Jérémie fut-il prophète pour les nations?" *ZAW* 27 (1907), pp. 75-78.

[5]L. C. Hay, "The Oracles Against the Foreign Nations in Jeremiah 46-51" (unpub. Ph.D. thesis, Vanderbilt University, 1960), p. 46.

[6]G. Ernest Wright, "The Nations in Hebrew Prophecy," *Encounter* 26 (1965), p. 231.

[7]John Bright, *Jeremiah* (AB 21; Garden City, New York: Doubleday & Company, 1865), p. LXXXVIII.

Nonetheless, his ministry is shaped no less than that of Isaiah by Israel's ancient traditions of holy war.

James Shenkel has shown the close connection between the prophetic *rîb* motif and the traditions of holy war in Jeremiah.[8] In particular he noted the striking passage in Jer. 23:16-22 where the prophet authenticates his mission, rejecting the false prophets and their message of "peace": "For who among them has stood in the council of Yahweh (עמד בסוד יהוה) to perceive (him) and to hear his word, or who has given heed to his word and listened?" The conceptual image is that of a herald reporting what he has seen and heard in the divine council. The same imagery is repeated in vss. 21-22:[9]

> I did not send the prophets, yet they ran; I did not speak to them, yet they prophesied. But if they had stood in my council (עמדו בסודי), then they would have proclaimed my words to my people, and they would have turned them from their evil way, and from the evil of their doings.

The true prophet, then, is the one who "assists at a judicial proceeding of Yahweh and his council and this is the basis of the prophetic *rîb* oracle, the expression of the divine lawsuit."[10] There is no report of the proceedings of the heavenly court in Jer. 23:16-22, but the sentence or judgment which the prophet is to proclaim is presented in vocabulary reminiscent of Israel's ancient war songs:

> Behold, the storm of Yahweh (סערת יהוה)! Wrath (חמה) has gone forth, a whirling tempest (סער); and it will burst upon the head of the wicked. The anger of Yahweh (אף יהוה) will not turn back until he has executed and accomplished the intents of his mind. (Jer. 23:19-20)

As Shenkel put it:[11]

> The image of Yahweh as head of the divine council has a triple aspect, that of king, judge and warrior. It is in the latter role that he executes the judgment given in the divine council. Hence there is an intimate connection betwen the *rîb* motif and the holy war motif. Succinctly stated the conceptual background is the

---

[8]James D. Shenkel, "Jeremiah and Holy War" (unpub. Old Testament seminar paper, Harvard University, Fall 1962).

[9]The verb עמד, "to stand," as used in Jer. 23:18,22 is a technical term for assistance at a judicial proceeding, as noted by Cross, "The Council of Yahweh in Second Isaiah," *JNES* 12 (1953), p. 274, n. 3.

[10]Shenkel, *op. cit.*, p. 4.

[11]*Loc. cit.*

following. Israel has broken covenant. A covenant lawsuit has been held in heaven, the witnesses of the original covenant have been summoned, and sentence imposed: guilty. The prophet is the officer of heaven who announces the verdict to those pronounced guilty. The imagery he employs in depicting Yahweh as warrior concerns Yahweh's punitive action in carrying out the sentence. This latter concern is the cardinal difference between the use made of the holy war motif in the prophets, and the ancient holy war ideology.

In the execution of divine judgment against Judah as conceived and expressed by Jeremiah, we find the same inversion of classical holy war traditions found in Isaiah's oracles. Yahweh is no longer the Divine Warrior waging battle in Israel's behalf; he is the divine suzerain of the nations coming in judgment against his own people. It should be noted that even in classical holy warfare Yahweh did not always fight in Israel's behalf, as witnessed by the story of Achan's sin in Joshua 7. Failure to maintain the standards of holiness demanded by the Divine Warrior resulted in military defeat. In Jeremiah, as was the case in the oracles of Isaiah, Yahweh is employing foreign armies as unwitting partners in his chastisement of disobedient Israel.

The most explicit text in Jeremiah which portrays judgment as holy war against Judah is found in Jer. 21:1-5.[12] King Zedekiah turned to Jeremiah to find out Yahweh's intentions in regards the siege of Jerusalem. As Shenkel has noted, the inhabitants of Jerusalem were still hoping for a holy war intervention on the part of Yahweh, as a hundred years earlier in the time of Sennacherib:[13]

> This is the word which came to Jeremiah from Yahweh, when King Zedekiah sent to him Pashur the son of Malchaiah and Zephaniah the priest . . . saying, "Inquire of Yahweh for us, for Nebuchadrezzar king of Babylon is making war against us; perhaps Yahweh will deal with us according to all his wonderful deeds, and will make him withdraw from us. (Jer. 21:1-2)

Jeremiah's response was the proclamation of holy war *against* Jerusalem delivered as the herald of the Divine Warrior:

> Then Jeremiah said to them: "Thus you shall say to Zedekiah, 'Thus says Yahweh, the God of Israel: Behold, I will turn back the weapons of war which are in your hands and with which you are fighting against

---

[12]Which falls in the "deuteronomic" (C) source in the well-known classification of Mowinckel.

[13]See J. Shenkel, *op. cit.*, pp. 6-7.

> the king of Babylon and against the Chaldeans who are besieging you outside the walls; and I will bring them together into the midst of this city. *I myself will fight against you* with outstretched hand and strong arm, in anger (באף), and in fury (בחמה), and in great wrath (בקצף גדול). . . .'" (Jer. 21:3-5; emphasis mine)

The expression "with outstretched hand and strong arm" is a cliché for expressing Yahweh's mighty acts on behalf of Israel, especially in the Exodus-Conquest.[14]

Other passages in the "deuteronomic" (C) source of Jeremiah display this same motif of the inversion of Yahweh's holy war. One of the more striking instances is found in chapter 27. The historical context is an apparent rebellion against Babylon involving Edom, Moab, Ammon, Tyre and Sidon (27:3). Jeremiah's oracle is addressed to the kings of these nations and the motif of submission is that Yahweh has handed them over to his "servant," Nebuchadnezzar:

> It is I who by great power and my outstretched arm have made the earth, with the men and animals that are on the earth, and I give it to whomever it seems right to me. Now I have given all these lands into the hand of Nebuchadnezzar, the king of Babylon, my servant . . . (Jer. 27:5-6)

Shenkel has shown that this inversion of holy war into divine judgment against Judah and her neighbors is by no means limited to the "deuteronomic" (C) source in Jeremiah.[15] The biographical materials (Mowinckel's "B" source) contain the same motif. The destruction of Jerusalem as presented in Jer. 19 is to be accomplished by hostile armies under Yahweh's control: "And in this place I will make void the plans of Judah and Jerusalem, and will cause their people to fall by the sword before their enemies, and by the hand of those who seek their life" (Jer. 19:7). Jeremiah's response to Pashur, who had him beaten and put in the stocks, is in the same vein (cf. Jer. 20:4-5).

Though these prose passages are perhaps the most explicit evidence, the poetic texts (Mowinckel's "A" source) are more graphic in their portrayal of Judah's chastisement in the imagery of warfare, with Yahweh in charge of the armies of Judah's enemies. Shenkel has discussed a number of examples.[16] In the vision of the boiling pot, one of the visions associated with Jeremiah's call, Yahweh declares that he is calling the kings of the north against Jerusalem and all the cities of Judah (1:13-16). In the oracle of Jer. 4:11-18, which Bright has entitled "The Stormwind of Judgment,"[17] the prophet

---

[14]Cf. Exod. 6:6; Deut. 4:34; 5:15; 26:8; I Kings 8:42; and Ps. 136:12. See also Shenkel, *ibid.*, p. 7.

[15]Shenkel, pp. 8-10.

[16]*Ibid.*, pp. 8-9.

has clearly linked the military assault of the unnamed destroyer with the punitive action of Yahweh. The oracle in Jer. 5:15-17 presents a similar picture:

	English	Hebrew	Syllables
	Look! I am bringing against you a nation from afar,		
	O house of Israel . . .		
	A nation whose language you know not;	גוי לא תדע לשנו	7
	Nor can you make out what they say.	[]לא תשמע מה ידבר	7

In subsequent lines the formidable military power of this nation is detailed along with the destruction they will cause in Judah.

Robert Bach has called attention to the ancient prophetic *Gattungen* of "summons to flight" and "summons to battle" preserved in the poetry of Jeremiah.[18] Most of these instances occur within the OAN tradition and will be discussed in detail later in this chapter. There are, however, two important passages in the poetic (A) source of Jeremiah which are generally regarded as reflecting his early preaching -- Jer. 4:5-8 and 6:1-5.

<u>Jeremiah 4:5-8</u>

Verse	English	Hebrew	Syllables
5	Proclaim it in Jerusalem;	הגידו ב(ירושלם)[a]	8
	And throughout Judah spread the news!	וב(יהודה) השמיעו [][b]	8
	Sound the trumpet through the land!	[]תקעו שופר בארץ	6
	Declare mobilization and say:	קראו מלאו[c] ואמרו	7
	"Assemble and let us go	האספו ונבואה	8
	Into the fortified cities!"	אל ערי []מבצר	5
6	Hoist the banner toward Zion!	שאו נס ציונה	6
	Flee for safety! Do not delay!	העיזו אל תעמדו	7
	(For) I am bringing calamity	[כי] רעה אנכי מביא	8/7
	Out of the north, a shatt'ring disaster.	מצפון []שבר גדול	6
7	The lion has gone up from his thicket;	עלה אריה מסבכו	8
	The destroyer of nations is on his way.	[ו]משחית גוים נסע	6/7
	He has left his base	יצא ממקמו	6
	To make your land a shambles.	לשום ארצך לשמה[d]	7/8
	Your cities will be ruins	עריך תצינה	11
	with no inhabitant (in them).	מאין יושב ⟨בהן⟩[e]	
8	So wrap yourself in sackcloth!	על זאת חגרו סקים	6
	Lament and wail!	ספדו והילילו	6
	For it has not turned back from us,	כי לא שב (ממנו)[f]	11
	Yahweh's fierce anger.	חרון אף יהוה	

---

[17] J. Bright, *Jeremiah*, p. 29.

[18] R. Bach, *Aufforderungen zur Flucht*; see p. 12, n. 53 above.

Notes to the Text of Jeremiah 4:5-8

[a]The two place names are exchanged to improve the metrical balance within this bicolon. If MT is retained, read the bicolon as a /b:1/ unit.

[b]The term ואמרו is deleted as a secondary expansion, perhaps from the following bicolon.

[c]See D. Winton Thomas, "מלאו in Jeremiah IV.5: A Military Term," *JJS* 3 (1952), pp. 47-52. From the study of the Hebrew text of Jer. 51:11; 12:6; Job 16:10; Gen. 48:19 and Isa. 31:4, in combination with the ancient versions, with the testimony of some Jewish commentators, and with the evidence of other Semitic languages, Thomas concludes that the root *mlʾ* can be used in the sense of "collect, assemblé, mass," and that the noun מלוא can mean "multitude, mass." The implied object of מלאו in the present context is מלוא and the phrase קראו מלאו means literally "proclaim, assemble a מלוא;" i.e., "assemble an assembly," a phrase which is equivalent to "proclaim mobilization." The Piel verbal form is taken in a declarative sense, hence "declare mobilization." The most instructive parallel usage is found in Jer. 12:6 where the phrase קראו אחריך מלא was correctly understood by the translators of LXX who rendered מלא as ἐπισυνηχθησαν, "are gathered together." Cf. the Arabic cognate which in the sixth form means "aided, assisted one another to do a thing." Arabic *malaʾun* and Syriac *mulaya* both mean "assembly." Cf. also Akk. *millu*, "band, company."

[d]The variant form *לשמה* can be read here to improve the meter, as Professor Cross has suggested; cf. Jer. 34:22.

[e]A conjectural emendation to improve the meter; cf. Jer. 4:29 and 50:3.

[f]Relocating this word to achieve better internal metrical balance within this strophe.

Jeremiah 4:5-8 in Outline

A. Summons to Flight (vss. 5-7b)

[1:1] ?	Proclaim the news in Judah!
[2(b1:1b)]	Muster the people and send them to safety!
[1b:b1]	The "Destroyer" has come.

B. Summons to Mourn (vss. 7c-8)

[1:(b:b):1]	Mourn, for Yahweh's wrath has not turned back from us.

The first strophe of this poem is a "summons to flight" in which the people of Judah/Jerusalem are told to flee to their fortified cities. The summons has a quality of irony, however, for there is no escape. The "lion," the "destroyer of nations" who has gone up to destroy the land of Judah is Yahweh himself. The Divine Warrior is "bringing calamity out of the north, a shatt'ring disaster." Military terminology is dominant here as D. Winton Thomas has shown.[19]

The prosodic-textual analysis of this summons to flight reveals an interesting adaptation of the qinah metrical pattern. In three successive four-part units there is poetic parallelism between the first long and short member but not the second. The pattern may be scanned 2(b:1::1b) / 1:b::b1.

The second strophe introduces a third type of "summons" oracle -- the summons to mourn, an important speech form within the OAN tradition, especially in Jeremiah. Within this poem the summons to mourn is essentially an announcement of judgment focusing attention on the threatening and foreboding aspects of the coming events.

Jeremiah 6:1-5 is somewhat similar in prosodic structure and content:

1	Flee for safety, people of Benjamin,	העזו בני בנימן	8
	from the midst of Jerusalem!	מקרב ירושלם	6
	Blow the trumpet in Tekoa,	[]בתקוע תקעו שופר	7
	And on Bet-hakkerem raise a signal!	ועל בית []כרם שאו משאת	8
	For calamity peers out of the north,	כי רעה נשקפה מצפון	9
	a shatt'ring disaster;	[]שבר גדול	3
2	The "delightful meadow" I will destroy,	[]נוה []מענגה דמיתי[a]	9
	O Daughter Zion.	בת ציון	3
3	Unto her shall come shepherds	אליה יבאו רעים	8
	and their flocks;	ועדריהם	4
	They shall pitch their tents round about,	תקעו [][b] אהלים סביב	8
	Each one shall graze the part he chooses.	רעו איש [] ידו[c]	5
4	Sanctify yourselves for battle against her!	קדשו עליה מלחמה	9
	Up! Let us attack in broad daylight!	קומו ונעלה בצהרים	9
	Alas! The daylight is waning!	אוי לנו כי פנה []יום	7
	Indeed, the shadows of evening lengthen.	כי ינטו צללי ערב	7
5	Up! Let us attack by night!	קומו ונעלה בלילה	8
	Let us destroy her strongholds!	[]נשחיתה ארמנותיה	8

<u>Notes to the Text of Jeremiah 6:1-5</u>

[a]The Hebrew text of this line is uncertain and is frequently emended. On the root *dmh* II, "(cause to) cease, destroy," cf. Jer. 47:5; Obad. 5; Isa. 15:1 and Ezek. 32:2 (all in OAN contexts).

[b]Deleting עליה *metri causa*.

[c]On this usage of יד cf. II Sam. 19:44 and II Kings 11:7.

---

[19]See D. Winton Thomas, "מלאו in Jeremiah IV.5: A Military Term," *JJS* 3 (1952), pp. 47-52.

Jeremiah 6:1-5 in Outline

A. Summons to Flight: To Men of Benjamin in Jerusalem (vss. 1-3)

[1b:b1] Flee for safety; assemble in Tekoa!

[2(1b:1b)] Zion shall be the habitation of shepherds.

B. Summons to Battle: To the Hosts Assembled Against Judah (vss. 4-5)

[1:1] Prepare yourselves for the attack!

[1:1] Daylight is waning.

[1:1] Attack by night!

The oracle in Jer. 6:1-5 consists of two strophes, the first of which is a summons to flight addressed to the people of Benjamin who are urged to flee south from the midst of Jerusalem. Again military terminology is dominant with the blowing of the trumpet (תקעו שופר) and the raising of a battle signal (שאו נס שאו משאת in Jer. 4:6).[20] The people are to take flight because the Divine Warrior is about to destroy Zion. Jerusalem is to be so devastated that her ruins will be the haunt of shepherds and their flocks, a familiar motif within the developing OAN tradition. In prosodic structure this summons to flight is another example of the qinah metrical pattern.

The second strophe is a summons to battle, apparently addressed to the enemy hosts assembled against Jerusalem. As herald of the divine suzerain of the nations, the prophet summons the hosts to battle with striking language. The troops are to "sanctify themselves" (קדשו) for battle, a clear reference to the sacral nature of the warfare, as Shenkel has noted.[21] This strophe is in the form of three balanced bicola which present an interesting picture. The command is to march up against Jerusalem immediately, "in broad daylight," as though the coming battle was indeed imminent. But then realizing that the vision, however vivid, is of an event somewhere in the future, the prophet alters the picture. It is too late in the evening to set out on a military campaign. Nonetheless, the prophet repeats the summons to battle, "attack by night!" Though perhaps delayed somewhat, the onslaught will come -- when least expected. The divine initiative behind this assault on Jerusalem is clearly evident in vs. 6 which again presents familiar imagery from the OAN tradition of Isaiah:

For thus says Yahweh:
"Hew down her trees!
Cast up a siege mound against Jerusalem!

---

[20] John Bright (*Jeremiah*, p. 43) translates this phrase "light the beacon," noting that משאת appears in the Lachish Letters (IV:10) as denoting a fire (or smoke) signal; cf. also Judg. 20:38,40.

[21] See J. Shenkel, *op. cit.*, p. 10.

[This is the city which must be punished,][22]
there is nothing but oppression within her."

Shenkel has cited three other poetic oracles in Jeremiah which depict Yahweh's holy war against Jerusalem -- Jer. 8:14-17; 15:5-9 and 18:13-17.[23] Jer. 8:14a is a summons to flight addressed to Judah: "Gather together, let us go into the fortified cities and perish there." From vs. 16 it is clear that the cause of terror is the approach of an army from the north. The poem in 18:13-17 is a judgment oracle against Judah. After the statement of the specific indictment (vs. 15), we again find the abandonment to the enemy as Yahweh's means of punishment:

> Like the east wind (רוח קדים), I will scatter them before the enemy;
> I will show them my back, not my face, in the day of their calamity.
> (Jer. 18:17)

As Hillers has noted, the language used in vs. 16 is reminiscent of that used in treaty-curses throughout the ancient Near East.[24]

The oracle in Jer. 15:5-9 merits more detailed analysis. In vs. 5 the prophet poses the question: Who will mourn for Jerusalem? Yahweh has rendered his decision: "Because you have rejected me, I will destroy you" (vs. 6). Yahweh's sentence against his people is in the form of a judgment/lament in qinah meter:[25]

7	I will winnow them with a fork,	[]אזרם במזרה	5
	In the towns of their land I will deprive them of children;	בשערי []ארץ שכלתי	7
	I will exterminate my people,	אבדתי [] עמי	5
	since they did not change their ways.	מדרכיהם לוא שבו	7
8	I will make their widows more in number	עצמו לי אלמנת⟨ם⟩[a]	8
	than the sand of the seas.	מחול ימים	4
	I bring against the mother of young warriors	הבאתי [][b] על אם בחור	7
	a destroyer by noon;	שדד בצהרים	6
	I cause to fall upon her suddenly	הפלתי עליה פתאם	8
	anguish and terror.	עיר ובהלות	5

---

[22] The bracketed words are a translation of MT; the Greek would be translated: "this is the city of falsehood." Cf. Shenkel, *ibid.*, p. 26, n. 17.

[23] Shenkel, p. 10.

[24] See D. R. Hillers, *Treaty-Curses and the Old Testament Prophets* (Rome: Pontifical Biblical Institute, 1964), p. 77.

[25] Notes to the text of Jer. 15:7-9 -- a) Reading with LXX χηραι αὐτων, "their widows." Cf. also Syr. and Targ. b) Deleting להם with LXX.

9 She who bore seven languishes;	אמללה ילדת [ ]שבעה	7
She gasps for breath.	נפחה נפשה	5
Her sun goes down while it is yet day;	באה שמשה בעד יומם	8
She is shamed, she is disgraced.	בושה [ ]חפרה	5

Jeremiah 15:7-9 in Outline

[bl:bl:lb] I will exterminate my people.

[2(lb:lb)] I will bring anguish and terror upon "mother" Jerusalem.

The imagery in this poem is vivid as Yahweh directs his holy war against Jerusalem because she has been unfaithful. The motif of the Divine Warrior stretching out his hand in judgment against Judah (vs. 6), has already been noted as a reflex of earlier poetic language from the Exodus-Conquest era.[26] The term בצהרים (here in parallel with פתאם), as denoting the rapidity of military siege operations, occurs also in Zeph. 2:4.[27]

Shenkel concluded his analysis of "Warfare Imagery and the Execution of Divine Judgment" in Jeremiah as follows:[28]

> It is evident from a consideration of all the texts which represent the three principal strata of materials in Jeremiah that have been cited, that the punitive intervention of Yahweh in Judah's history was expressed in terms of a military operation in which Yahweh was the principal agent, or in other words, that the conceptual imagery of ideology of holy war was a dominant motif.

The ideology of holy war was formative in the prophet's self-understanding. His call and confirmation into the prophetic office, his trust in Yahweh, his rejection of trust in human resources, his prophetic intercession, his rejection of the inviolability of Zion, his relation to the false prophets, and his "pacifism" must all be understood in light of the fact that Jeremiah understood himself primarily as the herald of the Divine Warrior, proclaiming holy war against Judah and Jerusalem, and by extension, to foreign nations as well.[29]

Jeremiah and the "Cup of Yahweh's Wrath"

The fact that chapter 25 of Jeremiah is somehow connected with the OAN collection of Jer. 46-51 is obvious. As Hay put it, "the drinking of the cup symbolizes the judgment of the nations, a judgment that is articulated in the oracles."[30] In the text of LXX the collection of foreign oracles appears

---

[26]See pp. 184-85 above. [27]See p. 156, n. a above.

[28]Shenkel, *op. cit.*, p. 11. [29]*Ibid.*, pp. 11-18.

[30]L. C. Hay, "Oracles Against Foreign Nations," p. 75.

after 25:13 and the "Cup of Wrath" pericope (25:15-38) was clearly regarded as the proper conclusion to this collection. Nonetheless, the relationship between ch. 25 and the OAN collection of chs. 46-51 is not entirely clear.

Cornill has shown that only in the MT form of the text does 25:1-13 form a suitable introduction to Jeremiah's OAN tradition.[31] There is a striking difference between the texts of LXX and MT in this chapter. In MT the discourse threatens Judah with destruction at the hands of Nebuchadnezzar king of Babylon, and then after 70 years Babylon in turn will be judged. LXX nowhere mentions Babylon or Nebuchadnezzar in this chapter. The vague reference in vs. 9 to the πατριαν ἀπο βορρα ("family/nation from the north") which Yahweh will send against Judah is in keeping with the general "enemy from the north" motif of Jeremiah's early preaching.[32] The desolation wreaked in both Judah and her neighbors by this unnamed foe is presented in typical language of ancient treaty-curses (vss. 9b-11a):

> . . . δωσω αὐτους εἰς ἀφανισμον και εἰς συριγμον και εἰς ὀνειδισμον αἰωνιον· [10]και ἀπολω ἀπ' αὐτων φωνην χαρας και φωνην εὐφροσυνης, φωνην νυμφιου και φωνην νυμφης, ὀσμην μυρου και φως λυχνου. [11]και ἐσται πασα ἡ γη εἰς ἀφανισμον . . .

> . . . I will make them a desolation, and a hissing and an everlasting reproach; and I will destroy from them the voice of joy, and the voice of gladness, the voice of the bridegroom and the voice of the bride, the scent of ointment, and the light of a candle. And all the land shall be a desolation . . .

In the summary judgment Judah is to be enslaved ἐν τοις ἔθνεσιν ("among the nations" -- vs. 12) for 70 years. Again the specification of Judah's enemy is vague. The reference to το ἔθνος ἐκεινος ("that nation") and την γην ἐκεινην ("that land") can be interpreted as a reference to Babylon, but this is by no means certain. Bright has argued that "the nation threatened in vs. 13 was originally Judah, while 'this book' was the (original) scroll of Jeremiah's prophecies."[33] As Cornill argued, the text of 25:1-13 has undergone a systematic editing which preceded the LXX and which MT carries much further.[34]

If Jer. 25:1-13, in its original form, does not form a proper introduction to Jeremiah's oracles against the nations, perhaps the "Cup of Wrath"

---

[31]Carl Heinrich Cornill, *Das Buch Jeremia* (Leipzig: Chr. Herm. Tauchnitz, 1905), p. 282.

[32]Cf. Jer. 1:13-15; 4:5-31; 5:15-17; 6:1-5; etc.

[33]J. Bright, *Jeremiah*, p. 163.

[34]C. H. Cornill, *Das Buch Jeremia*, p. 282. Cornill is following the arguments of F. Schwally as advanced in his study of the OAN tradition in *ZAW* 8 (1888), p. 183. See p. 2, n. 3 above.

pericope in 25:15-38 was the introduction and not the conclusion to this collection, as Cornill, Rudolph and others have suggested.[35] The relationship between 25:15-38 and chs. 46-51, however, does not appear to be so simple. The text of 25:15-38 has also undergone a complex development in the history of transmission and expansion. The difference between the texts of MT and LXX is again of primary importance in determining the relationship between these two parts of the book of Jeremiah.

In his doctoral dissertation, John G. Janzen has shown that the LXX represents an early recension of the text of Jeremiah which is not only significantly shorter, but also one that preserves superior readings in many instances.[36] The present writer has found the LXX most helpful in reconstructing Jeremiah's poetry. With the objective control of the historical development of Hebrew prosody, the Hebrew text reflected in LXX has been found to be generally superior to the expansionist text of MT.

The text of 25:15-38, as reconstructed with the aid of LXX, reveals a complex history of tradition. A poem against the nations in general (25:30-38) shows striking affinity to the 8th century OAN tradition of Amos. In Amos 1:2 the series of oracles against the nations was introduced by the quatrain:

Yahweh roars from Jerusalem;	יהוה מירושלם ישאג	9
From Zion he utters his voice.	ומיהודה יתן קולו	9
The pastures of shepherds dry up;	[]אבלו נאות []רעים	7
And the top of Carmel withers.	ויבש ראש []כרמל	6

This refrain (the first bicolon of which is also quoted in an OAN context in Joel 4:16) provides the formative theme of the poetry preserved in Jer. 25: 30-38.

<u>Jeremiah 25:30-38 (LXX 32:16-24)</u>

30 [You shall prophesy against them these words and say:]

Yahweh roars from the heights;	יהוה ממרום ישאג	7
From his holy abode his voice thunders.	[] מקדשו[a] יתן קולו	7
He roars mightily against his fold;	שאג ישאג על נוהו	8
Like the grape-treader's shout it rings out.	הידד כדרכים יענה	8

---

[35]*Ibid.*, p. 284; W. Rudolph, *Jeremia* (HAT I/12; Tübingen: J. C. B. Mohr, 1958, 2nd ed.), p. 141; and G. Fohrer, *Introduction to the Old Testament*, p. 397.

[36]Written originally in 1965, this work is now available in published form. See J. Gerald Janzen, *Studies in the Text of Jeremiah* (HSM 6; Cambridge: Harvard University Press, 1973).

	Against the inhabitants of the earth,	⟨ו⟩אל⟨י⟩[b] ישבי []ארץ	7
31	(His) clamor resounds to the ends of the earth.	בא שאון עד קצה []ארץ	7
	For Yahweh has an indictment against the nations;	כי ריב ליהוה בגוים	8
	He is arraigning all flesh for judgment;	נשפט הוא לכל בשר	7
	The wicked he will put to the sword.	[]רשעים נתנם לחרב	8
	--utterance of Yahweh.	נאם יהוה	
32	Thus says Yahweh:	כה אמר יהוה [][c]	-
	Look! The disaster spreads	הנה רעה יצאת	10
	from nation to nation;	מגוי אל גוי	
	A mighty tempest stirs	[]סער גדול יעור	10
	from the earth's farthest bounds.	מירכתי ארץ	

33 [Those slaughtered by Yahweh on that day shall extend from one end of the earth to the other. They shall not be buried; they shall be like dung upon the face of the earth.]

34	Howl, O shepherds! Cry!	הילילו []רעים וזעקו	8
	Roll on the ground, lords of the flock!	[]התפלשו אדירי []צאן	8
	(For) the time of your slaughter has come;	[כי] מלאו ימיכם לטבוח	10/9
	Down you'll go like the choicest rams.	[][d] ונפלתם ככ⟨ר⟩י[e] חמדה	9
35	There will be no refuge for the shepherds,	ואבד מנוס מן []רעים	8
	No escape for the lords of the flock.	[]פליטה מאדירי []צאן	8
36	Listen! A howling from the shepherds,	קול (יללת)[f] []רעים	6
	The cry of the lords of the flock!	(צעקת) אדירי []צאן	6
	For Yahweh is despoiling their pastures;	כי שדד יהוה [] מרעיתם	8
37	Their quiet sheepfolds are devastated,	ונדמו נאות []שלום	8
	Because of the fierce wrath of Yahweh.	מפני חרון אף יהוה	8
38	Like a lion he has left his lair,	עזב ככפיר סֻ⟨בְּ⟩כוֹ[g]	8
	Their land has become a shambles,	[][h] היתה ארצם לשמה	8
	Because of (his) dreadful anger.	מפני חרונהּ[i] יונה	8

<u>Notes to the Text of Jeremiah 25:30-38</u>

[a]Following LXX which reads ἀπο του ἁγιου αὐτου; cf. also the Old Latin, *de loco sancto suo*.

[b]Following LXX, και ἐπι καθημενους. The כל of MT is a frequent addition to the text of MT in Jeremiah.

[c]Deleting צבאות with LXX as an expansionary gloss. This term is another frequent addition to the text of MT in Jeremiah.

[d]The colon is too long. Delete ותפוצותיכם with LXX.

[e]A conjectural emendation based on LXX, οἱ κριοι, which is used to translate כרים in Ps. 65:14.

[f]The paired words are exchanged in this bicolon to improve the metrical balance.

[g]The proposed emendation involves a simple haplography and is based on the parallel usage in Jer. 4:7 (see p. 186 above). Cf. also Jer. 21:14 and 46:14 where MT סביביה and סביביך may also reflect a textual corruption of this same word.

[h]Omitting כי as an apparent dittography.

[i]Reading the *he* as a vowel letter for the third person singular masculine suffix rather than the article of the following word.

Jeremiah 25:30-38 in Outline

A. Theophanic Announcement: The Devastating Voice of Yahweh (vss. 30-31)

[3(1:1)] Yahweh's roaring resounds far and wide.

[1:1:1] Yahweh is arraigning the nations for judgment.

B. Announcement of Judgment (vss. 32-33)

[1:1] A mighty tempest is spreading disaster among the nations.

[prose] ? Those slaughtered by Yahweh shall cover the face of the earth.

C. Summons to Mourn (vss. 34-35)

[1:1] Howl, O rulers of the nations!

[1:1] The time of your slaughter has come.

[1:1] There is no escape.

D. Prophetic Vision: Yahweh as a Destroying Lion (vss. 36-38)

[1:1] Listen to the "shepherds" howl!

[1:1:1] Yahweh is destroying their "pastures."

[1:1:1] Like a lion he has gone up to ravage their land.

The first three bicola (vss. 30b-31a) are an expansion of the theme of Yahweh "roaring from Zion" as presented in Amos 1:2. The following tricolon presents the substance of Yahweh's "roar": the Divine Warrior/Judge is arraigning all the nations for judgment. Amos' theme of the "pastures of the shepherds withering" before Yahweh is expanded by Jeremiah in a remarkable manner. In imagery taken from Israel's ancient war songs, the coming disaster which "spreads from nation to nation" is portrayed as "a mighty tempest (סער גדול) which has come "from the earth's farthest bounds" (vs. 32). The rulers of the nations, addressed as "shepherds" (רעים) and "lords of the flock (אדירי צאן), are summoned to mourn their calamity for there is no escape from the wrath to come (vss. 34-35). The summons to mourn is in effect an announcement of judgment -- a terrible scene which the prophet envisions. The rulers of the nations howl in terror for Yahweh is devastating their lands (נאות, "sheepfolds," vss. 36-37). Like a lion Yahweh has gone up from his lair to vent his "dreadful anger" against the nations (vs. 38). The final tricolon forms a poetic inclusion with the opening series of three bicola. Both present Yahweh in the image of a roaring lion who has come up in fierce anger against the nations.

From the above prosodic-textual analysis and interpretation of Jer. 25: 30-38 it is clear that the passage in question is an integral part of the developing OAN tradition in the hands of Jeremiah, and as such must be associated with the individual oracles against foreign nations in chs. 46-51. But is this relationship merely that of an introduction or conclusion to the formal collection of Jeremiah's OAN tradition? The answer to that question lies in an analysis of the "Cup of Wrath" pericope in 25:15-29.

Weiser has denied that 25:15-38 once formed the introduction to the OAN tradition of chs. 46-51, as Rudolph and others maintain.[37] He argued that the enumeration of the individual nations in vss. 18-26 interrupts the stylistic continuity of the "Cup of Wrath" pericope (vss. 15-17, 27-29).[38] To Weiser the list of nations is a secondary addition to the text, made when the oracles were moved from their original place after 25:14, and so served as a kind of substitute for the original poems.[39] The "Cup of Wrath" pericope is then reduced by Weiser to six verses (25:15-17, 27-29) which appear in prose. These verses, as preserved in LXX, may be translated as follows:

> 15 Thus spoke Yahweh, the God of Israel:
> Take this cup of the wine of wrath from my hand,
> and make all the nations to whom I send you drink it.
> 16 They shall stagger and be crazed because of the
> sword which I am sending among them.
> 17 So I took the cup from Yahweh's hand and I made all
> the nations to whom Yahweh sent me drink it.
> 27 "Drink, be drunk and vomit! Fall and rise no more,
> because of the sword which I am sending among you."
> 28 And if they refuse to take the cup from your hand
> to drink, then you shall say --
> Thus spoke Yahweh: "You must drink!
> 29 For look! I begin to work evil at the city which
> is called by my own name, and shall you go unpunished?
> You shall not go unpunished, for I am summoning a sword
> against the inhabitants of the earth."

Again it should be noted that no specific nations are mentioned. The agent of Yahweh's wrath is "a sword" (vss. 16,29) which Yahweh has summoned.

---

[37] Arthur Weiser, *Das Buch des Propheten Jeremia Kapitel 25:15-52:34* (ATD 20; Göttingen: Vandenhoeck & Ruprecht, 1955), p. 231.

[38] J. W. Rothstein and P. Volz have influenced Weiser here.

[39] A Weiser, *op. cit.*, p. 231.

The imagery is that of holy war and the agent of Yahweh's destruction, presumably the Babylonians, is unimportant to the prophet. It is Yahweh's battle.

Weiser has argued that the motif of Yahweh's cup of wrath is not the invention of Jeremiah, as Cornill and others have suggested; but probably goes back to a sacral tradition of divine judgment, perhaps connected to an ancient ordeal custom as reflected in Num. 5:11ff.[40] Bright is also uncomfortable with making Jeremiah the author of this motif, though he does note that "the figure of 'the cup of wrath' . . . is first clearly witnessed in sayings and writings of this general period . . . and may well have been popularized by him and his followers."[41] Cross has suggested that the motif may reflect some ancient rite in which the cup contained blood rather than wine.[42] A possible reflex of this rite is found in the Ugaritic literature where the warrior goddess ʿAnat "drinks blood without a cup" in a gory battle scene.[43] In the context of holy war the cup of wine/blood may have been a victory cup used in cultic celebration. In typical reversal of imagery the cup of victory has become a cup of wrath or poison which the nations are forced to drink to their own destruction.

Bright has also reacted strongly to Weiser's excision of the list of nations from this pericope: ". . . although the list of peoples in vss. 18-26 has doubtless received expansion (but one would expect a list of some sort here!), the prophecy itself [vss. 15-29] may be credited to Jeremiah."[44] The shorter list of nations as preserved in LXX reads as follows (Jer. 25:18-26; LXX 32:4-12):

[4]την Ιερουσαλημ και τας πολεις Ιουδα	Jerusalem and the cities of Ju-
και βασιλεις αὐτου και ἄρχοντας αὐτου	dah, and his kings and his no-
του θειναι αὐτας εἰς ἐρημωσιν και εἰς	bles -- to make them a desolation
ἄβατον και αἰς συριγμον	and a waste and a thing of scorn.
[5]και τον Φαραω βασιλεα Αἰγυπτου και	And Pharaoh king of Egypt, and
τους παιδας αὐτου και τους μεγι-	his servants and his nobles, and
στανας αὐτου [6]και παντα τον λαον	all his people and all the hodge-
αὐτου και παντας τους συμμεικτους	podge (of races there).

---

[40]*Ibid.*, p. 232. Cf. also the discussion of L. C. Hay, *op. cit.*, pp. 85-86.

[41]J. Bright, *Jeremiah*, p. 164.

[42]Private communication.

[43]Cf. UT:ʿnt:II:6-35. The obvious parallel to this cup of wine/blood in the Eucharist of Christian tradition is intriguing.

[44]J. Bright, *Jeremiah*, p. 164.

και παντας τους βασιλεις ἀλλοφυλων, την 'Ασκαλωνα και την Γαζαν και την Ακκαρων και το ἐπελοιπον 'Αζωτου	And all the kings of the Philistines, Ashkelon and Gaza and Ekron and what remains of Ashdod.
7 και την 'Ιδουμαιαν και την Μωαβιτιν και τους υἱους Αμμων 8 και Βασιλεις Τυρου και Βασιλεις Σιδωνος και Βασιλεις τους ἐν τῳ περαν της ϑαλασσης	And Edom and Moab and the children of Ammon, and the kings of Tyre and the kings of Sidon and the kings of the coastland beyond the sea.
9 και την Δεδαν και την Θαιμαν και την Ρως και παντα περικεκαρμενον κατα προσωπον αὐτου 10 και παντας τους συμμεικτους τους καταλυοντας ἐν τῃ ἐρημῳ	And Dedan and Tema and Ros(?), and all those who clip the hair of their temples, and all the hodgepodge of peoples who dwell in the desert.
11 και παντας βασιλεις Αιλαμ και παντας βασιλεις Περσων 12 και παντας βασιλεις ἀπο ἀπηλιωτου	And all the kings of Elam, and all the kings of the Persians, and all the kings from the north.
τους πορρω και τους ἐγγυς, ἕκαστον προς τον ἀδελφον αὐτου, και πασας τας βασιλειας τας ἐπι προσωπου της γης.	Those far and near, each one with his brother, and all the kingdoms which are on the face of the earth.

The list of nations, as preserved in LXX, displays a carefully balanced structure. The series of five thought units concerned with specific foreign nations is framed by an introductory reference to Judah (vs. 4) and a concluding summation (vs. 12bc), to the effect that all the kingdoms of the earth are included. The order of the foreign nations listed is indeed interesting. The first two units present Egypt and Philistia, the most immediate threats to Judah in the Josianic period, and the first to fall before the might of Babylon in the closing decade of the 7th century. The third unit completes the list of Judah's traditional neighbors including each of the member nations listed in Jer. 27:3 as participants in the anti-Babylonian coalition of *ca.* 594. In the next two units the prophet turned to the insurgent Arab peoples and the emergent world powers beyond Babylon in the East.

Objections may be raised regarding the reconstruction of a prosaic list of nations in a form which suggests poetic composition. It should be noted, however, that lists do appear elsewhere in poetic contexts, such as the list of Moabite cities in Jer. 48:21-24. The best known extra-biblical example of an apparent prosaic list imbedded in a poetic context is the "Catalogue of Ships" in Homer's *Iliad*.[45] Moreover, the prose context in which the list

---

[45] See F. Dirlmeier, "Homerisches Epos und Orient," *Rheinisches Museum*

of nations is found contains evidence of an original poetic tradition. Verse 27 may be reconstructed in poetry:

Drink, be drunk and vomit!	שתו שכרו קי<א>ו	6
Fall and rise no more!	נפלו לא תקומו	6

Verses 15-16 may also reflect a possible original poetic unit:

Take the cup of wine from my hand!	קח כוס יין/חמה מידי	6/7
Make all the nations drink it!	השקיתה כל גוים	6
They shall reel in a drunken stupor before me.	התגעשו מפני	7

The reuse of this material in poetic form in the oracle against Edom (Jer. 49:12-13) suggests that Jer. 25:15-29 is a single literary unit. Jer. 49:12 reflects 25:28-29, in the "Cup of Wrath" pericope, whereas Jer. 49:13 reflects 25:18, in the list of nations. In its earliest form this tradition was probably poetic.

The historical setting of the original composition of 25:15-29 may have been *ca.* 601 and the widespread revolt against Nebuchadnezzar of Babylon. The prophet announced judgment against the rebelling nations, Judah included, for they had dared to challenge the political order sanctioned by Yahweh, the suzerain of the nations.

If indeed the original tradition of the cup of Yahweh's wrath in 25:15-29 was poetic, it is certainly prose in its present form, both in MT and LXX, and is probably neither the introduction nor the conclusion to Jeremiah's OAN tradition. The figure of the cup of Yahweh's wrath in Jer. 25 appears to be secondary to the more basic image of the "sword of Yahweh's wrath." Note that in vs. 16 the nations will "stagger and be crazed," not because of the cup of wine, but "because of the sword" which Yahweh is sending among them. Moreover, the only times that the motif appears elsewhere in Jeremiah are in the oracles against Edom (49:12-13) and Babylon (51:7), both of which have either suffered textual expansion after the destruction of Jerusalem in 587, or were in fact composed in the Exilic period. If the cup of Yahweh's wrath was a formative motif for the OAN tradition of Jeremiah, one would expect it

---

für Philologie 98 (1955), pp. 18-37; esp. p. 30. Cf. also Cyrus H. Gordon, *Ugaritic Literature* (Rome: Pontificium Institutum Biblicum, 1949), p. 6: ". . . when the Ugaritic poet begins Baal's plea for a house, he uses well-balanced stichoi in the best literary tradition; but as soon as the poet, in the course of the same plea, enumerates the houses of other gods (e.g., 51: IV:52-57), he gives a jejune listing, as unsatisfying to the modern esthete as Homer's Catalogue of the Ships is to most modern lovers of Homer." An interesting parallel usage of "the catalog" as a poetic device in English poetry is discussed by R. E. McFarland, "Thanksgiving in Seventeenth-Century Poetry," *Albion* 6 (1974), pp. 302-304.

to be more prominant within the formal OAN collection in chs. 46-51.

It is interesting to note that the motif of the cup of Yahweh's wrath proffered to the nations is not nearly as widespread a judgment motif as some scholars have assumed. The passage in Num. 5:11-28, which portrays an ancient ordeal custom for women suspected of adultery, has nothing to do with this literary motif. The references to Yahweh making Israel drink contaminated water (Jer. 8:14; 9:15 and 23:15) also have little, if anything, to do with this motif, but belong rather to the realm of typical language of treaty-curses in the ancient Near East.[46] The parable of the wine jars in Jer. 13: 12-14, though in some respects close to the motif in question, appears to be a take-off on a popular witticism of the day. The point there, as Bright has noted, is that Yahweh will fill the revelers (the inhabitants of Israel) "with drunkenness (i.e., He will rob them of ability to act), and will smash them like the jugs they joke about."[47]

There are but twelve occurrences of the motif of the cup of Yahweh's wrath proffered to the nations in the Old Testament, and only three of these are in Jeremiah (25:15-29; 49:12-13 and 51:7 -- where Babylon is "a golden cup in Yahweh's hand" from which all the nations must drink!). Four of the remaining occurrences are in pre-Exilic material, probably earlier than Jeremiah: Job 21:20, Ps. 60:5, Ps. 75:9 and Hab. 2:15-16. The five other occurrences are in Lam. 4:21, Ezek. 23:31-34, Isa. 51:17-23, Obad. 16 and Zech. 12:2 -- where Jerusalem has become the "cup of reeling to all the peoples round about!"

In the twelve passages where the motif occurs, six and possibly seven different nouns are used to portray the "cup": כד (Job 21:20), קשה (Ps. 60: 5), חמר (Ps. 75:9 in parallel with כוס), סף (Hab. 2:15 -- text emended, and Zech. 12:2), קבעת (Isa. 51:17,22 where it is glossed by כוס), כוס (Jer. 25: 15,17,28; Lam. 4:21; Ps. 75:9; Isa. 51:17,22; Ezek. 23:31-33; and Hab. 2:16), and possibly חרש (Ezek. 23:34). All of these terms with the exception of חרש appear in the Ugaritic literature as vessels from which wine may be drunk, along with some 13 or 14 other synonyms.[48] The very existence of at least two of these nouns has only become evident on the basis of recent study of the Ugaritic literature.

The four non-Jeremianic pre-Exilic occurrences of the motif in question may be reconstructed as follows:

---

[46]See D. R. Hillers, *Treaty-Curses and the Old Testament Prophets* (Rome: Pontifical Biblical Institute, 1964), pp. 63-64.

[47]J. Bright, *Jeremiah*, p. 94.

[48]See the list of Ugaritic terms for "vessels" in Cyrus H. Gordon, *Ugaritic Textbook* (Analecta Orientalia 38; Rome: Pontificium Institutum Biblicum, 1965), p. 536.

1) Job 21:20[49]

Let his descendants drain his cup;	7	יר⟨ו⟩ו[a] עינו[b] כדו
Let them drink of the wrath of Shaddai!	7	[]מחמת שדי ישתה

2) Psalm 60:5[50]

You made your people drain the chalice;	8	הר⟨ו⟩יתה עמך קשה
You made us drink wine that dazed us.	8	השקיתנו יין תרעלה

3) Psalm 75:9

For in Yahweh's hand there is a cup;	6	כי כוס ביד יהוה
The bowl is filled with wine --	6	ויין חמר מלא
He will draw and pour from this.	7	מסך ויגר מזה
O how its dregs will be drained;	7	אך שמריה ימצו
All the wicked of the earth will drink.	6	ישתו כל רשעי ארץ

4) Habakkuk 2:15-16[51]

Alas for the one who makes his neighbor drink from the cup of fierce wrath;	11	הוי משקה רעהו מסף[] חמת [] אף
He makes (them) drunk in order to look upon their nakedness.	11	שכר למען הביט על מעוריהם
You are sated with contempt instead of glory.	8	שבעת קלון מכבוד
Drink, yourself! Stagger!	8	שתה גם אתה []ה(רע)ל
It shall come round to you -- the cup of Yahweh's right hand;	10	תסוב עליך כוס ימין יהוה
Foul shame shall come upon your glory.	10	וקיקלון על⟨י⟩ כבודך

In five of the six pre-Exilic occurrences of the motif, counting Jer. 25:15-29 and 49:12-13, the cup is proffered to foreign nations or to the "wicked." In Jer. 25 Judah is included among the nations who are to drink the cup while in Ps. 60:5 Yahweh has given the cup to his own people who pray for

---

[49]Notes to the text: a) The root *rwh*, "to be saturated, drink one's fill," occurs elsewhere within OAN contexts where it was often confused with the root *r'h*, "to see." In its present context the word is parsed as a Pi. impf. *y^erawwû*. Cf. Jer. 46:10 and Isa. 34:5 where the root is used in a figurative sense with Yahweh's sword being "sated/drenched" with blood. See also Isa. 16:9; 34:7; 43:24; 55:10; Ps. 60:5; Jer. 31:25; Lam. 3:15 and Prov. 5:19; 11:25. b) Cf. Deut. 33:28 where עין יעקב appears as "Jacob's descendants." In the present context the antecedent of the pronoun is the "wicked" of vs. 17.

[50]This vs. is analyzed in context above, see pp. 120-22.

[51]These vss. are analyzed in context above, see pp. 177-78.

vengeance against the neighboring nations which formerly made up the Davidic Empire.

Among the Exilic occurrences of the motif, Lam. 4:21 presents a similar picture:

Rejoice and exult, O daughter Edom,	שישי ושמחי בת אדום	13
you who dwell in the land of Uz!	יושבת בארץ עוץ	
To you also the cup shall pass;	גם עליך תעבר כוס	13
you shall become drunk and lay yourself bare!	תשכרי ותתערי	

Judah has drunk the cup and now Edom shall have her turn. In Jer. 51:7 the cup itself is personified in bold metaphor:[52]

A golden cup was Babylon in Yahweh's hand,	כוס זהב בבל ביד יהוה	14
to make all the earth drunk;	משכרת כל [ ]ארץ	
From her wine the nations drank,	מיינה שתו גוים	13
consequently they reel (as drunken men).	על כן יתהללו [ ]	

Ezekiel has applied the motif only to Judah and Israel (ch. 23:32-34):[53]

You shall drink your sister's cup	כוס אחותך תשתי	13
which is deep and large;	[ ]עמקת ו[ ]רחבה	
You shall be laughed at and held in derision	תהיה לצחק וללעג	13
(for) it contains much;	מרבה להכיל	
You shall be filled with drunkenness and sorrow,	שכרון ויגון תמלאי	13
(for) it is a cup of horror.	כוס [ ][a] שממה	
The cup of your sister Samaria	כוס אחותך שמרון	13
you shall drink and drain it out;	[ ]שתית[ ]ה[b] ומצית [ ]	
Her bowl you shall smash to pieces and (with it)	חרש[ ]ה[c] תגרמי	13
you shall lacerate your breasts.	ושדיך תנתקי	

The usage of the motif in Obad. 16 is somewhat problematic as the cup as such is not mentioned. In the Day of Yahweh all the nations will drink and stagger(?),[54] as Judah did when Nebuchadnezzar destroyed Jerusalem. Only in Zion will there be refuge in that day of destruction (vs. 17). The fire of Jacob/Israel will consume the stubble of Esau/Edom (vs. 18), and the borders of Israel will once more be restored for those returning from exile (vss. 19-21). In the post-Exilic occurrence in Zech. 12:2 the motif appears in a

---

[52]This vs. is analyzed in context below, see pp. 262f.

[53]Notes to the text: a) Delete ו *שמה* with LXX. b) The particle אותה is prosaic. The suffix is retained and taken as accusative. c) The *ḥarāšehā* of MT is repointed as *ḥaršāh*, "her bowl, earthen vessel." Cf. Prov. 26:23 where חרש = "earthen vessel" (RSV).

[54]MT ולעו, "swallow (down)" or "talk wildly," is sometimes emended to read נעו, "reel, totter" (cf. Isa. 24:20 and 29:9).

prose context where Yahweh has made Jerusalem into a "cup of reeling" (סף רעל) for all the neighboring peoples.

The most important text for reconstructing the history of the motif of the cup of Yahweh's wrath proffered to the nations in judgment is that preserved in Isa. 51:17-23.

17	Rouse yourself!	התעוררי	4
	Rouse yourself!	התעוררי	4
	Rise up, O Jerusalem!	קומי ירושלם	5
	You have drunk from the hand of Yahweh	[]שתית מיד יהוה	10
	the cup of his anger;	[] כוס חמתו	
	The chalice of reeling	[] קבעת [][a] תרעלה	9
	you have drunk, you have drained.	שתית מצית	
18	There is no one to guide her	אין מנהל לה	12
	of all the sons she has borne;	מכל בנים ילדה	
	There is no one to grasp her hand	[]אין מחזיק בידה	13
	of all the sons she has reared.	מכל בנים גדלה	
19	These two things are now upon you --	שתים הנה קראתיך	12
	Who will condole with you?	מי ינוד לך	
	Violence and downfall, famine and sword;	[]שד ו[]שבר ו[]רעב ו[]חרב	12
	Who will comfort you?	מי ⟨י⟩נחמך[b]	
20	Your sons swoon,	בניך עלפו	12
	they lie down like antelope in a net;	שכבו [][c] כתוא מכמר	
	They are filled with the anger of Yahweh,	[]מלאים חמת יהוה	12
	with the rage of your God.	גערת אלהיך	
21	So listen to this, O afflicted one!	לכן שמעי נא זאת עניה	9
	You are drunk, but not with wine!	ושכרת ולא מיין	8
22	Thus your Lord, Yahweh, has spoken;	כה אמר אדניך יהוה	8
	For your God will defend the cause of his people:	ואלהיך יריב עמו	8
	"Look! I have taken from your hand	הנה לקחתי מידך	13
	the chalice of reeling;	(קבעת)[d] []תרעלה	
	The cup of my anger you shall not	[] (כוס) חמתי לא תוסיפי	13
	have to drink again.	לשתותה עוד	
23	I will put it in the hand of those who vex	ושמתיה ביד מוגיך	12
	and afflict you --	⟨ומעניך⟩[e]	
	Those who said to you, 'Bow down	[]אמרו לנפשך	12
	that we may walk over you.'	שחי ונעברה	
	And you flattened your back like the ground,	ותשימי כארץ גוך	8
	Like the street (for them) to walk upon."	וכחוץ לעברים	7

Notes to the Text of Isaiah 51:17-23

[a]Deleting כוס as a gloss, with Symmachus; cf. also LXX and Syr.

[b]Following 1QIsa[a], LXX, Vulg., and Syr. against MT אנחמך.

[c]Deleting בראש כל חוצות as an expansionary gloss, perhaps from Lam. 2:19 and 4:1.

[d]MT again glosses קבעת with כוס (cf. vs. 17 above). The order of the words has been reversed to improve the metrical balance. Note that קבעת appears with תרעלה in vs. 17 and כוס with חמתו.

[e]Restoring the text with 1QIsa[a]; cf. also LXX.

Isaiah 51:17-23 in Outline

A. Introduction (vs. 17)

[b:b:b] Summons to awaken: Get up, O Jerusalem!

[1:1] You have drunk the cup of wrath!

B. Lament over Jerusalem (vss. 18-20)

1. Jerusalem's plight (vs. 18)

[bl:bl] None of her sons remain to help her.

2. Jerusalem addressed (vss. 19-20)

[lb:lb] O desolate city, who is left to comfort you?

[bl:lb] Your sons lie silent because of Yahweh's wrath.

C. Oracle of Salvation/Judgment (vss. 21-23)

1. Prophetic announcement (vss. 21-22a)

[1:1] You are drunk, but not with wine.

[1:1] Your God will still defend the cause of his people.

2. Oracle from Yahweh (vss. 22b-23)

[1:1] I have removed the cup of wrath from your hand.

[1:1::1:1] I will give it to those who have trodden upon you.

Cross has discussed the larger context of this poem which combines notions of cosmic warfare with the themes of ritual conquest and a royal processional to Zion within the proto-apocalyptic thought of Second Isaiah.[55] These matters are not taken up here for our concern is the cup of Yahweh's wrath proffered to the nations as a judgment motif.

Engnell has argued that the "seizing of the hand of drunkenness," as portrayed in Isa. 51:17-23, stems originally from the royal ideology of the Jerusalem priesthood, in particular "to a special rite in the royal passion ritual."[56] He suggested that the "cup motif" in its original cultic-ideolog-

---

[55]See F. M. Cross, Jr., "The Divine Warrior," pp. 28-30; cf. also "New Directions in the Study of Apocalyptic," *JThC* 6 (1969), pp. 157-65.

[56]Ivan Engnell, *Studies in Divine Kingship in the Ancient Near East* (Up-

ical connection is preserved in Ps. 116:13.

> I will lift up the cup of salvation (כוס ישועות) and call on the name of Yahweh; I will pay my vows to Yahweh in the presence of all his people.

Nielsen has argued that the "cup of Yahweh's right hand" in Hab. 2:15-16 has acquired a special application, present also in Jeremiah and subsequent prophetic usage -- the punitive retribution of Yahweh.[57] Though some of Engnell's basic assumptions regarding the generalized patterns of mythic thought and ritual activity throughout the ancient Near East must be challenged, his basic understanding of the background of the "cup of wrath" motif in the Jerusalem temple cult may well be correct. The context, however, may have been that of ritual conquest and holy war rather than a "royal passion ritual." To Nielsen's observations regarding the usage of the motif in Habakkuk and Jeremiah, one should add that the cup as a judgment motif is also present in non-prophetic literature of the pre-Exilic period, namely Ps. 60:5 (probably Josianic), Ps. 75:9 and Job 21:20. In Jeremiah the motif is clearly found only in the prose sections of ch. 25 and in OAN material of questionable authenticity (49:12-13 and 51:7). Moreover, even in Jer. 25 the motif of Yahweh's cup of wrath is apparently secondary to the primary motif of Yahweh's sword extended against the nations.

The more basic connection between the formal collection of OAN material (Jer. 46-51) and ch. 25 is the poem preserved in 25:30-38. Since this poem is an expansion of the introduction to the OAN material in Amos 1-2, and since its pastoral motifs are dominant throughout chs. 46-51, one can conclude that the poem may have formed an introduction to Jeremiah's OAN collection. Nonetheless, the formal collection of oracles against foreign nations enjoyed an independent life, as witnessed by their inclusion as a sort of appendix to the book of Jeremiah in MT. Moreover, oracles against foreign nations in Jeremiah are not, in fact, limited to chs. 25 and 46-51. A prose oracle against Egypt is preserved in 43:8-13; 27:5-11 is an oracle against Edom, Moab, Ammon, Tyre and Sidon; and 9:25-26 is an oracle against Egypt, Judah, Edom, Ammon, Moab and the Arab peoples. Consequently we ought not to press too hard for a formal literary connection between Jer. 25 and 46-51, as though we could thus circumscribe Jeremiah's prophetic ministry to the nations. The history of tradition behind ch. 25 is much too complex to posit any simple answer to the question posed by the position of Jeremiah's OAN collection after 25:13 in LXX.

---

psala: Almqvist & Wiksells Boktryckeri A.-B., 1943), p. 210.

[57]E. Nielsen, "The Righteous and the Wicked in Habaqquq," *Studia Theologica* 6 (1953), p. 62.

The War Oracle and the OAN Tradition in Jeremiah

The oracles against the nations in Jer. 46-51 fall into three categories: Jeremianic oracles, which can be assigned to the prophet Jeremiah with some degree of confidence; archaic oracles, which are more timeless in nature and reflect both dependence on earlier OAN material and/or subsequent expansion and readaptation of an original core; and the exilic oracles against Babylon preserved in chs. 50-51.[58] Our analysis here will focus on the first and second of these categories where the oracles in question will be subjected to detailed prosodic-textual analysis. The oracles against Babylon in 50-51 will be analyzed separately, as their eschatological orientation reflects more clearly the transformation of the war oracle as we move from the classical prophetic tradition to the eschatological realm of what subsequently became apocalyptic.

1. Jeremianic OAN

The OAN collection in Jer. 46-51 consists of oracles against nine different nations. Of these the oracles against Qedar, Philistia, Egypt and Elam must be considered Jeremianic. In each case there is relatively little dependence on earlier OAN material and conceptual parallels elsewhere in the poetry of Jeremiah.

a. Oracle against Qedar [Jer. 49:28-33 (LXX 30:6-11)]

28	To Qedar, to the kings of the encampments;	לקדר [ ]לממלכת[a] חצ[ ]ר[b]	
	Thus saith Yahweh:	[ ][c] כה אמר יהוה	
	Rise up! March against Qedar!	קומו עלו אל קדר	7
	Destroy the Eastern People!	ושדדו בני קדם	7
29	Their tents and flocks shall be taken;	אהליהם וצאנם יקחו	9
	Their tent-cloths and all their gear,	יריעותיהם וכל כליהם	10
	And their camels shall be taken away from them.	וגמליהם יִשְׂאוּ להם	10
	Proclaim against them:	[ ]קראו[d] עליהם	5
	Terror (is) on every side!	מגור מסביב	5
30	Flee! Take to your heels!	נסו נדו מאד	5

[58]Cf. Otto Eissfeldt, "Jeremias Drohorakel gegen Ägypten und gegen Babel," in *Verbannung und Heimkehr*, ed. Arnulf Kuschke (W. Rudolph Festschrift, Tübingen: J. C. B. Mohr, 1961), pp. 31-37. Eissfeldt argued for an original Jeremianic kernel in ch. 50:17-20. The narrative in ch. 51:59-64 adds some substance to this interpretation as argued later in this chapter. Nonetheless, chs. 50-51 present unique problems of interpretation and must be placed in a separate category from chs. 46-49.

	Make your dwelling in inaccessible regions,	העמיקו לשבת	5
	O inhabitants of the encampments.	ישבי חצ[]ר [ ][e]	5
	For he has made a plan against you;	כי יעץ עליכם [ ][f] עצה	8
	He has formed a purpose against you.	[]חשב עלי⟨כ⟩ם[g] מחשבה	8
31	Rise up! March	קומו עלו	4
	against a nation at ease,	אל גוי שליו	4
	that dwells in confidence.	יושב לבטח [ ][e]	4
	Without gates,	לא דלתים	4
	without bars,	[]לא בריח לו	4
	they dwell in a remote place.	בדד ישכנו	5
32	Their camels will be for plunder;	והיו גמליהם לבז	9
	Their herds of cattle for spoil.	והמון מקניהם לשלל	9
	I will scatter them to the wind,	וזרתים ל[]רוח[h] קצוצי פאה	10
	those Crop-heads!		
	From every side I will bring their doom.	מכל עברי⟨ם⟩ ו-אביא[i] אידם	10
	--utterance of Yahweh.	נאם יהוה	
33	(His) encampments shall become	והיתה חצ[]ר	6
	a jackal's lair,	למעון תנים	5
	a howling waste forever.	שממה עד עולם	6
	No more shall any man live there,	לא ישב שָׁם[j] איש	6
	Nor human being settle there.	[]לא יגור בה בן אדם	7

Notes to the Text of Jer. 49:28-33

[a]Cf. I Chron. 29:30 כל ממלכות הארצות, "all the kings of the lands" [so J. M. Myers, *I Chronicles* (AB 12; Garden City, New York: Doubleday & Co., 1965), p. 200]. The word *mmlkt* appears in Phoenician with the meaning "royalty, king." Cf. also LXX τη βασιλισση της αὐλης.

[b]The place name Hazor makes little sense in this context. Read instead *ḥāṣēr*, "settlement, village, encampment." Cf. Isa. 42:11 where the term appears in a similar context: חצרים תשב קדר, "the villages that Kedar inhabits" (RSV). See also H. M. Orlinsky, "'Ḥaṣer in the Old Testament," *JAOS* 59 (1939), pp. 22-37.

[c]Deleting אשר הכה נבוכדראצור מלך בבל as an expansionary gloss.

[d]Repointing MT to read an imperative verbal form with LXX.

[e]Deleting נאם יהוה with LXX.

[f]Deleting נבוכדראצר מלך בבל as an expansionary gloss.

[g]Emending with a number of Heb. MSS, Cairo Geniza fragments and the witness of the ancient versions.

[h]Deleting כל as a secondary addition to the text.

[i]Reading the plural form of the substantive to make sense of the line and taking the *waw* as emphatic with the following verb at the suggestion of M.

Dahood (private communication).

[j]Reading the ballast variant to improve the metrical balance. Cf. 2QJer (fragments in *DJD* III, planche XIII) which reads שמה for שם of MT in Jer. 47:7.

Jeremiah 49:28-33 in Outline

A. Summons to Battle (vss. 28-29a)

[1:1]	Yahweh summons his hosts against Qedar.
[1:1:1]	Qedar is to be despoiled.

B. Summons to Flight (vss. 29b-30)

[b:b:b::b:b]	Take to your heels!
[1:1]	The "Destroyer" has formed a plot against you.

C. Summons to Battle (vss. 31-32a)

[b:b:b::b:b:b]	Yahweh summons his hosts against an unsuspecting foe.
[1:1]	Qedar is to be despoiled.

D. Oracle of Doom (vss. 32b-33)

[1:1]	I will scatter them to the wind.
[b:b:b::b:b]	Only desolate ruins will remain.

The oracle against Qedar is difficult to date. The Wiseman chronicle records a campaign of Nebuchadnezzar against the Arabs in December 599.[59] This historical reference is substantiated by Josephus (*Contra Apionem* I, 19). Unfortunately, however, the oracle in question contains no historical allusions by which it can be clearly related to this particular military campaign. Bright has suggested the possibility "that an earlier prophecy has been adapted (by Jeremiah) and reapplied" to a new situation.[60] In light of the insurgence of the Qedarite dominated league of Arab peoples in the middle of the 7th century, this is certainly possible, though in our estimation not likely.

There is one clue which suggests both Jeremiah's authorship and a date *ca.* 609-598. W. L. Holladay has argued that the phrase "terror on every side" (מגור מסביב) is based on a pun which plays on the name of Pashur, the priest who had Jeremiah beaten and placed in the stocks (Jer. 20:1-6).[61] Holladay

---

[59]D. J. Wiseman, *Chronicles of Chaldean Kings (626-556 B.C.)* (London: British Museum, 1956), p. 31f.

[60]J. Bright, *Jeremiah*, p. 338.

[61]See William L. Holladay, "The Covenant with the Patriarchs Overturned: Jeremiah's Intention in 'Terror on Every Side' (Jer 20:1-6)," *JBL* 91 (1972), pp. 305-20; and my response to his article, "'Terror on Every Side' in Jeremiah," *JBL* 92 (1973), pp. 498-502. Holladay argued "that the phrase *māgôr*

argues that Jeremiah's remark that, "Yahweh does not call your name Pashur, but מגור מסביב" marks the origin of this phrase in Jeremiah's usage. And since this same phrase is used in the oracle against Qedar (Jer. 49:29), that oracle probably does not precede the historical altercation between Jeremiah and Pashur which took place *ca.* 609-605. If the activities of the Qedarite league of Arab peoples were such as to necessitate a specific campaign on the part of Nebuchadnezzar in *ca.* 599/8, the oracle in question could have been written any time between *ca.* 609 and 598, when the judgment was in fact meted out.

In literary form the oracle consists of two major divisions, each beginning with a summons to battle in which Yahweh apparently summons his hosts to conquer and despoil the Arab peoples. The first summons to battle (vss. 28-29a) is followed by a summons to flight (vss. 29b-30), addressed to Qedar. The identity of the "Destroyer" who has formed his plot against these people is somewhat ambiguous. The easiest interpretation is perhaps that the "Destroyer" is Nebuchadnezzar; though it can also be argued that the "Destroyer" throughout the entire poem is the Divine Warrior himself, which is certainly the case in the concluding oracle of doom (vss. 32b-33).

The prosodic-textual analysis reveals poetic archaism on the part of Jeremiah. Aware of the mixed metrical patterns of Israel's ancient war poetry, Jeremiah has apparently tried to reproduce ancient metrical patterns, at least in part. The staccato effect of the series of short poetic lines, particularly in the summons to flight (vss. 29b-30) and the second summons to battle (vs. 31), is indeed effective from an aesthetic point of view. A sense of urgency is conveyed with force. The resultant metrical pattern of the poem as a whole, however, is without parallel in Israel's most ancient war poetry.

b. Oracle against Philistia [Jer. 47:1-7 (LXX 29:1-7)]

1	To the Philistines,	[][a] אל פלשתים [][b]	
2	thus saith Yahweh:	כה אמר יהוה	
	Look! Waters are rising up north;	הנה מים עלים מצפון	8
	They come as a torrent in flood.	והיו לנחל שוטף	7
	They will overflow the whole land,	[] ישטפו ארץ []מְלֹאָ[][c]	6
	Towns and those who dwell therein.	עיר וישבי בה	6

---

missābîb is the theological reversal of the name Pašḥur, heard or twisted as the Aramaic *pāš sᵉḥôr*, "fruitful on every side" (*pāš* being the participle of the verb *pwš*, occuring (*sic.*) in the targums in the meaning "be fruitful" to render the Hebrew *prh*);" (p. 307).

	Men cry out:	רזעקו [ ]אדם	6
	The inhabitants of the land wail --	והילל [ ][d] ירשב [ ]ארץ	6
3	At the sound of the galloping	מקול שעטת	10
	hoofs of his steeds;	פְּרָסוֹת אביריו	
	At the clank of his war chariots,	מרעש לרכבו	5
	The rumbling of their wheels.	המון גלגליו	5
	Fathers do not look back for their children,	לא הפנו אבות אל בנים	8
	So feeble are their hands in that day.	מרפיון ידים על היום	8
4	He has come to destroy all the Philistines,	[ ]בא לשדוד [ ]כל פלשתים	8
	To cut off from Tyre its last ally;	להכרית לצר [ ][e] שריד עזר	8
	Yahweh is destroying what is left of the coastland.	[ ][f] שדד יהוה [ ][g] שארית אי [ ][h]	8
5	Baldness has come upon Gaza;	באה קרחה אל עזה	7
	Devastated is Ashkelon,	נדמתה אשקלון	6
	The last of their strength.	שארית עמקם[i]	6
	How long will you whirl about,	עד מתי תתגו(רר)י[j]	11
6	O sword of Yahweh?	[ ][k] חרב ליהוה	
	How long until you are finally at rest?	עד אנה ל-תשקטי[l]	7
	Return to your scabbard!	האספי אל תערך	7
	Desist and be still!	הרגעי ודמו	11
7	(Yet) how can you rest?	איך תשקטי	
	Yahweh has given it orders against Ashkelon;	יהוה צוה לה אל אשקלון	9
	Against the sea coast expressly he has appointed it.	ואל חוף [ ]ים שָׁמָּה[m] יעדה	9

Notes to the Text of Jeremiah 47:1-7

[a]Deleting אשר היה דבר יהוה אל ירמיהו הנביא with LXX as an expansionary gloss.

[b]Deleting בטרם יכה פרעה את עזה with LXX as an expansionary gloss.

[c]To restore metrical balance either this colon must be shortened or the following one lengthened. MT may represent secondary expansion here, perhaps influenced by the occurrence of ארץ ומלואה in Jer. 8:16.

[d]Deleting כל to improve the metrical balance.

[e]Deleting ולצידון כל as an expansionary gloss. Vs. 4 has suffered considerable expansion in MT; cf. LXX and Syr.

[f]Deleting כי as secondary expansion.

[g]Deleting את פלשתים with LXX.

[h]Deleting כפתור with LXX.

[i]Interpreting עמק as "strength" with J. Bright, *Jerusalem*, p. 310. Bright cites the Ugaritic parallel of *ʿmq*, "strength," and the discussion of Driver, *Studies in Old Testament Prophecy*, ed. H. H. Rowley (T. H. Robinson

Festschrift, Edinburgh: T. & T. Clark, 1950), p. 61.

[j]Emending with 2QJer fragment which renders better sense here than the root *gdd*, "cut," of MT.

[k]Deleting הרי with LXX.

[l]Taking the *lamedh* as an asseverative particle; cf. W. L. Moran, *BANE*, p. 68.

[m]Reading the ballast variant form with 2QJer fragment which reads שמה here (see planche XIII in *DJD* III, p. 65.)

Jeremiah 47:1-7 in Outline

A. An Oracle of Doom Against Philistia (vss. 1-5c)

[1:1::1:1] Destruction is coming from the north.

[b:b:1:b:b] The people of Philistia will panic in battle.

[1:1] Fathers will forsake their children in that day.

[1:1:1] Yahweh has come to destroy the Philistines.

[1:1:1] Philistia is undone.

B. Song of Yahweh's Sword (vss. 5d-7)

[1b:1::1:1b] How long will you wreak vengeance?
Return to your scabbard!
Yet how can you do so?

[1:1] Yahweh has ordered his sword against Philistia.

The prosodic-textual analysis reveals a poem of two strophes which presents a war oracle of doom against Philistia (vss. 1-5c) and a song of Yahweh's sword (vss. 5d-7), the agent of Philistia's destruction. The first strophe portrays in vivid fashion the terror of battle, utilizing pairs of short cola to heighten the emotional content. The second strophe, in an unusual metrical pattern, presents the motif of Yahweh's sword of judgment -- a dominant motif in the OAN tradition of Jeremiah. Yahweh's sword is personified in the fashion of *Ba'l*'s two clubs in his combat with *Yamm* in the Ugaritic literature.[62] Yahweh has given his sword orders and consequently it whirls about wreaking destruction in Philistia, almost independent of Yahweh himself. Yahweh has expressly appointed it to destroy Ashkelon, the last of Philistia's strength (vss. 5,7).

Cornill has shown that this oracle exhibits no direct literary contact with the four other oracles against Philistia (Amos 1:6-8; Isa. 14:29-32; Ezek. 25:15-17 and Zeph. 2:4-7).[63] Tadmor sees fragments of a still earlier prophecy relating to a rebellion of Ashkelon against the Assyrian king Esar-

[62]See UT:68:12-28.

[63]See Cornill, *Das Buch Jeremia* (1905), p. 458.

haddon (*ca.* 681-670).[64] Though it is certainly possible that Jeremiah has reused earlier material here, it is not likely in this case. The poem as it stands is a unified whole which displays clear parallels to Jeremiah's poetry elsewhere and fairly clear historical allusions to events in the closing decade of the 7th century.

The oracle is introduced by a prose statement which dates the poem "before Pharaoh smote Gaza," an event which took place *ca.* 609. This chronological notation has been questioned by some critics since it is clear from vs. 2 that the "Destroyer" is coming from the north and hence could not be Egypt. As far as individual Philistine cities are concerned, the focus of attention is on Ashkelon (vss. 5,7). Ashdod is not mentioned in the poem, though numerous scholars emend the text so as to include that city along with Gaza and Ashkelon. Since Ashkelon fell to Nebuchadnezzar in November-December 604, this oracle was apparently composed sometime between *ca.* 609 and 604. Ashdod was destroyed by Necho sometime before 609, after a siege of some 29 years.[65] If Herodotus is to be trusted, Gaza also succumbed to Necho in *ca.* 609 when the Egyptian armies marched north to support crumbling Assyria against the rising Chaldeans.[66] If the interpretation of Albright, Bright and others of the Aramaic letter of King Adon of Ashkelon is correct, it would appear that Ashkelon had also accepted Egyptian suzerainty sometime prior to 604. At least in *ca.* 604, when Nebuchadnezzar's troops were marching south against Ashkelon, Adon made his futile plea for Egypt for help.[67] The assumption of vassalage to Egypt on the part of Ashkelon may have been a direct violation of political agreements reached under Josiah (d. 609) and hence the occasion of this oracle.

The identity of the "Destroyer" who is coming from the north is again somewhat ambiguous. The imagery of "waters" rising in the north to inundate the land suggests cosmic connotations. It would appear that the "Destroyer" here is once again the Divine Warrior marching in the van of a vast military

---

[64]Hayim Tadmor, "Philistia under Assyrian Rule," *BA* 29 (1966), p. 100, n. 52.

[65]Cf. Herodotus (book II, par. 157). See pp. 100 and 160 above.

[66]Herodotus (book II, par. 159).

[67]See p. 103, n. 135 above. The papyrus was originally published by A. Dupont-Sommer, "Un papyrus araméen d'époque Saite découvert à Saqqarah," *Semitica* 1 (1948), pp. 43-68. On historical interpretation see J. Bright, "A New Letter in Aramaic, Written to a Pharaoh of Egypt," *BA* 12 (1949), pp. 46-52; A. Malamat, *IEJ* 6 (1956), p. 251, n. 16; and J. A. Fitzmyer, "The Aramaic Letter of King Adon to the Egyptian Pharaoh," *Biblica* 46 (1965), pp. 41-55. On Greek evidence for the fall of Ashkelon see J. D. Quinn, "Alcaeus 48 (B16) and the Fall of Ascalon (604 B.C.)," *BASOR* 164 (1962), pp. 19-20.

host, presumably the Babylonians. The language in vs. 2 shows dependence on Jeremiah's poetry of the unnamed "foe from the north." In fact, if our textual reconstruction of vs. 2b is correct, the MT reflects corruption from Jer. 8:16 in the phrase ארץ ומלואה which overloads the metrical balance in 47:2. In the second strophe (vss. 5d-7) the "Destroyer" is the sword of Yahweh which is personified. The imagery is that of holy war with the Divine Warrior marching in battle against Philistia.

c. First Oracle against Egypt [Jer. 46:2-12 (LXX 26:2-12)]

2	Concerning Egypt:	למצרים	
	[Concerning the army of Pharaoh Necho, king of Egypt, which was by the river Euphrates at Carchemish; which Nebuchadrezzar, king of Babylon, smote in the fourth year of Jehoiakim, the son of Josiah, king of Judah.]		
3	Make ready with buckler and shield!	ערכו מגן וצנה	7
	Forward! To the battle!	וגשו למלחמה	7
4	Harness the horses!	אסרו [ ]סוסים	4
	Into the saddle -- horsemen!	[ ]עלו [ ]פרשים	5
	Fall into ranks -- with helmets on!	והתיצבו בכובעים	9
	Sharpen the lances!	מרקו [ ]רמחים	5
	Put on full armor!	לבשו [ ]סרינת	5
5	Why are they dismayed?	מדוע [ ][a] המה חתים	6
	They turn tail and flee.	נסגים אחור	5
	Their heroes are beaten back;	[ ]גבוריהם יכתו-(ם)[b]	7
	They flee pell-mell, without looking back.	נוס נסו ולא הפנו	7
	Terror is on every side!	מגור מסביב [ ][c]	5
6	The strong cannot flee;	אל ינוס (גבור)[d]	5
	The swift cannot escape.	[ ]אל ימלט (קל)	5
	In the north by the Euphrates,	צפונה על יד [ ][e] פרת	7
	They collapse, they fall.	כשלו ונפלו	7
7	Who is this that rises like the Nile,	מי זה כיאר יעלה	8
	Like rivers that surge to and fro?	כנהרות יתגעשו	8
8	The "waters" of Egypt rise like the Nile,	מימיו מצרים כיאר יעלה [ ][f]	9
	Saying, "I will rise up and cover the earth;	ויאמר אעלה אכסה ארץ	9
	I will destroy cities and their inhabitants."	אבידה עיר וישבי בה	9
9	Charge, O horses!	עלו [ ]סוסים	4
	Roll chariots!	[ ]התהללו [ ]רכב	5
	March, you soldiers --	ויצאו [ ]גבורים	7
	Men of Cush and Put, bearing shields;	כוש ופוט תפשי מגן	8
	Men of Lud, experts with the bow!	ולודים [ ][g] דרכי קשת	7

10	That day is Yahweh's,	[ ]יום [ ]הוא ל[ ]יהוה [ ][h]	5
	A day of vengeance, to avenge himself on his foes.	יום נקמה להנקם מצריו	11
	(His) sword shall devour;	ואכלה חרב	5
	It will be sated and glutted with their blood.	ושבעה ורותה מדמם	11
	For our God is having a sacrificial feast in the northern land,	כי זבח ל[ ]⟨אלהינו⟩[h] בארץ צפון	11
	By the river Euphrates.	אל נהר פרת	5
11	Go up to Gilead!	עלי גלעד	4
	Bring back balm, O virgin Daughter Egypt!	[ ]קחי צרי בתולת בת מצרים	9
	In vain you multiply remedies;	לשוא הרביתי[i] רפאות	8
	No cure have you.	תעלה אין לך	5
12	The nations have heard your ignominy;	שמעו גוים קלונך	7
	Your wailing has filled the earth.	[ ]צוחתך מלאה [ ]ארץ	7
	(For) warrior has stumbled against warrior;	[כי] גבור בגבור כשלו	9/8
	They both have fallen together.	יחדיו נפלו שניהם	8

<u>Notes to the Text of Jeremiah 46:2-12</u>

[a]Deleting ראיתי with LXX.

[b]Deleting the second *waw* as dittography and reading the *mem* as enclitic, with D. N. Freedman (see J. Bright, *Jeremiah*, p. 301, n. a-a). Read the substantive מנוס of MT as infinitive absolute followed by finite verb.

[c]Deleting נאם יהוה *metri causa*.

[d]The paired words are exchanged to improve the metrical balance.

[e]Deleting נהר with LXX.

[f]Omitting וכנהרות יתגעשו מים with LXX as an apparent dittography from the previous verse. The term מימיו was misunderstood and occasioned much difficulty here. The "waters" of Egypt make reference to the cosmic dimension of the military conflict; cf. H. G. May, "Some Cosmic Connotations of MAYIM RABBIM, 'Many Waters,'" *JBL* 74 (1955), pp. 9-21.

[g]Deleting תפשי as a variant to דרכי or perhaps a dittography from the previous colon.

[h]The phrase לאדני יהוה צבאות of MT reflects secondary expansion and leveling. LXX reads τῳ κυριῳ θεῳ ἡμων for the first occurrence and just τῳ κυριῳ for the second. These two readings have been accepted as more original than MT, but the order of their occurrence is reversed to improve the metrical balance.

[i]Cf. Jer. 2:33 where this archaic feminine ending appears again on a verbal form.

Jeremiah 46:2-12 in Outline

A. Summons to Battle: Yahweh summons his hosts against Egypt (vss. 3-4)
   [1:1::(b:b):1:(b:b)] Prepare yourselves for battle!

B. Prophetic Vision: Egypt's Defeat in Battle (vss. 5-6)
   [b:b] Why have they fled?
   [1:1::b:b:b] They have panicked because terror surrounds them.
   [1:1] Egypt is defeated by Babylon.

C. *Begründerung*: Egypt's Hubris (vss. 7-8)
   [1:1] Who is this who exalts himself?
   [1:1:1] Egypt's boast: "I will conquer the earth."

D. Summons to Battle (vs. 9)
   [b:b:b::1:1] Egypt summons troops, unwittingly opposing Yahweh.

E. Judgment/Lament over Egypt: Yahweh's Day of Vindication (vss. 10-11)
   [bl:bl:lb] In the day of battle Yahweh's sword consumes his foes.
   [bl:lb] There is no cure for Egypt's ruin.

F. Summary: Announcement of Judgment (vs. 12)
   [1:1] Egypt's demise is acknowledged by the nations.
   [1:1] Her warriors have fallen.

This oracle is perhaps the least challenged of any in Jeremiah's OAN collection as far as authenticity is concerned. As Bentzen has put it, we have in vs. 6 "an unmistakable reference to the battle of Carchemish in 605."[68] This oracle was probably composed just after Nebuchadnezzar shattered the forces of Pharaoh Necho at Carchemish on the Euphrates in the late spring or early summer of 605.[69]

The oracle begins with a summons to battle addressed to the hosts assembled against Egypt, composed in mixed meter reminiscent of ancient prosodic patterns. In vivid imagery the second strophe (vss. 5-6) presents the panic which gripped the Egyptian forces at the outset of battle -- terror surrounds them (מגור מסביב), there is no escape. The third strophe (vss. 7-8) presents the reason for Egypt's defeat. The Pharaoh has unwittingly exalted himself against Yahweh, the Divine Warrior. In summoning his troops to battle (vs. 9) he set the stage for his own destruction. The fifth strophe (vss. 10-11) expands the holy war imagery with the concept of Yahweh's devouring sword, a motif which is subsequently expanded in the proto-apocalyptic thought of Isaiah 34. Yahweh's sword is sated with blood (cf. Isa. 34:5-6a); and Yahweh has prepared a sacrificial feast beside the Euphrates (cf. Isa. 34:6b-7).

---

[68] A. Bentzen, *Introduction to the Old Testament*, II, p. 117.

[69] See J. Bright, *Jeremiah*, p. 308.

Vs. 11 picks up a familiar motif from Jer. 8:22 -- the balm of Gilead, which is unable to cure Egypt's wound. Mighty Egypt has fallen before the might of Babylon (vs. 12).

It is clear that Jeremiah attributed the destruction of Egypt to the activity of Yahweh who is engaged in holy war against Egypt. The Babylonian troops, in the prophet's mind, are merely the unwitting military hosts of the Divine Warrior. H. G. May has drawn attention to further cosmic connotations in vss. 7-8. The Nile (יאר) is in parallel with "rivers" (נהרות) which led May to conclude that, "Although the imagery of the inundation of the Nile is present, the "rivers" (*nehārōth*) suggest the insurgent waters, and the figure becomes that of creation completely engulfed by the waters, as in the flood of Noah."[70] He further noted that in Egypt the waters of the annual inundation of the Nile could be identified with the waters of chaos as seems to be the case in this poem.[71] In this oracle against Egypt the recrudescence of Canaanite mythology has found expression in combination with Israel's most ancient holy war traditions.

d. <u>Second Oracle against Egypt [Jer. 46:13-24 (LXX 26:13-24)]</u>

13 [The words which Yahweh spoke through Jeremiah concerning the coming of the king of Babylon to smite the land of Egypt:]

14	Announce it in Migdol!	הגידו [ ][a] במגדול	6
	Proclaim it in Memphis!	והשמיעו בנף [ ][b]	6
	Say, "Stand ready and be prepared!	אמרו התיצב והכן לך	9
	For the sword shall devour your thicket."	כי אכלה חרב סְבְ⟨כֶ⟩ךָ[c]	9
15	Why did your Bull Apis flee?	מדוע נס חף[d] אביריך	8
	He did not stand, Yahweh thrust him out;	לא עמד [כי] יהוה הדפו	9/8
	Your champion has stumbled, yea has fallen.	[ ]רַבְּ⟨ךָ⟩[e] כ[ ]של[f] גם נפל	8
16	Each one says to his neighbor:	איש אל רעהו [ ]יאמרו	9
	"Arise! Let us return to our people,	קומ(ו)[g] [ ]נשבה אל עמנו	9
	To the land of our birth,	[ ]אל ארץ מולדתנו	6
	Away from the oppressor's sword."	מפני חרב [ ]יונה	6
17	Proclaim a name for Pharaoh --	קראו שֵׁם[h] פרעה [ ][i]	5
	Big Noise, who missed his chance!	שאון העביר [ ]מועד	6
18	As I live, utterance of Yahweh:	חי אני נאם [ ] יהוה [ ][j]	-
	For as Tabor overtops the mountains,	כי כתבור בהרים	7
	As Carmel rises shear from the sea --	[ ]ככרמל בים יבוא	7
	He will come!		

[70] H. G. May, "Some Cosmic Connotations of MAYIM RABBIM, 'Many Waters,'" *JBL* 74 (1955), p. 16.

[71] *Ibid.*, p. 19.

19	Make ready your baggage for exile,	כלי גולה עשי לך	7
	O Virgin, dwelling in Egypt!	ירשבת בת⟨לת⟩[k] מצרים	7
	For Memphis shall be a waste;	כי נף לשמה[l] תהיה	7/8
	It shall be desolated, an uninhabited ruin.	רנצתה מאין ירשב	8
20	A beautiful heifer is Egypt,	עגלה יפה פיה מצרים	8
	Attacked by a fly from the north;	קרץ מצפון בא [ ][m]	5
21	Her mercenaries, too, in her midst,	גם שכריה בקרבה	8
	Are like fatted calves.	כעגלי מרבק	5
	They too turned tail and fled,	[ ][n] גם המה הפנו נסו יחדיו	9
	Not a one stood his ground;	לא עמדו	4
	For their day of disaster has come upon them,	כי יום אידם בא עליהם	8
	The time of their doom.	עת פקדתם	5
22	Quickly like a serpent she glides away,	קַו]לָהּ[o] כנחש ⟨זחל⟩[p]	7
	For in force they approach;	כי בחיל ילכו	6
	They come to her with axes,	[ ]בקרדמות באו לה	7
	Like men who fell trees.	כחטבי עצים	6
23	They cut down her forest, saith Yahweh,	כרתו יערה נאם יהוה	8
	Since it is impenetrable.	כי לא יחקר	5
	For they are more numerous than locusts;	כי רבו מארבה	6
	They are beyond count.	ואין להם מספר	6
24	Shamed is the Virgin Egypt,	הבישה בת⟨לת⟩[k] מצרים	8
	Caught in the clutch of the northern folk.	נתנה ביד עם צפון	8

Notes to the Text of Jeremiah 46:13-24

[a]Deleting במצרים והשמיעו with LXX.

[b]Deleting ובתחפנחס with LXX.

[c]Cf. LXX σμιλακα σου, "your yew-tree," which may render סבכך. Cf. also Jer. 21:14 where סביביה is in parallel with יערה, "her forest" (RSV).

[d]Reading נסחף of MT as two words with LXX.

[e]A conjectural emendation to make sense of a difficult line. LXX πληθος σου, "your multitude," may reflect the text as emended. The term is taken as the root *ryb* in the sense of "champion" as an epithet applied to a deity. Cf. Isa. 34:8 where C. C. Torrey sees ריב as an epithet of Yahweh [C. C. Torrey, *The Second Isaiah* (New York, 1928), p. 284]. Cf. also Jer. 50:34 and 51:36.

[f]The participial form is repointed as a perfect with LXX.

[g]The *he* of MT is taken as a vowel marker as the context would suggest a plural verbal form (so LXX). *Qere apud Orientales* reads קומו.

[h]Repointing the word with LXX ὄνομα, "name."

[i]Deleting מלך מצרים *metri causa*.

[j]Cf. LXX; this line has suffered secondary expansion.

[k]A conjectural emendation to restore metrical balance in this bicolon. Cf. Jer. 46:11 where both terms appear, i.e. בתולת בת מצרים. Though a simple haplography may account for this textual corruption, it seems more likely that the two terms in question served as ballast variants in the poet's formulaic repertoire. The "virgin" makes better sense in the present context. Cf. Syr. which reads both terms in the present context.

[l]The variant form לשממה may be read here to achieve closer metrical balance.

[m]Deleting the second בא as a dittography.

[n]Deleting כי as a prosaic expansion.

[o]A conjectural emendation to make better sense out of a difficult line. Cf. Jer. 4:13 and 46:6.

[p]Cf. LXX συριζοντος, "hissing," which may render the text as emended. Cf. Mic. 7:17 where נחש is used parallel to זחלי. MT ילך in the present context may be a dittography from the next colon.

Jeremiah 46:13-24 in Outline

A. Prophetic Announcement: Egypt is Humiliated (vss. 14-17)

[b:b::1:1]	Spread the news: The sword shall devour your thicket.
[1:1:]	Your Bull Apis could not stand before Yahweh.
[1:1::b:b]	The summons to flee was given by your own troops.
[b:b]	Give Pharaoh the name he deserves -- "Big Noise!"

B. Oracle of Doom against Egypt (vss. 18-19)

[rubric]	Oath formula
[1:1]	The coming of the "Destroyer" is certain.
[1:1::1:1]	Prepare for the ravages of exile, O Virgin Egypt!

C. Judgment/Lament over Egypt (vss. 20-23a)

[2(1b:1b)]	The heifer Egypt is chased by a stinging insect.
[1b:1b:1b]	Egypt flees in vain before a relentless foe.

D. Summary: Announcement of Judgment (vss. 23b-24)

[b:b]	Her enemy is a vast host.
[1:1]	The Virgin Egypt is deflowered.

The second oracle against Egypt is more difficult to date. The prose introduction of vs. 13 associates the oracle with "the coming of the king of Babylon to smite the land of Egypt." Since Nebuchadnezzar did not actually invade Egypt until *ca.* 568, the authenticity of this oracle has been sometimes challenged. It seems more likely, however, to assume that Jeremiah had regarded such an invasion as certain, and to have expected it imminently, particularly in the months following Egypt's defeat at Carchemish. Following Bright, we would see this oracle as composed "perhaps as Nebuchadnezzar's army appeared in force on the Philistine Plain (in 604) and threatened Egypt with invasion."[72]

The oracle begins with the announcement of Egypt's defeat in the imagery of the humbling of the sacred Bull Apis who is unable to stand before Yahweh. The messengers are urged to spread the news in Egypt that the sword will devour their thicket. The "thicket" (סבך) is sometimes the lion's lair from which the "Destroyer" set out against the nations (cf. Jer. 4:7). Here the "thicket" appears to be a place of refuge (cf. Jer. 21:14), perhaps for the Bull Apis, the forest which the "Destroyer" will hew down in search of the fleeing, panic-stricken Egyptians (vs. 22).

Again the identity of the "Destroyer" is somewhat ambiguous. The relentless foe described in vss. 22-23 is clearly designated "the northern folk" (עם צפון) and hence would be the Babylonians. On the other hand, it is also clear in vs. 15 that Apis, the sacred bull of the Egyptians, was thrust out by Yahweh. It is Yahweh's holy war which will destroy Egypt. The agents of Yahweh's warfare are the unwitting Babylonians. The coming of the "Destroyer" is certain (vss. 18-19); Egypt and her mercenaries, like a heifer (עגלה) and and fatted calves (עגלי מרבק) have fled before a stinging insect (vss. 20-21). The metaphor is compounded as the prophet declares that though Egypt slithers away into the recesses of her forest like a serpent (vs. 22), she will not escape. The "Destroyer" will search her out if he has to hew down all the trees of the forest in the process (vss. 22-23).

In both oracles against Egypt the judgment/lament, as a speech form, appears in the qinah meter (Jer. 46:10-11, 20-23a). It should be noted that the second oracle against Egypt here is lacking the military speech forms and the associated mixed metrical patterns of the first. The only summons oracle, as such, is a summons to flight placed on the lips of Egypt's own troops (vs. 16). In form the oracle is simply a prophetic announcement of doom directed against Egypt.

e. Oracle against Elam [Jer. 49:34-39 (LXX 25:14-26:1)]

34 [In the beginning of the reign of King Zedekiah there came this word concerning Elam:]

35 Thus saith Yahweh:	כה אמר יהוה [ ][a]	
I am breaking the bow of Elam,	⟨א⟩ני[b] שבר [ ] קשת עילם	7
Mainstay of their might.	ראשית גבורתם	6
36 I will bring the four winds,	והבאתי [ ][c] ארבע רוחות	8
From the four quarters of heaven.	מארבע קצות שמים	7

[I will scatter them to all these winds so that there shall not be a nation to which Elamite fugitives do not go.]

---

[72]See J. Bright, *Jeremiah*, p. 308.

37	I will terrify them before their foes,	והחתתי[ ]ם[d] לפני איביהם	11
	Before those who seek their life.	ולפני מבקשי נפשם	10
	I will bring disaster upon them,	והבאתי עליהם רעה	9
	My fierce anger.	[ ] חרון אפי [ ][e]	4
	I will send my sword after them,	ושלחתי אחריהם חרב<י>[f]	9
	Until I have consumed them.	עד כלותי[ ]ם[g]	4
38	I will establish my throne in Elam;	ושמתי כסאי בעילם	8
	I will destroy king and princes.	והאבדתי [ ][h] מלך ושרים [ ][e]	8

39 [But when it is all over, I will restore the fortunes of Elam.
--utterance of Yahweh.]

Notes to the Text of Jeremiah 49:34-39

[a]Deleting צבאות with LXX.

[b]Emending with LXX Συντριβητω.

[c]Deleting אל עילם *metri causa*.

[d]The text has suffered prosaic expansion and is restored with LXX which reads πτοησω αὐτους, "I will put them in fear."

[e]Deleting נאם יהוה with LXX.

[f]Emending with LXX μαχαιραν μου, "my sword."

[g]The text has suffered prosaic expansion and is restored with LXX which reads ἕως του ἐξαναλωσαι αὐτους, "until I have utterly destroyed them."

[h]Deleting משם *metri causa*.

Jeremiah 49:34-39 in Outline

A War Oracle Against Elam

[1:1] ?	I am breaking the bow of Elam.
[1:1::?]	I will scatter them in exile.
[1:1]	I will terrify them.
[1b:1b]	My sword will consume them.
[1:1]	I will establish my suzerainty in Elam.
[prose]	Afterwards I will restore Elam.

The oracle against Elam is dated to "the beginning of the reign of King Zedekiah" (i.e. *ca.* 597); and, as Bright has argued, there is no reason to question the accuracy of this date.[73] The history of Elam after its destruction by Asshurbanapal in *ca.* 639 is obscure. It seems to have regained its independence in *ca.* 626/5 as Assyria weakened.[74] Certain damaged lines in the Babylonian Chronicle refer to a campaign of Nebuchadnezzar against what

[73]See J. Bright, *Jeremiah*, p. 338.

[74]See D. J. Wiseman, *Chronicles of Chaldean Kings*, pp. 8-10 and 51.

may have been Elam in 596/5.[75] Elam later played a role in the overthrow of Babylon in 540/39.

The oracle in question is prosaic in nature and no doubt fragmentary. No human agent or reason for Elam's destruction is given. Yahweh is summoning the four winds from the four quarters of heaven to scatter the Elamites (vs. 36), and his sword to consume them (vs. 37). Elam's king and princes will be destroyed and Yahweh himself will establish his throne there (vs. 38).

The motif of Yahweh's sword of judgment commissioned to consume Elam is in keeping with the personification of Yahweh's sword in the oracle against Philistia (Jer. 47:6-7). The reference to Yahweh establishing his throne in Elam, however, introduces a new element, at least within the OAN tradition of Jeremiah. The statement appears to be eschatological in nature, somewhat similar to the additions to Isaiah's oracles against Egypt (Isa. 19:19-25) and Tyre (Isa. 23:17-18).

Thus, three of the five oracles which we have classified as Jeremianic OAN are firmly rooted in history. The oracle against Philistia and the two oracles against Egypt can be dated with some confidence to the period *ca.* 609-604. The political machinations of these nations in the years of uncertainty before Babylonian supremacy was established in the Levant are clearly evident. Though cosmic imagery and holy war ideology are dominant, it is clear that the prophet is concerned with real contemporary political events involving the nations concerned.

The oracle against Qedar is less specific but no less rooted in current political history, as far as the prophet Jeremiah is concerned. Thanks to our knowledge of the history of the Qedarite Arab confederation in this period and the happy coincidence of being able to date a specific cliché, we are able to pin this oracle down, at least within a decade (*ca.* 609-598). The speech forms used stress immediacy and the interpreter finds little pressure toward projecting the events presented into the future in any eschatological sense.

The oracle against Elam, on the other hand, borders on the eschatological. Perhaps with added knowledge about the political history of Elam after 639 this oracle too, like that against Qedar, will become more firmly rooted in the historical events at the turn of the 6th century B.C. But with our present knowledge of the history of Elam, and with the reference to Yahweh establishing his throne in distant Elam, replacing her king and princes, we appear to be entering a different realm of history. The prophet is projecting his message into the future where he sees a new day on the horizon, a day when pagan world powers will submit themselves to Yahweh, the suzerain of the nations.

---

[75] *Ibid.*, p. 73; see also pp. 36-38.

2. Archaic OAN

The second major division of Jeremiah's OAN tradition includes the oracles against Moab (ch. 48), Ammon (49:1-6), Edom (49:7-22) and Aram (49:23-27). Yehezkel Kaufmann has argued that this particular collection of oracles is pre-Jeremianic. He cited Jer. 28:8 as evidence of a pre-Jeremianic OAN tradition, which he suggests may have been called "Sefer Mišpaṭ Ha-Goyyim."[76] Other scholars have been impressed by the fact that historical allusions, where present within these oracles, seem to reflect a period prior to the death of Josiah in 609/8. In 1935 Bardtke developed an elaborate thesis in which he dated all of Jeremiah's OAN tradition to *ca.* 617, before the young prophet turned his attention to coming disaster for his own people.[77] Though Bardtke's main thesis must be rejected, many of his individual observations are of value,[78] particularly his discussion of the historical allusions within the oracles in question.

The oracle against Ammon provides a useful point of departure in analyzing the so-called "Archaic OAN" tradition in Jeremiah. This oracle is brief and shows relatively little evidence of subsequent expansion or readaptation to Exilic situations, as is the case in the oracles against Moab (cf. Jer. 48:29-47) and Edom (cf. 49:12-19). The oracle against Aram is unique in several respects and will be analyzed last in this section.

a. Oracle against Ammon [Jer. 49:1-6 (LXX 30:1-5)]

1	Concerning the Ammonites,	לבני עמון	
	Thus saith Yahweh:	כה אמר יהוה	
	Has Israel no sons?	הבנים אין לישראל	8
	Is not Jerusalem his heir?	אם יורש אין ל<ירושלם>[a]	8
	Why has Milcom taken possession of Gad?	מדוע ירש מִלְכֹּם[b] [ ] גד	7
	His people inhabit its towns.	[ ]עמו בעריו ישב	7
2	And so, look! The days are coming,	לכן הנה ימים באים	12
	utterance of Yahweh;	נאם יהוה	
	When I will make Rabbah to hear	והשמעתי אל רב(ה) [ ][c]	13
	the shout of battle.	תרועת מלחמה	
	She shall become a desolate mound,	והיתה לתל שממה	9
	Her villages burned with fire;	[ ]בנתיה באש תצתנה	9
	Israel shall evict his evictors.	וירש ישראל [ ] ירשיו [ ][d]	9

---

[76] Y. Kaufmann, *History of the Religion of Israel* (Heb.), III, pp. 38ff. and 415ff. See also B. Margulis, "Studies in the Oracles Against the Nations," pp. 17-18; who has summarized Kaufmann's argument.

[77] Hans Bardtke, "Jeremia der Fremdvölkerprophet," *ZAW* 53 (1935), pp. 209-39 and 54 (1936), pp. 240-62.

[78] O. Eissfeldt, *The Old Testament: An Introduction*, p. 364.

3	Howl, O Heshbon!	הלילי חשבון	5
	For Ai (?) is laid waste!	כי שדדה עי	5
	Cry aloud, daughters of Rabbah!	צעקנה בנות רבה	7
	Gird yourselves with sackcloth! Lament!	חגרנה שקים ספדנה	8
	Walk about with bodies gashed!	[ ]התשוטטנה בגד(ד)ות[e]	8
	For Milcom is going into exile,	כי מִלְכֹּם[b] בגולה ילך	8
	Together with his priests and nobles.	כהניו ושריו יחדיו	8
4	Why boast of (your) strength?	מה תתהללי בעמק-ם[f]	8
	Your strength is ebbing, O faithless daughter!	זב עמקך[f] [ ]בת [ ]שובבה	8
	She is trusting in her own treasures,	[ ]בטחה באצרתיה	9
	Saying: "Who can attack me?"	⟨אמרה⟩[g] מי יבוא אלי	8
5	Look! I am bringing terror upon you from every side;	הנני מביא עליך פחד [ ][h] מכל סביביך	12
	I will drive them in headlong flight, (and) no one will gather them.	ונדחת⟨י⟩ם[i] איש לפניו [ ]אין מקבץ [ ][j] [ ][k]	12

Notes to the Text of Jeremiah 49:1-6[79]

[a]The colon is too short in MT. LXX reads the plural αὐτοις which perhaps renders למו. Two Greek MSS, one in the hexaplaric group (233) and the other in the catena group (239), read ιερουσαλημ in place of "Israel" in the previous colon. The assonance provided by the root *yrš*, which precedes and follows the proposed emendation, lend some plausibility to the text as reconstructed.

[b]The word *malkām*, "their king," of MT is repointed to form the proper name of the Ammonite deity. Cf. Μελχολ of LXX.

[c]Deleting בני עמון with LXX and changing the construct state to the absolute.

[d]Deleting אמר יהוה with LXX.

[e]Changing the *resh* of MT to *daleth*; cf. Jer. 48:37. The root *gdd*, "cut," is used in the Hithpo. of cutting oneself as a religious practice, particularly in contexts of mourning. Cf. Jer. 16:6; 41:5 and elsewhere. This colon is missing in LXX.

[f]Accepting the reading of M. Dahood, "The Value of Ugaritic for Textual Criticism," *Bib* 40 (1959), pp. 166-67. Cf. also the discussion of Jer. 47:5 on p. 210 above. In the first occurrence of the root *ʿmq* here the final *mem* is taken as enclitic, with Dahood. The longer form of the second person singular suffix is read in the second instance to improve the metrical bal-

[79]For a discussion of the text of this oracle and the history of the phrase "terror on every side," see my article, "'Terror on Every Side' in Jeremiah," *JBL* 92 (1973), pp. 498-502.

ance and assonance in this quatrain.

[g]Emending with some Heb. MSS, LXX ἡ λεγουσα, and other ancient versions.

[h]Deleting נאם אדני יהוה צבאות as secondary expansion; cf. LXX.

[i]Emending with some Heb. MSS and Syr.

[j]Deleting לנדד with LXX.

[k]Deleting vs. 6 with LXX, as a later addition to the oracle.

Jeremiah 49:1-5 in Outline

A. Oracle of Judgment (vss. 1-2)

[1:1::1:1]	Accusation: Ammon has taken Israel's land.
	Sentence:
[1b:1b] ?	I will bring war to Ammon.
[1:1:1]	She shall become a desolate ruin, to be repossessed by Israel.

B. Summons to Mourn (vs. 3)

[b:b::1:1:1]	Make your lamentation, O Ammon!
[1:1]	Your god, your priests and nobles are going into exile.

C. Judgment/Lament over Ammon (vss. 4-5)

[1:1::1:1]	Ammon's hubris: She has boasted of her own strength saying: "Who can attack me?"
[1b:1b]	Yahweh's reply: "I will scatter them!"

The prosodic-textual analysis of this brief oracle against Ammon reveals a unified poem consisting of three strophes -- a summons to mourn (vs. 3) framed by two judgment oracles, which form a sort of poetic inclusion. Both the first and third strophes present a reason for Yahweh's judgment against Ammon, expressed in the third person, followed by an actual judgment oracle in the first person.

As numerous scholars have observed, this oracle lacks the spirit of vengefulness found elsewhere in the OAN material in Jeremiah. As Hyatt put it, "This oracle . . . seems almost to express sympathy for the Ammonites."[80] No source of Ammon's destruction is named, though the inference of vs. 2 is clearly that Israel is to be the benefactor of Ammon's demise -- "Israel shall evict his evictors."

The opening question asked in this oracle poses historical difficulties. The question is raised as to why Ammon is in possession of Gad/Gilead. As Bardtke put it, "Diese Zeit kann aber nur die Ära des Königs Josia sein und in dieser wieder die letzte Periode von der Kultusreformation bis zu seinem

---

[80]J. Philip Hyatt, "The Book of Jeremiah," *Interpreter's Bible*, ed. by G. A. Buttrick (Nashville: Abingdon Press, 1956), V, p. 1117.

Tode."[81] After the death of Josiah the matter of Israel dispossessing those who have dispossessed them in southern Transjordan makes little sense historically and none whatsoever after the Israelites themselves had gone into captivity. Landes has dated this oracle prior to the death of Josiah, at least in the events it reflects. On the basis of this date he went on to conclude that:[82]

> . . . by the beginning of the last decade of the seventh century B.C., the Ammonites had asserted their complete independence once again, had expanded as far west as the Jordan Valley, and had become the dominant state in southern Transjordan.

Landes also suggested that the oracle in question reflects the same historical situation as that in Zeph. 2:8-11.[83] We have already dated Zephaniah's oracle, on other grounds, to the beginning of Josiah's program of political expansion at the expense of the Assyrian provinces bordering Judah to the north, in *ca.* 628.[84]

The historical situation reflected in this poem is apparently the period of Judah's expansion into Transjordan under Josiah. Ammon faces judgment at the hands of the Divine Warrior for violating the covenant obligations inherent in the idealized Davidic Empire. In extending her borders Ammon has taken land which belongs to Israel (vss. 1-2). In "trusting in her own treasures" (vs. 4) she has provoked the wrath of Yahweh, the suzerain of David's empire. Consequently the Divine Warrior is bringing terror upon Ammon from every side (vs. 5). It should be noted, in passing, that the phrase here rendered "terror on every side" is not the stereotyped מגור מסביב of Jeremiah's later oracles, but a precursor of that cliché -- פחד מכל סביביך.[85]

b. Oracles against Edom [Jer. 49:7-22 (LXX 29:8-23)]

7	Concerning Edom, thus saith Yahweh:	לאדום כה אמר יהוה [ ][a]	
	Is there no longer any wisdom in Teman?	האין עוד חכמה בתימן	8
	Has good counsel vanished from the shrewd?	אבדה עצה מבנים	8
	Has their wisdom become vapid?	⟨ראם⟩[b] נסרחה חכמתם	8
8	Flee, turn tail! Remove your dwelling to far	נסו הפנו העמיקו לשבת	4+5
	reaches, O inhabitants of Dedan!	ישבי דדן	5
	For Esau's calamity I bring upon him,	כי איד עשו הבאתי עליו	4+5
	The time of his doom.	עת פְּקֻדָּת[ ]ו;[c]	5

[81] H. Bardtke, "Jeremia der Fremdvölkerprophet," *ZAW* 54 (1936), p. 250.

[82] George M. Landes, "A History of the Ammonites" (unpub. Ph.D. thesis, Johns Hopkins University, 1956), p. 305.

[83] *Ibid.*, p. 305.

[84] See pp. 160-61 above.

[85] See footnote 79 above, p. 223.

Verse	Translation	Hebrew	Syllables
9	If grape-gatherers came to you,	אם בצרים באו לך	7
	Would they not leave (only) gleanings?	לא ישארו עוללות	7
	If thieves (came) in the night,	אם גנבים בליל[d]	6
	Would they (not) destroy what they please?	ה-השחיתו דים	6
10	For I have exposed Esau;	כי [ ][e] חשפתי [ ] עשו	6
	I have uncovered his lairs,	גליתי [ ] מסתריו	6
	So that he cannot hide.	ונחבה לא יוכל	6
	The strength of his allies is shattered;	שדד זְרֹעַ[ ][f] [ ]אחיו	6
	His neighbors are no more.	[ ]שכניו [ ]איננו	6
11	Abandon your orphans! I will sustain them,	עזבה יתמיך אני אחיה	11
	And your widows may trust in me.	ואלמנתיך עלי תבטחו	11
12	For thus saith Yahweh:	כי כה אמר יהוה	-
	Those who were not bound to drink the cup	[ ][g] אין משפטם לשתות [ ]כוס	12
	have indeed drunk it!	שתו ישתו	
	Can you expect to go unpunished?	[ ]אתה ה-נקה[h] תנקה	12
	You shall not go unpunished.	לא תנקה [ ][i]	
13	[For I have bound myself by oath, utterance of Yahweh.]		
	For Bozrah shall be a horror	כי לשמה [ ][j] ולקללה	13
	and a curse;	תהיה בצרה	
	And all her cities shall be	וכל עריה תהיינה	13
	desolate wastes forever.	לחרבות עולם	
14	I have heard the report from Yahweh;	שמועה שמעתי מ[ ]יהוה	9
	An envoy has been sent to the nations.	[ ]ציר בגוים שלוח	6
	Assemble! March against her!	התקבצו [ ]באו עליה	9
	Up! To the battle!	[ ]קומו למלחמה	6
15	I will make you small among the nations,	[ ][k] קטן נתתיך בגוים	8
	Despised among men;	בזוי באדם	5
16	Your reputation for ferocity has deceived you,	תפלצתך השיאתך[l]	8
	Your arrogant pride.	זדון לבך	5
	You who dwell in the cleft of the rock,	שכני בחגוי סלע	7
	Who cling to the lofty height;	תפשי מרום גבעה	7
	Like an eagle you have made your nest high,	[ ][m] תגביה כנשר קנך	7
	From there I will fling you down.	משָׁם אורידך [ ][n]	7

17 [Edom shall be a desolation; everyone who passes by her will be shocked and whistle in awe at all the blows she has suffered,

18 just as was the case when Sodom and Gomorrah and their neighbors were overthrown -- Yahweh has spoken. No more will anyone live there; never again will any man settle there.]

19	Look! Like a lion which ascends	הנה כאריה יעלה	7
	From the thickets of the Jordan to the perennial pasture;	מגאון [] ירדן אל נוה איתן	10
	I will destroy her, I will chase them from her;	[][o] ארגיעה[p] אריצ(ם)[q] מעליה	10
	From her choicest rams I will select what I please.	[]מִבְחַר[r] אֱ⟨י⟩לֶיהָ[r] אפקד	7
	For who is there like me?	כי מי כמוני	5
	Who can hale me into court?	[]מי יעידני	5
	And who is the shepherd who can stand up to me?	ומי זה רעה [] יעמד לפני	10
20	Therefore, hear the plan which Yahweh has planned against Edom;	לכן שמעו עצת יהוה [] יעץ אל אדום	13
	The schemes which he has schemed against the inhabitants of Teman.	ומחשבותיו []חשב אל ישבי תימן	13
	Surely the little ones of their flock shall be dragged away;	אם לא יסחבו-ם[s] צעירי []צאן	10
	Surely the nurslings of their pasture shall be desolated.	אם לא יָשׁוֹם[t] עֲלֵיהֶם[u] נוהם	11
21	At the crash of their downfall the earth trembles;	מקול נפלם רעשה []ארץ	8
	The cry can be heard to the Sea of Reeds.	צעקה בים סוף נשמע [][v]	8
22	Look! Like an eagle he swoops and soars;	הנה כנשר ידאה / יעלה[w] []יפרש	8
	His wings are over her vintagers.	כנפיו על בֹּצְרֶ⟨י⟩הָ[x]	8

[The courage of Edom's warriors becomes, in that day, like that of a woman in labor.]

Notes to the Text of Jeremiah 49:7-22

[a]Deleting צבאות with LXX.

[b]A conjectural emendation to restore the metrical balance within this tricolon. On the use of this interrogative particle in the sequence ואם . . . ה cf. Isa. 49:24; 50:2; Jer. 5:9; 14:22; etc. The omission of the particle in MT may be the result of a simple haplography.

[c]Emending with Vulg. *Tempus visitationis eius*; cf. Syr. and Targ. Cf. also Jer. 50:31 where a similar reading has even stronger support in the versions and extant MSS.

[d]Taking the *he* as an interrogative particle with the following word to achieve closer metrical balance. A question is expected here and is so rendered in the RSV. On the shorter form בליל, "in the night," cf. Isa. 15:1, Prov. 31:18 and Lam. 2:19.

[e]Deleting אני *metri causa*.

[f]Cf. LXX ἐπιχειρα ἀδελφου, "forearm of his brother." On זרע with the meaning "strength" cf. Ps. 83:9; Job 35:9; Isa. 40:10; Jer. 17:5 and elsewhere.

[g]Deleting הנה with LXX and אשר as prosaic expansion.

[h]Reading the personal pronoun הוא as the interrogative particle to make better sense of this colon. Note that LXX clearly renders the first pronoun ואתה with και συ but gives no indication that the הוא of MT was present in the text.

[i]Deleting כי שתה תשתה with LXX.

[j]Deleting להרפה לחרב as secondary expansion; cf. LXX which omits one of these terms.

[k]Deleting כי הנה with LXX.

[l]MT השיא אתך is prosaic in form and probably reflects a dittography of the *aleph*; cf. LXX ἐνεχειρησε σοι.

[m]Deleting כי as secondary.

[n]Deleting נאם יהוה with LXX.

[o]Deleting כי as secondary.

[p]See M. D. Goldman, "The Meaning of *rg'*," *ABR* 4 (1954), p. 15; who argues that there exist two different roots *rg'*. Dahood renders *r^egā'îm* as "destruction" (*Psalms I*, p. 182).

[q]Emending with LXX, Syr., Targ., and Jer. 50:44[Q].

[r]A conjectural emendation suggested by W. Rudolph in the apparatus of *BHS*, which makes good sense of a very difficult verse. Note the similar pastoral imagery in vs. 20 following.

[s]Repointing MT as a Niphal *yissāḥ^ebû-m* with enclitic *mem*, as suggested by J. S. Kselman, "A Note on Jer 49,20 and Ze 2,6-7," *CBQ* 32 (1970), p. 580.

[t]Following Kselman (*ibid.*, p. 580) who reads *yāšōmmū* to agree in number with his reconstruction of the following word.

[u]Again following Kselman who reads the plural form of the noun *'ūl*, "young" (of animals or men). The use of the root *'wl* for animals is well attested; the active participle *'ālôt* ia a common word for ewes (cf. I Sam. 6:7,10; Gen. 33:13 and Ps. 78:71).

[v]Deleting קולה with LXX and Jer. 50:46.

[w]Taking these two words as variant readings; cf. LXX which omits one of these verbs here.

[x]Cf. LXX ὀχυρωματα αὐτης, "her strongholds," which may have rendered the text as reconstructed; cf. Zech. 9:12 where בצרון means "stronghold." On the meaning "vintager, grape-gatherer," cf. Jer. 49:9. On the use of נשר, "eagle," in contexts of military invasion cf. Jer. 4:13; 48:40; Lam. 4:19 and Ezek. 17:3. The imagery here is that of Yahweh soaring over the invading hosts as he leads them in battle against Edom.

Jeremiah 49:7-22 in Outline

I

A. Summons to Flight (vss. 7-9)

[1:1:1]	Has wisdom departed from Edom?
[b:b:b::b:b:b]	Go into hiding, for the time of Esau's calamity is at hand!
[1:1::1:1]	When it comes, will it not be total destruction?

B. Oracle of Doom (vs. 10)

[1:1:1]	I have exposed Esau.
[1:1]	Edom is without allies.

C. Summons to Entrust the Helpless to Yahweh (vs. 11)

[1:1]	Abandon your orphans and widows; I will sustain them.

II

A. Announcement of Judgment (vss. 12-13; cf. Jer. 25:15-29)

[1b:1b]	Edom, too, must drink the "Cup of Wrath."
[rubric]	Oath formula
[1:1]	Edom shall be utterly destroyed.

B. Summons to Battle and Oracle of Doom (vss. 14-16; cf. Obad. 1-4)

[1:b::1:b]	Yahweh has sent his message: March against Edom!
[1b:1b]	I will humble you.
[1:1::1:1]	I will dash you from the heights.

C. Eclectic Judgment/Lament and Oracle of Doom (vss. 17-22; cf. Jer. 50:40b, 44-46; 49:33b and 48:40)

[prose]	Edom shall become like Sodom and Gomorrah.
[b:1::1:b]?	Like a raging lion I will ravage Edom's flock.
[b:b:1]	Who is able to stand before me?
[1b:1b] ?	Yahweh has planned the battle against Edom.
[1:1]	Her young ones will be carried into exile.
[1:1::1:1]	Edom will fall before the "Destroyer." The crash of her fall will resound abroad. Like an eagle Yahweh soars over Edom's destroyers.
[prose]	The courage of Edom's soldiers will melt away.

The oracle against Edom (49:7-22) presents several major problems of interpretation. The literary relationship between this material and Obad. 1-14 has received perhaps the most attention in scholarly comment. Literary interdependence should also be noted between 49:12-13 and 25:15-29 and between 49:19-21 and 50:44-46. The fact that much of the material in this oracle against Edom is found elsewhere in Jeremiah (sometimes applied to Babylon) or in Obadiah, raises the question of authenticity. Is this oracle a unified whole composed by Jeremiah, or is it a later Exilic or post-Exilic fabrication from extant OAN tradition?

The questions of unity, authenticity and date are compounded by the content of vs. 11 which Cornill has described as "Ein überaus merkwürdiger Vers, in welchem Jahve selbst verheisst, sich der Wittwen und Waisen Edoms anzunehmen!"[86] In his recent doctoral dissertation, Cresson was even more forceful in his treatment of this verse which he dismissed as an intrusion of "sweetness and light" in the midst of a picture of doom that must be rejected as a "later intrusion which is foreign to 'Damn-Edom Theology.'"[87] It is difficult to explain this verse as a late insertion, however, as Streane has noted, for the attitude portrayed runs counter to "the attitude which later days would have assumed towards an enemy so bitterly hated."[88] The attitude of concern for orphans and widows who survive Edom's calamity makes better sense historically in the pre-Exilic period than it does after the fall of Jerusalem when the Edomites fought against Judah in league with Nebuchadnezzar.

It should also be noted that the basic theme of vs. 11 has important parallels in both early Israelite and Canaanite literature. In Ps. 68:5-6 Yahweh is described as "father of the fatherless and defender of the widows." The motif appears in the Ugaritic literature where *Dan'el* is described in a similar manner: "He judges the case of the widow; he defends the cause of the fatherless" (UT:2 Aqht:V:7-8). In the legend of Keret the motif is applied in negative fashion to king *Krt* by his son *Yṣb*:[89]

> You have allowed your hands to fall into negligence;
> You do not judge the case of the widow,
> nor defend the cause of the broken in spirit,
> nor drive away those who prey upon the poor!
> You do not feed the fatherless (that are) before you,
> nor the widow behind your back.

Concern for the widow and orphans is also expressed in Deut. 10:18 where Yahweh's justice is disclosed in his impartiality and in his defense of the legally helpless.

It seems likely that an earlier oracle against Edom, composed during the reign of Josiah, has been subsequently expanded by the addition of an eclectic oracle of doom taken largely from 25:15-29, the proto-Obadiah tradition (Obad. 1-4), and 50:44-46.[90] It is difficult to determine whether these

---

[86] D. C. H. Cornill, *Das Buch Jeremia*, pp. 479-80.

[87] Bruce C. Cresson, "Israel and Edom: A Study of the Anti-Edom Bias in Old Testament Religion" (unpub. Ph.D. thesis, Duke University, 1963), p. 78.

[88] A. W. Streane, *The Book of the Prophet Jeremiah* (Camb.-B, Cambridge: Cambridge University Press, 1881), p. 285.

[89] UT:127:45-50; cf. also UT:127:33-34 and Krt:97,185.

additions to the earlier oracle against Edom were by Jeremiah or, as seems more likely, by one of his followers in the Exilic period. An attempted revolt against Babylon in *ca.* 594 which included Edom, along with Moab, Ammon and Phoenicia, in which pressure was exerted on Judah to join the coalition (cf. Jer. 27:1-11), may have occasioned further oracles against Edom on the part of Jeremiah. On the other hand, Edom's despicable behavior in fighting against Judah in 587, and the fact that Edom herself escaped destruction at that time certainly occasioned bitter anti-Edom sentiment in various circles (cf. Lam. 4:21-22; Ps. 137:7-9 and Obad. 1-16) and could have occasioned expansion of Jeremiah's oracle(s) against Edom.

The so-called "original oracle against Edom" (vss. 7-11) consists of three strophes, the first of which contains a summons to flight addressed to Edom in a familiar metrical pattern, similar to that observed in the oracle against Qedar (49:29-30). The /b:b:b::b:b:b/ unit is framed by two questions which form a sort of inclusion. If there is any wisdom left in Edom (vs. 7), they will take flight (vs. 8); for Edom faces total destruction at the hands of an unnamed "Destroyer" (vs. 9; cf. Obad. 5). The second strophe is an oracle of doom in which Yahweh declares that there is no hiding place for Edom (vs. 10a), for she has no allies left (vs. 10b). A concluding note of hope is voiced in the assurance expressed by Yahweh that he will sustain Edom's helpless survivors in the coming calamity (vs. 11).

The judgment oracle in vss. 12-16 reflects a period after the death of Josiah and possibly after the fall of Jerusalem. The opening strophe is taken from the "Cup of Wrath" pericope in 25:15-29 and implies that Judah, who was not bound to drink the cup, has already drunk it and therefore Edom cannot expect to escape a similar fate (vs. 12). The very destruction applied to Jerusalem/Judah in 25:18 is here applied to Edom (vs. 13). The second strophe (vss. 14-16; cf. Obad. 1-4) is an oracle of doom -- the report which the herald of Yahweh has heard in the divine council and now delivers to the nations. It opens with a summons to battle, as the Divine Warrior summons the nations against Edom (vs. 14). Yahweh's judgment against Edom is then detailed: "I will humble you" (vss. 15-16a), "I will dash you from the heights" (vs. 16b). Vss. 14-16 are closely related to the literary tradition preserved in Obad. 1-4 and may stem from a pre-Jeremianic tradition.[91]

The final section of the oracles against Edom (vss. 17-22) is prosaic in nature and apparently taken from various parts of Jeremiah's extant OAN tradition. The prose expansion in vss. 17 and 18 is expressed in the typical

---

[90]The judgment oracle in Jer. 50:44-46 is probably more original than its setting here (vss. 19-21). See the discussion below on p. 232 and pp. 252-60.

[91]See the discussion above, pp. 162-65.

language of treaty-curses, with almost every phrase having parallels elsewhere in the OAN tradition of Jeremiah (cf. in particular 50:39-40). Vss. 19-21 appear to be an adaptation of an original oracle against Babylon (50:44-46). What was probably an original /1:1::1:1/ metrical pattern (cf. 50:44a) is here distorted into an awkward unit, which for all practical purposes must be read as prose. Vss. 20-21 continue the reuse of 50:45-46 with minor variants; particularly in vs. 21. Vs. 22a appears also in 48:40 where it is applied to Moab. Only vs. 22b is without parallel in Jeremiah's OAN tradition and it is clearly prose, at least in its present form. It would appear that these final verses in Jeremiah's collection of oracles against Edom are Exilic and/or post-Exilic additions to Jeremiah's OAN tradition, reflecting a time when a sense of feeling for the earlier metrical patterns has been lost.

c. Oracles against Moab [Jer. 48:1-47 (LXX 31:1-44)]

Vs.	English	Hebrew	
1	Concerning Moab, thus saith Yahweh:	למואב כה אמר יהוה [ ][a]	
	Alas for Nebo, for she is ravaged;	הוי אל נבו כי שדדה	8
	Taken is Kiriathaim!	[ ][a] נלכדה קריתים	6
	The citadel is humbled and shattered;	הבישן[ ] [ ]משגב וחת[ ][b]	6
2	No more is the glory of Moab.	אין עוד תהלת מואב	7
	At Heshbon they plot evil (against her):	בחשבון חשבו [ ][c] רעה	8
	"Let us cut her off from being a nation!"	[ ][d] נכריתנה מגוי	6
	With a loud voice, O Madmen, you shall wail;	גם[e] מדמן תדמי	6
	Hard after you comes (my) sword.	אחריך תלך חרב⟨י⟩[f]	7
3	The voice of crying echoes from Horonaim;	קול צעקה מחרונים	8
	Devastation and utter destruction!	שד ושבר גדול	5
4	Smashed is Moab!	נשברה מואב	5
	The cry is heard as far as Zoar!	השמיעו זעקה (צֹעֲרָה)[g]	8
5	For up the slopes of Luhith,	כי מעלה [ ]לח(י)ת בבכי	12
	weeping profusely they climb;	יעלה בכי	
	At the descent of Horonaim,	[ ][h] במורד חורנים [ ][i]	12
	a cry of destruction is heard.	צעקת שבר שמעו	
6	Flee! Run for your lives!	נסו מלטו נפשכם	7
	Remain in the desert (like a wild ass)!	ותי(ו)-נה [ ][j] במדבר	7
7	Because you trust in your own achievements,	כי יען בטחך במעשיך [ ][k]	7
	You also shall be captured.	גם את[l] תלכדי	7
	Chemosh shall go into exile,	ויצא כמ(ו)ש בגולה	8
	Together with his priests and nobles.	כהניו ושריו יחדו[m]	8
8	The destroyer has come against every town,	יבא שדד אל כל עיר	13
	not a town shall escape;	ועיר לא תמלט	
	The Valley shall be destroyed and	ואבד [ ]עמק ונשמד [ ]מישר	13
	the Plain plundered, saith Yahweh.	אמר יהוה	

9	Provide salt for Moab,	תנו ציץ למואב	6
	Her cities shall be utterly ruined;	[][m] נצ(ה) תצ(ה) []עריה	7
	They shall become a desolate waste,	לשמה תהיינה	6
	Where nobody dwells.	מאין יושב בָהֵנָ	7
10	[Cursed be he who does Yahweh's work with slackness,		
	who withholds his sword from shedding blood.]		
11	Secure is Moab from his youth;	שאנן מואב מנעוריו	8
	He is undisturbed on his lees --	ושקט הוא אל שמריו	8
	Never having been decanted,	[]לא הורק מכלי אל כלי	7
	Never having gone into exile;	ובגולה לא הלך	7
	Thus he has retained his flavor,	על כן עמד טעמו בו	7
	And his aroma is not changed.	וריחו לא נמר	6
12	[And so, look! The days are coming -- utterance of Yahweh -- when I will		
	send him decanters who will decant and empty his vessels; and his jars		
	they will smash. 13 Moab shall be disappointed in Chemosh, as the house		
	of Israel was disappointed in Bethel, in whom they placed their trust.]		
14	How can you say:	איך תאמרו	-
	"We are heroes,	גבורים אנחנו	6
	Men who are valiant in battle?"	[]אנשי חיל למלחמה	7
15	Destroyed is Moab, (its) city and fortress;	שדד מואב []עיר[][n] ומבחר	8
	Its soldiers have gone down to the slaughter.	בחוריו ירדו לטבח [][o]	8
16	Moab's ruin is close at hand;	קרוב איד מואב לבוא	7
	Its downfall comes at top speed.	[]רעתו מהרה מאד	7
17	Grieve for him, all you his neighbors,	נדו לו כל סביביו	7
	All who know his name;	וכל ידעי שמו	7
	Say: "Imagine it being broken,	אמרו איכה נשבר	6
	That mighty rod, that splendid scepter!"	מטה עז מקל תפארה	8
18	Come down from (your) glory (and) sit in the	רדי מכבוד []שבי בצמה	10
	dry ground, O inhabitress of Dibon!	ישבת [][p] דיבון	4
	For Moab's destroyer is upon you;	כי שדד מואב עלה בך	9
	He has stormed your strongholds.	שחת מבצריך	5
19	Stand by the wayside!	אל דרך עמדי	4
	Watch, O inhabitress of Aroer (Desolation?)!	צפי ישבת ערוער	8
	Question the fugitive and runaway!	שאלי נס ונמלט[]	6
	Ask: "What has happened?"	אמרי מה נהיתה	6
20	Humbled is Moab for he is shattered!	הביש מואב כי חַת[][b]	6
	Wail! Cry out!	הילל(ו) []זעק(ו)	5
	Proclaim it across the Arnon,	הגידו בארנון	6
	That Moab lies waste.	כי שדד מואב	5
21	Judgment has come on the tableland,	[]משפט בא אל ארץ []מישר	7
	On Holon and on Jahaz.	אל חלון ואל יהצה	7

[and Mephaath; 22 on Dibon, Nebo, and Beth-diblathaim; 23 on Kiriathaim,
Beth-gamul, and Beth-meon; 24 on Kerioth, on Bozrah, and on all the cities
of Moab, both far and near.]

25	The horn of Moab is cut off;	נגדעה קרן מואב	6
	His arm is broken.	[]זרעו נשברה [][q]	6
26	[Make him drunk, for he has set himself up	השכירהו כי על יהוה הגדיל	
	against Yahweh. Moab will wallow in his	וספק מואב בקיאו	
	vomit; he will become a laughingstock.	והיה לשחק גם הוא	
27	Was not Israel a laughingstock to you?	ואם לוא השחק היה לך ישראל	
	Was she (not) caught in the company of	אם בגנבים נמצאה (ב)[]מד[]בר[r]	
	thieves in the wilderness, when she fled away?]	(כ)י בו תתנודד	
28	Forsake the towns!	עזבו עדים	4
	Make the rocks your home,	[]שכנו בסלע	4
	O inhabitants of Moab!	ישבי מואב	5
	Be like the dove that nests	[]היו כיונה תקנן	8
	high on the sides of the gorge.	בעברי פי פחת	5
29	I have heard of Moab's pride,	שמע<תי>[s] גאון מואב	10
	excessive pride;	גאה מאד	
	His arrogance, his swagger,	גבהו [][t] וגאותו	10
	his lofty conceit.	ורם לבו	
30	I myself know his insolence;	אני ידעתי [][u] עברתו	8
	False are his boasts, false his deeds.	[]לא כן בדיו לא כן עשו	8
31	And so I wail for Moab;	על כן על מואב איליל	7
	For the whole of Moab I cry.	[]למואב כלה אזעק	7
	For the men of Kir-heres I mourn;	אל אנשי קיר חרש <א>הגה[v]	7
32	O fountain of Jazer, I weep for you.	מבכ[][w] יעזר אבכה לך [][x]	7
	Your tendrils have reached beyond the sea;	נטישתיך עברו ים	8
	All the way from Jazer they extended.	עדי מיעזר[y] נגעו	8
	On your summer fruit and your vintage	על קיצך ועל בצירך	12
	the destroyer has descended;	שדד נפל	
33	Gladness and joy have vanished	ונאספה שמחה וגיל	12
	from the land of Moab.	[][z] מארץ מואב	
	Wine from the presses is gone;	[]יין מיקבים הָשְׁבַּת[á]	7
	The treader of grapes treads no more;	(ו)לא ידרך []ד(ו)<ך>[b́]	6
	The shout of harvest is no longer voiced.	הידד לא הידד-ם[ć]	6
34	The cry of Heshbon (resounds) to Elealeh;	זעקת[ć] חשבון עד אלעלה	8
	As far as Jahaz their voice is heard.	עד<י>[d́] יהץ נתנו קולם	8
	From Zoar (it resounds) as far as Horonaim,	מצער עד חרנים	7
	And Eglath-shelishiyah.	<ו>עגלת[é] שלשיה [][f́]	7

35 I will stop Moab	והשבתי למואב [][g]	7
From offering sacrifices on high places,	מעלה ⟨עלה על⟩[h] במה	7
From making sacrifices to his gods.	ומקטיר לאלהיו	7
36 And so my heart for Moab	על כן לבי למואב	7
wails like a flute;	כחללים יהמה	6
My heart for the men of Kir-heres	[]לבי אל אנשי קיר חרש	7
wails like a flute.	כחלילים יהמה	6
For that accumulated treasure is lost;	על כן יתרת עשה אבדו	9
The waters of Nimrin are desolate.	(מי נמרים למשמות יהיו)[f]	9
37 Every head in every covert is shorn,	[][i] כל ראש ⟨בכל סך⟩[j] קרחה	7
And every beard cut off.	וכל זקן גרעה	7
On every hand are gashes,	על כל ידים גדדת	7
And on every waist sackcloth.	ועל⟨י כל⟩[k] מתנים שק	7
38 On every rooftop of Moab,	⟨ו⟩על⟨י⟩[l] כל גגות מואב	8
In all his squares there is mourning.	[]ברחבתי(ו)[b] כלה מספד	8
For I have broken Moab,	כי שברתי [] מואב	6
Like an unwanted pot.	ככלי אין חפץ בו [][g]	6
39 How shattered they are! They howl!	איך חת(ו)[m] הילילו	6
How Moab turns tail in flight!	איך הפנה ערף מואב	6
They are shamed! Moab has become an object of derision,	בושו[n] היה מואב לשחק	9
A shock to all those around him.	[]למחתה לכל סביביו	9
40 For thus saith Yahweh:	כי כה אמר יהוה [][o]	
41 The towns are captured,	נלכדה []קריות	6
The strongholds seized.	[]מצדות נתפשה [][o]	6
42 Destroyed as a people is Moab,	[]נשמד מואב מעם	6
Because he has defied Yahweh.	כי על יהוה הגדיל	6
43 Terror, trapfall, and trap	פחד ופחת ופח	5
are upon you, O Moab.	עליך [][p] מואב [][o]	5
44 He who flees from the terror	[]נ[]ס[q] מפני []פחד	5
falls into the trapfall;	יפל אל⟨ו⟩[r] []פחת	5
And he who climbs from the trapfall	ו[]עלה מן []פחת	5
is caught in the trap.	ילכד בפח	5
For I will bring these things upon Moab,	כי אביא אל[]ה[s] אל מואב	7
In the year of their doom.	⟨ב⟩שנת[t] פקדתם [][o]	7

Notes to the Text of Jeremiah 48:1-47

[a]Deleting the phrase צבאות אלהי ישראל and the term הבישה with LXX.

[b]Reading the masculine form with משגב, "stronghold, citadel." The feminine form of this verbal root (חתת, "be shattered") has apparently been

leveled through in this chapter. Cf. vss. 20 and 39. The reading of משגב as a place name led to the feminine forms הבישה and חתה in MT. The feminine suffix in vs. 38 (וברחבתיה) is further evidence of this general confusion. Moab is taken as masculine throughout this chapter in the present analysis.

[c]Deleting עליה *metri causa.*

[d]Deleting לכו with LXX.

[e]Following M. Dahood, "Ugaritic Studies and the Bible," *Gregorianum* 43 (1962), p. 70; who interprets the particle גם as meaning "with a loud voice." Cf. also A. Kuschke, "Jeremia xlviii, 1-8. Zugleich ein Beitrag zur historischen Topographie Moabs," *Verbannung und Heimkehr* (W. Rudolph Festschrift, Tübingen: J. C. B. Mohr, 1961), p. 185.

[f]LXX reads μαχαιρα. ὅτι which probably renders חרב כי. Since the particle כי overloads the meter in the following verse, it seems preferable to take the Hebrew text reflected in LXX as a dittography from an original חרבי. The emendation improves the metrical balance allowing the qinah pattern to extend throughout this opening strophe.

[g]Following LXX εἰς Ζογορα; cf. also Isa. 15:5 עד-צער.

[h]Deleting כי as dittography with LXX.

[i]Deleting צרי with LXX; cf. also Isa. 15:5.

[j]Taking the verb as second masculine plural with the energic ending, as suggested by D. N. Freedman (in Bright, Jeremiah, p. 314, n. e–e). The word כערוער is deleted *metri causa*, a secondary expansion perhaps from יעערו of Isa. 15:5.

[k]Deleting ובאוצרותיך as a doublet. LXX reads only ὀχυρωμασι σου, "your stronghold," for the two terms of MT and perhaps represents a third alternate reading (במעזיך? or במצדותיך?) as suggested in the commentaries.

[l]Following 2QJer fragment which reads אתה thus improving the metrical balance in this quatrain.

[m]The *waw* is taken here as a suffix rather than as a conjunction attached to the following verb in MT. Cf. the parallel passage in Jer. 49:3.

[ṁ]Deleting כי *metri causa* and reading the root נצה, "fall in ruins," for MT נצא, "fly;" cf. LXX ἀφη ἀναφθησεται, "(her cities) shall become desolate."

[n]See the discussion of Byron E. Shafer, "מבחור/מבחר = 'Fortress,'" *CBQ* 33 (1971), pp. 393-94; who has reconstructed this verse on the basis of LXX. The reading suggested here differs only in the deletion of the pronominal suffix on עירה, "its city."

[o]Deleting נאם המלך יהוה צבאות שמו with LXX.

[p]Deleting בת as a dittography with LXX.

[q]Deleting נאם יהוה with LXX.

[r]A conjectural emendation to make sense of a most difficult verse. LXX omits מבי דבריך perhaps due to an haplography since ὅτι ἐπολεμεις αὐτον may render an original כי בו תתגודד. On the meaning of גנבים in this context

cf. Deut. 24:7 where the "thieves" have stolen men and made slaves of them, thereby violating covenant stipulations.

[s]Emending with LXX ἤκουσα, "I have heard." MT probably reflects textual conflation with Isa. 16:6. Cf. also 2QJer fragment which reads שמער נא.

[t]Deleting וגאונו as textual conflation from Isa. 16:6. The LXX reading ὕβρισε λιαν ὕβριν reflects only two of the three synonyms in MT. The presence of either of the second or third terms as conflation from the parallel passage in Isa. 16:6 is easier to explain than the secondary addition of גבהו.

[u]Deleting נאם יהוה with LXX.

[v]Emending with *Qere apud Orientales* as cited in *BHS*. The parallel verb in each of the other three cola of this quatrain is in the first person.

[w]See G. M. Landes, "The Fountain at Jazer," *BASOR* 144 (1956), p. 31; who relates the term here to Ug. *npk*, "(water) source, fountain, well."

[x]Deleting הגפן שבמה *metri causa*, as secondary conflation from Isa. 16:8.

[y]A conjectural emendation which involves only a slight redivision of the consonantal text of MT. Cf. LXX πολεις which renders ערים in place of עד ים of MT.

[z]Deleting מכרמל ו with LXX; cf. Isa. 16:10 as the probable source of this expansion.

[á]Repointing the verb as Hophal and taking the *yodh* as *waw* conjunction with the following word.

[b́]A conjectural emendation in an attempt to render sense of an obviously corrupt text; cf. Isa. 16:10.

[ć]Taking the *mem* as enclitic, rather than the preposition, to improve both the metrical balance and sense.

[d́]The ballast variant of the preposition improves the metrical balance and is not in fact a textual emendation per se, as the *yodh* here may be taken as a shared consonant.

[é]Restoring the *waw* with LXX.

[f́]Deleting כי גם as prosaic expansion and relocating this colon to the end of vs. 36 below. The position of the same colon in a different context in Isa. 15:6 probably accounts for the dislocation here.

[ǵ]Deleting נאם יהוה *metri causa*.

[h́]Accepting the emendation proposed by Rudolph in the apparatus to *BH*[3]. Rudolph suggested an haplography of עלה and the restoration of the preposition על with LXX, Aquila, Symmachus and Targ.

[í]Deleting כי with LXX.

[j́]LXX adds ἐν παντι τοπῳ which may render the text as reconstructed; on τοπος = סך cf. Pss. 42:5 and 76:3.

[ḱ]Restoring the text with LXX και ἐπι πασης.

[ĺ]Restoring the *waw* with LXX and reading the ballast form of the preposition to improve the metrical balance.

[ḿ]Reading the plural form of the verb to form closer parallelism with the following verb and to improve the metrical balance. The *he* of MT may have been a vowel marker for the û-vowel.

[ń]Redividing the words to preserve the same alternation between plural verbal form when applied to the people of Moab and singular with Moab itself, as observed in the previous verse.

[ó]Following the shorter Hebrew text reflected in LXX, the MT pluses of vss. 40-47 are here omitted.

[ṕ]Deleting יושב *metri causa*; cf. Isa. 24:17 for the probable source of this conflation.

[q́]Taking the *Qere* reading in agreement with the parallel in Isa. 24:18.

[ŕ]Reading the ballast variant form of the preposition to strengthen the metrical balance.

[ś]Emending with LXX ταυτα, "these things," for MT אליה.

[t́]Restoring the *beth* with LXX; lost by haplography.

Jeremiah 48:1-44 in Outline

I

A. Judgment/Lament over Moab (vss. 1-5)

[lb:bl:lb] Moab's glory is shattered, she will be a nation no longer.

[bl:lb:bl] The noise of mourning resounds as far as Zoar.

[lb:bl] The sound of weeping is heard at Luhith and Horonaim.

B. Summons to Flight (vss. 6-8)

[b:b::b:b] Hide in the wilderness to escape captivity!

[l:l] Moab's god and her rulers will be exiled.

[l:l] ? Not a town shall be spared.

C. Summons to Desolate the Ruins of Moab (vss. 9-10)

[b:b::b:b]? Salt the ruins and make Moab uninhabitable.

[prose] Apodictic curse -- directed against those who refuse to participate in Yahweh's war against Moab.

D. Oracle of Doom (vss. 11-16)

[l:l] Moab is like good aged wine.

[l:l] He has never been shaken in exile.

[l:l] Hence he has retained his "shalom."

[prose] I will empty and smash his vessels.

Moab will share Israel's fate.

[l:l] ? How can you say: "We are heroes, valiant in battle?"

[l:l::l:l] Moab's "heroes" will be slaughtered, her ruin is close at hand.

E. Summons to Mourn (vss. 17-19)

[1b:b1] Grieve for Moab, his splendor is no more!

[1b:1b] Humble yourself, Dibon, for the "Destroyer" has come!

[b1:1b] Inquire of the refugees!

F. Announcement of Judgment

[b:b::b:b] Make lamentation for Moab is shattered!

[1:1] The tableland (north of the Arnon) is destroyed.

[prose] Judgment has come to all the cities of Moab.

[1:1] The "horn" (strength) of Moab is cut off.

[prose] Make Moab drunk so he can wallow in his vomit!
Moab will be a laughingstock to Israel as Israel was to him.

G. Summons to Flight (vs. 28)

[b:b:b::1:b] Seek safety in the wilderness!

II

A. Judgment/Lament over Moab (vss. 29-36; cf. Isa. 16:6-10; 15:4-7)

[1:1::1:1] I know about Moab's excessive pride.

[1:1::1:1] I mourn for Moab.

[1:1] Her "tendrils" have extended far.

[1:1] The "Destroyer" descends to destroy her produce.

[1:1:1] The wine of Moab will be no more.

[1:1::1:1] Moab's cry of terror resounds far and wide.

[1:1:1] I will bring Moab's idolatry to an end.

[1:1] ? My heart "wails like a flute" for Moab.

[1:1] All Moab's goodness is gone.

B. Oracle of Doom (vss. 37-44; cf. Isa. 15:2-3; 24:17-18)

1. Moab -- a grief stricken people (vss. 37-38a)

[1:1::1:1] Everyone displays signs of mourning.

[1:1] Everywhere in Moab there is mourning.

2. Moab -- destroyed by Yahweh (vss. 38b-39)

[1:1::1:1] I have shattered Moab like an unwanted pot.

[1:1] Moab has become an object of derision.

3. Summary (vss. 40-44)

[b:b::b:b] Moab is destroyed because he defied Yahweh.

[3(b:b)] A threefold peril -- there is no escape.

[1:1] I, Yahweh, will bring these things upon Moab.

Chapter 48 of Jeremiah consists of a series of poems, together with prose comments, directed against Moab. Commentaries are not agreed as to the actual number of individual poems nor to exactly where each separate unit leaves off and a new one begins.[92] The major difficulty confronting the interpreter is the unusual length of this oracle against Moab. As Cornill put it, the oracle takes a unique place among Jeremiah's oracles against the nations because of "seine monströse Länge von 47 massorethischen Versen."[93] A careful prosodic-textual analysis has failed to reveal any neat division of material into separate oracles. It is fairly easy to determine the limits of the various poetic strophes but the larger groupings of these strophes is not always certain.

As the text stands, the chapter is basically a single literary unit which contains several distinct forms of prophetic speech, including summons to flight, summons to mourn, prophetic laments, announcements of judgment, and oracles of doom. The imagery is in almost constant flux with heralds proclaiming their messages, fugitives fleeing the ravaged cities and mourners lamenting the destruction of Moab. Prose sections break up the movement of thought. Sometimes the prose elements seem to reflect an underlying poetic original (i.e., vss. 10?, 12-13 and 26-27). Elsewhere the prose elements appear to be secondary expansions of the original text (vss. 21b-24).

The dating of the material preserved in Jer. 48 is extremely difficult. Presumably Moab, like Judah, submitted to the Babylonians when Nebuchadnezzar advanced into Palestine after defeating the Egyptians at Carchemish in 605. When Jehoiakim rebelled in *ca.* 600-598, Moab remained loyal to Babylon and even assisted the Babylonians against Judah (II Kings 24:2). This is certainly one occasion when anti-Moab sentiment blazed forth and may have occasioned the material preserved here. A second possible occasion for an oracle against Moab is the attempted rebellion against Babylon in *ca.* 594 in which Moab was involved and which Jeremiah opposed (Jer. 27:1-11). A third possibility has been suggested by Bardtke, and a few others, which deserves serious consideration -- the period of the political expansion of Judah under Josiah (*ca.* 628-609).

---

[92]Bardtke divided the chapter into three divisions: 1-13, 14-27 and 28-47. Dimon-Haran found four essential units (1-6, 16-24, 29-38 and 45-47) which have been expanded in the course of transmission and readaptation of the material to new situations. Bright saw five divisions: 1-10, 11-17, 18-28, 29-39 and 40-47. A. S. Peake also listed five major divisions but chose to divide the second and third between vss. 19 and 20. Rudolph broke Bright's fifth division into two parts (it would perhaps be more accurate to say that Bright combined these two divisions of Rudolph) thus obtaining six divisions. Numerous other variations of these possible sub-divisions of the chapter appear in the commentaries, most ranging between three and six major sub-units.

[93]C. H. Cornill, *Das Buch Jeremia* (Leipzig: Chr. Herm. Tauchnitz, 1905), p. 462.

Bardtke argued that the historical setting of both Jer. 48 and 49:1-6 was the political extension of Judah between 622 and *ca.* 617.[94] He saw a reflection of Josiah's cultic reform in vs. 13, arguing that both the northern kingdom of Israel and Moab had forsaken their loyalty to Yahweh in favor of Bethel and Chemosh respectively. For this action Israel had been punished in the fall of Samaria in 722. Moab's punishment, long overdue, was now to be meted out by Yahweh himself.

The summons to desolate the ruins of Moab (vs. 9) makes good sense within the context of a summons to battle against an unfaithful member of the Covenant League of the idealized Davidic Empire. Even the apodictic curse against those who refuse to participate in Moab's destruction ought not to be dismissed too quickly as a late prosaic addition to the text. Bach described the curse in 48:10 as "ein Rudiment aus dem heiligen Krieg" and compared it to the apodictic series of curses in Deut. 27:15ff.[95] A further parallel in the Song of Deborah (Judg. 5:23) where Meroz is cursed for not participating in the battle against Sisera and the Canaanites should also be noted. The two curses are similar in both content and construction:

Curse Meroz, says the messenger of Yahweh;	אורו מרוז אמר[מלאך] יהוה	10/8
Bitterly curse her inhabitants;	ארו ארור ישביה	8
For they did not come to Yahweh's aid,	כי לא באו לעזרת יהוה	9
To the help of Yahweh with warriors.	לעזרת יהוה בגבורים	9
Cursed be he who does Yahweh's work with slackness,	ארור עשה [מלאכת יהוה] רמיה	11/7
Who withholds his sword from shedding blood.	ארור מנע חרבו מדם	8

Both verses fall within the category of battle-curses and are to be understood in terms of the institution of holy war in ancient Israel.

Bardtke also called attention to the list of place names preserved in Jer. 48 and 49:1-6 arguing that they constitute the territorial claims of the tribes of Reuben and Gad in Transjordan. He followed Alt in dating the related lists in Joshua 13 and Numbers 32 to the reign of Josiah.[96] The earlier dating of the Joshua lists as advanced by Cross and Wright does not alter the major thrust of Bardtke's argument.[97] Josiah was concerned with reestab-

---

[94]Hans Bardtke, "Jeremia der Fremdvölkerprophet," *ZAW* 54 (1936), p. 242.

[95]Robert Bach, *Die Aufforderungen zur Flucht und zum Kampf im alttestamentlichen Prophetenspruch* (WMANT 9; Neukirchen: Neukirchen Verlag, 1962), p. 88, n. 2.

[96]H. Bardtke, *op. cit.*, p. 241, n. 3.

[97]See F. M. Cross, Jr. and G. E. Wright, "The Boundary and Province Lists of the Kingdom of Judah," *JBL* 75 (1956), pp. 202-26.

lishing the Davidic Empire and one justification of his projected political expansion in the former Assyrian provinces of Israel, Gilead, Megiddo, Dor and Ashdod was certainly the historical claim to this territory from the days of Israel's Covenant League.

In the present analysis the lengthy oracle against Moab has been divided into two major divisions: vss. 1-28 and 29-44. The first division is further divided into seven strophic units (1-5, 6-8, 9-10, 11-16, 17-19, 20-27 and 28). The second major division shows considerable dependence on earlier OAN material, particularly Isa. 15:2-7 and 16:6-11.[98] Vss. 43-44 appear again in Isa. 24:17-18. William Millar has argued that these verses are original to the so-called "Isaiah Apocalypse" and are secondarily added to the oracle against Moab in Jer. 48.[99] As was the case in the concluding section of the oracles against Edom (49:12-21), we have in 48:29-44 an eclectic oracle of doom which may be secondary to the poetic tradition preserved in vss. 1-28.

One should also note the difference between LXX and MT, especially in vss. 40-47. Recent studies in both the Qumran literature and LXX indicate that the Palestinian text behind MT in Jeremiah was conflated and expanded through the addition of standard clichés and material from proximate and parallel passages.[100] The shorter Hebrew text reflected in LXX has been taken as the more original text at numerous points in this section. Consequently vss. 45-47 are deleted as secondary expansion from Num. 21:28 and 24:17b. Other major omissions occur in vss. 40-41 which apparently are more original in Jer. 49:22.

As to the date of the poetic material in vss. 1-28, the one conclusion that can be made with any degree of certainty is that vs. 13 reflects a pre-Exilic situation. The comparison of Chemosh with Bethel and the remark that the God of the Israelites (Bethel) could not prevent the disaster that fell

---

[98]According to A. S. Peake, *Jeremiah* (The New-Century Bible, New York: Henry Frowde, 1911), p. 235: "(Jer. 48:29-38) is almost entirely derived from Isa. xv, xvi, and is not an improvement on the original."

[99]William R. Millar, "Isaiah 24-27 and the Origin of Apocalyptic" (unpub. Ph.D. thesis, Harvard University, 1970), pp. 59-62. It should be noted that such questions of originality are difficult, if not impossible, to demonstrate. Millar also made the remark that, "The entirety of Jeremiah 48 is a collection of separate oracles against Moab drawn together secondarily" (p. 59, n. 3). Such a conclusion overstates the evidence as our prosodic-textual analysis has shown.

[100]See F. M. Cross, Jr., "The History of the Biblical Text in Light of the Discoveries in the Judaean Desert," *HTR* 57 (1964), esp. pp. 287, 297-99. See also J. G. Janzen, "Double Readings in the Text of Jeremiah," *HTR* 60 (1967), pp. 446-47 and his doctoral thesis as cited on p. 11, n. 50 above.

on the northern kingdom certainly makes little sense after 587. As Eissfeldt put it, "after the downfall of the southern kingdom itself there could hardly be so spiteful and self-righteous an attitude towards the northern kingdom."[101] Just how much of the rest of this section (vss. 1-28) is to be taken as contemporary with vs. 13 is not certain; and a more precise date within the pre-Exilic period for any of this material is difficult to determine.

A possible reflection of the Josianic period is also found in the second major division (vs. 32) where the "tendrils" of Moabite political control are portrayed as reaching beyond the Dead Sea and spreading out from Jazer in southern Gilead. After the death of Ahab (*ca.* 850), the entire region of southern Gilead was conquered by Mesha of Moab. The northern kingdom of Israel recovered control of this region under Jeroboam II (*ca.* 783-748). In *ca.* 734 this region was incorporated into the Assyrian provincial system as part of *Gal'aza*. During the revolt of Shamashshumukin in Babylon (*ca.* 652-648) Moab was free to extend her political influence northward once again. Under Kamashhalta (*ca.* 650-640) Moab defeated the Qedarite forces of Ammuladin and almost certainly regained control of southern Gilead.[102] By *ca.* 628 Josiah was challenging Moab for possession of the former Assyrian province of *Gal'aza*. It is quite possible that the political events of *ca.* 650-630 are reflected in the lament over Jazer in 48:32.

If our reconstruction of the text of vs. 26 is correct, we may have here a reference to events of *ca.* 587 when the fugitives of Judah were held in derision by the Moabites. The case perhaps cannot be proved, but it does seem likely that the lengthy oracle against Moab in Jer. 48 reflects original oracular poems uttered during the reign of Josiah, augmented by material from *ca.* 600-598, 594 (?) and/or 587-582 when earlier material was up-dated. In its present form the chapter is a collection of these various anti-Moab traditions, editorially arranged in a manner that defies specific historical analysis in matters of detail.

d. Oracle against Aram [Jer. 49:23-27 (LXX 30:12-16)]

23	Concerning Damascus:	לדמשק	
	Dismayed are Hamath and Arpad,	בושה חמת וארפד	7
	For disastrous news they have heard;	כי שמעו[ ] רע[ ][a] שמעו	6
	They melt away (in terror) like Yamm, they quiver in fear,	נמג[ ] (כ)ים דאג(ו)[b]	7
	They cannot be calmed.	השקט לא יוכל⟨ו⟩[c]	6

---

[101] O. Eissfeldt, *The Old Testament: An Introduction*, p. 363; see also "Der Gott Bethel," *ARW* 28 (1930), pp. 1-30.

[102] See the discussion above on pp. 95-96.

24	Faint is Damascus,	רפתה דמשק	5
	She turns to flee,	הפנתה לנוס	5
	Panic has seized her!	[]רטט החזיקה [][d]	4
25	How utterly forsaken she is --	איך ל-עזבה[e]	5
	The city renowned,	עיר תהלה	4
	The joyous town.	קרית משושי[f]	5/4
26	And so (your) choice young men shall fall in your squares;	לכן יפלו בחורי⟨ם⟩[g] ברחבתי⟨ך⟩[g]	13
	All (your) men of war shall lie lifeless, utterance of Yahweh.	[]כל אנשי []מלחמה ידמו []^h נאם יהוה [][i]	13
27	For I will kindle a fire in the wall of Damascus,	והצתי אש בחומת דמשק	10
	That will consume the strongholds of Ben-hadad.	ואכלה ארמנות בן הדד	10

Notes to the Text of Jeremiah 49:23-27

[a]A conjectural emendation to restore metrical balance in this quatrain. On the use of the masculine noun שמע in this sense cf. Jer. 50:43 and Isa. 23:5. See also Jer. 6:24 שמענו שמעו.

[b]A conjectural emendation which involves minimal change in the consonantal text. LXX reads two verbs in this colon. The first word נמג is read as infinitive absolute and the last word דאגו as third person plural in parallel with שמעו of the previous colon. The source of difficulty in this colon was the reference to *Yamm* of Canaanite mythology which was misunderstood in transmission of this oracle.

[c]Restoring a third person plural verb in parallel with שמעו and דאגו of the two previous cola; cf. LXX δυνωνται, "they shall (not) be able."

[d]Deleting צרה וחבלים אחזתה כיולדה with LXX; cf. Jer. 6:24 and 50:43b.

[e]Taking the *lamedh* as the asseverative particle which renders better sense in this context.

[f]The *yodh* is retained as the archaic genitive ending; most of the versions omit the suffix.

[g]Following LXX νεανισκοι ἐν πλατειαις σου. MT probably represents secondary conflation with the parallel passage in Jer. 50:30.

[h]Deleting ביום ההוא with LXX; a secondary conflation from Jer. 50:30.

[i]Deleting צבאות with LXX.

Jeremiah 49:23-27 in Outline

A. Prophetic Vision: The Panic of Aram (vss. 23-25)

[b:b::b:b] Hamath and Arpad are dismayed over disastrous news.

[b:b:b::b:b:b] Damascus is in utter panic.

B. Yahweh's Declaration of Judgment (vss. 26-27)

[1:1] Your armies, Aram, will be decimated.

[1:1] I will destroy the strongholds of Ben-hadad.

Note: vs. 24c (here deleted with LXX) = Jer. 6:24, 50:43b
26 = Jer. 50:30
27 = Amos 1:4,14

Though the shortest of Jeremiah's oracles against the nations, the oracle against Damascus is one of the more interesting. It is extremely difficult to fit this oracle into the known events of Jeremiah's lifetime. R. H. Pfeiffer called the oracle deliberately archaic, maintaining that: "It reflects the Assyrian conquests in the second half of the eighth century (cf. 49:27, which quotes Amos 1:4) rather than the time of Jeremiah, when these cities were no longer powerful."[103] He then proceeded to date the oracle to the late fifth century B.C., as an example of late prophetic archaism. Bright represents another group of scholars who, rejecting Pfeiffer's post-Exilic date, are still unable to fit the oracle into their understanding of Jeremiah's ministry:[104]

> . . . it is possible that we are dealing with an anonymous saying much older than Jeremiah, perhaps of eighth-century date, which has been reapplied to Damascus perhaps in connection with one of Nebuchadrezzar's campaigns . . .

Bright took note of the single reference to Aram in connection with events of Jeremiah's life in II Kings 24:2, where Aramean troops (sometimes emended to "Edomite" troops) are mentioned along with Chaldeans, Moabites and Ammonites in the pacification of Judah in *ca.* 600-597; but did not find this a suitable occasion for the original composition of this oracle.

A prosodic-textual analysis reveals a carefully constructed poem of two strophes, the first of which is in short meter. The first quatrain describes the reaction to bad news on the part of distant Hamath and Arpad. They are utterly dismayed and quake in fear. Like *Yamm* in his mythical combat with *Ba'l*, they melt away, they collapse in terror.[105] The focus of attention is not on Hamath and Arpad, however, but on Damascus whose panic is presented in a pair of short tricola (vss. 24-25). The staccato effect of this metrical unit is indeed striking.

---

[103]Robert H. Pfeiffer, *Introduction to the Old Testament* (New York: Harper & Brothers, 1941), p. 508.

[104]J. Bright, *Jeremiah*, p. 337.

[105]The reference is perhaps to the defeat of *Yamm* and the powers of chaos by mighty *Ba'l-Haddu* in the mythic cycle of *Ba'l* and *'Anat* (cf. UT:68:1-28).

The second strophe (vss. 26-27) is a pair of long bicola which present the actual oracle as such. Yahweh declares that the armies of Aram and the city of Damascus will be destroyed. The destruction of Damascus is couched in language borrowed from the earlier OAN tradition of Amos (cf. Amos 1:1,14).

The original setting of this oracle may well have been the period of political expansion under Josiah (*ca.* 628-609). If our reconstruction of Psalm 60 is correct, we may have an interesting poetic parallel to Jeremiah's oracle against Aram. In response to the divine oracle assuring victory over Moab, Edom and Philistia the king responded:[106]

> Would that he would bring me to the citadel of Tyre!
> Would that he would lead me as far as Aram!

The king of Israel is requesting of the Divine Warrior that the full extent of David's empire be restored. It would appear, as Bright has surmised,[107] that when Assyria collapsed, the Aramean peoples of Syria regained their freedom alongside resurgent Judah. The Aramean states were still legitimately part of the ideal Davidic Empire, at least in the eyes of the official theology in Jerusalem; and hence, when Yahweh had completed the restoration of David's empire he would also reestablish his suzerainty over Aram. Damascus would once again face the judgment of Yahweh and this time the Divine Warrior would finish the job, once and for all.

From the above analysis it is clear that the so-called "Archaic OAN" tradition in Jeremiah (48:1-49:27) displays characteristic features that set it off as distinct from the "Jeremianic OAN" tradition (46-47, 49:28-39). The oracles in the former category tend to show layers of development which reflect a more complex history of tradition than the latter. Moreover, the oracles against Ammon, Edom, Moab and Aram can be interpreted as stemming originally from the period of the political expansion of Judah under Josiah. In subsequent periods, beginning in *ca.* 605, these oracles were collected and expanded to fit new historical situations, perhaps in *ca.* 600-597, 594 and 587-582. The specific war oracles, composed in the decade *ca.* 609-598, against Qedar, Philistia, Egypt and Elam did not lend themselves so well to such expansionary reuse in the decade before and after the destruction of Jerusalem.

The two divisions observed in Jeremiah's OAN tradition in chs. 46-49 reflect two different stages in the ministry of the prophet, before and after the death of Josiah. The "Archaic OAN" tradition reflects the political expansion of Judah under Josiah and is akin to the OAN tradition of Zephaniah. The "Jeremianic OAN" tradition reflects the turbulent final decade of the 7th

---

[106] See pp. 120-26 above.

[107] J. Bright, *Jeremiah*, p. 337.

century when Judah was caught up in the power struggle between Egypt and Babylon. The abortive revolt of Jehoiakim (*ca.* 600-597) and the subsequent collapse of Judah before the might of Babylon marked the end of an era in the mind of Jeremiah. His subsequent OAN tradition, beginning with the oracle against Elam (*ca.* 597) reveals a growing eschatological orientation which will become more evident in our analysis of the oracles against Babylon in Jeremiah 50-51.

Jeremiah 50-51 and Early Apocalyptic

The lengthy collection of oracular poems concerning Babylon in chs. 50-51 presents numerous problems to the interpreter. Sheer bulk is not the least of these problems. The two chapters are made up of 110 verses (in MT), thus constituting almost as much material as the entire OAN tradition preserved in chs. 46-49 (121 verses). As was the case in the oracles against Moab (ch. 48), there are relatively few obvious divisions within these chapters which form clear boundaries for individual poems. The lack of scholarly consensus concerning the literary structure of this material as a whole reveals the need for a new methodology in our approach to this important OAN tradition.

The analysis here is based on a detailed prosodic-textual study of the Hebrew text, utilizing both our knowledge of the historical development of Hebrew poetry and the evidence from the various ancient versions, especially LXX. Once the limits of the individual metrical units are thus determined, the smaller units are grouped into poetic strophes and the strophes into still larger units of thought which are presented in outline form. The reconstructed text and literary units are then subjected to form-critical analysis in an attempt to relate the specific forms of prophetic speech found in these particular oracles to the developing OAN tradition studied thus far.

1. Jeremiah 50:1-46 (LXX 27:1-46)

1	The word which Yahweh spoke		הדבר אשר דבר יהוה
	concerning Babylon:		אל בבל [ ][a]
2	Declare among the nations!	6	הגידו בגוים
	Set up a banner (and) proclaim!	6	[ ][b] שאו נס השמיעו
	Do not conceal the news!	6	⟨ו⟩אל[c] תכחדו
	Say: Babylon is taken!	7	אמרו נלכדה בבל
	Bel is confounded! Merodach is dismayed!	7	הביש בל חת מרדך [ ][d]
3	A nation from the north has risen against her,	9	[ ][e] עלה עליה גוי מצפון
	Who will make her land a desolation;	9	הוא ישית [ ] ארצה לשמ⟨מ⟩ה[f]
	So that none shall dwell there,	7	ולא יהיה יושב בה
	Neither man nor beast.	7	מאדם [ ]עד בהמה [ ][g]

Verse	Translation	Hebrew	Syllables
4	In those days, (and) at that time,	בימים []המה []בעת []היא [][q]	8
	The people of Israel shall come,	יבאו בני ישראל	8
	Together with the people of Judah.	[][h] ובני יהודה יחדו	8
	They shall walk along weeping,	הלוך ובכו ילכו	8
	Seeking (Yahweh) their God.	[][i] אלהיהם יבקשו	8

5 [They shall ask the way to Zion. Thence they shall set their faces saying: "Come, let us join ourselves to Yahweh, for the everlasting covenant
shall not be forgotten."]

Verse	Translation	Hebrew	Syllables
6	Lost sheep are my people,	צאן אבדות הָי(וּ)[j] עמי	8
	Their shepherds led them astray on the mountains;	רעיהם התעום ⟨על⟩[k] הרים	8
	They turned aside from mountain to hill,	שובבו[][l] מהר אל גבעה	8
	They wandered, they forgot their fold.	הלכו שכחו רבצם	8
7	All who found them have devoured them;	כל מוצאיהם אכלום	8
	Their enemies said: "We are guiltless.	[]צריהם אמרו לא נאשם	8
	It is because they have sinned against Yahweh,	תחת אשר חטאו ליהוה	9
	Their true habitation, the hope of their fathers."	נוה צדק []מקוה אבותיהם	9
8	Ho! Flee from the midst of Babylon and from the land of the Chaldeans!	(הוי)[m] נדו מתוך בבל ומארץ כשדים	12
	Go forth! Be like he-goats before the flock!	[]צאו[n] היו כעתודים לפני צאן	12

9 [For look! I am rousing (an enemy) against Babylon, a horde of mighty
nations from the northern land.]

Verse	Translation	Hebrew	Syllables
	They will take positions against her;	וערכו לה	5
	By them she will be taken.	משם תלכד	5
	Their arrows are like a trained soldier;	חציו כגבור משׂכיל[o]	7
	They will not return empty-handed.	לא ישוב⟨ו⟩[p] ריקם	6
10	So Chaldea shall be for spoil;	והיתה כשדים לשלל	9
	Her spoilers shall have their fill.	כל שלליה ישבעו [][q]	9
11	{Rejoice / Have your triumph} you plunderers of my heritage!	[][r] {תשמח(ו) / תעלז(ו)}[s] שסי נחלתי	8
	Prance about, like a calf in the grass,	[][r] תפוש(ו) כעגל⟨י ב⟩דש(א)[t]	8
	And neigh like stallions!	ותצהל(ו) כאברים	8
12	Deeply shamed your mother will be,	בושה אמכם מאד	7
	Disgraced she who bore you --	חפרה יולדתכם	7
	The lowest of the nations, a desert;	[][u] אחרית גוים [][v] ערבה	7
13	Through the wrath of Yahweh (she will be) uninhabited.	מקצף יהוה לא תשב	7

	She shall become an empty solitude;	והיתה שממה כלה	9
	All who pass by Babylon will be appalled,	כל עבר על בבל ישם	8
	And whistle in awe at such calamity.	וישרק על כל מכותיה	9
14	Set yourselves in array against Babylon round about!	עדכו על בבל סביב	7
	All you who bend the bow, shoot (at her)!	כל דרכי קשת י(ר)ו [][w]	7
	Do not spare the arrows!	אל תחמלו אל חץ [][x]	6
15	Raise a battle-cry against her!	הריעו עליה	6
	She surrenders!	סביב נתנה ידה	7
	Her bastions (?) are fallen!	נפלו אש(יו)תיה[y]	7
	Her walls are battered down!	נהרסו חומותיה	7
	(For) this is Yahweh's vindication --	[כי] נקמת יהוה היא	6/5
	Take vengeance upon her!	הנקמו בה	5
	As she has done, so do to her!	כ⟨י⟩[z] עשתה עשו לה	7
16	Deprive Babylon of the man who sows,	⟨ה⟩כרתו[ż] זורע מבבל	8
	Of the man who wields the sickle in harvest.	[]תפש מגל בעת קציר	8
	Because of the sword of the oppressor,	מפני חרב [] יונה	6
	Each one returns to his own people;	איש אל עמו יפנו	6
	Each one flees to his own land.	[]איש לארצו ינסו	7
17	A scattered flock is Israel;	שה פזורה ישראל	7
	Lions have chased him.	אריות הדיחו⟨הו⟩[â]	7
	First the king of Assyria devoured him;	[]ראשון אכלו מלך אשור	8
	Now lately the king of Babylon has gnawed his bones.	[]זה []אחרון עצמו [][b̄] מלך בבל	9

18 [Therefore, thus saith Yahweh: "Look! I will punish the king of Babylon
and his land as I punished the king of Assyria."]

19	I will bring Israel back to his habitation;	[]שבבתי [] ישראל אל נוהו	10
	He shall pasture on Carmel and Mount Ephraim.	[]רעה ⟨ב⟩כרמל [][c̄] ובהר אפרים	10
	In Gilead his appetite shall be satisfied,	[] ⟨ב⟩גלעד[d̄] תשבע נפשו	7
20	In those days, (and) in that time.	בימים []הם []בעת []היא [][q]	7

[Iniquity shall be sought in Israel, and there shall be none; and sin in Judah, and none shall be found; for I will pardon the remnant I spare.]

21	Against the land of Merethaim, march!	על []ארץ מרתים עלה [][ê]	7
	Against the inhabitants of Pekod, attack!	[]אל יושבי פקוד חרב[f̄]	8
	Devote to destruction, utterance of Yahweh!	והחרם [][ḡ] נאם יהוה	7
	Do just as I have commanded you!	[]עשה ככל [] צויתיך	8

22	The din of battle, a mighty crash	קול מלחמה [][h] ושבר גדול	12
	in the land of Chaldea!	⟨בארץ כשדים⟩[h]	
23	How broken it is and shattered --	איך נגדע וישבר	11
	the hammer of the whole earth!	פטיש כל []ארץ	
	How Babylon has become a horror	איך היתה לשמה	12
	among the nations!	בבל בגוים	
24	You set a snare for yourself and were trapped,	יָקֹשְׁתִּי[i] לך וגם נלכדת	8
	O Babylon, ere you knew it.	בבל ואת לא ידעת	7
	You were caught and held fast,	נמצאת וגם נתפשת	6
	For you dared to challenge Yahweh.	כי ביהוה התגרית	7
25	Yahweh has opened his armory;	פתח יהוה [] ארצרו	7
	He is bringing forth his weapons of wrath.	ויוצא [] כלי זעמו	7
	For Yahweh has a task (to do);	כי מלאכה [][j] לן] יהוה [][k]	7
	God is in the land of Chaldea.	⟨אלהים⟩[k] בארץ כשדים	7
26	Come upon her from every side!	באו לה מקצ⟨ה⟩[l]	6
	Break open her granaries!	פתחו מאבסיה	6
	Pile her up as a swath of grain!	סלוה כמ[]ע(מר)ים[m]	8
	Devote her to destruction!	[]החרימוה	4
	Leave her no remnant!	אל תהי לה שארית	7
27	Let all her fruit be laid waste!	חָרְבוּ כל פְּרְיָהּ[n]	5
	They go down to the slaughter,	ירדו לטבח	5
	Alas for them!	הוי עליהם	4
	For their day has come,	כי בא יומם	4
	The time of their doom.	עת פקדתם	5
28	[Hark! Fugitives and refugees come from the land of Babylon to announce in Zion the vindication of Yahweh our God.][o]		
29	Summon a host against Babylon,	השמיעו אל בבל רב[][p]	7
	From all those who draw the bow!	מכל דרכי קשת	6
	Encamp against her on every side!	חנו עליה סביב	7
	Let no one escape!	אל יהי ⟨לה⟩[q] פלטה	7
	Repay her as her deeds deserve!	שלמו לה כפעלה	7
	As she has done, do so to her!	כן]עשתה[r] עשו לה	7
	For it is against Yahweh she has rebelled,	כי אל יהוה זדה	6
	Against the Holy One of Israel.	אל קדוש ישראל	6
30	And so, her young men shall fall	לכן יפלו בחוריה	13
	in (her) squares;	ברחבת[][s]	
	All her men of war shall perish,	[]כל אנשי מלחמתה ידמו	13
	utterance of Yahweh.	[][t] נאם יהוה	

31	Look! I am against you, O Arrogant One;	הנני אליך זדון [][ú]	8
	The day has come, the time when I will doom you.	כי בא יום[][v́] עת פְּקַדְתִּיךָ[ẃ]	8
32	The arrogant One has stumbled and fallen,	[]כשל זדון []נפל	6
	And no one will lift him up.	ואין לו מקים	5
	I have kindled a fire in his forest,	והצתי אש ב⟨י⟩ער[]ו[x́]	8
	That will rage through all his environs.	ואכלה כל סביב[]יו[ý]	8
33	Thus saith Yahweh:	כה אמר יהוה [][ź]	-
	Oppressed are the people of Israel,	עשוקים בני ישראל	8
	And the people of Judah as well.	ובני יהודה יחדו	8
	Their captors hold them fast;	[][ä] שביהם החזיקו בם	7
	(For) they have refused to let them go.	⟨כי⟩[b̈] מאנו שלחם	7
34	But their Redeemer is strong,	⟨ו⟩גאלם[c̈] חזק	6
	Yahweh of Hosts is his name.	יהוה צבאות שמו	7
	Their Champion will surely defend their cause,	ריב יריב [] ריבם[d̈]	5+5
	and so give rest to the land;	למען הרגיע []ארץ	
	He will discomfit the inhabitants of Babylon.	והרגיז לישבי בבל	9
35	A sword against the Chaldeans,	חרב על כשדים [][ë]	4+6
	against the inhabitants of Babylon;	[]אל ישבי בבל	
	Against her officers and her wise men.	[]אל שריה ואל חכמיה	10
36	A sword against her diviners -- they shall become fools;	חרב אל []בדי⟨ה⟩[f̈] ונאלו	9
	A sword against her warriors -- they shall panic.	חרב אל גבוריה וחתו	9
37	A sword against the rabble in her midst,	חרב [][g̈] אל [][ḧ] ערב [] בתוכה	6
	They shall be as women.	והיה לנשים	6
	A sword against her treasures -- they shall be plundered.	חרב אל ארצרת[][ï] ובזזו	9
38	A sword against her waters -- they shall be dried up.	חרב אל מימיה ויבשו	9
	For it is a land of idols --	כי ארץ פסלים היא	6
	In terror they shall reel (as drunken men).	[]באימים יתהללו	7
39	And so demons and fiends shall live there,	לכן ישבו ציים [] איים	9
	And ostriches shall inhabit her.	וישבו בה בנות יענה	9
	She shall never be peopled again;	[]לא תשב עוד לנצח	7
	She shall remain uninhabited age after age.	[]לא תשכון עד דור ודור	7
40	As God overthrew Sodom,	כמהפכת אלהים [] סדם	9
	And Gomorrah and their neighboring towns;	ו[]עמרה ו[]שכניה [][j̈]	9
	No more shall any man live there,	לא ישב שָׁמָּ איש	6
	Nor human being settle there.	[]לא יגור בה בן אדם	7

41	Look! A people comes from the north,	הנה עם בא מצפון	7
	A mighty nation (and) many kings;	[]גוי גדול []מלכים רבים	8
	They are astir from the farthest reaches of the earth.	יעדו מירכתי ארץ	8
42	They are armed with bow and blade;	קשת וכידן יחזיקו	7
	Cruel are they, without pity.	אכזרי [][k] []לא ירחמו	8
	Their sound is like the thunder of the sea (as) they come riding upon horses;	קולם כים יהמה ועל סוסים ירכבו	13
	Drawn up in battle array, as men (prepared) for war against you, Daughter Babylon!	ערוך כאיש למלחמה עליך בת בבל	13
43	The king of Babylon has heard the news, his hands hang limp;	שמע מלך בבל [] שמעם []רפו ידיו	11
	Anguish has gripped him, pangs as (a woman) in childbirth.	צרה החזיקתהו חיל כיולדה	11
44	Look! Like a lion which goes up,	הנה כאריה יעלה	7
	From the Jordan to perennial pasture;	מ[]ירדן[l] אל נוה איתן	8
	Yea, I will chase them from her,	כי [][m] אריצם מעליה	8
	Of her choicest rams I will select what I choose.	(ומבחר) א⟨י⟩ליה[n] אפקד	8
	For who is there like me?	כי מי כמוני	5
	Who can hale me into court?	[]מי יועדני	5
	What shepherd is there that can stand before me?	ומי זה רעה [] יעמד לפני	10
45	And so, hear the plan which Yahweh has planned against Babylon,	לכן שמעו עצת יהוה [] יעץ אל בבל	13
	The schemes which he has schemed against (the inhabitants of) Chaldea.	ומחשבתיו [] חשב אל ⟨ישבי⟩[o] כשדים	13
	Surely the little ones of their flock shall be dragged away;	אם לא יסחבו-ם צעירי []צאן	10
	Surely the nurslings of (their) pasture shall be desolated.	אם לא יַשֹּׁם⟨ו⟩ עֲלֵיהֶם נוה[p]	10
46	At the shout: "Babylon is taken!"	מקול נתפשה בבל	7
	The earth is rocked;	נרעשה []ארץ	4
	The cry is heard among the nations!	[]זְעָקָה[q] בגוים נשמע	7

Notes to the Text of Jeremiah 50:1-46

[a]Deleting אל ארץ כשדים ביד ירמיהו הנביא with LXX.

[b]Deleting והשמיעו *metri causa*. Cf. LXX ἀκουστα ποιησατε which may reflect an haplography in the Hebrew text behind LXX: בגוים [שאו נס] השמיעו. MT represents a conflation of the two subsequent textual traditions.

[c]Adding the *waw* with LXX και μη κρυφητε; lost by haplography.

[d]Deleting הבישו עצביה חתו גלוליה with LXX as an expansionary gloss.

[e]Deleting כי as a dittography; cf. LXX τρυφερα. ὁτι which probably renders מרד כי, a corruption of מרדך.

[f]Reading the alternate form of this substantive to improve the meter; cf. vs. 13 below.

[g]Deleting נדו הלכו with LXX.

[h]Deleting המה *metri causa*.

[i]Deleting ואת יהוה *metri causa*.

[j]Following the *Qere*; cf. Jer. 5:31 where עמי takes a plural verb.

[k]Emending with LXX ἐπι τα ὄρα.

[l]Deleting the *mem* as dittography and reading the third person plural form of the verb in parallel with הלכו in the next colon.

[m]A conjectural emendation to make sense of the word יהוה at the end of the previous vs. in MT. Cf. Zech 2:10 הוי הוי ונסו מארץ צפון.

[n]Following the *Qere*.

[o]Reading the root *śkl* with some Heb. MSS, LXX, Syr. and Symmachus.

[p]Reading the plural form of the verb to improve the meter, taking the subject as "their arrows" rather than "a trained soldier."

[q]Deleting נאם יהוה with LXX.

[r]Deleting כי as secondary expansion. Note that LXX omits the second כי in the first colon of vs. 11.

[s]Taking these two terms as variants.

[t]Emending with LXX ὡς βοΐδια ἐν βοτανη.

[u]Deleting הנה with LXX.

[v]Cf. LXX which reads only ἔρημος for the three synonyms of MT.

[w]Reading ידו of MT as ירו with LXX and some Heb. MSS and deleting אליה *metri causa*.

[x]Deleting כי ליהוה חטאה with LXX.

[y]Following the *Qere*; a *hapax legomenon* of uncertain meaning.

[z]The particle אשר is not at home in poetry of this period.

[ż]Cf. LXX ἐξολεθρευσατε; the *he* was lost by haplography.

[á]Emending with LXX ἐξωσαν αὐτον; lost by haplography.

[b́]Deleting נבוכדראצר with LXX.

[ć]Emending with LXX ἐν τῳ Καρμηλῳ; the *beth* was probably lost by haplography. The term והבשן is deleted with LXX.

[d́]Emending with LXX ἐν τῳ Γαλααδ.

[é]Deleting עליה *metri causa*; possibly a dittography from עלה.

[f́]On the root *ḥrb* as a denominative of *ḥereb*, i.e. "put to the sword," cf. vs. 27 below, as it appears in MT.

[ǵ]Deleting אחריהם with LXX.

[h́]Emending with LXX φωνη πολεμου και συντριβη μεγαλη ἐν γῃ Χαλδαιων.

[í]Taking the term as an archaic 2nd fem. verbal form; cf. Jer. 2:20.

[j]Deleting היא with LXX.

[k]Deleting צבאות . . . אדני as secondary; cf. LXX τῳ κυριῳ θεῳ.

[l]Cf. Jer. 51:31 and LXX οἱ καιροι αὐτης, "her times."

[m]A conjectural emendation for the difficult כמו-ערמים of MT; cf. Aquila ὥσπερ σωρευοντες which may render the text as reconstructed.

[n]Pointing with LXX τους καρπους αὐτης and Aquila καρπον αὐτης. According to the prosodic analysis presented here this colon must be taken with vs. 26 rather than the remainder of vs. 27. Consequently the usual interpretation of MT, "Putting all her bulls to the sword," must be rejected. The imagery is that of grain being laid waste. For a similar use of the root *ḥrb* see Jer. 2:12.

[o]Deleting the reference to the temple (נקמת היכלו) with LXX.

[p]Redividing this word to improve the metrical balance.

[q]Following the *Qere* and the ancient versions.

[r]Deleting כל אשר as secondary.

[s]Deleting the suffix in an attempt to restore the metrical balance.

[t]Deleting ביום ההוא with LXX.

[u]Deleting נאם אדני יהוה צבאות as secondary; cf. LXX λεγει κυριος.

[v]Deleting the suffix in an attempt to restore the metrical balance; cf. vs. 27 above for the apparent source of this textual expansion.

[w]This bicolon may also be read with LXX as follows:

Look! I am against you,	12 הנני אליך זדון נאם יהוה
O Arrogant One, utterance of Yahweh;	
For your day has come, the time of your doom.	11 כי בא יומך עת פקדתיך

[x]Emending with LXX ἐν τῳ δρυμῳ αὐτης; cf. Jer. 21:14.

[y]Emending with Jer. 21:14 and some Heb. MSS.

[z]Deleting צבאות with LXX.

[ä]Deleting וכל *metri causa*.

[b̈]Emending with LXX ὅτι οὐκ ἠθελησαν.

[c̈]Emending with LXX και ὁ λυτρουμενος.

[d̈]On ריב, "Champion," as an epithet for Yahweh cf. Isa. 34:8 and the discussion above on p. 217, n. e.

[ë]Deleting נאם יהוה with LXX.

[f̈]This colon is missing in LXX. Emend the suffix with Theodotion, Vulg., Syr. and other witnesses.

[g̈]Delete אל סוסיו ואל רכבו ו as a secondary expansion, perhaps from Jer. 51:21. Elsewhere in the present context the pronominal suffixes are feminine.

[ḧ]Deleting כל with LXX.

[ï]Deleting the pronominal suffix *metri causa*.

[j̈]Deleting נאם יהוה *metri causa*.

[k̈]Deleting המה *metri causa*.

[l]Deleting גאון with LXX.

[m]Deleting ארגעה *metri causa*. LXX ὅτι ταχεως ἐκδιωξω αὐτους apparently reflects the presence of this term, perhaps reflecting an original reading of ברגע, "in a moment," or the like. On the meaning of the root *rg'* see p. 228, n. p above.

[n]A conjectural emendation suggested in the apparatus of *BHS*, which makes good sense of a difficult verse. See p. 228, n. r above.

[o]Emending with LXX and some Heb. MSS.

[p]For details on the reconstruction and interpretation of this verse cf. p. 228, nn. s, t, and u above and the literature cited there.

[q]Emending with the Syriac; cf. Jer. 49:21.

<u>Jeremiah 50:1-46 in Outline</u>

An Eschatological Oracle of War, Judgment and Salvation

A. Announcement of Judgment and Salvation (vss. 2-5)

[b:b:b::1:1] Summons to proclaim the news: Babylon is taken!
[1:1::1:1] A nation from the north will destroy her.
[1:1:1::1:1] Israel and Judah will return repentant.
[prose] They will ask the way to Zion in order to renew their covenant with Yahweh.

B. Lament over Israel and Summons to Return (vss. 6-10)

1. The Plight of Israel (vss. 6-7)

[1:1::1:1] My people are lost sheep who were led astray.
[1:1::1:1] Their enemies devoured them because they have forsaken Yahweh.

2. Summons to Return (vss. 8-10)

[1b:b1] Flee from Babylon!
[prose] I am bringing a horde of nations against her.
[b:b::b:b] They will defeat Babylon in battle.
[1:1] Chaldea will be despoiled.

C. War Oracle against Babylon and Promise of Restoration to Israel (vss. 11-32)

1. Announcement of Judgment against Babylon (vss. 11-13)

[1:1:1] Enjoy yourself while you can, Babylon!
[1:1::1:1] Your glory will be turned into shame.
[1:1:1] Those who pass by will be shocked at the sight of Babylon's calamity.

2. Summons to Battle and Vision of Babylon's Defeat (vss. 14-16)

[b:b::b:b] Set yourself in array and raise the battle shout!
[b:b:b] Her walls are battered down!
[b:b::1:1:1] Take vengeance upon Babylon!
[b:b:b] Her captives flee.

3. Lament/Salvation Oracle: Plight and Hope of Captive Israel (vss. 17-20)

[1:1::1:1] Israel has been ravaged by Assyria and Babylon.

[prose] I will punish Babylon's king as I did Assyria's king.

[1:1::1:1] I will return Israel to her home in that day.

[prose] I will pardon the remnant I spare.

4. Summons to Battle and Vision of Babylon's Defeat (vss. 21-27a)

[1:1::1:1] March against "Merethaim/Pekod"! Exterminate them!

[bl:lb:lb] Babylon is shattered, a horror among the nations.

[1:1::1:1] You trapped yourself, Babylon, by opposing Yahweh.

[1:1::1:1] Yahweh has loosed the arsenal of his wrath against Babylon.

[b:b::1:b::1:b] "Devote" Babylon to total destruction!

5. Judgment/Lament over Babylon (vss. 27b-28)

[b:b::b:b] Alas for Babylon, her doom has come!

[prose] Fugitives announce in Zion Yahweh's vindication.

6. Summons to Battle (vss. 29-30)

[b:b::b:b] Encamp against her on every side, let no one escape!

[b:b::b:b] Repay her for defying the Holy One of Israel!

[1:1] Babylon's warriors shall perish!

7. Announcement of Babylon's Defeat (vss. 31-32)

[1:1] I, Yahweh, am against you to destroy you.

[b:b::1:1] The "Arrogant One" will be consumed by the fire of my wrath.

D. Announcement of Salvation and Judgment (vss. 33-40)

1. Assurance of Deliverance to Israel (vss. 33-34)

[1:1::1:1] The people of Israel and Judah are held captive.

[b:b::b:b:1] Their Redeemer is Yahweh who will vindicate their cause.

2. Song of Yahweh's Sword -- The Sword is Extended: (vss. 35-38)

[1:1::1:1] Against Babylon's military might.

[b:b] Against the rabble within her.

[1:1] Against her wealth and her "waters."

[b:b] Babylon's people shall real in terror (as drunken men).

3. Oracle of Doom (vss. 39-40)

[2(1:1::1:1)] Babylon shall become an uninhabited ruin forever.

E. An Eclectic Oracle of Doom against Babylon (vss. 41-46)

1. The Enemy from the North (vss. 41-43; cf. Jer. 6:22-24)

[1:1:1::1:1] A ruthless nation is stirring in the North.

[bl:lb] They come in battle array against you, Babylon!

[lb:lb] The king of Babylon recoils in terror at the news.

2. The Lion of the Jordan (vss. 44-45; cf. Jer. 49:19-20)

[1:1::1:1] I will go up like a lion to ravage Babylon.

[b:b:1] Who can stand before me?

[1:1::1:1] Yahweh intends to desolate their sheepfold.

3. Summation (vs. 46; cf. Jer. 49:21)

[1:b:1] The sound of Babylon's fall resounds among the nations.

The prosodic-textual analysis of Jer. 50 reveals a single literary unit made up of five major divisions: vss. 2-5, 6-10, 11-32, 33-40 and 41-46. The chapter illustrates several important factors in the transformation of the war oracle within Old Testament prophecy which apparently took place during the first half of the 6th century B.C. The first strophe (vss. 2-5), which is introductory in nature, is a three-part announcement of judgment and salvation, followed by a prose comment. The staccato-like affect of the opening verse of this metrical unit is reminiscent of prosodic patterns observed in earlier war poetry. The herald is summoned to announce the defeat of Babylon (vs. 2) at the hands of a nation from the north which has risen against her (vs. 3). Vs. 4 introduces a new element to the developing OAN tradition which is expanded further in the prose comment in vs. 5. The focus of the announcement is no longer the judgment which the enemy nation faces, but the assurance of salvation to Israel. In earlier OAN material the deliverance of Israel is nowhere so explicitly linked to the judgment of one of Israel's national foes. Where earlier this particular element of the war oracle was an announcement of judgment, here we have an announcement of judgment and salvation which sets the stage for what is to follow.

The second major poetic unit (vss. 6-10) is made up of two strophes, a lament over Israel's plight in exile and a summons to return to Jerusalem. Picking up the pastoral language, so dominant elsewhere in Jeremiah's OAN tradition, Israel is likened to sheep whose leaders (רעים, "shepherds") led them astray such that they have been devoured by their enemies (vss. 6-7). The second strophe (vss. 8-10) introduces a new form of prophetic speech to the developing OAN tradition. The earlier summons to flight, addressed to the people who faced destruction at the hands of the Divine Warrior in the ensuing battle, has here become a summons to return to Jerusalem, addressed to the exiled Israelites.

In Jeremiah's earlier OAN tradition (chs. 46-49) the summons to flight was not always to be taken literally, as was perhaps the case in the war oracles of Israel's ancient Covenant League. We need not assume that the enemy people were actually given the prophet's advice to vacate their homeland.[108]

---

[108]See the discussion of Isaac Rabinowitz, "Towards a Valid Theory of Biblical Literature," in *The Classical Tradition: Literary and Historical Studies in Honor of Harry Caplan*, ed. Luitpold Wallach (Ithaca: Cornell University Press, 1966), pp. 315-28.

At times the setting in chs. 46-49 with respect to the summons to flight as a form of prophetic speech is almost sarcastic, bordering on the mocking lament as a form of battle curse hurled at the enemy. It must be remembered that these oracles were delivered in Judah, and that the prophet's primary concern was apparently that of shaping foreign policy within his own nation relative to the foreign nation in question.

In 50:8-10 the summons to flight of earlier prophecy has been given new meaning. The prophet's concern is no longer the immediate political-military situation and the shaping of foreign policy per se. His concern is with the "lost sheep of Israel." Like Moses of old, he is seeking to encourage and strengthen the enslaved children of Israel in order to bring them out of bondage and back to Jerusalem, at the appointed time. The great redemptive event which the prophet envisions is not necessarily so imminent as many scholars have assumed, and ought not to be used as the primary category in dating this poetic material. The prophet's concern here is to make the exiled people of Israel remember their heritage in Palestine, to make them "think Jerusalem" so as to sustain them in the long interval before the arrival of that great day when the Divine Warrior will once again act to redeem his chosen people and to restore them to their land of promise. The prophet is concerned with real history, but his summons to return is eschatological in nature. It anticipates an event which the prophet believes will certainly take place, but at some unspecified time in the future.

The major section of this chapter (50:11-32) is a war oracle proper which again has undergone an important transformation from what we have observed within the OAN tradition up to this point. The war oracle is not simply an oracle of doom or judgment leveled at a national foe of Israel. Though in literary form this material is clearly a war oracle uttered against Babylon, with its summonses to battle and announcements of military defeat, it is also a promise of restoration to exiled Israel (cf. especially vss. 19-20). The war oracle is made of seven strophic units, every other one of which is a summons to battle, with the first and last strophes forming a poetic inclusion.

The war oracle opens with an announcement of judgment against Babylon who is urged to enjoy herself while she can, for the day is coming when the "great reversal"[109] will take place -- Babylon, the devastator, will herself be devastated (vss. 11-13)!

The three summonses to battle (vss. 14-16, 21-27a and 29-30) also show evidence of certain transformations in literary form. They are no longer

---

[109]To borrow a phrase from Martin Kessler in a paper read at the annual meeting of the Society of Biblical Literature in Toronto in November 1969, "Oracles Against the Nations: Jeremiah 50 and 51."

simply individual summonses to battle; they now have other elements incorporated into them. In each case the literary form includes a prophetic vision of Babylon's defeat incorporated into it, or an announcement of Babylon's defeat in battle closely attached. The second summons (vss. 21-27a) also includes a summons to devote Babylon to the sacred ban of Israel's most ancient holy war traditions (vss. 26-27a):

> Come upon her from every side!
> Break open her granaries!
> Pile her up as a swath of grain!
> Devote her to destruction (החרימוה)!
> Leave her no remnant!
> Let all her fruit be laid waste!

Other familiar themes occur within these three summonses to battle. It is Yahweh's sword that will exterminate the Babylonians (vs. 21). The fire of his wrath will consume them (vss. 25,32).

Interspersed between the summonses to battle are two brief laments which are integrally connected with the more explicit military forms of prophetic speech. The first lament (vss. 17-20) is tied to the previous summons to battle through the description of Babylon's various captives fleeing to their homes upon the defeat of Babylon (vs. 16). It presents the plight of Israel, one of these captive nations, who was ravaged first by Assyria and now by Babylon (vs. 17). Yahweh has a *rîb* against Babylon and will not only punish their king; he will also return a forgiven remnant of his own people to Zion (vss. 18-20). The second lament (vss. 27b-28) presents the plight of Babylon and in effect is an announcement of judgment. In the day of their doom the Babylonians will go down to the slaughter (vs. 27), while the Israelite fugitives announce in Zion Yahweh's vindication (vs. 28).

The fourth major section of this oracle against Babylon (vss. 33-40) is an announcement of salvation and judgment which expands some of the themes already introduced. Israel is oppressed and her captors refuse to release her (vs. 33); but Yahweh, her Redeemer, is a mighty warrior who will vindicate their cause (vs. 34). Vss. 35-38 present a "Song of Yahweh's Sword," for indeed the sword of Yahweh's wrath is extended against Babylon. The Divine Warrior will wage his holy war against Babylon whose people shall reel in terror as drunken men (vs. 38). Babylon, like all the other nations will have tasted Yahweh's wrath, will become an uninhabited ruin forever (vss. 39-40).

The concluding section of this oracle against Babylon (vss. 41-46) has been called an eclectic oracle of doom since almost all of this material appears elsewhere in the book of Jeremiah. Vss. 41-43 are clearly an adaptation of an earlier prophecy against Judah (cf. Jer. 6:22-24), while vss. 44-46 appear also in the additions to the oracles against Edom in 49:19-21.

The opening strophe of this concluding oracle of doom is an adaptation of what is perhaps the classic presentation of Jeremiah's unnamed "foe from the north," a motif which was introduced in vs. 3 at the very beginning of this oracle against Babylon. The concluding /1:b:1/ unit in vs. 46 forms a remarkable poetic inclusion with the opening metrical unit in vs. 2. The news is proclaimed: "Babylon is taken!" The announcement of doom resounds among the nations. The whole earth is rocked by the news of the defeat of mighty Babylon. The oracle of doom for Babylon and ultimate salvation for Israel, preserved here in Jer. 50, no doubt exerted a powerful influence within the struggling Jewish community during the Exilic period.[110]

Scholars have made much of the fact that the sentiment against Babylon, as developed in Jer. 50-51, is contrary to the pro-Babylonian policy reflected elsewhere in Jeremiah's preaching. This conclusion is based, for the most part, on a faulty interpretation of the nature and purpose of the OAN tradition here in question. Jeremiah's advice to "serve the king of Babylon and live" (Jer. 27:17) and his much discussed letter to the exiles to prepare for a lengthy stay in Babylon are not in opposition to the sentiment against Babylon as portrayed in Jer. 50-51.

It is the failure to appreciate the major transformation of the entire prophetic tradition in the years following the first deportation under Nebuchadnezzar in 597, that has produced the widely divergent interpretations of Jer. 50-51. As Malamat has shown, the exile of King Jehoiachin to Babylon in 597 was a major turning point in the prophetic ministry of Jeremiah.[111] Jeremiah rejected the interpretation of those who continued to look to the exiled king as the legitimate "Davidic" king of Judah and who preached a speedy return and restoration of their king in Jerusalem. To Jeremiah the concept of the Davidic king as Yahweh's anointed, the Messiah, took on much deeper meaning. Jeremiah knew that the kingdom of Judah, as restored by Josiah, had died with the conquest of Nebuchadnezzar. Hence, as early as 597, he advised the people in exile to:

> Build houses and live in them; plant gardens and eat their produce. Take wives and have sons and daughters; take wives for your sons, and give your daughters in marriage, that they may bear sons and daughters; multiply there and do not decrease. But seek the welfare of the city where I (Yahweh) have sent you into exile, and pray to Yahweh on its behalf . ... (Jer. 29:5-7)

At the same time Jeremiah also firmly believed that Yahweh was not through

---

[110]Cf. also the related literary tradition in Isaiah 13-14, 21.

[111]Abraham Malamat, "Jeremiah and the Last Two Kings of Judah," *PEQ* 83 (1951), pp. 81-87.

with his people:

> For thus says Yahweh: "When seventy years are completed for Babylon, I will visit you, and I will fulfil to you my promise and bring you back to this place. . . . I will restore your fortunes and gather you from all the nations and all the places where I have driven you, says Yahweh, and I will bring you back to the place from which I sent you into exile." (Jer. 29:10-14)

If indeed Yahweh's mighty redemptive act was to be projected into the distant future, beyond the life-span of virtually all his hearers; then, Jeremiah also knew how absolutely essential it was to preserve the heritage and hope of Israel throughout this interim period. The assurance that the Divine Warrior would one day humble even mighty Babylon is a theme that is altogether consonant with what we know of the prophet "to the nations," particularly in the years of his maturity after 597.

In several respects the OAN tradition preserved in Jer. 50 is close to the thought world of Second Isaiah, and probably stems from the literary circle of that great prophetic figure of the Exilic period. Nonetheless, it is also clear that this remarkable eschatological poem against Babylon is thoroughly Jeremianic in language, as virtually all commentators have noted. We ought not to dismiss too quickly the possibility of Jeremiah's authorship of oracles against Babylon which helped to shape this and other OAN material of the Exilic period.

2. Jeremiah 51:1-40 (LXX 28:1-40)

1	Thus saith Yahweh:	כה אמר יהוה	
	Look! I am rousing against Babylon,	הנני מעיר על בבל	8
	Against the inhabitants of Chaldea,	[ ]אל ישבי ⟨כשדים⟩[a]	9
	a destroying wind.	רוח משחית	
2	I will send winnowers to Babylon;	ושלחתי לבבל זרים	9
	They will winnow her, they will empty her land.	וזרוה [ ]יבקקו [ ] ארצה	10
	Yahweh is against her from every side;	[ ] (יהוה)[b] עליה מסביב	8
3	In the evil day God will tread down.	ביום רעה אל ידרך	7
	God himself will rise up in full armor;	[ ]אל יתעל בסרינו	7
	He will tread down those who draw the bow.	(ידרך הדרך קשתו)[c]	7
	Do not spare her young men!	[ ]אל תחמלו אל בחוריה	9
	Exterminate her entire army!	⟨ו⟩החרימו[d] כל צבאה	8
4	They shall fall slain in the land of the Chaldeans,	[ ]נפלו חללים בארץ כשדים	10
	Thrust through in the streets;	ומדקרים בחוצותיה	10
5	For Israel and Judah have not been widowed,	כי לא אלמן ישראל ויהודה	11
	Of their God, of Yahweh of Hosts.	מאלהיו מיהוה צבאות	10

Verse	Translation	Hebrew	Syllables
	The land is filled with offense	[] ארץ[][e] מלאה אשם	12
	against the Holy One of Israel;	מקדוש ישראל	
6	Flee from the midst of Babylon!	נסו מתוך בבל	6
	Let each man save his own life!	[]מלטו איש נפשו	6
	Do not be struck down in her punishment,	אל תדמו בעונה	8
	(For) it is Yahweh's time of vindication!	[][f] עת נקמה היא ליהוה	8
	As she deserves, so He is repaying her.	גמול הוא משלם לה	7
7	A golden cup was Babylon in Yahweh's hand,	כוס זהב בבל ביד יהוה	9
	to make all the earth drunk;	משכרת כל []ארץ	5
	From her wine the nations drank,	מיינה שתו גוים	7
	and so they reel (as drunken men).	על כן יתהללו [][g]	6
8	Suddenly she fell, she is broken;	פתאם נפלה [][h] []תשבר	8
	wail over her!	הילילו עליה	6
	Take ointment for her wounds;	קחו צרי למכאובה	8
	perhaps she may be healed.	אולי תרפא	5
9	We treated Babylon but she was not cured.	רפאנו [] בבל ולא נרפתה	10
	Forsake her! Let us go each to his own land;	עזבוה ונלך איש לארצו	10
	For her judgment reaches to the heavens,	כי נגע אל []שמים משפטה	9
	It ascends to the skies.	ונשא עד⟨י⟩[i] שחקים	8
10	Yahweh has brought forth our deliverance,	הוציא יהוה [] צדקתינו	8
	Come! Let us tell in Zion	באו []נְסַפְּרָה בציון []	8
	What Yahweh our God has done!	מעשה יהוה אלהינו	8
11	Sharpen the arrows!	הברו []חצים	5
	Prepare the shields (?)!	מלאו []שלטים[j]	5
	[Yahweh has stirred up the spirit of the king(s) of the Medes, for he is against Babylon; his purpose is to destroy her. For this is the vengeance of Yahweh, the revenge for his temple.]		
12	Against (her) walls signal attack!	אל חומת [][k] שאו נס	6
	Strengthen the watch!	החזיקו []משמר	5
	Post the sentries!	הקימו שמרים	6
	Take up concealed positions!	הכינו []ארבים	6
	[For Yahweh has made a plan; he has done as he promised to the inhabitants of Babylon.]		
13	You who dwell by many waters,	שכנתי על מים רבים	7
	Together with rich treasures,	⟨ועל⟩[l] רבת אוצרת	7
	Your end has come, your life's thread is cut.	בא קצך אמת בצעך	7
14	For Yahweh has sworn by himself:	נשבע יהוה [][m] בנפשו	8
	"Yea, I will fill you with men like locusts;	[][n] אם מלאתיך אדם כילק	8
	They shall shout (their) triumph over you."	וענו עליך הידד	7

15	Yahweh made the earth by his power;	〈יהוה〉[o] עשה ארץ בכחו	8
	He established the world by his wisdom,	מכין תבל בחכמתו	8
	By his skill he stretched out the heavens.	[]בתבונתו נטה שמים	9
16	The waters of the heavens roar with thunder;	(לקולת יֶהֱמַיִן)[p] מים בשמים	10
	He brings up the storm clouds from the ends of the earth.	ויעל〈ה〉[q] נשאים מקצה ארץ	10
	Lightning to cause rain he made;	ברקים למטר עשה	8
	He brings forth the wind from his storehouse.	[]יצא רוח מאצרתיו	8
17	All men are stupid and without knowledge;	נבער כל אדם מדעת	7
	Every goldsmith is shamed by his idol.	הביש כל צרף מפסל	7
	For the figures he casts are a sham,	כי שקר נסכו	8
	there is no breath (of life) in them;	[]לא רוח בם	
18	They are worthless, a work of delusion,	הבל המה מעשה תעתעים	8
	At the time of their doom they will perish.	בעת פקדתם יאבדו	9
19	Not like these is the Portion of Jacob,	לא כאלה חלק יעקוב	7
	For he who forms all things is his inheritance;	כי יוצר []כל הוא [][r] נחלתו	8
	Yahweh of Hosts is his name.	יהוה צבאות שמו	7
20	My mace are you,	מפץ אתה לי	5
	My weapon of war.	כְלִי מלחמה	5
	With you I shatter nations;	ונפצתי בך גוים	8
	With you I strike down kings.	והשחתי בך ממלכות	9
21	With you I shatter horse and rider;	ונפצתי בך סוס ורכבו	11
	With you I shatter chariot and driver.	ונפצתי בך רכב ורכבו	11
22	With you I shatter husband and wife;	ונפצתי בך איש ואשה	10
	With you I shatter old man and youth.	ונפצתי בך זקן ונער [][s]	10
23	With you I shatter shepherd and flock;	ונפצתי בך רעה ועדרו	11
	With you I shatter farmer and team.	ונפצתי בך אכר וצמדו	11
	With you I shatter princes and wisemen;	〈ונפצתי בך שרים וחכמים〉[t]	12
	With you I shatter governors and prefects.	ונפצתי בך פחות וסגנים	12

24 [I will repay Babylon and all the inhabitants of Chaldea for all the evil which they have done in Zion before your very eyes, utterance of Yahweh.]

25	Look! I am against you, O Destroying Mountain,	הנני אליך הר []משחית [][u]	9
	You who destroyed the whole earth;	[]משחית [] כל []ארץ	4
	I will stretch out my hand against you.	ונטיתי [] ידי עליך	9
	I will roll you down from those crags;	וגלגלתיך מן הסלעים	10
	I will make of you a burnt-out mountain.	ונתתיך להר שרפה	10

Verse	Translation	Hebrew	Syllables
26	No more shall they quarry from you a cornerstone,	[]לא יקחו ממך אבן לפנה	11
	Or stone for foundations;	[]אבן למוסדות	5
	For you shall be a waste forever, utterance of Yahweh.	כי שממות עולם תהיה נאם יהוה	11
27	Raise the battle signal among the nations!	שאו נס (בגוים)[v]	6
	Sound the trumpet in the land!	תקעו שופר (בארץ)[v]	6
	Consecrate nations against her!	קדשו עליה גוים	8
	Summon against her the kings	השמיעו עליה ממלכות	9
	Of Ararat, Minni, and Ashkenaz!	אררט מני ואשכנז	9
	Appoint a marshal (?) against her!	פקדו עליה טפסר	7
	Bring up the cavalry like bristly locusts!	העלו סוס כילק סמר	7
28	Consecrate nations against her --	קדשו עליה גוים	8
	The king of the Medes and the land under his dominion,	[] מלך[] מדי [] (ו[]ארץ ממשלתו)[w]	8
	His governors and all his prefects!	[] פחותי⟨ו⟩ ו[]כל סגני⟨ו⟩[x]	8
29	The land trembles and writhes,	ותרעש []ארץ ותחל	7
	For the plan of Yahweh stands --	כי קמה [][y] מחשֶׁבֶת[z] יהוה	7
	To make the land of Babylon a desolation,	לשום [] ארץ בבל לשמה	8
	A place where no one dwells.	⟨ו⟩מאין[a] יושב ⟨שמה⟩[b]	7
30	The warriors of Babylon have ceased fighting,	חדלו גבורי בבל להלחם	12
	They remain in the strongholds;	ישבו במצדות	7
	Their courage has failed, they have become like women.	נשתה גבורתם היו לנשים	12
	Her buildings are set on fire;	הציתו משכנתיה	8
	The bars (of her gates) are broken.	נשברו בריחיה	7
31	Runner after runner comes running,	רץ לקראת רץ ירוץ	7
	Courier after courier,	[]מגיד לקראת מגיד	7
	To tell the king of Babylon	להגיד למלך בבל	7
	That his city is taken.	כי נלכדה עירו	6
32	At the remote fords they are seized,	מקצה[c] []מעברות נתפשו []	9
	The marshes are set on fire,	[]אגמים שרפו באש	8
	The soldiers are gripped with panic.	[]אנשי []מלחמה נבהלו	8
33	For thus saith Yahweh:	כי כה אמר יהוה [][d]	-
	Daughter Babylon is like a threshing floor when it is time to tread it;	בת בבל כגרן עת הַדְּרִיכָהּ	9
	In but a little while the time of her harvest will come.	עוד מעט []באה עת []קציר לה	9

34	He devoured me, he consumed me,	אכלנ(י) הממנ(י)[e]	8
	Did Nebuchadrezzar, king of Babylon;	נבוכדראצר מלך בבל	8
	He set me down an empty dish.	הציגנ(י) כלי ריק	7
	He gulped me down as (would) a monster,	בלענ(י) כתנין	7
	He filled his maw with my tidbits;	מלא כרשו מעדני	8
35	He cleansed away my violence.	הדיחנ(י) חמסי	7
	My flesh be upon Babylon,	[]שארי על בבל	6
	Saith Zion's inhabitress;	תאמר ישבת ציון	6
	My blood be on the land of Chaldea,	[]דמי אל ⟨ארץ⟩[f] כשדים	6
	Saith Jerusalem.	תאמר ירושלם	6
36	And so, thus saith Yahweh:	לכן כה אמר יהוה	-
	Look! I will take up your defense;	הנני רב [] ריבך	6
	I will surely vindicate you.	ונקמתי [] נקמתך	7
	I will dry up her sea;	והחרבתי [] ימה	6
	I will make her springs run dry.	והבשתי [] מקורה	7
37	Babylon shall become a ruin-heap,	והיתה בבל לגלים	9
	A jackal's lair, where no one dwells.	מעון תנים [][g] ⟨ו⟩מאין יושב	9
38	Like lions they roar in chorus;	יחדו ככפרים ישאגו	9
	Like lions' cubs they growl --	נערו כגורי אריות	9
39	While they fret I make ready their banquet.	בחמם אשית [] משתיהם	8
	I will besot them so they become tipsy;	והשכרתים למען יעלזו	9
	Then they'll sleep a perpetual sleep,	וישנו שנת עולם	8
	They shall never wake up, utterance of Yahweh.	[]לא יקיצו נאם יהוה	8
40	I will haul them like lambs to the slaughter,	אורידם ככרים לטבוח	8
	Like so many rams and goats.	⟨ו⟩כאילים[h] עם עתודים	8

Notes to the Text of Jeremiah 51:1-40

[a]Emending with LXX Χαλδαιους for MT לב קמי, an atbash for Chaldea. Cf. vs. 41 where ששך appears as an atbash for Babylon (בבל) and Jer. 25:25-26 where ששך appears again along with זמרי which may be a secondary corruption of זמכי, an atbash for עילם. The use of such a cipher for "Chaldea" suggests an Exilic date for the Palestinian text of Jer. 51 as reflected in MT. Such a subterfuge makes historical sense in the context of the Exile, but scarcely in a later period when the Babylonian empire had vanished.

[b]A conjectural emendation to make better sense of a most difficult passage. The כי of MT is deleted with LXX which reads οὐαι ἐπι Βαβυλωνα. The source of the corruption probably stems from an early misunderstanding of the meaning of the following verse.

[c]Jer. 51:3 is the source of much confusion in all extant witnesses to

the textual transmission. The reconstruction proposed here retains the consonantal text of MT with a relocation of one colon which was suggested by Professor Cross (private communication). On the use of אל as the name of the Divine Warrior cf. Jer. 32:18 and 51:56. The verbal root *drk* has a long history within Israel's ancient war poetry; cf. Num. 24:17 where דרך appears in parallel with קם in a military context where the "stars of Jacob"/"tribes of Israel" prevail over Moab. For a discussion of this verbal root in light of Ugaritic parallels see W. F. Albright, "The Oracles of Balaam," *JBL* 63 (1944), p. 219, n. 82.

[d]The *waw* is added with LXX to improve the metrical balance of this bicolon. It may have been lost by haplography.

[e]The prosodic structure of this metrical unit is problematic. The כי of MT is deleted as secondary along with the pronominal suffix on ארצם which may be a secondary dittography.

[f]Deleting the כי as secondary so as to improve the metrical balance within this tricolon.

[g]Deleting גוים with LXX; perhaps a vertical dittography from the previous colon.

[h]Deleting ו בבל *metri causa*; on the secondary insertion of "Babylon" cf. Jer. 51:2 (LXX); 51:12? and 25:1,9,11 and 12.

[i]Reading the ballast form of the preposition to improve the meter.

[j]The meaning of both words in this colon is uncertain. On the use of the verbal root *ml'* in a military context, see D. W. Thomas, "מלאו in Jeremiah IV.5: A Military Term," *JJS* 3 (1952), pp. 47-52. The noun שלט seems to denote a shield of some sort in II Sam. 7:7 and II Kings 11:10. Y. Yadin has suggested that it is some kind of dart, *The Scroll of the War of the Sons of Light against the Sons of Darkness*, p. 134. LXX, "fill the quivers," appears to be a gloss.

[k]Deleting בבל *metri causa*.

[l]Emending with LXX και ἐπι πληθει. On the use of על in the sense of "together with" cf. Jer. 3:18. Another possible reading would be to insert ועם which would be easier to explain in terms of scribal haplography.

[m]Deleting צבאות with LXX.

[n]Deleting the כי as secondary.

[o]Emending with the Old Latin, Syriac and Jer. 10:12(LXX).

[p]A conjectuaal emendation to make sense of MT לקול תתו המון. The reading "thunder" (קולת) is suggested by the context as the term appears in parallel with "storm clouds," "lightning" and "wind" within this quatrain. On the verbal form in question cf. Isa. 17:12 and Ps. 83:3. The term קולות appears twelve times elsewhere in the Old Testament, each time in the meaning of "thunder": Exod. 9:23,28,29,33,34; 19:16; 20:18; I Sam. 12:17,18; Job 28:26: 38:25 and Ps. 93:4.

[q]The longer verbal form is read to improve the meter.

[r]Deleting ושבט with LXX.

[s]Deleting ונפצתי בך בחור ובתולה as a variant reading for one of the members of this bicolon. LXX reads a bicolon here but omits a different colon. The reconstruction suggested here achieves closer metrical balance.

[t]A conjectural emendation to supply a balancing colon for the reference to "governors and prefects" which stands alone in both MT and LXX. The reconstruction is based on Jer. 51:57(MT).

[u]Deleting נאם יהוה with LXX.

[v]These two terms are interchanged to improve the metrical balance.

[w]MT as it stands is prosaic. The reconstruction here is based on LXX τον βασιλεα των Μηδων και πασης της γης. The ארץ ממשלתו of MT is substituted for πασης της γης of LXX to achieve closer metrical balance.

[x]The masculine pronominal suffixes are restored with LXX ἡγουμενους ἀύτου και παντας στρατηγους αὐτου.

[y]Deleting על בבל *metri causa*.

[z]Reading the sing. form of the noun with LXX, Syr. and some Heb. MSS.

[á]Restoring the *waw* with LXX.

[b́]A conjectural emendation to improve the metrical balance; cf. Jer. 49: 18,33.

[ć]Following LXX this word is taken with vs. 32 rather than with 31 as in MT. The resultant reading improves both meter and sense.

[d́]Deleting צבאות אלהי ישראל with LXX.

[é]The first person pronominal suffix is restored throughout these two tricola with the *Qere*, LXX and other ancient versions.

[f́]A conjectural emendation for ישבי of MT to improve the metrical balance. These two words are formulaic equivalents elsewhere in Jeremiah's OAN material.

[ǵ]Deleting שמה ושרקה with LXX. The further omission of מעון תנים in LXX may be explained as a secondary haplography. The *waw* on the following word is restored with LXX.

[h́]The *waw* is restored here with LXX.

<u>Jeremiah 51:1-58 in Outline</u>

I

A. War Oracle against Babylon and Promise of Restoration to Israel (vss. 1-14)

1. Oracle of Judgment and Summons to Holy War (vss. 1-3)

[1:1::1:1] I am sending winnowers to winnow Babylon.

[1:1::1:1] Yahweh himself will tread down her warriors.

[1:1] "Devote" Babylon to total destruction!

2. Announcement of Judgment (vss. 4-5b)

[1:1::1:1] Babylon's soldiers shall be slain by Israel's "spouse."

3. Summons to Flight/Return (vss. 5c-6)

[1:b:b] Flee from the midst of wicked Babylon!

[1:1:1] Do not be struck down in her punishment!

4. Judgment/Lament over Babylon (vs. 7)

[1b:1b] Babylon was the "Cup in Yahweh's Right Hand" proffered to to the nations in judgment.

5. Summons to Mourn (vs. 8)

[1b:1b] Weep for fallen Babylon, apply ointment to her wounds!

6. Summons to Flight/Return (vss. 9-10)

[1:1::1:1] There is no cure for Babylon! Forsake her!

[1:1:1] Let us proclaim in Zion the work of Yahweh!

7. Summons to Battle (vss. 11-12)

[b:b] Prepare your weapons!

[prose] Yahweh has stirred up the Medes against Babylon to avenge his temple.

[b:b::b:b] Prepare to attack the city of Babylon!

[prose] Yahweh has accomplished his purpose against Babylon.

8. Oracle of Doom against Babylon (vss. 13-14)

[1:1:1] Your end has come!

[1:1:1] Yahweh has sworn that your enemies will shout their triumph over you.

B. A Hymn of Praise and Folly (vss. 15-19)

1. The Greatness of Yahweh (vss. 15-16)

[1:1:1] It is Yahweh who created the universe.

[1:1::1:1] The forces of the heavens are at his command.

2. The Folly of Idolatry (vss. 17-19)

[1:1::1:1:1] The idols of stupid men are nothing but lifeless sham.

[1:1:1] Jacob/Israel belongs to Yahweh.

C. The Song of Yahweh's Hammer (i.e. Babylon) (vss. 20-24)

[b:b] You are my weapon of war.

[5(1:1)] With you I shatter nations.

[prose] But I will take vengeance upon you, O Babylon.

D. War Oracle against Babylon (vss. 25-40)

1. Oracle of Doom against Babylon (vss. 25-26)

[1:b:1] I am against you, O Destroying Mountain.

[1:1] I will make of you a burnt-out mountain.

[1:b:1] You shall become a worthless ruin forever.

2. Summons to Battle (vss. 27-28)

[b:b]	Raise the battle signal among the nations!
[1:1:1]	Consecrate the northern kings for battle!
[1:1]	Assemble for battle!
[1:1:1]?	Consecrate the king of the Medes against Babylon!

3. Vision of Babylon's Defeat in Battle (vss. 29-32)

[1:1::1:1]	Babylon will be destroyed according to Yahweh's plan.
[1:b:1]	Their warriors have become like women.
[1:1]	Her buildings are ablaze, the city-gates broken down.
[1:1::1:1]	Runners carry the news of calamity to their king.
[1:1:1]	The entire land is taken, her soldiers in panic.

4. Judgment/Lament over Babylon (vss. 33-35)

[rubric]	Messenger formula
[1:1]	Babylon is a threshing floor waiting to be trodden upon.
[2(1:1:1)]	Nebuchadnezzar feasted upon my people.
[b:b::b:b]	The guilt remains on the people of Chaldea.

5. Oracle of Doom against Babylon and Deliverance for Israel (vss. 36-40)

[rubric]	Messenger formula
[b:b::b:b]	I will vindicate you, my people.
[1:1]	Babylon shall become an uninhabited ruin.
[1:1:1]	While the Babylonians roar I prepare a banquet.
[1:1:1]	I will make them thoroughly drunk.
[1:1]	I will haul them to their slaughter.

II

A. An Eclectic Judgment/Lament against Babylon (vss. 41-43; cf. 50:23,40b)

[1:1] ?	Babylon has become a horror among the nations.
[1:1]	The forces of chaos have surged over Babylon.
[1:1::1:1	Babylon has become an uninhabited ruin.

B. Prophetic Announcement of Judgment/Salvation (vss. 44b-49a; in MT only)

[b:b::b:b] ?	Summons to flight/return
[prose]	Rumors come and go year after year.
[prose]	The days are coming when I will punish the idols of Babylon.
[1:1::1:1]	Heaven and earth will rejoice over Babylon's fall to the destroyer from the north.

C. Oracle of Judgment and Salvation (vss. 44a, 49b-57)

1. Yahweh's Decree (vs. 44a)

[1:1:1]	I will make Bel disgorge what he has swallowed.

2. Summons to Flight/Return (vss. 49b-51)

[1:b:b]	Babylon has fallen -- flee from her midst!

[1:1] Remember Jerusalem!

[1:1:1] We are shamed for strangers have entered Yahweh's sanctuary.

3. Oracle of Doom against Babylon (vss. 52-53)

[1:1:1] The days are coming when I will punish her idols.

[1:1:1] Mighty Babylon will be despoiled.

4. Announcement of Babylon's Defeat (vss. 54-56)

[2(1:1::1:1)] A mighty crash resounds for Yahweh is destroying Babylon.

[lb:bl] ? Yahweh is defeating her to vindicate himself.

5. Yahweh's Decree (vs. 57)

[1:1] ? I will make her leaders utterly drunk.

D. A Great Summation (vs. 58)

[rubric] Messenger formula

[lb:lb] ? Babylon's great wall shall be razed to the ground.

[1:1] Nations toil for nought (cf. Hab. 2:13).

The prosodic-textual analysis of Jer. 51 reveals a two-part structure somewhat similar to that observed in chs. 48 (Moab) and 49:7-22 (Edom). The first major section (vss. 1-40) displays a more or less unified structure consisting of two war oracles against Babylon (vss. 1-14, 25-40) separated by what we have called "A Hymn of Praise and Folly" (vss. 15-19) and "The Song of Yahweh's Hammer" (vss. 20-24). The second division (vss. 41-58) is made up of miscellaneous additions to the collection which are divided into four sections.

A brief three-part judgment/lament against Babylon (vss. 41-43), most of which appears again in Jer. 50:23 and 40b, is followed by an eschatological oracle of war, judgment and salvation which is interrupted by an announcement of judgment and salvation (vss. 44b-49a), found only in MT where it appears to have been inserted between the first two strophes of the larger oracle of vss. 44-57.[112] This Masoretic plus is prosaic in nature and has been described by Leslie as "eschatological and messianic":[113]

It deals with the convulsions caused by alarming news and with turbulent

---

[112]The relationship between this Masoretic plus and its larger context poses difficult problems which led to the decision to omit the detailed textual reconstruction of Jer. 51:41-58 from the present study. This material is presented in outline form and pertinent sections are presented in greater detail in the body of the general discussion in the following pages.

[113]See Elmer A. Leslie, *Jeremiah, Chronologically Arranged, Translated and Interpreted* (New York and Nashville: Abingdon Press, 1954), p. 310.

> events which will precede the time of the end. The Jews are not to be thrown into anxiety by these convulsions and alarms, but are to view them as the necessary preliminaries to the breaking in of the time of salvation.

The fact that this Masoretic plus appears to be a literary unit in itself which seems to disrupt the prosodic continuity of the larger oracle of war, judgment and salvation in which it is imbedded, suggests that what we have here is not an instance of homoeoteleuton or homoeoarchton, as is so frequently suggested, but a secondary expansion of the text. Secondary expansion is found elsewhere in the Palestinian text of Jeremiah's OAN tradition as reflected in MT: i.e. 46:25-28 (Egypt), 48:45-47 (Moab) and 49:6 (Ammon). It is interesting to note that eschatological elements dominate these other additions as well. At some unspecified time in the future, Egypt will be restored as in earlier times (46:26). Jacob/Israel will be restored after Yahweh has made a full end of all the nations among whom they are scattered (46:27-28); and the fortunes of Moab and Ammon will be restored as well (48:47 and 49:6).

The most important sections of Jer. 51 as far as our purposes are concerned are vss. 1-14 and 25-40, the two war oracles against Babylon which have been subjected to detailed prosodic-textual analysis. Each of these oracles displays important features relative to the transformation of the prophetic war oracle which apparently took place during the opening decades of the 6th century B.C.

The first of these two war oracles consists of eight strophic units, the first of which presents a striking picture, which unfortunately has been distorted by an apparent scribal haplography in vs. 3. In the text, as reconstructed, Yahweh himself is declaring holy war against Babylon. He has stirred up a destroying wind (vs. 1) and is sending winnowers to utilize this wind to "harvest" Babylon (vs. 2). Yahweh himself will tread down Babylon (vs. 3). In that day of disaster (ביום רעה) the Divine Warrior himself will tread upon the warriors of Babylon as one treads upon a threshing floor in time of harvest (cf. Jer. 51:33).[114] This opening announcement of judgment against Babylon is concluded with an explicit summons to holy war against Babylon (vs. 3b) whose entire army is to be "devoted" (החרימו) to destruction.

The second and third strophes (vss. 5-6) are closely related, consisting of an announcement of salvation to Israel followed by a summons to return to Jerusalem. Though the land is filled with offense against the Holy One of Israel, the people "have not been widowed of their God" (vs. 5). The exiled Israelites are summoned to flee from Babylon in the day of Yahweh's wrath lest they be destroyed along with Babylon. As a literary form the summons

---

[114]Cf. also Jer. 50:26-27 where the imagery of Babylon's granaries is used in a summons to holy war against Babylon.

to flight/return in vs. 6 is almost identical to earlier occurrences of this speech form. It is only the larger literary context that reveals the transformation this oracular speech form has undergone, from a form of judgment speech to a message of hope.

The fourth and fifth strophes of this war oracle (vss. 7-8) are of primary interest in this study. The judgment/lament against Babylon in vs. 7 contains one of the three occurrences in Jeremiah of the motif of Yahweh's cup of wrath proffered to the nations in judgment. As Hab. 2:13 is quoted in the "Great Summation" in 51:58, it seems likely that Jeremiah is here referring to Hab. 2:15-16 where the "cup in Yahweh's right hand" is proffered by an unnamed nation "who makes his neighbors drink from the cup of (Yahweh's) fierce wrath . . . in order to look upon their nakedness" (Hab. 2:15). Though the unnamed subject of Habakkuk's series of "woes" may originally have been Assyria, his prophecy was certainly interpreted to apply to Babylon in the present context.[115] Babylon's turn has come and the prophet summons Israel to mourn for her (vs. 8). The summons to mourn is closely tied to another summons to flight/return which constitutes the sixth strophe of this war oracle. Since Babylon is beyond cure, the exiles are summoned to forsake her, in that day, and to proclaim again in Zion the mighty redemptive acts of Yahweh (vss. 9-10).

The summons to battle (vss. 11-12) which makes up the seventh strophe has been expanded by two prose insertions. The underlying speech form is in the familiar staccato-like /b:b/ units. The prose insertions appear to be interpretive in nature and are clearly secondary to the original poetic oracle. Later transmitters of this tradition realized that it was the Medes who were destined to fulfill this prophecy of Babylon's destruction (vs. 11b). Looking back in hind-sight they declared that, indeed, Yahweh "has done as he promised to the inhabitants of Babylon" (vs. 12c).

The war oracle in 51:1-14 concludes with an announcement of doom against Babylon (vss. 13-14). Her enemies will shout their victory triumph over defeated Babylon. The nature of this shout of triumph is expressed in the term הידד which is also used of the shouting in harvest (Isa. 16:10, Jer. 48:33), and of the vintage shout at the time of the treading of grapes (Jer. 25:30). The allusions conveyed in this "shout" of triumph form a poetic inclusion of sorts with the grim harvest scene of the opening strophe in vss. 1-3 of this oracle.

The second war oracle against Babylon (51:25-40) reveals the least evidence for the transformation of the war oracle as such. The oracle is made up of five strophes which, for the most part, preserve intact the speech forms of the older prophetic war oracles. The first strophe (vss. 25-26) is

---

[115]Cf. Jer. 51:7 and the discussion above on pp. 178-79.

an announcement of judgment against Babylon in which the Divine Warrior declares that he has stretched out his hand to destroy the "Destroying Mountain" of Babylon (vs. 25). Expanding the metaphor, Yahweh declares that Babylon shall become a "burnt-out mountain," an empty shell, no longer capable of supplying even quarried stone for the builder (vss. 25c-26).

The summons to battle in vss. 27-28 is of particular interest because it provides a helpful clue for dating this particular oracle. The command to raise a battle signal (שאו נס) and sound the trumpet (תקעו שופר) are familiar clichés from Israel's most ancient traditions of holy war. The nations of Ararat, Minni and Ashkenaz are to be consecrated (קדשו) for holy war against Babylon (vs. 27). In his study of the history of these three peoples, I. M. Diakonov has concluded that this historical reference makes little sense after 590 B.C. In particular Diakonov assigned the date of 593 to Jer. 51:27. He argued that:[116]

> . . . following the campaigns against Assyria, the Medes had entered into a relationship with the Mannai, the Urartians, and a remnant of the Scyths (Ashkenaz) remaining in Asia in which the three latter were at first tributary but semi-independent politically and that this status continued until after 593.

According to Diakonov the final destruction of Urartu by the Medes took place *ca.* 593-90.[117] In the account of Herodotus, the outbreak of hostilities between the Medes and Lydians began in 590. Diakonov argues that the Medes would not have ventured into Asia Minor in 590 if matters were not firmly under control in their home territory. This means that by 590 the Mannai and Scyths (Ashkenaz) were completely assimilated into Media, and hence a reference to these two peoples along with Urartu (Ararat) as the celebrated foe from the north, "consecrated" to carry out Yahweh's holy war against Babylon, can only mean a date prior to 590, and certainly before the destruction of Jerusalem in 587. The original historical reference to these northern peoples apparently has been reinterpreted in the Exilic period with the addition of vs. 28. Though the text of this verse is difficult to reconstruct, the original unit was probably a poetic tricolon meant to either replace or to clarify the tricolon in vs. 27, as the earlier reference was clearly incorrect from an historical point of view. The first line of each tricolon is identical. It was not the kings of the northern lands of the Urartians, Mannai and Scyths, but rather the king of the Medes whom Yahweh

---

[116] I. M. Diakonov, *ИСТОРИЯ МИДИИ* (Moscow: Academy of Sciences, 1956), pp. 316-17; translation that of Elizabeth von Voigtlander, "A Survey of Neo-Babllonian History," p. 115.

[117] *Ibid.*, pp. 317-18.

was preparing to destroy Babylon.

The third major section of this war oracle against Babylon is a five-part strophe which portrays an oracular vision of Babylon's defeat in battle (vss. 30-32). Babylon's warriors become like women, her buildings are ablaze, the city-gates are torn down (vs. 30). The king of Babylon, in distant refuge, is informed by couriers of Babylon's calamity (vs. 31). The couriers are seized at the distant fords, the marshes are set ablaze, and Babylon's soldiers are in panic for the entire land has fallen (vs. 32).

The prophet then takes up a judgment/lament against Babylon (vss. 33-35) in which the nation is described as "a threshing floor when it is time to tread it" (vs. 33). Nebuchadnezzar has devoured Israel as a monster fills his maw with tidbits (vs. 34). But in so doing he has cleansed Israel, rinsing off her violence; and now he in turn stands guilty, together with his people, of violence done against Yahweh's people (vs. 35).

The concluding oracle of doom against Babylon (vss. 36-40) is, by implication, an oracle of deliverance for Israel. It should be noted, however, that there is no summons to flight/return as such in this oracle. The focus throughout is on the judgment facing Babylon at the hands of the Divine Warrior/King/Judge of the nations. Yahweh declares that he will once again take up the legal defense (ריב) of his people; and the sea (ים) and springs (מקור) of Babylon will be dried up (vs. 36). Babylon shall become an uninhabited ruin (vs. 37). The language here is typical of earlier war oracles, though perhaps somewhat restrained in respect to military imagery per se, at least within this particular strophe. The closing scene presents a striking motif in that Babylon is compared to lions' cubs growling in chorus awaiting their dinner (vs. 38). While they fret, Yahweh prepares a banquet where the roles will be reversed in typical prophetic fashion -- the eater shall be eaten! Yahweh declares that he will besot them until they are in a drunken stupor, and then haul them to their slaughter "like so many rams and goats" (vss. 39-40).

In several respects the war oracle in 51:25-40 stands closer to the Jeremianic OAN tradition of chs. 46-47, 49:28-39 than either of the other two war oracles against Babylon (50:1-46 and 51:1-14).[118] The focus of attention in 51:25-40 is clearly on the nation judged. The language used reflects that of ancient treaty curses and the motivation for judgment is clearly stated. The Chaldean king, along with his people, bears guilt for the "flesh and blood" of the people of Israel whom Nebuchadnezzar has consumed (vss. 34-35).

---

[118]To these three war oracles one should also add Jer. 51:44-57, the two oracles against Babylon in Isa. 13:1-22 and 21:1-10, and the taunt against the king of Babylon in Isa. 14:4-21 which are also 6th century in date and reflect a close literary relationship to the material analyzed here.

On the basis of historical inference from vs. 27, this oracle has been dated to *ca.* 593, with Diakonov. It is indeed possible that this oracle is in fact the scroll described in the narrative of 51:59-64 which is attached to the poetic OAN tradition against Babylon. In his recent paper on Jeremiah 50-51, presented before the Society of Biblical Literature in Toronto, Kessler made much of the connection between this narrative and the preceding poetic oracles, arguing that the symbolic act described in the narrative provides the *Sitz im Leben* for at least the kernel behind this collection of oracular poems against Babylon. In the fourth year of Zedekiah's reign (*ca.* 594/3), according to the narrative, Jeremiah sent a scroll with Seraiah who accompanied King Zedekiah to Babylon. The scroll contained "all the evil that should come upon Babylon" (vs. 60) which Seraiah was to read and then proclaim: "O Yahweh, you have said concerning this place that you will cut it off, so that nothing shall dwell in it, neither man nor beast, and it shall be desolate for ever" (Jer. 51:62). Seraiah was then to bind a stone to the scroll and cast it into the middle of the Euphrates and utter a further curse: "Thus shall Babylon sink, to rise no more, because of the evil that I am bringing upon her" (51:64).

The year 594 saw another instance of symbolic prophecy on the part of Jeremiah, for this is the time that Jeremiah put on the wooden yoke to dramatize his conviction that Judah and her neighbors should submit to the yoke of Babylon and not revolt again (Jer. 27-28). This pro-Babylonian policy on the part of Jeremiah in respect to the foreign policy of Judah does not mean that he excluded Babylon from his OAN tradition. It only means that his oracles against Babylon were of a different sort. Jeremiah's OAN tradition against Babylon was not aimed at shaping foreign policy on the part of Judah in the immediate historical situation, but was instead formulated for the express benefit of the people of Israel, so as to fortify them that they might remain loyal to Yahweh in the long interim period before the curse would be fulfilled.

Jeremiah was a "prophet to the nations" and as such he had much to say about Babylon. As an agent of judgment against Judah, Nebuchadnezzar was called the unwitting "servant of Yahweh" (Jer. 25:9; 27:6; 43:10). That Jeremiah's pro-Babylonian policy was an historical necessity of the moment is clear. Nonetheless, he took pains to assure the exiles of 597 that after 70 years they would return with the vessels of the temple which Nebuchadnezzar had taken. Jeremiah was a true "Yahwist" and he knew that the suzerain of the nations had ushered in a new day for his people. Israel's survival would be found only in submission to the political yoke of Babylon, coupled with a vigorous spiritual independence and an ultimate rejection of Babylon's political yoke as well, in Yahweh's own time.

A further argument for a pre-Exilic date for at least part of the OAN tradition in Jer. 50-51 should be mentioned. It is frequently argued that the references to the temple in these chapters assume its destruction. The most commonly cited text in this argument is 51:11 which, as we have already shown, is a secondary prose expansion and not part of the original oracles against Babylon. An interesting reference to the temple appears in the oracle of war, judgment and salvation in 51:49b-51, which in literary form is a summons to flight/return:[119]

49b	Yea, to Babylon have fallen	גם לבבל נפלו	12
	all the slain of the earth!	חללי כל []ארץ	
50	You who have escaped her sword,	פלטים מֵחַרְבָּהּ[a]	6
	Go! Do not wait!	לכו אל תעמדו	6
	Remember Yahweh from afar!	זכרו מרחוק [] יהוה	7
	Let Jerusalem come to mind!	[]ירושלם תעלה על לבב[][b]	8
51	We are shamed for we have heard of her reproach;	בשנו כי שמענו חרפה	8
	Our faces are covered with ignominy,	כסתה כלמה פנינו	9
	(For) strangers have entered the sanctuary of Yahweh.	[][c] באו זרים על מקדש[][d] יהוה	9

The reference to Jerusalem's shame because "strangers have entered the sanctuary of Yahweh" certainly makes better sense in the decade 597-87 than it does after the temple was reduced to rubble. Strangers have entered the temple and taken its treasures, but the temple itself is still standing. Jeremiah made much of the fact that the vessels of the temple were taken by Nebuchadnezzar in 597 and that the remaining treasures would also be taken (cf. 27:16ff). References to vengeance for Yahweh's temple do not, in all cases, require the final destruction of that temple.

If our prosodic-textual analysis of Jer. 50-51 is substantially correct, it appears that we have here a nucleus of oracles against Babylon from the hand of the prophet Jeremiah himself, composed in the first decade of the 6th century, which were subsequently expanded and transformed in the decades following the destruction of Jerusalem in 587. Just how far the hand of Jeremiah extends in this transformation is not certain. The war oracle in 51:25-40 is almost certainly the work of Jeremiah, composed prior to the outbreak

---

[119] Notes to the text of Jer. 51:49b-51 -- [a]Cf. LXX ἐκ γης, πορευεσθε which apparently redivides the consonantal text of MT as reconstructed here. [b]The shorter form of this noun is read without a suffix to improve the metrical balance. [c]Deleting כי with LXX. [d]The *yodh* is deleted as dittography. Cf. LXX ἑις τα ἅγια ἡμων . . . κυριου and Vulg. *super sanctificationem domus Domini* which seem to reflect either a longer text than MT or to interpret the difficult מקדשי יהוה of MT. Both Syriac and Targum seem to reflect the text as reconstructed here.

of hostilities between the Medes and Lydians in *ca.* 590. The remarkable oracle in 51:1-14 may also be the work of Jeremiah from a somewhat later period, perhaps *ca.* 590-580. The remarkable holy war imagery with Yahweh/El treading upon Israel's foes in the grim harvest scene of vss. 1-3 is certainly in tune with the holy war ideology so dominant elsewhere in Jeremiah's prophetic tradition. The summons to flight as a speech form is still preserved intact in vs. 6. The only occurrence of the summons to mourn in the oracles against Babylon is also found in this oracle (vs. 8).

The war oracle in Jer. 50 comes from a still later period in time when the transformation of the war oracle and its related speech forms is more complete. In this oracle the various speech forms have begun to disintegrate, merging with one another in a remarkable manner. The end result is a new form of prophetic speech -- an eschatological oracle of war, judgment and salvation.[120] A sort of dual tension permeates the work. What was an announcement of judgment earlier is now both an announcement of judgment for Babylon and an explicit announcement of salvation for Israel. A lament over Israel's plight is at the same time a summons to participate in a "new Exodus" from Babylon to Zion. The summons to battle is set over against a lament or salvation oracle. The "foe from the north" is not only a mighty nation, it is the "Lion of the Jordan," the Divine Warrior himself who will ravage the flock of his foe and desolate their sheepfold.

The beginnings of this transformation of the war oracle are already evident in Jeremiah's oracle against Elam (49:34-39) which we have dated to *ca.* 597. Yahweh's declaration that he will establish his throne in Elam (49:38) looks beyond the here and now of contemporary history to the culmination of history, when the "Suzerain of the Nations" will vindicate himself with respect to pagan world powers. The war oracle in 51:25-40, which we have dated to *ca.* 593, also reflects the early stages of this transformation. The older prophetic speech forms are still intact but the oracle itself has become essentially a form of curse hurled at the enemy nation, rather than a political or propaganda work designed to undergird or to actually shape foreign policy within the national state of Judah.

The destruction of Jerusalem and its temple in 587 was no doubt a powerful impulse to speed up this transformation of the war oracle. The older war oracle was now completely loosed from its political and cultic moorings within the royal court and the Jerusalem temple. With the destruction of the political and religious institutions of Jerusalem, the prophet faced a new

---

[120]The war oracle in Jer. 51:44-57, which must be dated prior to the destruction of the temple in 587 (cf. vs. 51 and the discussion above on p. 276), falls into this same literary category at a somewhat earlier stage in its development.

task -- the preservation of Yahweh's people in exile. Speech forms were modified to this end. The war oracle remained a viable form, but it was put to new uses. The battle against Yahweh's national foes was given an eschatological orientation and a cosmic scope designed to encourage the people of Israel to continue to place their hope and trust in Yahweh, the Divine Warrior, in a most difficult time when Israel's very existence was challenged.

Further aspects of this transformation of the war oracle from its primary concern with the contemporary world of international politics to the trans-historical realm of early apocalyptic would require detailed analysis of the OAN tradition in Ezekiel, Second Isaiah, Zechariah 9:1-17 and Joel 4:9-17. It is sufficient here to note that the great cosmic battle at the end of the age, a concept which eventually produced the remarkable "Scroll of the War of the Sons of Light against the Sons of Darkness" in the apocalyptic community at Qumran, has deep roots within the developing OAN tradition in Old Testament prophecy. That apocalyptic battle in which the Divine Warrior finally annihilates his foes is foreshadowed in the use of the war oracle on the part of Jeremiah and his followers in the first half of the 6th century B.C.

CONCLUSION

For various reasons the oracles against the nations (OAN) in Old Testament prophecy have received relatively little attention in biblical research of the past century. In the present study relevant OAN material has been subjected to detailed prosodic-textual analysis, form critical study, and historical interpretation in an attempt to trace the historical development of the war oracle in ancient Israel from earliest times to *ca.* 580 B.C. Amos 1-2 and Jeremiah 46-51, the natural foci in any analysis of the OAN tradition, form the two poles around which this analysis has taken shape. These two collections are relatively easy to control in respect to historical setting and textual reconstruction. Moreover, they constitute the two central poles in the development of prophecy itself as an historical phenomenon in ancient Israel. Amos was the first of the classical "writing prophets" whereas Jeremiah witnessed the destruction of both the institutions of temple and kingship in Jerusalem and hence reflects that transitional period between classical prophecy and what eventually became apocalyptic.

The use of the war oracle in ancient Israel has a long and complex history. Obtaining a war oracle was an essential part of military strategy throughout the ancient Near East. In Israel the more mechanical means of oracular divination were used from earliest times, but were displaced from the time of Samuel by the prophets of Israel who saw themselves as the heralds of the Divine Suzerain, the spokesmen of the *imperium* of Yahweh. The rise of the monarchy in Israel saw a split in the administration of this *imperium*. Though David assumed the executive control of Israel and Judah, first as military commander (*nāgîd*) and later as king (*melek*), the prophet remained an active agent of Yahweh's *imperium*, particularly in military matters. He alone retained the authority to summon the tribal levy of the Covenant League in holy warfare. Thus when Rehoboam summoned the levy of Judah and Benjamin against the ten northern tribes, he was successfully checked by the prophet Shemaiah who delivered an oracle from Yahweh to the king and his troops declaring that they were not to fight the people of Israel (I Kings 21:21-24).

The ninth century saw the resurgence of the prophetic movement in northern Israel and with it a renascence of Israel's ancient holy war traditions. The prophet emerged once again as a dominant political force over against the king, especially in military matters. One of the earliest examples of an oracle against a foreign nation, as a form of prophetic speech, stems from this period. In I Kings 20:28 a certain "man of God" delivered an oracle against Aram to Ahab, king of Israel, which is both a war oracle and a judgment speech.

The transformation of the war oracle from the domain of military tactics to a literary mode of judgment speech is developed further in the OAN tradition of Amos 1-2. In the hands of Amos the member nations of the former Davidic Empire are each judged in a highly stylized manner for violation of the treaty stipulations of their "covenant of brotherhood." Though the form of each judgment speech against the foreign nations is identical to that observed in the earlier oracle against Aram in I Kings 20:28, the focus of attention is now the nation of Israel. Motifs from the war songs of Israel's Covenant League are incorporated into the poetic composition, which is essentially a reversal of Yahweh's Holy War as celebrated in the ritual conquest traditions. The Divine Warrior will lead his hosts in battle against his own people, because they have spurned their covenant obligations.

The framework of the idealized Davidic Empire as the legal basis for judgment speeches against the nations is expanded in the OAN tradition from Amos to Jeremiah. Isaiah's oracles against Assyria, Egypt, Ethiopia, and the insurgent Arab tribes of the East are based on the concept of the universal sovereignty of Yahweh as suzerain of the nations. The dominant intent of the OAN tradition in the hands of Isaiah, Nahum, Zephaniah and Jeremiah from *ca.* 720-609 appears to be political. The war oracle as a judgment speech against both Israel and foreign nations persists, but the major thrust of the formal OAN tradition of this period is aimed at shaping foreign policy in Judah with respect to the nations concerned.

The death of Josiah in 609/8 and the conquests of Nebuchadnezzar from *ca.* 605-597 mark the end of an era in the developing OAN tradition, and the beginning of the second major transformation of the prophetic war oracle in ancient Israel. Beginning with Habakkuk and Jeremiah's oracle against Elam (Jer. 49:34-39) the focus of attention in the OAN tradition shifts from the contemporary events of political history to the realm of eschatology. The primary intent of this literary mode is no longer that of shaping foreign policy per se, but the preservation of the people of Israel in the impending crisis which challenges their very existence. The fall of Jerusalem in 597 and its final destruction at the hands of Nebuchadnezzar in 587 serve to complete this transformation. Loosed from its moorings in the royal court and the temple cult, the war oracle within the OAN tradition evolves rather quickly from prophetic eschatology to early apocalyptic. Though Jeremiah 50-51, in its present form, is part of the Exilic tradition of oracles against Babylon, akin to Isaiah 13-14 and 21, the hand of Jeremiah can be traced in the early stages of this transformation. The war oracle in Jer. 51:25-40 is to be dated *ca.* 593, and 51:44-57 to *ca.* 597-587. The war oracle in 51:1-14 is somewhat later in date, perhaps *ca.* 590-580, and may also be the work of Jeremiah.

This study of the war oracle in Old Testament prophecy is basically an inductive analysis of the large and important literary tradition known as the oracles against the nations. Two major transformations of the war oracle are observed. In the 10th-8th centuries the war oracle as a tactical element in military strategy was transformed into the literary mode of a prophetic judgment speech against both military foes and the nation of Israel, together with her political allies. In the opening decades of the 6th century the war oracle was again transformed from the world of international politics to the trans-historical realm of early apocalyptic.

The details of this latter transformation would require careful analysis of the OAN tradition in Ezekiel, Second Isaiah, Zechariah 9:1-17 and Joel 4: 9-17. It is sufficient here to note that the transformation of speech forms observed in Jeremiah 50-51 suggests that the process was already virtually complete by the middle of the 6th century, before the fall of Babylon. The subsequent use of the prophetic war oracle in early apocalyptic has deep roots in earlier usage within the developing OAN tradition of Old Testament prophecy.

BIBLIOGRAPHY

I. *Books and Monographs*

Aharoni, Yohanan, and Michael Avi-Yonah. *The Macmillan Bible Atlas*. London: Collier-Macmillan Limited, 1968.

Aimé-Giron, Noël. *Textes araméens d'Egypte*. Le Caire: Impr. de l'Institut français d'archéologie orientale, 1931.

Aisleitner, Joseph. *Wörterbuch der ugaritischen Sprache*, 2nd ed. O. Eissfeldt, ed. Berlin: Akademie-Verlag, 1965.

Albright, William F. *Archaeology and the Religion of Israel*, 4th ed. Baltimore: The Johns Hopkins Press, 1956.

________ *The Biblical Period from Abraham to Ezra*, 4th ed. Harper Torchbooks. New York: Harper & Row, 1963.

________ *From the Stone Age to Christianity. Monotheism and the Historical Process*, 2nd ed. Anchor Books. Garden City, N. Y.: Doubleday, 1957.

________ *Samuel and the Beginnings of the Prophetic Movement*. Cincinnati: Hebrew Union College Press, 1961.

________ *Yahweh and the Gods of Canaan. A Historical Analysis of Two Contrasting Faiths*. Garden City, N. Y.: Doubleday, 1968.

Alt, Albrecht. *Essays on Old Testament History and Religion*, trans. R. A. Wilson. Anchor Books. Garden City, N. Y.: Doubleday, 1968.

________ *Israel und Aegypten. Die Politischen Beziehungen der Könige von Israel und Juda zu den Pharaonen*. Leipzig: J. D. Hinrichs, 1909.

________ *Kleine Schriften zur Geschichte des Volkes Israel*, 3 vols. München: C. H. Beck, 1953-59.

Bach, Robert. *Die Aufforderungen zur Flucht und zum Kampf im alttestamentlichen Prophetenspruch*. WMANT, 9. Neukirchener Verlag, 1962.

Bächli, Otto. *Israel und die Völker. Eine Studie zum Deuteronomium*. AThANT, 41. Zurich: Zwingli-Verlag, 1962.

Barthélemy, D., J. T. Milik, R. de Vaux, P. Benoît, M. Baillet, and J. A. Sanders. *Discoveries in the Judaean Desert, I-IV. Qumran Cave I, Les Grottes de Murabba'ât, Les 'Petites Grottes' de Qumrân, The Psalms Scroll of Qumrân Cave 11*. Oxford: Clarendon Press, 1955-65.

Baumbartner, Walter. *Hebräisches und Aramäisches Lexicon zum Alten Testament*. Dritte Auflage, Lieferung I und II. Leiden: E. J. Brill, 1967, 1974.

Bentzen, Aage. *Introduction to the Old Testament*, 2 vols., 7th ed. Copenhagen: G. E. C. Gad Publisher, 1967.

Blommerde, Anton C. M. *Northwest Semitic Grammar and Job.* Biblica et Orientalia, 22. Rome: Pontifical Biblical Institute, 1969.

Borger, R. *Die Inschriften Asarhaddons, König von Assyrien.* Archiv für Orientforschung, Beiheft 9. Graz, 1956.

Breasted, James H. *Ancient Records of Egypt. From the Earliest Times to the Persian Conquest, Edited and Translated with Commentary.* Vol. IV. Chicago: University of Chicago Press, 1906.

Brichto, Herbert C. *The Problem of "Curse" in the Hebrew Bible.* JBL Monograph, XIII. Philadelphia: SBL, 1963.

Bright, John. *A History of Israel.* Philadelphia: Westminster Press, 1959.

_________ *Jeremiah.* AB, 21. Garden City, N. Y.: Doubleday, 1965.

Brooke, A. E., N. McLean, and H. St. J. Thackeray (eds.). *The Old Testament in Greek.* Cambridge: Cambridge University Press, 1906-1930.

Brown, F., S. R. Driver, and C. A. Briggs. *A Hebrew and English Lexicon of the Old Testament.* Oxford: Clarendon Press, 1962 (c1907).

Brownlee, William H. *The Text of Habakkuk in the Ancient Community from Qumran.* JBL Monograph, XI. Philadelphia: SBL, 1959.

Buccellati, Giorgio. *Cities and Nations of Ancient Syria. An Essay on Political Institutions with Special Reference to the Israelite Kingdoms.* Studi Semitici, 26. Istituto di Studi del Vicino Oriente: Università di Roma, 1967.

Bury, J. B. (gen. ed.). *The Cambridge Ancient History. Vol. III, The Assyrian Empire.* Cambridge: At the University Press, 1929.

Buttrick, George A. (gen. ed.). *The Interpreter's Dictionary of the Bible. An Illustrated Encyclopedia.* 4 vols. New York and Nashville: Abingdon Press, 1962.

Cameron, George C. *History of Early Iran.* Chicago: University of Chicago Press, 1936.

Cathcart, Kevin J. *Nahum in the Light of Northwest Semitic.* Biblica et Orientalia, 26. Rome: Biblical Institute Press, 1973.

Childs, Brevard S. *Isaiah and the Assyrian Crisis.* SBT, Second Series, 3. London: SCM Press, 1967.

Clements, R. E. *Prophecy and Covenant.* SBT, 43. London: SCM Press, 1965.

_________ *Prophecy and Tradition.* Oxford: Blackwell, 1975.

Clifford, Richard J. *The Cosmic Mountain in Canaan and the Old Testament.* HSM, 4. Cambridge: Harvard University Press, 1972.

Cornill, Carl H. *Das Buch Jeremia.* Leipzig: Chr. Herm. Tauchnitz, 1905.

Coste, Erich. *Die Weissagungen des Propheten Jeremias Wider die Fremden Völker.* Leipzig: Druck von W. Drugulin, 1895.

Cross, Frank M., Jr. *The Ancient Library of Qumran and Modern Biblical Studies,* rev. ed. Anchor Books. Garden City, N. Y.: Doubleday, 1961.

Cross, Frank M., Jr. *Canaanite Myth and Hebrew Epic. Essays in the History of the Religion of Israel.* Cambridge: Harvard University Press, 1973.

Cross, Frank M., Jr., and David N. Freedman. *Early Hebrew Orthography. A Study of the Epigraphic Evidence.* American Oriental Series, 36. New Haven: American Oriental Society, 1952.

________ *Studies in Ancient Yahwistic Poetry.* Baltimore: The Johns Hopkins University, 1950.

Dahood, Mitchell, S.J. *Psalms I, II and III. Introduction, Translation and Notes.* The Anchor Bible, vols. 16, 17 and 17A. Garden City, N. Y.: Doubleday, 1966-70.

________ *Ugaritic-Hebrew Philology.* Rome: Pontifical Biblical Institute, 1965.

Diakonov, I. M. *ИСТОРИЯ МИДИИ.* Moscow: Academy of Sciences, 1956.

Dijk, H. J. van. *Ezekiel's Prophecy on Tyre.* Rome: Pontifical Biblical Institute, 1968.

Donner, Herbert. *Israel Unter den Völkern. Die Stellung der Klassischen Propheten des 8. Jahrhunderts v. Chr. zur Aussenpolitik der Könige von Israel und Juda.* SVT, XI. Leiden: E. J. Brill, 1964.

Drioton, Étienne. *L'Egypt Pharaonique.* Paris: A. Colin, 1959.

Driver, Samuel R. *The Book of the Prophet Jeremiah.* New York: Charles Scribner's Sons, 1906.

________ *Notes on the Hebrew Text and Topography of the Books of Samuel. With an Introduction on Hebrew Palaeography and the Ancient Versions,* 2nd ed. Oxford: Clarendon Press, 1913.

Duhm, Bernard. *Das Buch Jeremiah.* KHC, 11. Tübingen: J. C. B. Mohr, 1901.

Eissfeldt, Otto. *Der Gott Karmel.* Berlin: Akademie-Verlag, 1953.

________ *The Old Testament. An Introduction including the Apocrypha and Pseudepigrapha, and also the works of similar type from Qumran. The History of the Formation of the Old Testament,* trans. Peter R. Ackroyd. New York and Evanston: Harper & Row, 1965.

________ *Philister und Phönizer.* Der Alte Orient, 34/3. Leipzig: J. C. Hinrichs, 1936.

Ellermeier, Friedrich. *Prophetie in Mari und Israel.* Theologische und Orientalische Arbeiten, 1. Herzberg am Harz: Verlag Erwin Jungfer, 1968.

Elliger, K., and W. Rudolph (eds.). *Biblia Hebraica Stuttgartensia.* Stuttgart: Württembergische Bibelanstalt, 1968-

Engnell, Ivan. *Studies in Divine Kingship in the Ancient Near East.* Uppsala: Almqvist & Wiksells Boktryckeri AB, 1943.

________ *A Rigid Scrutiny. Critical Essays on the Old Testament,* trans. John T. Willis. Nashville: Vanderbilt University Press, 1969.

Erlandsson, S. *The Burden of Babylon. A Study of Isaiah 13:2-14:23.* Coniectanea Biblica, Old Testament Series, 4. Lund: Gleerup, 1970.

Fohrer, Georg. *History of Israelite Religion,* trans. David E. Green. New York and Nashville: Abingdon Press, 1972.

________ *Introduction to the Old Testament,* trans. David E. Green. New York and Nashville: Abingdon Press, 1968.

Fredriksson, Henning. *Jahwe als Krieger. Studien zum alttestamentlichen Gottesbild.* Lund: C. W. K. Gleerup, 1945.

Gadd, C. J. *The Fall of Nineveh. The Newly Discovered Babylonian Chronicle no. 21,901 in the British Museum.* London: Trustees of the British Museum, 1923.

Gardiner, Sir Alan Henderson. *Egypt of the Pharaohs.* A Galaxy Book. Oxford: Clarendon Press, 1966 (c1961).

Gauthier, H. *Livre des Rois d'Egypte, III. Memoires publies par les Membres de l'Institut Français d'Archeologie Orientale,* Tome 19. Paris, 1913.

Glueck, Nelson. *Explorations in Eastern Palestine.* 4 vols. AASOR 14 (1933-34), 15 (1934-35), 18-19 (1937-39), and 25-28 (1945-48). New Haven: American Schools of Oriental Research.

Gordon, Cyrus H. *Ugaritic Literature. A Comprehensive Translation of the Poetic and Prose Texts.* Rome: Pontifical Biblical Institute, 1949.

________ *Ugaritic Textbook. Grammar, Texts in Transliteration, Cuneiform Selections, Glossary, Indices.* Analecta Orientalia, 38. Rome: Pontifical Biblical Institute, 1965.

Gottwald, Norman K. *All the Kingdoms of the Earth.* New York: Harper, 1964.

________ *Studies in the Book of Lamentations,* rev. ed. SBT, 14. London: SCM Press, 1962.

Gray, John. *I & II Kings: A Commentary.* OTL. London: SCM Press, 1964.

Gressman, Hugo. *Der Messias.* FRLANT, 43. Göttingen: Vandenhoeck & Ruprecht, 1929.

________ *Der Ursprung der israelitisch-jüdischen Eschatologie.* FRLANT, 6. Göttingen: Vandenhoeck & Ruprecht, 1905.

Gross, Walter. *Bileam: Literar- und formkritische Untersuchung der Prosa in Num 22-24.* StANT, 38. Munich: Kösel-Verlag, 1974.

Guillaume, Alfred. *Prophecy and Divination.* London: Hodder and Stoughton, 1938.

Gunkel, Hermann. *Ausgewählte Psalmen,* 4th rev. ed. Göttingen: Vandenhoeck & Ruprecht, 1917.

________ *Einleitung in die Psalmen. Die Gattungen der religiösen Lyric Israels.* Göttingen: Vandenhoeck & Ruprecht, 1933.

________ *Die Psalmen übersetzt und erklärt.* HzAT 11/2. Göttingen: Vandenhoeck & Ruprecht, 1926.

Haldar, Alfred. *Associations of Cult Prophets among the Ancient Semites.* Uppsala: Almqvist & Wiksells Boktryckeri AB, 1945.

________ *Studies in the Book of Nahum.* Uppsala: Lundequistska Bokhandeln, 1947.

Hanson, Paul David. *The Dawn of Apocalyptic. The Historical and Sociological Roots of Jewish Apocalyptic Eschatology.* Philadelphia: Fortress, 1975.

Hentschke, Richard. *Die Stellung der vorexilischen Schriftpropheten zum Kultus.* BZAW, 75. Berlin: Alfred Töpelmann, 1957.

Herdner, Andrée. *Corpus des tablettes en cunéiformes alphabétiques.* 2 vols. Paris: Imprimerie Nationale, 1963.

Herodotus. *The Persian Wars,* trans. A. D. Godley. 4 vols. Loeb Classical Library. London: Heinemann, 1920-25.

Hillers, Delbert R. *Treaty-Curses and the Old Testament Prophets.* Biblica et Orientalia, 16. Rome: Pontifical Biblical Institute, 1964.

Humbert, Paul. *La "Terou'a." Analyse d'un rite biblique.* Neuchatel: Secrétariat de l'Université, 1946.

Janzen, J. Gerald. *Studies in the Text of Jeremiah.* HSM, 6. Cambridge: Harvard University Press, 1973.

Janzen, Waldemar. *Mourning Cry and Woe Oracle.* BZAW, 125. Berlin and New York: Walter de Gruyter, 1972.

Jean, Charles-Francois (ed.). *Archives Royales de Mari, II: Lettres.* Musée du Louvre, Département des Antiquités Orientales, 23. Paris: Paul Geuthner, 1950.

Jean, Charles, and J. Hoftijzer. *Dictionnaire des Inscriptions sémitiques de l'ouest.* Leiden: E. J. Brill, 1965.

Jenni, Ernst. *Die politischen Voraussagen der Propheten.* AThANT, 29. Zürich: Zwingli-Verlag, 1956.

Jeremias, Jörg. *Kultprophetie und Gerichtsverkündigung in der späten Königszeit Israels.* WMANT, 35. Neukirchener Verlag, 1970.

Johnson, Aubrey R. *The Cultic Prophet in Ancient Israel,* 2nd ed. Cardiff: University of Wales Press, 1962.

Josephus. *Jewish Antiquities,* trans. H. St. J. Thackeray (et al.). 5 vols. Loeb Classical Library. London: William Heinemann, 1928-

________ *The Life; Against Apion,* trans. H. St. J. Thackeray. Loeb Classical Library. London: William Heinemann, 1926.

Kaiser, Otto. *Isaiah 1-12. A Commentary.* OTL. Philadelphia: Westminster Press, 1972.

Kaufmann, Yehezkel. *The Babylonian Captivity and Deutero-Isaiah,* trans. C. W. Efroymson. New York: Union of American Hebrew Congregations, 1970.

Kaufmann, Yehezkel. *The Religion of Israel*, abridgement and trans. Moshe Greenberg. Chicago: University of Chicago Press, 1960.

_________ *Tôldôt Ha-Emûnah Ha-Yisrē'elît.* 4 vols. Tel Aviv: Bialik Institute-Dvir, 1937-56.

Kienitz, F. K. *Die politische Geschichte Ägypten vom 7. bis zum 4. Jahrhundert vor der Zeitwende.* Berlin: Akademie-Verlag, 1953.

Kittle, Rudolph, et al (eds.). *Biblia Hebraica*, 7th ed. Stuttgart: Würtembergische Bibelanstalt for The American Bible Society, New York, 1962.

Klauber, Ernst G. *Assyrische Beamtentum nach Briefen aus der Sargonidenzeit.* Leipziger semitische Studien, 5/3. Leipzig: J. C. Hinrichs, 1910.

Koehler, Ludwig, and Walter Baumgartner (eds.). *Lexicon in Veteris Testamenti Libros*, 2nd ed. Leiden: E. J. Brill, 1953.

König, F. W. *Geschichte Elams.* Leipzig: J. C. Hinrichs, 1931.

Kraus, Hans-Joachim. *Psalmen.* 2 vols. BK, 15. Neukirchener Verlag, 1960.

_________ *Worship in Israel. A Cultic History of the Old Testament*, trans. Geoffrey Buswell. Richmond, Virginia: John Knox Press, 1965.

Kupper, Jean-Robert. *Archives Royales de Mari, III: Lettres.* Musée du Louvre, Département des Antiquités Orientales, 24. Paris: Geuthner, 1948.

Langlamet, F. *Gilgal et les Récits de la Traversée du Jourdain (Jos. III-IV).* Cahiers de la Revue Biblique, 11. Paris: J. Gabalda, 1969.

Lauha, Aarre. *Zaphon. Der Norden und die Nordvölker im Alten Testament.* Helsinki: Der Finnischen Literaturgesellschaft, 1943.

Leslie, Elmer A. *Jeremiah, Chonologically Arranged, Translated and Interpreted.* New York and Nashville: Abingdon Press, 1954.

Lisowsky, Gerhard. *Konkordanz zum Hebräischen Alten Testament.* Stuttgart: Württembergische Bibelanstalt, 1958.

Luckenbill, Daniel D. *Ancient Records of Assyria and Babylonia.* 2 vols. Chicago: University of Chicago Press, 1926.

_________ *The Annals of Sennacherib.* University of Chicago Oriental Institute Publications, II. Chicago: University of Chicago Press, 1924.

Lutz, Hanns-Martin. *Jahwe, Jerusalem und die Völker. Zur Vorgeschichte von Sach 12,1-8 und 14,1-5.* WMANT, 27. Neukirchener Verlag, 1968.

Maier, Walter A. *The Book of Nahum. A Commentary.* Saint Louis: Concordia Publishing House, 1959.

Mays, James L. *Amos. A Commentary.* OTL. Philadelphia: Westminster, 1969.

Mandelkern, Solomon. *Veteris Testamenti Concordantiae Hebraicae atque Chaldaicae.* Tel-Aviv: Sumptibus Schocken Hierosolymis, 1962.

McKay, John. *Religion in Judah under the Assyrians.* SBT, Second Series, 26. Naperville, Ill.: Alec R. Allenson, 1973.

Meissner, Bruno. *Könige Babyloniens und Assyriens. Charakterbilder aus der altorientalischen Geschichte.* Leipzig: Quelle & Meyer, 1926.

Mendenhall, George E. *The Tenth Generation. The Origins of the Biblical Tradition.* Baltimore and London: Johns Hopkins University Press, 1973.

Meulenaere, Herman de. *Herodotos over de 26ste Dynastie (II,147-III,15).* Louvain: Leuvense Universitaire Uitgaven, 1951.

Meyers, Jacob M. *I and II Chronicles.* 2 vols. AB, 12 and 13. Garden City, N.Y.: Doubleday, 1965.

Miller, Patrick D., Jr. *The Divine Warrior in Early Israel.* HSM, 5. Cambridge: Harvard University Press, 1973.

Montgomery, James A. *A Critical and Exegetical Commentary on the Books of Kings.* ICC. Edinburgh: T. & T. Clark, 1951.

Moscati, Sabatino. *The World of the Phoenicians.* New York: Praeger, 1968.

Mowinckel, Sigmund. *Zur Komposition des Buches Jeremia.* Kristiania: J. Dybwad, 1914.

_________ *Prophecy and Tradition. The Prophetic Books in the Light of the Study of the Growth and History of the Tradition.* Oslo: Dybwad, 1946.

_________ *The Psalms in Israel's Worship,* trans. D. R. Ap-Thomas. 2 vols. New York and Nashville: Abingdon Press, 1962.

Noth, Martin. *The History of Israel,* trans. from 2nd German ed. by S. Godman as revised by P. R. Ackroyd, 2nd ed. New York and Evanston: Harper & Row, 1960.

Parker, Richard A., and Waldo H. Dubberstein. *Babylonian Chronology 626 B.C. - A.D. 75,* 3rd ed. Providence: Brown University, 1956.

Pfeiffer, Robert H. *Introduction to the Old Testament.* New York: Harper & Brothers, 1941.

Plöger, Otto. *Theocracy and Eschatology,* trans. S. Rudman. Richmond, Virginia: John Knox Press, 1968.

Pritchard, James B. (ed.). *Ancient Near Eastern Texts Relating to the Old Testament,* 2nd ed. Princeton: Princeton University Press, 1955.

_________ *The Ancient Near East. Supplementary Texts and Pictures Relating to the Old Testament.* Princeton: Princeton University Press, 1969.

Rad, Gerhard von. *Der Heilige Krieg im alten Israel,* 4. Auflage. Göttingen: Vandenhoeck & Ruprecht, 1965.

_________ *Old Testament Theology, II. The Theology of Israel's Prophetic Traditions,* trans. D. M. G. Stalker. New York: Harper & Row, 1965.

_________ *Studies in Deuteronomy,* trans. David Stalker. SBT, 9. London: SCM Press, 1953.

Ralphs, Alfred, and Joseph Ziegler. *Septuaginta. Vetus Testamentum Graecum Auctoritate Academiae Litterarum Gottingensis editum.* Göttingen: Vandenhoeck & Ruprecht, 1931-

Reventlow, Henning G. *Das Amt des Propheten bei Amos.* FRLANT, 80. Göttingen: Vandenhoeck & Ruprecht, 1962.

Richter, Wolfgang. *Die sogenannten vorprophetischen Berufungsberichte. Eine literaturwissenschaftliche Studie zu I Sam. 9,1-10,16, Ex 3f. und Ri 6, 11b-17.* FRLANT, 101. Göttingen: Vandenhoeck & Ruprecht, 1970.

Robinson, Theodore H. *Die Zwölf kleinen Propheten. Hosea bis Micha.* HAT, 14. Tübingen: J. C. B. Mohr, 1964.

Rudolph, W. *Jeremia,* 2te Auflage. HAT, 12. Tübingen: J. C. B. Mohr, 1958.

Sabottka, Liudger. *Zephanja. Versuch einer Neuübersetzung mit philologischem Kommentar.* Biblica et Orientalia, 25. Rome: Biblical Institute Press, 1972.

Saggs, H. W. F. *The Greatness that was Babylon.* New York: Hawthorn, 1962.

Schmoekel, Hartmut. *Jahwe und die Fremdvölker. Der Werdegang einer religiösen Idee.* Breslauer Studien zur Theologie und Religionsgeschichte, 1. Breslau: Maruschke & Berendt, 1934.

Schmerl, Christian. *Die Völkerorakel in den Prophetenbüchern des Alten Testaments.* Würtzburg: Richard Mayr, 1939.

Schottroff, Willy. *Der altisraelitische Fluchspruch.* WMANT, 30. NeuKirchener Verlag, 1969.

Schulz, Hermann. *Das Buch Nahum. Eine redaktionskritische Untersuchung.* Berlin and New York: Walter de Gruyter, 1973.

Schwally, Friedrich. *Die Reden des Buches Jeremia gegen die Heiden. XXV. XLVI-LI.* Giessen: Druck von Wilhelm Keller, 1888.

________ *Semitische Kriegsaltertümer, I. Der heilige Krieg im Alten Israel.* Leipzig: Dietrich, 1901.

Simons, J. *The Geographical and Topographical Texts of the Old Testament.* Leiden: E. J. Brill, 1959.

Smend, Rudolf. *Jahwekrieg und Stämmebund,* 2nd ed. FRLANT, 84. Göttingen: Vandenhoeck & Ruprecht, 1966. Translated by Max G. Rogers as *Yahweh War & Tribal Confederation. Reflections upon Israel's Earliest History.* Nashville and New York: Abingdon, 1970.

Smith, Sidney. *Babylonian Historical Texts Relating to the Capture and Downfall of Babylon.* London: Methuen and Co., 1924.

Soggin, J. Alberto. *Joshua. A Commentary.* OTL. Philadelphia: Westminster, 1972.

Stenning, J. F. *The Targum of Isaiah.* Oxford: Clarendon Press, 1949.

Stolz, Fritz. *Jahwes und Israels Kriege. Kriegstheorien und Kriegsfahrungen im Glaube des alten Israels.* AThANT, 60. Zürich: Theologischer Verlag, 1972.

Stonehouse, G. G. V. *The Books of the Prophets Zephaniah and Nahum.* The Westminster Commentaries. London: Methuen & Co., 1929.

Thiele, Edwin R. *The Mysterious Numbers of the Hebrew Kings,* rev. ed. Grand Rapids, Mich.: William B. Eerdmans, 1965.

Unger, Arthur. *Babylon, die heilige Stadt nach der Beschriebung der Babylonier.* Berlin: W. de Gruyter, 1931.

Vandier, Jacques. *L'Egypt*, 3rd ed. Paris: Presses Universitaires de France, 1952.

Vaux, Roland de. *Ancient Israel.* New York: McGraw-Hill, 1961.

Vetter, D. *Seherspruch und Segensschilderung. Ausdruksabsichten und sprachliche Verwirklichungen in den Bileam Spruchen von Num 23 und 24.* Stuttgart: Calwer, 1974.

Volz, Paul. *Der Prophet Jeremia.* KAT, X. Leipzig: A. Deichert, 1928.

________ *Studien zum Text des Jeremia.* BWAT, 25. Leipzig: Hinrichs, 1920.

Vuilleumier, René, and Carl-A. Keller. *Michée, Nahoum, Habacuc, Sophonie.* Commentaire de l'Ancien Testament, XIb. Neuchâtel: Delachaux et Niestlé, 1971.

Ward, William A. (ed.). *The Role of the Phoenicians in the Interaction of Mediterranean Civilizations. Papers presented to the Archaeological Symposium at the American University of Beirut, March 1967.* Beirut: American University of Beirut, 1968.

Waterman, Leroy. *Royal Correspondence of the Assyrian Empire. Translated into English with a transliteration of the text and a commentary.* 4 vols. Ann Arbor: University of Michigan Press, 1930-36.

Weber, Max. *Ancient Judaism*, trans. Hans H. Gerth and Don Martindale. New York: The Free Press, and London: Collier-Macmillan Ltd., 1967.

Weiser, Artur. *Das Buch des Propheten Jeremia.* 2 vols. ATD, 20. Göttingen: Vandenhoeck & Ruprecht, 1952-55.

________ *Das Buch der zwölf Propheten.* ATD, 24. Vol. I, 4te Auflage. Gottingen: Vandenhoeck & Ruprecht, 1963.

________ *The Old Testament: Its Formation and Development*, trans. Dorothea M. Barton. New York: Association Press, 1961.

________ *Die Profetie des Amos.* BZAW, 53. Giessen: Töpelmann, 1929.

________ *Samuel, seine geschichtliche Aufgabe und religiöse Bedeutung.* FRLANT, 81. Göttingen: Vandenhoeck & Ruprecht, 1962.

Westermann, Claus. *Basic Forms of Prophetic Speech*, trans. Hugh White. Philadelphia: Westminster Press, 1967.

Whitaker, Richard E. *A Concordance of the Ugaritic Literature.* Cambridge: Harvard University Press, 1972.

Wiseman, Donald J. *Chronicles of Chaldean Kings (626-556 B.C.).* London: Trustees of the British Museum, 1956.

Wright, G. Ernest. *Biblical Archaeology*, rev. ed. Philadelphia: Westminster Press, 1962.

________ *The Book of Isaiah.* LBC, 11. Richmond, Virginia: John Knox Press, 1968.

________ *The Old Testament and Theology.* New York: Harper & Row, 1969.

________, and Floyd V. Filson. *The Westminster Historical Atlas to the Bible*, rev. ed. Philadelphia: Westminster Press, 1956.

Yadin, Yigael. *The Art of Warfare in Biblical Lands in the Light of Archaeological Study.* 2 vols. New York: McGraw-Hill, 1963.

________ *The Scroll of the War of the Sons of Light against the Sons of Darkness*, trans. Batya and Chaim Rabin. Oxford University Press, 1962.

Zeissl, Helene von. *Äthiopen und Assyrer in Ägypten. Beiträge zur Geschichte der ägyptischen "Spätzeit."* Ägyptologische Forschungen, 14. Glückstadt: J. J. Augustin, 1944.

Zyl, A. H. von. *The Moabites.* POS, 3. Leiden: Brill, 1960.

II. *Articles*

Albright, William F. "The Assyrian March on Jerusalem, Isa. x, 28-32," *AASOR* 4 (1922-23), pp. 134-40.

________ "The Assyro-Tyrian Synchronism and the Chronology of Tyre," *Annuaire de l'Institut de Philologie et d'Histoire Orientales et Slaves* 13 (1955), pp. 1-9.

________ "A Catalogue of Early Hebrew Lyric Poems (Psalm LXVIII)," *HUCA* 23 (1950-51), pp. 1-39.

________ "The Earliest Forms of Hebrew Verse," *JPOS* 2 (1922), pp. 69-86.

________ "The Elimination of King 'So'," *BASOR* 171 (1963), p. 66.

________ "Further Light on Synchronisms between Egypt and Asia in the Period 935-685 B.C.," *BASOR* 141 (1956), pp. 23-27.

________ "The Nebuchadnezzar and Neriglissar Chronicles," *BASOR* 143 (1956), pp. 28-33.

________ "New Light on Early Recensions of the Hebrew Bible," *BASOR* 140 (1955), pp. 27-33.

________ "The Oracles of Balaam," *JBL* 63 (1944), pp. 207-33.

________ "The Psalm of Habakkuk," in *Studies in Old Testament Prophecy*, ed. H. H. Rowley. New York: Charles Scribner's Sons (1950), pp. 1-18.

________ "The Seal of Eliakim and the Latest Preëxilic History of Judah, with Some Observations on Ezekiel," *JBL* 51 (1932), pp. 77-106.

________ "Some Remarks on the Song of Moses in Deuteronomy XXXII," *VT* 9 (1959), pp. 339-46.

________ "The Song of Deborah in the Light of Archaeology," *BASOR* 62 (1936), pp. 26-31.

Alt, Albrecht. "Das System der Assyrischen Provenzen auf dem Boden des Reiches Israel," *ZDPV* 52 (1929), pp. 220-242.

________ "Zelte und Hütten," in *Kleine Schriften zur Geschichte des Volkes*

Israel, III. München: C. H. Beck, 1959, pp. 233-42.

Anderson, Bernhard W. "Exodus Typology in Second Isaiah," in *Israel's Prophetic Heritage*. Essays in honor of James Muilenburg, ed. B. W. Anderson and W. Harrelson. New York: Harper & Brothers, 1962, pp. 177-95.

Bach, Robert. "Gottesrecht und Weltliches Recht in der Verkündigung des Propheten Amos," in *Festschrift G. Dehn*. Neukirchener Verlag, 1957, pp. 23-24.

Baltzer, K. "Considerations Regarding the Office and Calling of the Prophet," *HTR* 61 (1968), pp. 567-81.

Bardtke, Hans. "Jeremia der Fremdvölkerprophet," *ZAW* 53 (1935), pp. 209-39 and 54 (1936), pp. 240-62.

Baumgärtel, F. "Die Formel *n^{e}ʾum jahwe*," *ZAW* 73 (1961), pp. 277-90.

Beaucamp, É. "Amós 1-2. O Pesha' de Israel e o das Nações," *Actualidades Biblicas*. Petrópolis, 1971, pp. 325-30.

Beek, M. A. "The Meaning of the Expression 'The Chariots and the Horsemen of Israel' (2 Kings 2,12)," *OTS* 17 (1971), pp. 1-10.

Begrich, J. "Das priestliche Heilsorakel," *ZAW* 52 (1934), pp. 81-92.

Bentzen, Aage. "The Ritual Background of Amos i 2 - ii 16," *OS* 8 (1950), pp. 85-99.

Borger, R. "Das Ende des ägyptischen Feldnerrn Sib'e = סוא," *JNES* 19 (1960), pp. 46-52.

Brekelmans, C. "Le ḥerem chez les prophètes du royaume du nord et dans le Deutéronome," *Bibliotheca Ephemeridum Theologicarum Lovaniensum* 12-13 (1959), pp. 377-83.

Bright, John. "A New Letter in Aramaic Written to a Pharaoh of Egypt," *BA* 12 (1949), pp. 46-52.

Brownlee, William H. "The Placarded Revelation of Habakkuk," *JBL* 82 (1963), pp. 319-25.

Bruston, Ch. "Jérémia fut-il prophéte pour les nations?," *ZAW* 27 (1907), pp. 75-78.

Buchanan, G. W. "Eschatology and the 'End of Days'," *JNES* 20 (1961), pp. 188-93.

Budde, Karl. "Uber die Kapital 50 und 51 des Buches Jeremia. I und II," *Deutsche Theologie* 23 (1878), pp. 428-70, 529-62.

Cazelles, H. "Sophonie, Jérémie, et les Scythes en Palestine," *RB* 74 (1967), pp. 24-44.

Childs, Brevard S. "The Enemy from the North and the Chaos Tradition," *JBL* 78 (1959), pp. 187-98.

Christensen, Duane L. "The Acrostic of Nahum Reconsidered," *ZAW* 87 (1975), pp. 17-30.

_________ "Num 21:14-15 and the Book of the Wars of Yahweh," *CBQ* 36 (1974), pp. 359-60.

________ "The Prosodic Structure of Amos 1-2," *HTR* 67 (1974), pp. 427-36.

________ "'Terror on Every Side' in Jeremiah," *JBL* 92 (1973), pp. 498-502.

Clifford, R. J. "The Use of *Hôy* in the Prophets," *CBQ* 28 (1966), pp. 458-64.

Cohen, Chayim. "The 'Widowed' City," in *The Gaster Festschrift. Journal of the Ancient Near Eastern Society of Columbia University* 5 (1974), pp. 75-81.

Cohen, S. "The Political Background of the Words of Amos," *HUCA* 36 (1965), pp. 153-60.

Coote, Robert B. "Amos 1:11: RḤMYW," *JBL* 90 (1971), pp. 206-208.

Coppens, J. "Les Oracles de Biléam," in *Mélanges Eugène Tisserant I.* Studi e Testi 231. Vatican City: Biblioteca Apostolica Vaticana, 1964, pp. 67-80.

Cross, Frank M., Jr., and David N. Freedman. "The Blessing of Moses," *JBL* 67 (1948), pp. 191-210.

________ "Josiah's Revolt Against Assyria," *JNES* 12 (1953), pp. 56-58.

________ "The Song of Miriam," *JNES* 14 (1955), pp. 237-50.

Cross, Frank M., Jr., and G. Ernest Wright. "The Boundary and Province Lists of the Kingdom of Judah," *JBL* 75 (1956), pp. 202-226.

Cross, Frank M., Jr. "The Contribution of the Discoveries at Qumran to the Study of the Biblical Text," *IEJ* 16 (1966), pp. 81-95.

________ "The Council of Yahweh in Second Isaiah," *JNES* 12 (1953), pp. 274-77.

________ "The Development of the Jewish Scripts," *BANE* (1961), pp. 170-264.

________ "The Divine Warrior in Israel's Early Cult," *Studies and Text III: Biblical Motifs*, ed. A. Altmann. Cambridge: Harvard, 1966, pp. 11-30.

________ "Epigraphic Notes on Hebrew Documents of the Eighth-Sixth Centuries B.C.: II. The Murabbaʿât Papyrus and the Letter Found Near Yabneh-Yam," *BASOR* 165 (1962), pp. 34-46.

________ "The History of the Biblical Text in the Light of Discoveries in the Judaean Desert," *HTR* 57 (1964), pp. 281-299.

________ "New Discoveries in the Study of Apocalyptic," *JThC* 6 (1969), pp. 157-65.

________ "The Song of the Sea and Canaanite Myth," *JThC* 5 (1968), pp. 1-25.

Dahood, Mitchell. "Some Northwest-Semitic Words in Job," *Bib* 38 (1957), pp. 306-320.

________ "Hebrew-Ugaritic Lexicography I-XII," *Bib* 44-55 (1963-74), *passim.*

________ "Ugaritic Studies and the Bible," *Gregorianum* 43 (1962), pp. 55-79.

________ "The Value of Ugaritic for Textual Criticism," *Bib* 40 (1959), pp. 160-70.

Daiches, S. "Balaam -- a Babylonian *Bārū*," *Hermann Hilprecht Anniversary Volume*. Leipzig, 1909, pp. 60-70.

Davies, G. Henton. "The Ark of the Covenant," *Annual of the Swedish Theological Institute in Jerusalem* 5 (1967), pp. 30-47.

Diman-Haran, M. See Menahem Haran.

Dubberstein, Waldo H. "Assyrian-Babylonian Chronology (669-612 B.C.)," *JNES* 3 (1944), pp. 38-42.

Dupont-Sommer, A. "Un papyrus araméen d'époque Saite découvert à Saqqarah," *Semitica* 1 (1948), pp. 43-68.

Eissfeldt, Otto. "Das Datum der Belagerung von Tyrus durch Nebuchadnezar," *FuF* 9 (1933), pp. 421-22.

________ "El and Yahweh," *JSS* 1 (1956), pp. 25-37.

________ "Der Gott Bethel," *ARW* 28 (1930), pp. 1-30.

________ "Israelitische-philistäische Grenzverschiebungen von David bis auf die Assyrerzeit," *ZDPV* 66 (1943), pp. 115-28.

________ "Jahwe als König," *ZAW* 44 (1928), pp. 81-105.

________ "Jeremias Drohorakel gegen Ägypten und gegen Babel," in *Verbannung und Heimkehr*, ed. Arnulf Kuschke. Tübingen: J. C. B. Mohr, 1961, pp. 31-37.

________ "Die Komposition der Bileam-Erzählung," *ZAW* 57 (1939), pp. 212-41.

________ "Kultzelt und Tempel," *Alter Orient und Altes Testament* 18 (1973), Neukirchener Verlag, pp. 51-55.

Erlandsson, Seth. "Jesaja 11:10-16 och dess historiska bakgrund," *Svensk exegetisk årsbok* 36 (1971), pp. 24-44.

Fensham, F. Charles. "Common Trends in Curses of the Near Eastern Treaties and *Kudurru*-Inscriptions Compared with Maledictions of Amos and Isaiah," *ZAW* 75 (1963), pp. 155-76.

________ "Malediction and Benediction in Ancient Near Eastern Vassal-Treaties and the Old Testament," *ZAW* 74 (1962), pp. 1-9.

________ "The Treaty between the Israelites and Tyrians," SVT 17 (1969), pp. 71-87.

Fish, T. "War and Religion in Ancient Mesopotamia," *BJRL* 23 (1939), pp. 387-402.

Fishbane, Michael. "The Treaty Background of Amos 1:11 and Related Matters," *JBL* 89 (1970), pp. 313-18.

Fitzmyer, J. A. "The Aramaic Letter of King Adon to the Egyptian Pharaoh," *Bib* 46 (1965), pp. 41-55.

Fohrer, Georg. "Vollmacht über Völker und Königreiche. Beobachtungen zu den prophetischen Fremdvölkerspruchen anhand von Jer 46-51," *Forschung zur Bibel* 2 (1972), pp. 145-53.

Freedman, David N. See Frank M. Cross, Jr.

________ "The Babylonian Chronicle," *BA* 19 (1956), pp. 50-60.

Gadd, C. J. "The Harran Inscriptions of Nabonidus," *Anatolian Studies* 8 (1958), pp. 35-92.

Ginsberg, H. L. "An Aramaic Contemporary of the Lachish Letters," *BASOR* 111 (1948), pp. 24-27.

_________ "Judah and the Transjordan States from 734 to 582 B.C.E.," in *Alexander Marx Jubilee Volume*. English section. New York: The Jewish Theological Seminary of America, 1950, pp. 347-68.

Glueck, Nelson. "Some Ancient Towns in the Plains of Moab," *BASOR* 91 (1943), pp. 7-26.

Goedicke, Hans. "The End of 'So, King of Egypt'," *BASOR* 171 (1963), pp. 64-66.

Goldman, M. D. "The Meaning of רגע," *ABR* 4 (1954), pp. 7-16.

Graham, W. C. "The Interpretation of Nah 1,9-2,3," *AJSL* 44 (1927/28), pp. 37-48.

Gray, John. "The Diaspora of Israel and Judah in Obadiah v. 20," *ZAW* 65 (1953), pp. 53-59.

_________ "The Period and Office of the Prophet Isaiah in the Light of a New Assyrian Tablet," *ET* 63 (1952), pp. 263-65.

Hallo, W. "From Qarqar to Carchemish: Assyria and Israel in the Light of New Discoveries," *BA* 23 (1960), pp. 34-61.

Hanson, Paul D. "The Song of Heshbon and David's *Nîr*," *HTR* 61 (1968), pp. 297-320.

Haran, Menahem. "An Archaic Remnant in Prophetic Literature" (Heb.), *BIES* 13 (1946/47), pp. 7-15.

_________ "Some Problems of the Historical Background of 'Prophecies of the Nations' in the Book of Amos" (Heb.), *Yediot* 30 (1966), pp. 56-69.

Holladay, John S., Jr. "Assyrian Statecraft and the Prophets of Israel," *HTR* 63 (1970), pp. 29-51.

_________ "The Day(s) the Moon Stood Still," *JBL* 87 (1968), pp. 166-78.

Holladay, W. L. "The Covenant with the Patriarchs Overturned: Jeremiah's Intention in 'Terror on Every Side' (Jer 20:1-6)," *JBL* 91 (1972), pp. 305-20.

Hyatt, J. Philip. "The Book of Jeremiah," *The Interpreter's Bible*. New York and Nashville: Abingdon Press, 1956, V, pp. 775-1142.

_________ "The Date and Background of Zephaniah," *JNES* 7 (1948), pp. 25-29.

_________ "Jeremiah and War," *Crozer Quarterly* 20 (1943), pp. 52-58.

_________ "New Light on Nebuchadrezzar and Judaean History," *JBL* 75 (1956), pp. 277-84.

_________ "The Peril from the North in Jeremiah," *JBL* 59 (1940), pp. 499-513.

Iwry, S. "New Evidence for Belomancy in Ancient Palestine and Phoenicia," *JAOS* 81 (1961), pp. 27-34.

Janzen, John G. "Double Readings in the Text of Jeremiah," *HTR* 60 (1967), pp. 446-47.

Kaiser, Otto. "Der geknickte Rohrstag. Zum geschichtlichen Hintergrund der Überlieferung und Weiterbildung der prophetischen Ägyptensprüche im 5. Jahrhundert," *Alter Orient und Altes Testament* 18 (1973), pp. 99-106.

Kapelrud, A. S. "God as Destroyer in the Preaching of Amos and in the Ancient Near East," *JBL* 71 (1952), pp. 33-38.

Kingsbury, E. C. "The Prophets and the Council of Yahweh," *JBL* 83 (1964), pp. 279-86.

Kitchen, K. A. "Late-Egyptian Chronology and the Hebrew Monarchy," in *The Gaster Festschrift. Journal of the Ancient Near Eastern Society of Columbia University* 5 (1974), pp. 225-33.

Kselman, John S. "A Note on Jer 49,20 and Ze 2,6-7," *CBQ* 32 (1970), pp. 579-81.

Kuschke, A. "Jeremia 48,1-8. Zugleich ein Beitrag zur historischen Topographie Moabs," *Verbannung und Heimkehr*, ed. Arnulf Kuschke. Tübingen: J. C. B. Mohr, 1961, pp. 181-96.

Landes, George M. "The Fountain at Jazer," *BASOR* 144 (1956), pp. 30-37.

Lind, M. C. "The Concept of Political Power in Ancient Israel," *Annual of the Swedish Theological Institute in Jerusalem* 7 (1970), pp. 4-24.

Linder, J. "Weissagung über Tyrus, Is. Kap. 23," *ZKTh* 62 (1940), pp. 217-21.

Lipínski, Edouard. "Juges 5.4-5 et Psaume 68.8-11," *Bib* 48 (1967), pp. 185-206.

Löhr, Max. "Alphabetische und Alphabetisierende Lieder im Alten Testament," *ZAW* 25 (1905), pp. 173-98.

Long, B. "2 Kings III and Genres of Prophetic Narrative," *VT* 23 (1973), pp. 339-41.

________ "Prophetic Call Traditions and Reports of Visions," *ZAW* 84 (1972), pp. 494-500.

Malamat, Abraham. "Amos 1:5 in the Light of the Til Barsip Inscriptions," *BASOR* 129 (1953), pp. 25-26.

________ "The Ban in Mari and in the Bible," *OuTWP* 7 (1966), pp. 134-42.

________ "'*Ḥăṣērim*' in the Bible and Mari" (Heb.), *Yediot* 27 (1963), pp. 180-84.

________ "The Historical Background of the Assassination of Amon, King of Judah," *IEJ* 3 (1953), pp. 26-29.

________ "The Historical Setting of Two Biblical Prophecies on the Nations," *IEJ* 1 (1950/51), pp. 149-59.

________ "Jeremiah and the Last Two Kings of Judah," *PEQ* 83 (1951), pp. 81-7.

________ "Josiah's Bid for Armageddon," *The Gaster Festschrift. Journal of the Ancient Near Eastern Society of Columbia University* 5 (1974), pp. 267-79.

________ "The Last Kings of Judah and the Fall of Jerusalem. An Historical-Chronological Study," *IEJ* 18 (1968), pp. 137-56.

________ "The Last Wars of the Kingdom of Judah," *JNES* 9 (1950), pp. 218-27.

________ "Organs of Statecraft in the Israelite Monarchy," *BA* 27 (1965), pp. 34-65.

Mauchline, John. "Implicit Signs of a Persistent Belief in the Davidic Empire," *VT* 20 (1970), pp. 287-303.

May, H. G. "Some Cosmic Connotations of MAYIM RABBIM, 'Many Waters'," *JBL* 74 (1955), pp. 9-21.

Mazar, Benjamin. "The Aramean Empire and its Relations with Israel," *BA* 25 (1962), pp. 98-120.

________ "The Philistines and the Rise of Israel and Tyre," *The Israel Academy of Sciences and Humanities*, I/7. Jerusalem: Magnes Press, 1964.

McCullough, W. S. "Israel's Eschatology from Amos to Daniel," *Studies on the Ancient Palestinian World*, ed. J. W. Wevers and D. B. Redford. University of Toronto Press, 1972, pp. 86-101.

Mendenhall, George E. "The Census Lists of Numbers 1 and 26," *JBL* 77 (1958), pp. 52-66.

________ "God of Vengeance, Shine Forth!" *Wittenberg Bulletin* (Wittenberg College, Springfield, Ohio) 45 (1948), pp. 37-42.

________ "Law and Covenant in Israel and the Ancient Near East," *BA* 17 (1954), pp. 26-46, 49-76.

Michaud, Henri. "La Vocation du 'Prophète des Nations'," *Máqqel shâqédh. Hommage à Welhelm Vischer*. Montpellier: Causse Graille, Castelnau, 1960, pp. 157-64.

Miller, Patrick D., Jr. "The Divine Council and the Prophetic Call to War," *VT* 18 (1968), pp. 100-107.

________ "El, the Warrior," *HTR* 60 (1967), pp. 411-31.

________ "Fire in the Mythology of Canaan and Israel," *CBQ* 27 (1965), pp. 256-61.

________ "God the Warrior. A Problem in Biblical Interpretation and Apologetics," *Interpretation* 19 (1965), pp. 39-46.

Milne, Nicol. "Prophet, Priest and King and Their Effect on Religion in Israel," *Abr-Nahrain* 2 (1960-61), pp. 55-67.

Moran, William L. "The Ancient Near Eastern Background of the Love of God in Deuteronomy," *CBQ* 25 (1963), pp. 77-87.

________ "The Hebrew Language in Its Northwest Semitic Background," *BANE* (1961), pp. 59-84.

Morgenstern, J. "The Universalism of Amos," *Essays Presented to L. Baeck*. London: East & West Library, 1954, pp. 106-26.

Muilenburg, James. "Form Criticism and Beyond," *JBL* 88 (1969), pp. 1-18.

Müller, H. P. "Phönizien und Juda in exilisch-nachexilischer Zeit," *Die Welt des Orients* 6 (1971), pp. 189-204.

________ "Zur Funktion des Mythischen in der Prophetie des Jesaja," *Kairos* 13 (1971), pp. 266-81.

Muntingh, L. M. "Political and International Relations of Israel's Neighbouring Peoples According to the Oracles of Amos," *OuTWP* 7 (1966), pp. 134-42.

Naveh, J. "A Hebrew Letter from the Seventh Century B.C.," *IEJ* 10 (1960), pp. 137-39.

Nielsen, E. "La guerre considerée comme une religion et la religion comme une guerre," *Studia Theologica* 15 (1961), pp. 93-112.

________ "The Righteous and the Wicked in Habaqquq," *Studia Theologica* 6 (1953), pp. 54-78.

North, F. "The Oracle against the Ammonites, Jer. 49:1-6," *JBL* 65 (1946), pp. 37-43.

Nötscher, F. "Prophetie im Umkreis des alten Israel," *Biblische Zeitschrift* 10 (1966), pp. 161-97.

Oded, B. "The Historical Background of the Syro-Ephraimite War Reconsidered," *CBQ* 34 (1972), pp. 153-65.

________ "Observations on Methods of Assyrian Rule in Transjordania after the Palestinian Campaign of Tiglath-Pileser III," *JNES* 29 (1970), pp. 177-86.

Oppenheim, A. Leo. "Zur keilschriftlichen Omenliteratur," *Or* 5 (1936), pp. 199-228.

Orlinsky, H. M. "'*Ḥāṣēr* in the Old Testament," *JAOS* 59 (1939), pp. 22-37.

Pakozdy, L. M. "Theologische Redaktionsarbeit in der Bileam-Perikope (Num. 22-24)," *Von Ugarit nach Qumran. Beiträge zur alttestamentlichen und altorientalische Forschung.* BZAW, 77. Berlin: Töpelmann, 1958, pp. 161-76.

Plöger, O. "Priester und Prophet," *ZAW* 63 (1951), pp. 157-192.

Porter, J. R. "The Background of Joshua III-IV," *Svensk exegetisk årsbok* 36 (1971), pp. 5-23.

Priest, J. "The Covenant of Brothers," *JBL* 84 (1965), pp. 400-406.

Quell, G. "Jesaja 14,1-23," *Festschrift für Friedrich Baumgärtel*, ed. J. Herrmann. Erlangen Universitätsbund, 1959, pp. 131-57.

Quinn, J. D. "Alcaeus 48 (B16) and the Fall of Ascalon (604 B.C.)," *BASOR* 164 (1962), pp. 19-20.

Rabinowitz, Isaac. "Towards a Valid Theory of Biblical Literature," *The Classical Tradition. Literary and Historical Studies in Honor of Harry Caplan*, ed. Luitpold Wallach. Ithaca: Cornell University, 1966, pp. 315-28.

Richter, W. "Zu den 'Richtern Israels'," *ZAW* 77 (1965), pp. 40-72.

Ross, James F. "Prophecy in Hamath, Israel and Mari," *HTR* 63 (1970), pp. 1-28.

________ "The Prophet as Yahweh's Messenger," *Israel's Prophetic Heritage*, B. W. Anderson and W. Harrelson. New York: Harper, 1962, pp. 98-107.

Rost, Leonhard. "Das Problem der Weltmacht in der Prophetie," *ETL* 41 (1965), pp. 5-19.

Rowton, M. B. "Jeremiah and the Death of Josiah," *JNES* 10 (1951), pp. 128-30.

Rudolph, Wilhelm. "Die angefochtenen Völkersprüche in Amos 1 und 2," *Schalom. Studien zu Glaube und Geschichte Israels*, ed. K.-H. Bernhardt. Stuttgart: Calwer Verlag, 1971, pp. 45-49.

________ "Jesaja xv-xvi," *Hebrew and Semitic Studies Presented to Godfrey Rolles Driver*, ed. D. W. Thomas, and W. D. McHardy. Oxford: Clarendon Press, 1963, pp. 130-43.

________ "Jesaja 23:1-14," *Festschrift für Friedrich Baumgärtel*, ed. J. Herrmann. Erlangen Universitätsbund, 1959, pp. 166-74.

Saggs, H. W. F. "Assyrian Warfare in the Sargonid Period," *Iraq* 25 (1963), pp. 145-54.

Schmidt, W. "Die deuteronomistische Redaktion des Amosbuches," *ZAW* 77 (1965), pp. 168-92.

Schottroff, W. "Horonaim, Nimrim, Luhith, und der Westrand des 'Landes Altaroth.' Ein Beitrag zur historischen Topographie des Landes Moab," *ZDPV* 82 (1966), pp. 163-208.

Seeligman, I. H. "On the History and Nature of Prophecy in Israel" (Heb.), *Eretz-Israel* 3 (1954), pp. 125-32.

Selms, A. van. "Amos' Geographic Horizon," *OuTWP* 7 (1966), pp. 166-69.

Seybold, K. "Das Herrscherbild des Bileamorakels Nu 24, 15-19," *ThZ* 29 (1973), pp. 1-19.

Shafer, Byron E.. "מבחור/מבצר = 'Fortress'," *CBQ* 33 (1971), pp. 389-96.

Smith, Louise P., and Ernest R. Lacheman. "The Authorship of the Book of Zephaniah," *JNES* 9 (1950), pp. 137-42.

Soggin, J. A. "Der prophetische Gedanke über den heiligen Krieg als Gericht gegen Israel," *VT* 10 (1960), pp. 79-83.

Soper, B. K. "For Three Transgressions and for Four: A New Interpretation of Amos i 3," *ET* 71 (1959/60), pp. 86-87.

Stade, B. "Der 'Völkerprophet' Jeremiah und der jetzige Text von Jer. Kap. 1," *ZAW* 26 (1906), pp. 97-123.

Stinespring, W. F. "No Daughter of Zion," *Encounter* 26 (1965), pp. 133-41.

Tadmor, Hayim. "The Campaigns of Sargon II of Assur," *JCS* 12 (1958), pp. 22-42, 77-100.

________ "Chronology of the Last Kings of Judah," *JNES* 15 (1956), pp. 226-30.

________ "Introductory Remarks to a New Edition of the Annals of Tiglath-Pileser III," *Israel Academy of Sciences and Humanities*, II/9. Jerusalem: Magnes Press, 1967, pp. 168-86.

________ "The Last Three Decades of Assyria," 25th International Congress of Orientalists, *Trudi* I (Moscow, 1960), pp. 240-41.

________ "Philistia Under Assyrian Rule," *BA* 29 (1966), pp. 86-102.

Talmon, S. "The New Hebrew Letter from the Seventh Century B.C. in Historical Perspective," *BASOR* 176 (1964), pp. 29-38.

Thomas, D. Winton. "מלאו in Jeremiah IV.5: A Military Term," *JJS* 3 (1952), pp. 47-52.

Tsevat, Matitiahu. "God and the Gods in Assembly. An Interpetation of Psalm 82," *HUCA* 40-41 (1969-70), pp. 123-37.

Tur-Sinai (Torczyner), Harry. "Lachish Letter IV," *JQR* 39 N.S. (1948-49), pp. 365-77.

Tur-Sinai, N. H. "Was There an Ancient 'Book of the Wars of the Lord'?" (Heb.), *BIES* 24 (1959/60), pp. 146-48.

Vaux, Roland de. "Notes d'Histoire et de Topographie Transjordannienes," *RB* 50 (1941), pp. 16-47.

Vogt, Ernst. "Jesaja und die drohende Eroberung Palästinas durch Tiglatpileser," *Forschung zur Bibel* 2 (1972), pp. 249-55.

________ "Die neubabylonische Chronic über die Schlact bei Karkemisch und die Einnahme von Jerusalem," SVT 4 (1957), pp. 67-96.

Vries, S. J. de. "The Acrostic of Nahum in the Jerusalem Liturgy," *VT* 16 (1966), pp. 476-81.

Weidner, Ernst. "Silkan(he)ni, König von Muṣri, ein Zeitgenosse Sargons II," *AfO* 14 (1941), pp. 44-45.

________ "Hochverrat gegen Nebuchadnezar II," *AfO* 17 (1954/55), pp. 1-5.

Weippert, M. "Heiliger Krieg in Israel und Assyrien. Kritische Anmerkungen zu Gerhard von Rads Konzept des 'Heiligen Krieges in Israel'," *ZAW* 84 (1972), pp. 460-93.

________ "Jahwekrieg und Bundesfluch in Jer 21, 1-7," *ZAW* 82 (1970), pp. 396-409.

Weiss, M. "On the Traces of a Biblical Metaphor II. Joel 4:15-17; Amos 1:2; Jer. 25:3" (Heb.), *Tarbiẓ* 34 (1964), pp. 211-23, 303-18.

________ "For Three Transgressions and for Four" (Heb.), *Tarbiẓ* 36 (1966), pp. 307-18.

Williams, Donald L. "The Date of Zephaniah," *JBL* 82 (1963), pp. 77-88.

Williams, J. G. "The Alas-Oracles of the Eighth Century Prophets," *HUCA* 38 (1967), pp. 75-91.

Woudstra, M. H. "A Prophet to the Nations. Reflections on Jeremiah's Call to the Prophetic Office," *Vox Reformata* 18 (1972), pp. 1-13.

Wright, G. Ernest. See Frank M. Cross, Jr.

________ "Fresh Evidence for the Philistine Story," *BA* 29 (1966), pp. 70-86.

________ "The Lawsuit of God: A Form-Critical Study of Deuteronomy 32," *Israel's Prophetic Heritage*, ed. B. W. Anderson and W. Harrelson. New

York: Harper & Brothers, 1962, pp. 26-67.

__________ "The Nations in Hebrew Prophecy," *Encounter* 26 (1965), pp. 225-37.

__________ "The Provinces of Solomon," *Eretz-Israel: Archaeological, Geographical, Historical Studies*. E. L. Sukenik Volume. Jerusalem: Israel Exploration Society, 1967, pp. 58-68.

Würthwein, Ernst. "Kultpolemik order Kultbescheid? Beobachtungen zu den Thema 'Prophetie und Kult'," *Tradition und Situation: Studien zur alttestamentlichen Prophetie*, ed. E. Würthwein. Göttingen: Vandenhoeck & Ruprecht, 1963, pp. 115-31.

Wyk, W. C. van. "Allusions to 'Prehistory' and History in the Book of Nahum," *De Fructu Oris Sui. Essays in Honour of Adrianus van Selms*. POS, 9. Leiden: E. J. Brill, 1971, pp. 222-32.

III. *Unpublished Materials*

Ackerman, James A. "An Exegetical Study of Psalm 82." Unpub. Th.D. thesis, Harvard University, 1966.

Asami, Sadao. "The Central Sanctuary in Israel in the Ninth Century B.C." Unpub. Th.D. thesis, Harvard University, 1964.

Chaney, Marvin L. "Mythology and Holy War in Isaiah 34:1-17 and 51:9-11." Old Testament Seminar paper, Harvard University, Fall, 1965.

Cogan, W. J. "Imperialism and Religion: Assyria, Judah and Israel in the Eighth and Seventh Centuries B.C." Ph.D. thesis, University of Pennsylvania, 1971. Available now in published form through Scholars Press, SBL Monograph Series.

Cresson, Bruce C. "Israel and Edom: A Study of the Anti-Edom Bias in Old Testament Religion." Unpub. Ph.D. thesis, Duke University, 1963.

Dumbrell, William. "The Midianites and Their Transjordanian Successors." Unpub. Th.D. thesis, Harvard University, 1970.

Glock, Albert E. "Warfare in Mari and Early Israel." Unpub. Ph.D. thesis, University of Michigan, 1968.

Gold, Victor R. "Studies in the History and Culture of Edom." Unpub. Ph.D. thesis, Johns Hopkins University, 1951.

Graesser, Carl. "The Imperial Policy of Josiah." Old Testament Seminar paper, Harvard University, Fall, 1962.

Hay, Lawrence C. "The Oracles Against the Foreign Nations in Jeremiah 46-51." Unpub. Ph.D. thesis, Vanderbilt University, 1960.

Hayes, John H. "The Oracles Against the Nations in the Old Testament: Their Usage and Theological Importance." Unpub. Th.D. thesis, Princeton Theological Seminary, 1964.

Jones, G. H. "An Examination of Some Leading Motifs in the Prophetic Oracles against the Nations." Ph.D. thesis, University of Wales, 1970.

Kaufman, Ivan T. "The Significance of Oracles Concerning Foreign Nations." Old Testament Seminar paper, Harvard University, Fall, 1962.

_________ "Holy War and Foreign Policy in Eighth Century Prophecy." Old Testament Seminar paper, Harvard University, Fall, 1961.

Kessler, Martin. "Oracles Against the Nations: Jeremiah 50 and 51." A paper read before the Society of Biblical Literature at Toronto on November 19, 1969.

Klein, Ralph. "The Chaos Motif in the Northern Menace in Jeremiah." Old Testament Seminar paper, Harvard University, Fall, 1962.

Krahmalkov, Charles. "Studies in Amorite Grammar." Unpub. Ph.D. thesis, Harvard University, 1965.

Landes, George M. "A History of the Ammonites." Unpub. Ph.D. thesis, Johns Hopkins University, 1956.

Macy, Howard R. "The Legal Metaphor in Oracles Against Foreign Nations in the Pre-Exilic Prophets." Unpub. M.A. thesis, Earlham School of Religion, 1970.

Margulis, Barry B. "Studies in the Oracles Against the Nations." Unpub. Ph.D. thesis, Brandeis University, 1966.

Millar, William R. "Isaiah 24-27 and the Origin of Apocalyptic." Unpub. Ph.D. thesis, Harvard University, 1970.

Miller, Patrick D., Jr. "Warfare in the Davidic Era." Old Testament Seminar paper, Harvard University, Fall, 1959.

Miscall, Peter. "The Concept of the Poor in the Old Testament." Unpub. Ph.D. thesis, Harvard University, 1972.

Moon, C. H. S. "Israel's Relations with Edom During the Period of the Divided Kingdom." Ph.D. thesis, Emory University, 1970.

Poulton, A. W. "The Martial Poetry of Greece and Israel." Unpub. Ph.D. thesis, Brandeis University, 1971.

Purvis, James D. "The Holy War in Early Israel." Old Testament Seminar papar, Harvard University, Fall, 1959.

Rahtjen, Bruce D. "The Philistine Amphictyony." Unpub. Ph.D. thesis, Duke University, 1964.

Ramey, G. G. "The Horse and Chariot in Israelite Religion." Unpub. Th.D. thesis, The Southern Baptist Theological Seminary, 1968.

Robertson, David A. "Linguistic Evidence in Dating Early Hebrew Poetry." Ph.D. thesis, Yale University, 1970. Available in published form through Scholars Press, SBL Dissertation Series.

Shenkel, James D. "Jeremiah and Holy War." Old Testament Seminar paper, Harvard University, Fall, 1962.

Stone, Michael. "The Language of Holy War in the Prophets of the Eighth Century." Old Testament Seminar paper, Harvard University, Fall, 1961.

Voigtlander, Elizabeth N. von. "A Survey of Neo-Babylonian History." Unpub. Ph.D. thesis, University of Michigan, 1963.

SUPPLEMENTARY BIBLIOGRAPHY

IV. Selected Articles by Duane L. Christensen Since 1975

"The March of Conquest in Isaiah X 27c-34," *VT* 26 (1976), pp. 385-99.

"Two Stanzas of a Hymn in Deuteronomy 33," *Bib* 65 (1984), pp. 382-89.

"Zephaniah 2:4-15: A Theological Basis for Josiah's Program of Political Expansion," *CBQ* 46 (1984), pp. 669-82.

"Huldah and the Men of Anathoth: Women in Leadership in the Deuteronomic History," *SBL Seminar Papers* 23 (1984), pp. 399-404.

"Prose and Poetry in the Bible: The Narrative Poetics of Deuteronomy 1:9-18," *ZAW* 97 (1985), pp. 179-89.

"Form and Structure in Deuteronomy 1-11," in *Das Deuteronomium: Enstehung, Gestalt und Botschaft*, ed. N. Lohfink. Bibliotheca Ephemeridum Theologicarum Lovaniensium, 68. Leuven: University Press, 1985, pp. 135-44.

"The Song of Jonah: A Metrical Analysis," *JBL* 104 (1985), pp. 217-31.

"Andrzej Panufnik and the Structure of the Book of Jonah: Icons, Music and Literary Art," *Journal of the Evangelical Theological Society* 28 (1985), pp. 133-40.

"The *Numeruswechsel* in Deuteronomy 12," in *Proceedings of the Ninth World Congress of Jewish Studies*, vol. 4. Division A: The Period of the Bible. Jerusalem: World Union of Jewish Studies, 1986, pp. 61-68.

"Job and the Age of the Patriarchs in Old Testament Narrative," *Perspectives in Religious Studies* 13 (1986), pp. 225-28.

"Biblical Geneaologies and Eschatological Speculation," *Perspectives in Religious Studies* 14 (1987), pp. 59-65.

"Narrative Poetics and the Interpretation of the Book of Jonah," in *Directions in Biblical Hebrew Poetry*, ed. E. R. Follis. JSOT Supplement, 40. Sheffield: Sheffield Academic Press, 1987, pp. 29-48.

"The Acrostic of Nahum Once Again: A Prosodic Analysis of Nahum 1,1-10," *ZAW* 99 (1987), pp. 409-15.

"A New Israel: The Righteous from among All Nations," in *Israel's Apostasy and Restoration: Essays in Honor of Roland K. Harrison*, ed. A. Gileadi. Grand Rapids: Baker Book House, 1988, pp. 250-59.

"Nahum," in *Harper's Bible Commentary*, ed. J. L. Mayes et al. San Francisco: Harper & Row, 1988, pp. 736-38.

"The Book of Nahum: The Question of Authorship Within the Canonical Process," *Journal of the Evangelical Theological Society* 31 (1988), pp. 51-58.

"The Book of Nahum as a Liturgical Composition: A Prosodic Analysis," *Journal of the Evangelical Theological Society* 32 (1989), pp. 159-69.

"The Identity of 'King So' in Egypt (2 Kings XVII 4)," *VT* 39 (1989), pp. 140-53.

"Dtn 33,11 – A Curse in the 'Blessing of Moses'?," *ZAW* 101 (1989), pp. 278-82.